Jews in Post-Holocaust Germany, 1945–1953

This is the story of the reemergence of the Jewish community in Germany after the near total destruction of the Holocaust. In western Germany, the community needed to overcome deep cultural, religious, and political differences before uniting. In eastern Germany, the small Jewish community struggled against Communist opposition. After coalescing, both Jewish communities, largely isolated by the international Jewish community, looked to German political leaders and the two German governments for support. Through relationships with key German leaders, they achieved stability by 1953, when West Germany agreed to pay reparations to Israel and to individual Holocaust survivors and East Germany experienced a wave of antisemitic purges. Using archival materials from the Jewish communities of East and West Germany as well as governmental and political party records, Geller elucidates the reestablishment of organized Jewish life in Germany and the Jews' critical ties to political leaders.

Jay Howard Geller is Assistant Professor of History at the University of Tulsa. His articles have appeared in the Leo Baeck Institute *Year Book*, the *Journal of Military History*, and *Adenauer, Israel und das Judentum*, edited by Hanns Jürgen Küsters.

JEWS IN POST-HOLOCAUST GERMANY, 1945–1953

JAY HOWARD GELLER

University of Tulsa

CAMBRIDGE UNIVERSITY PRESS

PUBLISHED BY THE PRESS SYNDICATE OF THE UNIVERSITY OF CAMBRIDGE
The Pitt Building, Trumpington Street, Cambridge, United Kingdom

CAMBRIDGE UNIVERSITY PRESS
The Edinburgh Building, Cambridge, CB2 2RU, UK
40 West 20th Street, New York, NY 10011-4211, USA
477 Williamstown Road, Port Melbourne, VIC 3207, Australia
Ruiz de Alarcón 13, 28014 Madrid, Spain
Dock House, The Waterfront, Cape Town 8001, South Africa

http://www.cambridge.org

© Cambridge University Press 2005

First published 2005

Printed in the United States of America

Typeface Baskerville 11/12.5 pt   *System* LaTeX 2$_\varepsilon$ [TB]

A catalog record for this book is available from the British Library.

Library of Congress Cataloging in Publication Data
Geller, Jay Howard.
Jews in post-Holocaust Germany, 1945–1953 / by Jay Howard Geller.
p. cm.
Includes bibliographical references and index.
ISBN 0-521-83353-1 – ISBN 0-521-54126-3 (pb.)
1. Jews – Germany – History – 1945–   2. Holocaust survivors – Germany –
History – 20th century.   3. Jews – Germany – Politics and government –
20th century.   4. Germany – Ethnic relations.   I. Title.
DS135.G332G39   2004
305.892′4043′09045–dc22   2004045672

ISBN 0 521 83353 1 hardback
ISBN 0 521 54126 3 paperback

Contents

Acknowledgments

Researching and writing a book such as this one requires the assistance of many people, to whom I am greatly indebted. The West German portions of this book have their origins in my doctoral dissertation, written under the supervision of Professor Henry Ashby Turner, Jr., of Yale University. Professors Paul M. Kennedy and Paula Hyman also served on my dissertation committee. I thank them all for their help and suggestions. The East German sections of this book stem from an article published in the Leo Baeck Institute *Year Book* in 2002. The anonymous readers for that publication helped to improve the manuscript, and the *Year Book*, under the editorship of John Grenville, Gabriele Rahaman, and Joel Golb, has permitted the reprinting of portions of that article. At various conferences, notably the German Studies Association, the New England Historical Association, the Midwest Jewish Studies Association, and the Yale International Security Studies Colloquium, I received useful suggestions from many individuals, including Frank Nicosia, Rebecca Boehling, David Weinberg, and Robert Melson.

The anonymous readers who reviewed the manuscript for Cambridge University Press provided suggestions that improved this text immeasurably, and I am extremely grateful to them. I also express my thanks to Andy Beck and Malinda Barrett of Cambridge University Press, with whom it has been a pleasure to work.

A number of institutions provided this project with financial support, without which this book would scarcely be possible. They include the Friedrich-Ebert-Stiftung, the Leo Baeck Institute of New York, the Deutscher Akademischer Austauschdienst, the Fox International Fellowship Program, Yale University, and the University of Tulsa. Their generosity cannot truly be repaid.

So many individuals helped with the research for this project that I am unable to enumerate them all. The staffs of the following archives were generous with their time and patience as I made my way through innumerable documents: American Jewish Archive; Amherst College Library, Archives and Special Collections; Archiv des Liberalismus (Friedrich-Naumann-Stiftung); Archiv für Christlich-Demokratische Politik (Konrad-Adenauer-Stiftung); Archiv der sozialen Demokratie (Friedrich-Ebert-Stiftung); Bundesarchiv Koblenz and Bundesarchiv Berlin; Center for Jewish History, YIVO; Landesarchiv Berlin; National Archives and Record Administration; Parlamentsarchiv des Deutschen Bundestages; Politisches Archiv of the Auswärtiges Amt; Stiftung Bundeskanzler-Adenauer-Haus; Stiftung "Neue Synagoge-Berlin Centrum Judaicum" Archiv; U.S. Holocaust Memorial Museum Archive and Library; and Zentralarchiv zur Erforschung der Geschichte der Juden in Deutschland. A few individuals provided assistance greater than any researcher could reasonably expect, and they deserve particular mention: Christoph Stamm and Wolfgang Stärcke, Gabriele Jakobi and Monica Nägele-Dreher, Raymond Pradier and Monika Wittmann, Brigitte Kaff and staff, Ina Remus, Leslie Swift, Barbara Welker, and Peter Honigmann and Eva Blattner. Hans Peter Mensing not only helped with my research, but he has continued to support this project and my scholarly career, for which I thank him. Sue Roberts, chief librarian for European history and coordinator of humanities collections at Sterling Memorial Library at Yale University, was wonderful in tracking down and procuring rare materials. In the course of research for this book, I had occasion to speak with or to correspond with several eyewitnesses to the events described below. Fritz Heine, Jochen Abraham Frowein, and Lilli Marx were very generous with their time and their memories. Notably, I am grateful to the Zentralrat der Juden in Deutschland for granting me (then) unprecedented access to its records.

In conceptualizing and writing this book, I have incurred nearly as many debts as I have in researching for it. So many people have patiently listened to me develop my ideas or even read earlier versions of this text that I apologize if I have failed to mention any of them. Harold James and Stephen Kotkin inspired me as an undergraduate and continued to offer their encouragement as I conceived this project. In a graduate class with Kevin Repp, while discussing emancipation and German-Jewish relations in an earlier era, this topic began to take shape. My friend and teacher Toni Attwell read the entire dissertation manuscript and patiently made suggestions to make this historian a better writer. For his encouragement, suggestions, and assistance, Charles Lansing receives my particular gratitude. A word of thanks also goes to my friends and colleagues Bernd Braun, Greg Caramenico, Mark Choate, Astrid Eckert, Will Gray, Jim Heinzen, Jeffrey Kopstein, Thomas Maulucci, Patricia Nordeen, Dan Rogers, Jeremi Suri, George Williamson, and Joachim Wintzer. Moreover, at the University of Tulsa, Chris Ruane patiently read and commented on the manuscript, while Andrew Burstein and Nancy Isenberg helped me to promote it, and John Bowlin acted as a sounding board. I thank them all.

My deepest thanks go to those closest to me. Over the years, my parents, Salem and Barbara Geller, have never failed to offer their love and support. As I completed this project, that encouragement, affection, and assistance was augmented by that of my wife Valerie Anne Geller, née Glauberg, some of whose relatives, tragically, were not permitted to share in this story.

Acronyms and Abbreviations

OMGUS	Office of Military Government of the United States
PW and DP	Prisoners of war and displaced persons
SED	Sozialistische Einheitspartei Deutschlands (Socialist Unity Party of Germany)
SHAEF	Supreme Headquarters, Allied Expeditionary Force
SPD	Sozialdemokratische Partei Deutschlands (Social Democratic Party of Germany)
SRP	Sozialistische Reichspartei (Socialist Reich Party)
UN	United Nations
UNRRA	United Nations Relief and Rehabilitation Administration
USFET	United States Forces, European Theater
VVN	Vereinigung der Verfolgten des Naziregimes (Association of Victims of the Nazi Regime)
WJC	World Jewish Congress

ARCHIVES AND CITATIONS

Abt.	Abteilung
ACDP	Archiv für Christlich-Demokratische Politik (of the Konrad-Adenauer-Stiftung)
ADL	Archiv des Liberalismus (of the Friedrich-Naumann-Stiftung)
AdsD	Archiv der sozialen Demokratie (of the Friedrich-Ebert-Stiftung)
AJA	American Jewish Archive
Amherst-A&SC	Amherst College, Archives and Special Collections
B	Bestand
BAB	Bundesarchiv, Berlin
BAK	Bundesarchiv, Koblenz
CJA	Stiftung "Neue Synagoge-Berlin Centrum Judaicum" Archiv
CJH	Center for Jewish History
LAB	Landesarchiv Berlin
N	Nachlass

NARA	National Archives and Records Administration, College Park, Maryland
PAAA	Politisches Archiv, Auswärtiges Amt
Rep.	Repertorium (used at Landesarchiv Berlin)
SAPMO	Stiftung Archiv Parteien und Massenorganisationen
StBKAH	Stiftung Bundeskanzler-Adenauer-Haus
USHMM	United States Holocaust Memorial Museum
YIVO	YIVO Institute for Jewish Research (formerly Yidisher Visnshaftlekher Institut)
ZA	Zentralarchiv zur Erforschung der Geschichte der Juden in Deutschland

Introduction

By the 1930s, Jews had been living in Germany for at least 1600 years. Although they faced tremendous persecution during the Middle Ages, their communities persisted, and German Jews were among the first to enjoy the fruits of post-emancipatory integration. Germany became a beacon for Jewish immigration, and the Jewish community of Germany was among the most culturally assimilated in the world. Most German Jews considered themselves at home in German culture and society, and their participation in the First World War is a testament to their devotion to Germany. Despite this high degree of integration – or possibly because of it – German Jewry still faced persecution. Conservative bastions of society, including the army and the professorate, remained largely impervious to Jewish participation before 1914. Throughout the nineteenth century, there were anti-Jewish riots, though they did not find state sanction until the advent of the Nazi regime.[1] In the 1930s and 1940s, Hitler and his followers unleashed an all-encompassing genocide designed to make Germany, and all of Europe, free of Jews. No aspect of European Jewish life or society was safe from Nazi supervision and destruction. The very nature of the genocide has caused some historians to term it "the war against the Jews."[2] Despite this overt goal, the Nazis failed, and Jewish life continued – even in Germany.

[1] For a distillation of views on the topic, see Christhard Hoffmann, Werner Bergmann, and Helmut Walser Smith, eds., *Exclusionary Violence: Antisemitic Riots in Modern Germany* (Ann Arbor: University of Michigan Press, 2002). One of the most poignant observations of the failure of the so-called German-Jewish symbiosis is Gershom Scholem's essay "Against the Myth of the German-Jewish Dialogue," in Gershom Scholem, *On Jews and Judaism in Crisis: Selected Essays*, ed. Werner J. Dannhauser (New York: Schocken, 1976), originally "Wider den Mythos vom deutsch-jüdischen 'Gespräch,'" in *Auf gespaltenem Pfad. Zum neunzigsten Geburtstag von Margarete Susman*, ed. Manfred Schlösser (Darmstadt: Erato, 1964).

[2] Lucy Dawidowicz, *The War against the Jews, 1933–1945* (New York: Holt, Rinehart and Winston, 1975).

After social exclusion, concentration, and the ultimate decimation of German Jewry, not long after the war's end, Germany witnessed a miraculous reemergence of Jewish life. A German Jewish population, comprised of those who had gone underground, emigrated, or survived the camps, refounded religious congregations and other Jewish institutions. Moreover, the renascent German Jewish community was joined by an influx of Eastern European Holocaust survivors who did not wish to remain in their homelands after their liberation from the concentration camps. Together, they formed a fractious community, divided on cultural, religious, and even political grounds.

This is a book about Jews, Jewish institutions, and Jewish issues in Germany in the critical first decade immediately after the Second World War. It tells a multifaceted story focusing on the reestablishment of the Jewish community in Germany, on the community's interest representation, and on the manner in which German political elites related to Jewish issues – including the reconstruction of the community, restitution, and reparations – as German society rebuilt itself. Despite the Jewish community's small size, the very presence of Jews in Germany had importance, both providing interlocutors for a reconciliatory dialogue and serving as reminders of Germany's historic failings.

In the years immediately after the war – coinciding with the years of Allied occupation of Germany – instability characterized the reemerging Jewish community. The majority of the Jews living in Germany did not wish to remain there, preferring to settle in Palestine; however, a significant minority of Jews did wish to stay in Germany. Their enduring presence proved confounding and controversial to Jews around the world who felt that Germany was no place for a Jew to live after 1945, and especially not after 1948, when the establishment of the state of Israel permitted an exodus of Jewish refugees from Europe.

As a small group, acting largely without the support of Jews abroad, the community in Germany needed cohesion. Overcoming social and religious differences, Jews in Germany united for the purposes of political representation. Simply put, they needed a coordinated voice to advocate their interests, both to the German governments and to Jewish groups around the world. Two organizations took up this task. In West Germany, the principal representative was the Central Council of Jews in Germany (Zentralrat der

Juden in Deutschland). This group's origins, internal structure, leadership, and relations with the Bonn government and Jewish groups abroad stand at the center of this study. In East Germany, the State Association of Jewish Communities in the German Democratic Republic (Landesverband der Jüdischen Gemeinden in der Deutschen Demokratischen Republik) functioned as the Central Council's equivalent or nominal subsidiary. Its struggle on behalf of the Jews of eastern Germany, showcased in chapters 3 and 5, forms an interesting contrast to the western experience. Despite the differing political conditions each faced, both groups relied heavily on personal ties between their leaders and influential Germans, a policy that had the potential for great success and catastrophic failure.

At the same time that the Jewish community was coalescing and organizing, non-Jewish Germans sought to rebuild their society. Starting in 1949, two German states came into being, and German administrations assumed most governmental functions previously under Allied control. In western Germany, winning support for liberal democracy, which had failed before 1933, was not easy. Politicians faced critical decisions regarding any confrontation with the legacy of Germany's crimes against humanity, most particularly against the Jewish people of Europe. While dealing with these issues in an open and forthright manner would have reflected a renewal of civil society and progressive public discourse, it also had the potential to alienate millions of Germans who did not unqualifiedly reject the previous regime. The decisions made by state and party leaders regarding the Jews and Jewish issues are central to understanding the conditions under which the Jewish community developed.

In many ways, Germany's break with its past and its official relationship with the Jews characterized its progress toward a democratic, liberal future. This study seeks to clarify the manner in which German politicians and political parties addressed Jewish-related issues. In particular, it examines Jews' relationships with state and party leaders. Because of the recent German past, Jewish leaders, representing a small community (between 20,000 and 40,000), acquired an influence greater than their constituency would have merited under normal circumstances.

In the most overt sense, this study poses a number of questions. How did the Jewish community of Germany form after the tragedy of the Holocaust? What was the nature of the community, and how did it regard itself? What were its relations to other Jewish groups in Israel and throughout the Diaspora? How did the state and individual German leaders deal with the Jewish community? How were Jewish or Jewish-related issues regarded by the political class in both German states? Was there a difference in domestic Jewish-German relations and Israeli-German relations, possibly colored by German Jewry's own relations with Israel? This book attempts to answer these questions and to demonstrate their interconnectedness.

My examination begins even before the defeat of Nazi Germany, as Allied officials began considering the reintegration of Jews into German society and the fate of refugees after the war. Indeed, from 1945 to 1949, the Allied occupation governments were the primary focus of policy formation, including policy on Jewish matters. While German politicians certainly did consider and debate Jewish-related matters before the advent of German statehood, prior to 1949 – even afterward to some degree – the Jews in Germany concentrated their lobbying efforts on the military occupation governments. Thus, as this study traces the reestablishment of the organized Jewish community, it also elucidates the relationship between that community and the Allies, and in particular the Americans, whose zone had the largest Jewish community.

In some senses, the years 1945 to 1949 were merely a prelude to the story of renewed Jewish life in Germany. In September 1949, a West German government formed; the following month, an East German government came into being. After the Israeli war of independence, tens of thousands of displaced persons left Germany for the new Jewish state. In 1950, the Jewish community, having been reduced to a core population, overcame its internal divisions and united for representative purposes under the Central Council of Jews in Germany. By the autumn of 1950, the community had a hierarchical organization and German partners for dialogue in the West German federal government and the government of East Germany. Therefore, after the pivotal transitional years of 1949–1950, explicated in chapters 1 and 2, this study focuses on the policies of the governments and leading political parties regarding Jewish issues and the relationship of those bodies with the western Central Council and the eastern State Association. Additionally, an examination of the Central Council's troubled relationship with

Jewish groups in other countries, including Israel, elucidates the challenges facing the community.

Concentrating on political and collective aspects, particularly on the national or federal level, my analysis reaches its terminal point in the year 1953. That year, West Germany established its policy regarding Jewish survivors of the Holocaust, ratifying a treaty for reparations to Israel and foreign Jewish groups and legislating reparations to individual victims of the Nazis. At the same time, the West German Interior Ministry began an institutionalized relationship with the Central Council, supporting it through regular subsidies. Finally, in 1953, with the goal of reparations achieved, the Central Council began an internal reorganization and reorientation. It sought to change from primarily a political advocacy group to the principal coordinator of Jewish social and cultural life in Germany. The year 1953 was also critical for East German Jewry. Following a precedent already established elsewhere in the eastern bloc, the Communist Party began a purge of Jewish and philosemitic members. Additionally, the regime harassed and arrested the leadership of the Jewish community. Ultimately, the community's leaders fled East Germany, necessitating a state-supervised reorganization of the State Association and the individual Jewish communities in eastern German cities. The patterns of German-Jewish political rapport that were established by the end of 1953 prevailed for the next twelve to fifteen years, if not longer, as both Jewish communities settled into a routine of bureaucratized administration and institutionalized relations with the state.

As noted, during the era of Allied occupation, the largest segment of the Jewish population in Germany was comprised of displaced persons (DPs) from Eastern Europe. Many of these Jewish Holocaust survivors simply found themselves on German soil on 8 May 1945; others fled postwar conditions in Poland and Romania. Although they could not emigrate to British-occupied Palestine, they could stay in the Allied occupation zones of western Germany, where they felt relatively secure. While waiting for their final settlement status to change, these refugees recreated in Germany a version of Jewish Eastern Europe. Their DP camps eventually became loci of Jewish culture and education, and Zionist politics thrived in the camps. This refugee community, with its renaissance of Eastern European y*iddishkayt*, has become a popular topic of examination for historians in America, Germany, and Israel. Among the earlier studies of the displaced persons in postwar Germany are works by Mark Wyman and Wolfgang Jacobmeyer.[3] More recently, Jewish displaced persons specifically have received increased attention. Angelika Königseder and Juliane Wetzel have thoroughly examined the structure of political and social life in many of the different DP camps in the occupation zones. Their investigation looks at DP life until the dissolution of the camps. Angelika Eder deals with cultural matters. In contrast, Zeev Mankowitz examines many aspects of DP life and politics, but his analysis concentrates on the years 1945–1946, with later years receiving less attention. Additionally, his story, rich in detail, is primarily a Zionist one.[4] Hagit Lavsky and Joanne Reilly have focused on the Belsen displaced persons camp, located in the British zone of occupation. In fact, Belsen was one of the most organized and successful camps, eventually becoming a locus of Jewish life in northern Germany – inside or out of DP camps. Lavsky also argues that it was the breeding ground for a grassroots-organized, Zionist civil society.[5] Rather than focusing on a single camp or zone, Michael Brenner has incorporated the story of the DPs into the wider history of Jewish resettlement in postwar Germany. Using newspapers and other scholars' works, which contain rich quotations, Ruth Gay has constructed a ground-level view of DP life in Germany. Atina Grossmann has examined the displaced persons and the question of gender as part of a larger project on the

---

3 Mark Wyman, *DP: Europe's Displaced Persons, 1945–1951* (Philadelphia: Associated University Press, 1989); Wolfgang Jacobmeyer, *Vom Zwangsarbeiter zum Heimatlosen Ausländer. Die Displaced Persons in Westdeutschland 1945–1951* (Göttingen: Vandenhoeck und Ruprecht, 1985).

4 Angelika Königseder and Juliane Wetzel, *Lebensmut im Wartesaal. Die jüdischen DPs (Displaced Persons) im Nachkriegsdeutschland* (Frankfurt: Fischer, 1994); Angelika Eder, "Kultur und Kulturveranstaltungen in den jüdischen DP-Lagern," in *Leben im Land der Täter: Juden in Nachkriegsdeutschland (1945–1952)*, ed. Julius H. Schoeps (Berlin: Jüdische Verlagsanstalt, 2001); Zeev W. Mankowitz, *Life between Memory and Hope: The Survivors of the Holocaust in Occupied Germany* (Cambridge: Cambridge University Press, 2002).

5 Hagit Lavsky, *New Beginnings: Holocaust Survivors in Bergen-Belsen and the British Zone in Germany, 1945–1950* (Detroit: Wayne State University Press, 2002); Joanne Reilly, *Belsen: The Liberation of a Concentration Camp* (London: Routledge, 1998). Wolfgang Jacobmeyer alleges that the DPs' Zionism was not a deeply held political conviction, but merely a reaction to the desperate contemporary political situation. Wolfgang Jacobmeyer, "Jüdische Überlebende als 'Displaced Persons.' Untersuchungen zur Besatzungspolitik in den deutschen Westzonen und zur Zuwanderung osteuropäischer Juden 1945–1947," *Geschichte und Gesellschaft* 9, no. 3 (1983): 423–424.

displaced persons and debates on victimhood during the Allied occupation.[6]

While most scholars dwell on the irony of traditional eastern Jewish culture thriving in post-Hitler Germany, their ultimate focus is not on the permanence of this Jewish life in Germany, but rather on its transience. As Hagit Lavsky has argued, this transitional phase of internment in Germany helped to rehabilitate these Jews, both physically and culturally. Restored to health, the DPs had the highest birthrate of Jews anywhere in the world after World War II. To a large degree, the population made the transition from Yiddish Eastern European culture to a more modern Hebrew, Zionist orientation. By the time the refugees left Germany, they were a lively, politicized population, eager to aid in the construction of the new Jewish state.

Although most DPs did depart for Israel after 1947, it is critical to note that many remained in Germany. The merger of the German Jewish community and the residual displaced persons community marked the real establishment of a new and enduring Jewish community in postwar Germany. Thus, with a focus on that new community and its political development, it is critical to regard the DPs, or at least some of them, as future constituents of the Central Council of Jews in Germany. However, their presence in Germany complicated the situation of the Jewish community. Though some eastern Jews had lived in Germany before 1933, these newcomers were culturally alien to Germany, and differences between them and German-born Jews manifested themselves as political tensions. Thus, in addition to examining some aspects of the DPs' Zionist politics, relations between eastern Jews and German-born Jews require elucidation, both before the founding of the Central Council (chapters 1 and 2) and after the coalescence of the community (chapter 8).

The Jewish communities of both West and East Germany are the subject of a number of studies. Henry Maor's dissertation,

[6] Michael Brenner, *After the Holocaust: Rebuilding Jewish Lives in Postwar Germany*, trans. Barabra Harshav (Princeton: Princeton University Press, 1997); Ruth Gay, *Safe among the Germans: Liberated Jews after World War II* (New Haven: Yale University Press, 2002); Atina Grossmann, "Victims, Villains, and Survivors: Gendered Perceptions and Self-Perceptions of Jewish Displaced Persons in Occupied Postwar Germany," *Journal of the History of Sexuality* 11, nos. 1/2 (January/April 2002), and *Victims, Victors, and Survivors: Germans, Allies, and Jews in Occupied Postwar Germany, 1945–1950* (Princeton: Princeton University Press, forthcoming).

written nearly thirty-five years ago, is generally considered the first scholarly examination of the topic; however, it is little more than a statistical and sociological overview of the community's composition.[7] Since the mid-1980s, there has been a profusion of sociological analyses. While many do address the history of the community's politics and role in German society, few undertake a serious archival examination of the community's origins.[8] This study seeks to root its analysis in archival evidence. A number of scholars have looked at psychological or sociological phenomena related to being Jewish in Germany or to Jewish-Christian social relations, topics not surveyed here.[9] More recently, Michael Brenner's study provides an introduction to the renewed Jewish community, terminating its analysis in 1950, the year of the Central Council's establishment, and Ruth Gay gives a view of the community's genesis before quickly moving forward to the present day, with an emphasis on individuals and personal stories.[10] My analysis reintroduces Jewish institutions, particularly political representative bodies, to the story of the renewal of Jewish life in Germany. Without these groups, the community could never have received the critical support it did from non-Jewish political leaders.

[7] Harry Maor, "Über den Wiederaufbau der jüdischen Gemeinden in Deutschland seit 1945," Dr.phil. diss., Universität Mainz, 1961.

[8] Micha Brumlik et al., eds., *Jüdisches Leben in Deutschland seit 1945* (Frankfurt: Jüdischer Verlag bei Athenäum, 1986); Anson Rabinbach and Jack Zipes, eds., *Germans and Jews since the Holocaust: The Changing Situation in West Germany* (New York: Holmes and Meier, 1986); Erica Burgbauer, *Zwischen Erinnerung und Verdrängung – Juden in Deutschland nach 1945* (Hamburg: Rowohlt, 1993); Michael Cohn, *The Jews in Germany, 1945–1993: The Building of a Minority* (Westport: Praeger, 1994); Uri Kaufmann, *Jewish Life in Germany Today*, trans. Susan Schwarz (Bonn: Inter Nationes, 1994); Günther Ginzel, ed., *Der Anfang nach dem Ende. Jüdisches Leben in Deutschland bis heute* (Düsseldorf: Droste, 1996).

[9] Micha Brumlik, "Zur Identität der zweiten Generation deutscher Juden nach der Shoah in der Bundesrepublik," in *Jüdisches Leben*, ed. Brumlik et al.; Jael Geis, *Übrig sein. Leben "danach": Juden deutscher Herkunft in der britischen und amerikanischen Zone Deutschlands 1945–1949* (Berlin: Philo, 2000); Peter Sichrowsky, *Strangers in Their Own Land: Young Jews in Germany and Austria Today*, trans. Jean Steinberg (New York: Basic Books, 1986), originally *Wir wissen nicht was morgen wird, wir wissen wohl was gestern war. Junge Juden in Deutschland und Österreich* (Cologne: Kiepenhauer und Witsch, 1985); Susan Stern, ed., *Speaking Out: Jewish Voices from United Germany* (Chicago: edition q, 1995); Lynn Rapaport, *Jews in Germany after the Holocaust: Memory, Identity and Jewish-German Relations* (Cambridge: Cambridge University Press, 1997); Micha Brumlik, ed., *Zuhause, keine Heimat? Junge Juden und ihre Zukunft in Deutschland* (Gerlingen: Bleicher, 1998); Leslie Morris and Jack Zipes, eds., *Unlikely History: The Changing German-Jewish Symbiosis, 1945–2000* (New York: Palgrave, 2002).

[10] Brenner, *After the Holocaust*; Gay, *Safe among the Germans*.

Adding to the variegation of existing examinations is a host of local histories. German historians, in particular, have focused on the history of individual Jewish communities.[11] While these studies add to the general understanding of the Jewish experience in the postwar years and illustrate the great difficulty in reestablishing Jewish life in Germany, they cannot address many of the wider issues relating to the survival of Jewish life in Germany. In a highly politicized atmosphere, replete with debates on victimhood and on the postwar state's relationship with the past, the Jewish community of Germany only fared as well as it did because it organized on a nationwide level and sought recognition of Jewish demands from the West German federal government as well as the East German government. This study seeks to elucidate the supraregional and national coordination of the Jewish community in Germany to demonstrate the success of this model of organization.

Although there were some basic similarities between the Jewish community of East Germany and the community in West Germany (reconstitution of the community, centralizing organization, critical relations with state elites), the eastern Jewish community faced a unique set of difficulties. An increasingly centralized society and authoritarian government confronted it with serious challenges, not the least of which was regime-sanctioned antisemitism. This special circumstance has made the East German Jewish community

---

[11] Monika Berthold-Hilpert, "Die frühe Nachkriegsgeschichte der jüdischen Gemeinde Fürth (1945–1954)," in *Menora. Jahrbuch für deutsch-jüdische Geschichte* 9 (1998), ed. Julius H. Scheops (Munich: Piper, 1998); Monika Berthold-Hilpert, "Jüdisches Leben in Franken nach 1945 am Beispiel der Gemeinde Fürth," in *Jüdisches Leben in Franken*, ed. Gunnar Och and Hartmut Bobzin (Würzburg: Ergon, 2002); Barbara Johr, "Die Jüdische Gemeinde Bremen – Neugründung und Wiederaufbau 1945 bis 1961," *Arbeiterbewegung und Sozialgeschichte. Zeitschrift für die Regionalgeschichte Bremens im 19. und 20. Jahrhundert* 7 (July 2001); Ina Lorenz, "Jüdischer Neubeginn im 'Land der Mörder'? Die Wiederanfänge der Hamburger Jüdischen Gemeinde in den Nachkriegsjahren," in *Leben im Land der Täter*, ed. Schoeps; Anke Quast, *Nach der Befreiung. Jüdische Gemeinden in Niedersachsen seit 1945, das Beispiel Hannover* (Göttingen: Wallenstein Verlag, 2001); Donate Strathmann, *Auswandern oder Hierbleiben? Jüdisches Leben in Düsseldorf und Nordrhein 1945–1960* (Essen: Klartext, 2003); Alon Tauber, "Die Entstehung der Jüdischen Nachkriegsgemeinde [Frankfurt am Main], 1945–1949," in *Wer ein Haus baut, will bleiben. 50 Jahre Jüdische Gemeinde Frankfurt am Main. Anfänge und Gegenwart*, ed. Georg Heuberger (Frankfurt: Societäts-Verlag, 1998); Juliane Wetzel, *Jüdisches Leben in München, 1945–1951. Durchgangsstation oder Wiederaufbau?* (Munich: Stadtarchiv München, 1987); Jürgen Zieher, "Kommunen und jüdische Gemeinden von 1945 bis 1960. Studien zu Dortmund, Düsseldorf und Köln," Dr.phil. diss., Technische Universität Berlin, 2002; Ulrike Offenberg, "Die jüdische Gemeinde zu Berlin 1945–1953," in *Leben im Land der Täter*, ed. Schoeps.

a point of particular interest for scholars. Early studies of community did not have the advantage of the archival sources available since 1990, and they relied almost exclusively on interviews and memoirs.[12] More recently, scholars have explored many aspects of the small Jewish community in the east.[13] Despite a strong focus on relations with the state and Communist Party, the central role of the State Association and its internal debates have not figured as prominently as merited. In fact, even before the Jewish communities in western Germany united, the Jews of eastern Germany founded their umbrella organization, the State Association, under the politically active leadership of Julius Meyer. In chapters 3 and 5, the importance of the State Association to Jewish life in the east and the efficacy of Meyer's leadership receive critical examination.[14]

This is a story both about the Jews themselves and their relations with non-Jewish, German political elites. An important factor impacting these relations was the manner in which members of German society remembered the years 1933 to 1945. Naturally, those years had a very different meaning to Jewish Germans than to non-Jewish Germans. Moreover, interpretations of the recent past differed among various German social groups, and political leaders in West Germany viewed the legacy of the Nazi past differently from their counterparts in the east. Not only did the treatment of the past reflect German society's self-image after 1945, it also had practical ramifications for German interactions with Jewish victims of the Nazi regime. The historiography of memory has clarified our understanding of politics and society in postwar Germany; however, my work concentrates on the importance of political

[12] Robin Ostow, *Jews in Contemporary East Germany: The Children of Moses in the Land of Marx* (New York: St. Martin's, 1989), originally *Jüdisches Leben in der DDR* (Frankfurt: Jüdischer Verlag, 1988); Vincent von Wroblewsky, ed., *Zwischen Thora und Trabant: Juden in der DDR* (Berlin: Aufbau, 1993).

[13] Mario Keßler, *Die SED und die Juden – zwischen Repression und Toleranz. Politische Entwicklungen bis 1967* (Berlin: Akademie, 1995); Lothar Mertens, *Davidstern unter Hammer und Zirkel. Die Jüdischen Gemeinden in der SBZ/DDR und ihre Behandlung durch Partei und Staat, 1945–1990* (Hildesheim: Georg Olms, 1997); Ulrike Offenberg, *"Seid vorsichtig gegen die Machthaber." Die jüdischen Gemeinden in der SBZ und der DDR 1945–1990* (Berlin: Aufbau, 1998); Lothar Mertens, "Schwieriger Neubeginn. Die Jüdischen Gemeinden in der SBZ/DDR bis 1952/1953," in *Leben im Land der Täter*, ed. Schoeps.

[14] On Julius Meyer and the State Association, also see Jay Howard Geller, "Representing Jewry in East Germany, 1945–1953: Between Advocacy and Accommodation," in Leo Baeck Institute, *Year Book* 47 (2002), ed. J. A. S. Grenville (Oxford: Berghahn, 2002).

institutions to postwar German Jewish life and the manner in which those institutions handled overtly Jewish or Jewish-related issues.

Both Germanys wrestled with the legacy of the Nazi years as they tried to build new governments and societies. The integration into society or into the government of Nazi fellow-travelers, not to mention actual party members, was a serious challenge for the Bonn administration. Even as West Germany dealt with the historical legacy it had inherited, a good number of individuals with questionable pasts were installed in positions of influence.[15] Administrators frequently remained in their positions of authority without a significant change in personal attitude.[16] For politicians, the dilemma of dealing with the Nazi legacy in practical terms (e.g., reparations to the Nazis' victims, disposition of the camps, questions of architectural preservation after the wartime bombings, reinstatement of discredited officials, veterans' affairs, the national anthem question) remained ever-present.[17] Meanwhile, disputed

---

[15] Norbert Frei, ed., *Karrieren im Zwielicht. Hitlers Eliten nach 1945* (Frankfurt: Campus, 2001); Norbert Frei, *Vergangenheitspolitik. Die Anfänge der Bundesrepublik und die NS-Vergangenheit* (Munich: Beck, 1996), in English as *Adenauer's Germany and the Nazi Past: The Politics of Amnesty and Integration*, trans. Joel Golb (New York: Columbia University Press, 2002).

[16] Some German officials failed to cease some Nazi-era bureaucratic measures, such as the use of the word "Jew" on identification cards. Frank Stern, "The Historic Triangle: Occupiers, Germans and Jews in Postwar Germany," in *West Germany under Construction: Politics, Society, and Culture in the Adenauer Era*, ed. Robert G. Moeller (Ann Arbor: University of Michigan Press, 1997). For more on antisemitism and philosemitism, see Frank Stern, *The Whitewashing of the Yellow Badge: Antisemitism and Philosemitism in Postwar Germany*, trans. William Templer (Oxford: Pergamon, 1992), originally *Im Anfang war Auschwitz: Antisemitismus und Philosemitismus im deutschen Nachkrieg* (Gerlingen: Bleicher, 1991).

[17] The literature on memory of the past is increasingly voluminous. Among the many books that deal with some of these issues are Aleida Assmann and Ute Frevert, *Geschichtsvergessenheit/Geschichtsversessenheit. Vom Umgang mit deutschen Vergangenheiten nach 1945* (Stuttgart: Deutsche Verlags-Anstalt, 1999); Martin Broszat, ed., *Zäsuren nach 1945. Essays zur Periodisierung der deutschen Nachkriegsgeschichte* (Munich: Oldenbourg, 1990); James H. Diehl, *The Thanks for the Fatherland: German Veterans after the Second World War* (Chapel Hill: University of North Carolina Press, 1993); Helmut Dubiel, *Niemand ist frei von der Geschichte. Die nationalsozialistische Herrschaft in den Debatten des Deutschen Bundestages* (Munich: Carl Hanser, 1999); Konrad H. Jarausch and Michael Geyer, *Shattered Past: Reconstructing German Histories* (Princeton: Princeton University Press, 2003); Rudy Koshar, *Germany's Transient Pasts: Preservation and National Memory in the Twentieth Century* (Chapel Hill: University of North Carolina Press, 1998); Harold Marcuse, *Legacies of Dachau: The Uses and Abuses of a Concentration Camp, 1933–2001* (Cambridge: Cambridge University Press; 2001); Moeller, ed., *West Germany under Construction*; Robert G. Moeller, *War Stories: The Search for Usable Past in the Federal Republic of Germany* (Berkeley: University of California Press, 2001); Robert G. Moeller, "What Has 'Coming to Terms with the Past' Meant in Post–World War II Germany? From History to Memory to the 'History of Memory,' "

claims to victimhood and the instrumentalization of the memory of Nazi persecution had a critical impact on the East German government and, naturally, its relationship with Jews.[18] As that state perceived itself to be the very antithesis of the Nazi regime, its conception of National Socialism and of the effects of Nazi policy were critical in defining what East Germany would be. Soon, the internal debate on memory adversely affected the Jewish community, and demonstrations of memory of the Nazi past ossified into a routine of so-called antifascist commemoration.

Not only governments, but also members of civil society engaged in debate over the meaning and legacy of the Nazi years. Reflecting on the inheritance of the Nazi era and the Second World War, many groups regarded themselves as victims and sought redress of grievances. In West Germany, a veritable competition over victimhood erupted, fueled, in part, by the desire for political influence and demands for material support.[19] Germans living under occupation quickly forgot the war and characterized themselves as victims of an oppressive regime not unlike the Nazi regime.[20] Women who lost their husbands in the war were considered victims.[21] Those who had lost property in the war saw themselves as victims and were not inclined to support the victims of German aggression. This group of so-called war-damaged became an important constituency in West German politics.[22] Even German industry considered itself to be a victim of the Nazi era, and it

Central European History 35, no. 2 (June 2002); Hanna Schissler, ed., *The Miracle Years: A Cultural History of West Germany, 1949–1968* (Princeton: Princeton University Press, 2001).

[18] Thomas C. Fox, *Stated Memory: East Germany and the Holocaust* (Rochester: Camden House, 1999); Frevert, "Wider die deutsche Misere: Geschichtspolitik und Geschichtspropaganda," in Assmann and Frevert, *Geschichtsvergessenheit/Geschichtsversessenheit;* Karin Hartewig, *Zurückgekehrt. Die Geschichte der jüdischen Kommunisten in der DDR* (Cologne: Böhlau, 2000); Jeffrey Herf, *Divided Memory: The Nazi Past in the Two Germanys* (Cambridge: Harvard University Press, 1997); Jutta Illichmann, *Die DDR und die Juden: Die deutschlandpolitische Instrumentalisierung von Juden und Judentum durch die Partei- und Staatsführung der SBZ/DDR von 1945 bis 1990* (Frankfurt: Peter Lang, 1997).

[19] Some of these issues are reviewed in the introduction and part 3 of Alon Confino and Peter Fritzsche, eds., *The Work of Memory: New Directions in the Study of German Society and Culture* (Urbana: University of Illinois Press, 2002).

[20] Josef Foschepoth, "German Reaction to Defeat and Occupation," in *West Germany under Construction*, ed. Moeller; Marcuse, *Legacies of Dachau*, 63.

[21] Elizabeth D. Heineman, *What Difference Does a Husband Make?: Women and Marital Status in Nazi and Postwar Germany* (Berkeley: University of California Press, 1999).

[22] Michael L. Hughes, *Shouldering the Burdens of Defeat: West Germany and the Reconstruction of Social Justice* (Chapel Hill: University of North Carolina Press, 1999).

viewed Allied measures – including the trials of collaborationist industrialists – as an attack on German capitalism.[23] In general, "Germans preferred to dwell on their own suffering at the front and during the bombardment at home, and on their expulsion from the eastern parts of the Reich."[24]

Considering the political and social climate that prevailed in the postwar years, the consensus that something had to be done for Jewish victims quickly evaporated. To represent their interests and to press their claims, Jews in Germany relied on the ties forged to political leaders by the leaders of the Central Council. In fact, this strategy did bear fruit. In addition to the official role played by Hendrik George van Dam, secretary general of the Central Council, Karl Marx, publisher of the community's principal newspaper, slowly became something of an unofficial adviser to West German president Theodor Heuss on Jewish matters. Although Heuss has been considered the regime's representative who was most receptive to Jewish needs, there has been no examination of his critical

[23] S. Jonathan Wiesen, *West German Industry and the Challenge of the Nazi Past, 1945–1955* (Chapel Hill: University of North Carolina Press, 2001).

[24] Jarausch and Geyer, *Shattered Past*, 8. Debate over the meaning of the Nazi years continued long after the immediate postwar years. Scholars and philosophers, such as Theodor Adorno, asked just what "coming to terms with the past" meant. The issue is implicitly raised at every German commemoration of the Holocaust and of the war. At one such event in 1985, West German president Richard von Weizsäcker posed the question of whether the defeat of May 1945 was not also a liberation for the Germans. Popular reactions to recent examinations of the war and the Holocaust, notably to the German-language publication of Daniel Goldhagen's *Hitler's Willing Executioners* and to the so-called *Wehrmachtsausstellung*, are strong indicators that there is no consensus on the issue of memory and responsibility. On the Goldhagen controversy in Germany, see, among others, Daniel Jonah Goldhagen, *Hitlers willige Vollstrecker. Ganz gewöhnliche Deutsche und der Holocaust*, trans. Klaus Kochmann (Munich: Siedler, 1996); Johannes Heil and Rainer Erb, eds., *Geschichtswissenschaft und Öffentlichkeit. Der Streit um Daniel J. Goldhagen* (Frankfurt: Fischer, 1998). On the *Wehrmachtsausstellung*, which chronicled war crimes and atrocities committed by ordinary German soldiers during World War II, see, among others, Hamburger Institut für Sozialforschung, *Vernichtungskrieg. Verbrechen der Wehrmacht 1941 bis 1944. Ausstellungskatalog*, ed. Hannes Heer and Birgit Otte (Hamburg: Hamburger Edition, 1996); Hans-Günther Thiele, *Die Wehrmachtsausstellung. Dokumentation einer Kontroverse: Dokumentation der Fachtagung in Bremen am 26. Februar 1997 und der Bundestagsdebatten am 13. März und 24. April 1997* (Bonn: Bundeszentrale für Politische Bildung, 1997). More recently, there has been a new wrinkle in the debate on victimhood and memory of the Nazi years as some writers have raised the question of whether the Germans were victims of unnecessary or willful violence and atrocities by the Allies. Among the most notable exponents in this controversial debate are Günter Grass, *Crabwalk*, trans. Krishna Winston (New York: Harcourt, 2003), originally *Im Krebsgang: Eine Novelle* (Göttingen: Steidel, 2002); W. G. Sebald, *On the Natural History of Destruction*, trans. Anthea Bell (New York: Random House, 2003), originally *Luftkrieg und Literatur* (Frankfurt: Fischer, 2001); and Jörg Friedrich, *Der Brand. Deutschland im Bombenkrieg 1940–1945* (Munich: Propyläen, 2002).

symbiotic relationship with Marx, nor has there been much written explicitly on Heuss's philosemitism in forty years.[25] Meanwhile, Chancellor Konrad Adenauer developed his own relationship with Jewish leaders, namely Israeli diplomats and Nahum Goldmann of the World Jewish Congress.[26] The Jewish community also found strong support among the Social Democratic opposition, including party leader Kurt Schumacher.[27] The decisively important relations between the Jews and Heuss, Adenauer, and Schumacher, among others, stand at the center of the following examination of German-Jewish political relations.

Much of the scholarship on Jewish issues in German political discourse focuses on West German relations with Israel, and in particular reparations to Israel and Jewish groups around the world.[28] The importance of these reparations for Israel in material terms and West Germany in symbolic ones cannot be underestimated. This study reexamines some of those issues; however, with an emphasis on the Jewish community within Germany, I have also

[25] Theodor Heuss, *An und über Juden. Aus Schriften und Reden (1906–1963)*, ed. Hans Lamm, with a foreword by Karl Marx (Düsseldorf: Econ, 1964). The closest thing to a biography of Marx is a festschrift, a book about his newspaper, and a few shorter pieces: Marcel W. Gärtner, Hans Lamm, and E. G. Löwenthal, *Vom Schicksal Geprägt. Freundesgabe zum 60. Geburtstag von Karl Marx* (Düsseldorf: n.p., 1957); Ralph Giordano, *Narben, Spuren, Zeugen. 15 Jahre Allgemeine Wochenzeitung der Juden in Deutschland* (Düsseldorf: Verlag Allgemeine Wochenzeitung der Juden in Deutschland, 1961); Lilli Marx, "Renewal of the German-Jewish Press," interview by Michael Brenner, in *After the Holocaust*, ed. Brenner; "Karl Marx," in Verein EL-DE Haus, *Unter Vorbehalt. Rückkehr aus der Emigration nach 1945*, ed. Wolfgang Blaschke, Karola Fings, and Cordula Lissner (Cologne: Emons, 1997), 154–155.

[26] Jay Howard Geller, "Das Bild Konrad Adenauers vom Judentum und seine Beziehungen zu Vertretern jüdischer Organisationen nach 1945," in *Adenauer, Israel und das Judentum*, ed. Hanns Jürgen Küsters (Bonn: Bouvier, 2004).

[27] Shlomo Shafir, "Das Verhältnis Kurt Schumachers zu den Juden und zur Frage der Wiedergutmachung," in *Kurt Schumacher als deutscher und europäischer Sozialist*, ed. Willy Albrecht (Bonn: Abteilung Politische Bildung der Friedrich-Ebert-Stiftung, 1988).

[28] Lily Gardner Feldman, *The Special Relationship between West Germany and Israel* (Boston: George Allen and Unwin, 1984); Nana Sagi, *German Reparations: A History of the Negotiations*, trans. Dafna Alon (New York: St. Martin's, 1986); Kai von Jena, "Versöhnung mit Israel? Die deutsch-israelische Verhandlungen bis zum Wiedergutmachungsabkommen von 1952," *Vierteljahreshefte für Zeitgeschichte* 34, no. 4 (October 1986); Ludolf Herbst and Constantin Goschler, eds., *Wiedergutmachung in der Bundesrepublik Deutschland* (Munich: R. Oldenbourg, 1989); Constantin Goschler, *Wiedergutmachung. Westdeutschland und die Verfolgten des Nationalsozialismus (1945–1954)* (Munich: R. Oldenbourg, 1992); George Lavy, *Germany and Israel: Moral Debt and National Interest* (London: Frank Cass, 1996); Dominique Trimbur, *De la Shoah à la reconciliation: La question des relations RFA-Israël [1949–1956]* (Paris: CNRS Éditions, 2000); Niels Hansen, *Aus dem Schatten der Katastrophe. Die deutsch-israelischen Beziehungen in der Ära Konrad Adenauer und David Ben Gurion* (Düsseldorf: Droste, 2002).

investigated the role of German Jewry in making those reparations a reality. As it seemed increasingly likely that West Germany would pay significant reparations to Jewish recipients, the wider, international Jewish community did not remain immune to in-fighting and competition for compensation funds. The Jews in Germany did not always have cordial relations with their coreligionists and presumptive allies abroad.

In East Germany, the competitive cult of victimhood had more serious ramifications. As Jeffrey Herf has shown, the ruling Communist Party of the German Democratic Republic virtually predicated its claim to leadership of society on the legacy of victimhood under the Nazis. Moreover, it openly downplayed or denigrated the suffering of Jewish victims in comparison to the travails of Communist resisters. When the Jewish community pressed for reparations, many Communist leaders of East Germany regarded these demands as a potential threat. In their opinion, Jewish claims to victimhood and demands for reparations represented a rejection of the state's assertion of no responsibility for the past and its self-characterization as antifascist – the antithesis of the Nazi state. Catherine Epstein has expanded on Herf's analysis of intraparty competition and Jewish issues, and Karin Hartewig has specifically examined the fate of Jewish communists in the German Democratic Republic.[29] Other scholars, including Michael Wolffsohn, Jutta Illichmann, Angelika Timm, and Thomas Fox, have looked at the manner in which East Germany used the memory of Nazi persecution of the Jews for its own political purposes, including the manipulation of the relationship with Israel.[30]

Herf, Epstein, and Hartewig have looked at relations between Jews and the Communist regime in great detail from the perspective of the Communist Party's internal workings. Wolffsohn, Illichmann, Timm, and Fox focus on the uses and abuse of Jewish history by the regime. Similar to the first group, this study examines East German debates on victimhood from the non-Jewish, governmental perspective, but it also integrates the Jewish community's

[29] Herf, *Divided Memory;* Catherine Epstein, *The Last Revolutionaries: German Communists and Their Century* (Cambridge: Harvard University Press, 2003); Hartewig, *Zurückgekehrt.*
[30] Michael Wolffsohn, *Eternal Guilt?: Forty Years of German-Jewish-Israeli Relations,* trans. Douglas Bokovoy (New York: Columbia University Press, 1993), originally *Ewige Schuld? 40 Jahre deutsch-jüdisch-israelische Beziehungen* (Munich: Piper, 1993); Illichmann, *Die DDR und die Juden;* Angelika Timm, *Hammer, Zirkel, Davidstern. Das gestörte Verhältnis der DDR zu Zionismus und Israel* (Bonn: Bouvier, 1997); Fox, *Stated Memory.*

perspective, relying on documentation from the State Association of Jewish Communities in the GDR.

Between 1945 – when it was not clear whether Jewish life would successfully continue in Germany – and 1953, a unified and organized Jewish community emerged, despite tremendous obstacles. Moreover, as both Germanys struggled with their own relationship to the past, they were forced to confront a vocal and needy Jewish community. Some political leaders repeated prejudiced patterns of behavior, while others engaged with the Jewish community and fostered its growth and stability. The unlikely and extraordinary series of events that laid the earliest foundations for the vibrant Jewish community of contemporary Germany is this story.

CHAPTER 1

Liberation, Disunity, and Divided Organization in Western Germany

Long after the German surrender on 8 May 1945, millions of victims of Nazi terror continued to suffer from the war's devastating consequences. During the first months after the war, nearly seven million displaced persons (DPs), having lost their homes as a result of the war or having been deported by German occupiers, crowded into western Germany. Several hundred thousand Jewish concentration camp inmates – known in Jewish circles as the *Sherit Ha'pletah*, the saving remnant – numbered among these uprooted Europeans. Gathered in DP camps, these Yiddish-speaking, often religious Eastern European Jews (called *Ostjuden* in German) initially comprised the majority of the Jewish population in the three western zones of Allied occupation. Jewish Holocaust survivors who, before the war, had been Germans by culture and citizenship (called *Yekkes* in Yiddish) formed a minority of the fragmented Jewish community in occupied Germany. Many had survived the war living underground in Germany or in so-called privileged marriages (i.e., with a non-Jewish spouse), and few were religious.[1] After the war, thousands more returned to Germany, hoping to resume their prewar lives. Resettling primarily in cities, not in displaced persons camps, they interacted more with their local German governments than with the Allied authorities. Thus, from the beginning, the Jewish population in western Germany was culturally and physically divided.

Although most Jewish displaced persons intended to leave Germany for America or Palestine as soon as possible, they quickly organized themselves politically after their liberation.

[1] Gay, *Safe among the Germans*, 99–112; Michael Brenner, "East European and German Jews in Postwar Germany, 1945–1950," in *Jews, Germans, Memory: Reconstructions of Jewish Life in Germany*, ed. Y. Michal Bodemann (Ann Arbor: University of Michigan Press, 1996), 52.

While initially on a camp-by-camp basis, their organizations soon reached the regional and zonal levels, interacting with the Allied occupation authorities. Meanwhile, Jews fleeing antisemitism in Eastern Europe entered Germany, augmenting the refugees' numbers. The Allied occupiers were unprepared for a further massive influx of Jewish Holocaust survivors, and American authorities struggled to deal with what they termed "infiltration" of their occupation zone as they balanced their own security needs and humanitarian concern for the Jewish displaced persons.

The overwhelming majority of Jewish displaced persons in western Germany lived in the American zone of occupation, and their political activities were critically important. However, as the historian Hagit Lavsky has shown, the Bergen-Belsen DP camp in the British zone also developed into a leading center of Jewish self-administration. In fact, its success in fomenting a renaissance of Jewish life on German soil and its variegated, active Zionist political scene prepared thousands for life in Israel. By contrast, the Jewish displaced persons community in the French zone accounted for less than 1 percent of the total in western Germany and had "hardly any significance" to the wider history of Jewry in postwar Germany.[2]

For the native Jews of Germany who wished to resume their lives in the land of their birth, restitution and reparations remained primary concerns. Interacting with German administrators and governmental officials, they attempted to refound religious communities and to reestablish Jewish institutions, such as schools and retirement homes. To aid in the representation of their interests, they united on a regional basis and nominally on a trizonal basis in an association comprising the German Jewish communities in the American, British, and French zones of occupation. While some local groups had ties to the displaced persons' organizations, their interzonal union did not.

TWO JEWISH COMMUNITIES, TWO PATTERNS OF ASSISTANCE

As early as April 1945, Cologne had the first reestablished Jewish community on German soil, and throughout the summer of 1945,

---

[2] Brenner, "East European and German Jews in Postwar Germany, 1945–1950," in *Jews, Germans, Memory*, ed. Bodemann, 49; Lavsky, *New Beginnings*; Königseder and Wetzel, *Lebensmut im Wartesaal*, 10 and 81.

the community largely relied on the beneficence of then-mayor Konrad Adenauer. He aided Herbert Lewin, whom he character- ized as "chief doctor of the Jewish hospital of Cologne," in journey- ing to Theresienstadt in Czechoslovakia to collect all the Cologne citizens still in the camp. He also gave Lewin a certificate of en- dorsement to help him with his Jewish communal work.[3] Native German Jews, most of whom wished to remain in Germany, looked to local government leaders for support.

The Berlin Jewish community, the largest and most vibrant in Germany before the war, faced greater obstacles but still relied on local officials for assistance. Until July 1945 the erstwhile German capital was solely under Soviet occupation, and, as illustrated in chapter 3, the factor of Communist antisemitism would criti- cally impact Jewish life there. Once new Jewish groups sprang up to replace Nazi-era bodies, they received assistance from Siegmund Weltlinger, the official governmental adviser for Jewish affairs ap- pointed by the municipal office for religious affairs under Pastor Peter Buchholz.[4] Weltlinger spearheaded early efforts to care for Jewish Berliners and to centralize Jewish institutions in the city, and as seen below, his relations with the local Christian Democrats certainly facilitated that task.

In contrast to the German Jews living in towns and cities, Jewish displaced persons gathered in camps or assembly centers and re- lied on the American, British, and French armies of occupation for support. Based on their experience after previous wars, the Allies expected a displaced persons problem and began planning for that eventuality even before hostilities ended. In December 1943, Supreme Headquarters of the Allied Expeditionary Force (SHAEF) Civil Affairs Division established a small Refugees Sec- tion. Additionally, forty-four nations founded the United Nations Relief and Rehabilitation Administration (UNRRA) in November 1943, and it undertook voluntary relief work in areas under Allied

---

[3] Letter from Konrad Adenauer to the Czech authorities, 8 August 1945; certificate for Dr. Herbert Lewin, 11 August 1945; Konrad Adenauer, *Briefe 1945–1947*, ed. Hans Peter Mensing, Rhöndorfer Ausgabe, ed. Rudolf Morsey and Hans-Peter Schwarz (Berlin: Siedler, 1983), 69 and 72.

[4] "Bericht (26. Juni 1945)," 26 June 1945, LAB, E Rep. 200–22, 41. Interestingly, in November 1947 the Jewish adviser noted that the Allies, not the German administra- tion of the city of Berlin, had demanded the formation of the adviser's office. "Bericht über die Bedeutung und das Aufgabengebiet des Beirats für kirchliche Angelegenheiten," 24 November 1947, LAB, E Rep. 200–22, 38.

control. The American army asked the new group for 450 teams with thirteen staff members each, but UNRRA did not have that many personnel at its disposal. Allied headquarters classified refugees as stateless or as United Nations, ex-enemy, or enemy nationals. There were also special categories for those persecuted for religious, racial, or political reasons. This complicated and overlapping categorization would later hinder the army's project for separation and repatriation of displaced persons. Moreover, as officers on the ground would discover, not all those classified as "displaced" wished to be repatriated, and some were even unwilling to associate with their own compatriots.[5]

American intelligence operatives underestimated the extent and misjudged the nature of the postwar displaced persons problem. The Jewish Desk of the Office of Strategic Services, forerunner of the Central Intelligence Agency, handled questions arising from the persecution of Jews and prepared a report in June 1944 on the Jewish question in postwar Germany. The report's author naively suggested that eliminating discriminatory laws in Germany and stressing equal treatment for Jews would restore the status of the German Jews.[6] Virtually no provision was made for special treatment of Jews in the distribution of relief. Throughout the initial postwar months, the American army adhered to this policy, severely disadvantaging the expropriated and impoverished German Jews. Significantly, the report dealt almost exclusively with German Jews, even though the Holocaust had a disproportionately greater effect on Polish Jewry, and Polish Jews would be the primary concentration camp survivors. American analysts did not understand the circumstances facing German Jews in the post-Nazi era, nor did they foresee the massive influx of unrepatriable Eastern European Jews into Germany.

Only as Allied armies began to occupy Germany did their commanders and policy experts perceive the potential size of the displaced persons situation, but without acknowledging the uniquely Jewish element. In April 1945, the American Seventh

5 For information on the relationship between UNRRA and SHAEF, see Jacobmeyer, *Vom Zwangsarbeiter zum Heimatlosen Ausländer,* and George Woodbridge, *UNRRA: The History of the United Nations Relief and Rehabilitation Administration* (New York: Columbia University Press, 1950), 1:3, 2:482–484, and 2:507–518.
6 "Military Government and Problems with Respect to the Jews of Germany," 14 June 1944, NARA, RG 226, Records and Research Relating to the Analysis, Jewish Desk, box 2, folder "Allied Military Government and the Jewish Problem."

Army circulated a memorandum entitled "Repatriation Procedure," which dealt with refugees from Eastern Europe, omitting
mention of Jews. Even when the army did recognize groups of
displaced persons as United Nations allies, Jews did not receive
recognition as a distinct national or ethnic group.[7] In April 1945,
to aid with repatriation, an important goal, the Americans established a Displaced Persons Executive to work with UNRRA. Furthermore, in May 1945, UNRRA proposed collaborating with the
American Joint Distribution Committee, and Brigadier General
Stanley R. Mickelsen approved of the plan one month later.[8] Commonly known as "the Joint" and established by American Jews as
a refugee-aid organization during World War I, the organization
cooperated with the United Nations and the U.S. army to establish
displaced persons camps, officially known as "assembly centers."
There, refugees would be housed, clothed, and physically reha-
bilitated. Even before the war's end, Joseph Schwartz, European
director of the Distribution Committee, wrote UNRRA, offering
to provide fifteen to twenty staff members, a wholly inadequate
number.[9] In any case, petty bureaucratic obstacles prevented the
voluntary organizations from placing relief workers in the camps
until July and August. Still, the Joint Distribution Committee in the
American zone and the Jewish Relief Unit in the British zone provided an invaluable service to Jewish Holocaust survivors, and in
later years their efforts received praise from such prominent Jewish
leaders as Nahum Goldmann and Hendrik George van Dam.[10]

By July 1945, the four occupying powers had managed to repatri-
ate nearly four million of the seven million DPs, and by September,
six million DPs had returned home. However, the western powers' armies faced the growing problem of nonrepatriable persons,
including Poles, Balts, Ukrainians – and Jews. By late 1945, the
western Allies had ceased forcible repatriation of Soviet citizens,

---

7 "Displaced Persons" and "Repatriation Procedure," 4 April 1945, USHMM, RG 19.024,
  fiche 1; directive from Major John Pederson, 24 May 1945, USHMM, RG 19.024,
  fiche 2.
8 "Administrative Memorandum no. 39," 16 April 1945; letter from Brigadier General
  Stanley R. Mickelsen to UNRRA, 5 June 1945; CJH/YIVO, RG 294.1, folder 90 and
  folder 517.
9 Letter from Joseph Schwartz to UNRRA, 7 May 1945, CJH/YIVO, RG 294.1, folder 517.
10 Nahum Goldmann, *Mein Leben als deutscher Jude* (Munich: Albert Langen-Georg Müller,
  1980), 373–374; Hendrik George van Dam, "Die Juden in Deutschland nach 1945,"
  in *Judentum: Schicksal, Wesen und Gegenwart*, ed. Franz Böhm and Walter Dirks, vol. 2
  (Wiesbaden: Franz Steiner, 1965), 893.

reflecting the deterioration of relations with the USSR. Meanwhile, many Eastern Europeans who had refused repatriation lost their protected displaced persons status as a result of an intense screening procedure. While some simply had no desire to live under a communist regime, many non-Jewish displaced persons had politically compromised themselves through collaboration with the Nazis during the occupation of their homelands.

Throughout the summer of 1945, the number of Jewish refugees in the American zone was rapidly increasing as Jews left their erstwhile concentration camps. While army memoranda provided for displaced persons camps based on nationality, "Jewish" did not qualify as a nationality, leading to horrific situations. For example, the western occupiers often placed Hungarian Jews in camps with non-Jewish Hungarians who had been Nazi collaborators only a few months before, and the American Third Army in southern Germany, under orders from General George Patton, forcibly repatriated Polish Jews. At last, on 20 June, U.S. army units received orders to establish special camps for nonrepatriable refugees, and nine days later, further orders allowed the AJDC and UNRRA to run the camps.[11]

The American army did have some dealings with the much smaller German Jewish community, whose members lived primarily in cities and towns among the non-Jewish German population. Allied authorities interpreted the abolition of religious discrimination to mean no special privileges for any religious group. Therefore, they treated German Jews the same as non-Jewish Germans – as former enemies. However, by the end of July, American headquarters in Europe ordered the Third and Seventh Armies to treat ex-enemy nationals who had been in concentration camps the same way they would treat UN nationals. Even though this directive included a large number of German Jews, many soldiers all but ignored the orders.

In fact, relations between soldiers and displaced persons were deplorable. Emaciated and dehumanized by their years in the concentration camps, most survivors did not resemble normal human beings, and many disregarded the most elemental aspects of hygiene, according to American soldiers. These soldiers, with no training in relief work, could not understand the plight of

[11] "Memorandum," undated [February 1946], CJH/YIVO, RG 294.1, folder 90.

Hitler's victims and often treated them brutally. Many Americans identified with the conquered Germans, whom they saw as clean and orderly, in contrast to the starved and dirty concentration camp survivors. As the historian Leonard Dinnerstein has noted, many of the young American soldiers involved in the occupation of Germany had never seen people as physically or emotionally broken as the DPs and could, in no way, relate to their charges. On the other hand, the soldiers appreciated the Germans' deference to the Americans and readily consorted with German women.[12] George Patton repeatedly criticized the Jewish survivors, referring to them as "lower than animals" while commenting on their hygiene and living conditions.[13]

THE HARRISON REPORT AND ITS EFFECTS

Despite the Allies' best intentions, the situation was desperate. Critically lacking experience and resources, the American army, when confronted with the squalor of the concentration camps, was hard pressed to rectify the situation as it converted the camps into displaced persons assembly centers. Even after repatriating millions of displaced persons and adjusting its policy regarding nonrepatriable displaced persons, the U.S. army did not drastically improve the quality of life for those remaining in camps. Chronic shortages of adequate housing and clothing persisted; the diet provided for the refugees was nutritious but monotonous and often tasteless; and sanitary conditions remained abysmal. American Jews, including Treasury Secretary Henry Morgenthau, were exceptionally concerned, and by the summer of 1945, pressure had mounted to do something about the displaced persons' condition.[14] Earl G. Harrison, dean of the law school of the University of Pennsylvania and special State Department envoy in occupied Germany, was to be the agent of change.

Acting on a suggestion from Morgenthau and reacting to pressure from American Jews, a core Democratic Party constituency, President Truman ordered Harrison sent to Germany to inspect

---

[12] Leonard Dinnerstein, *America and the Survivors of the Holocaust* (New York: Columbia University Press, 1982), 52–55.
[13] George S. Patton, *The Patton Papers, 1940–1945*, ed. Martin Blumenson, vol. 2 (Boston: Houghton Mufflin, 1974), 751 inter alia.
[14] Dinnerstein, *America and the Survivors*, 34–35.

the situation. Accompanied by Joint Distribution Committee official Joseph Schwartz, among others, he toured displaced persons centers throughout western Germany in July 1945, and he met with many prominent Jewish leaders then in Europe, including Chaim Weizmann. The abject conditions in the displaced persons camps and the relationship between the residents and the occupation authorities shocked Harrison. While most Jews wanted to go to Palestine or America, he noted in his journal that they were "sitting and waiting. Have no feeling of liberation. Cannot leave without pass and curfew." Moreover, they were not allowed to live outside camps and had to manage with limited supplies, while Germans benefited from captured stocks of Nazi goods.[15] Despite improvement in their health conditions, the Jewish displaced persons needed more medical supplies and clothing. In many cases, they had to decide between retaining their striped prisoners' uniforms or wearing discarded Nazi uniforms. Harrison also criticized the inadequate food and buildings provided for them. Although the Jews no longer faced the threat of death, they saw little change in their daily lives.[16]

Earl Harrison's report for President Truman critically impacted the situation of the Jewish survivors. He called the Jews, who still lived isolated and "under guard behind barbed-wire fences," liberated "more in a military sense than actually." He added that since they had been persecuted specifically as Jews, they should be recognized as having needs different from those of other refugee groups. In an oft-quoted passage, he condemned the example that the Americans were setting for the German population:

As matters now stand, we appear to be treating the Jews as the Nazis treated them except that we do not exterminate them. They are in concentration camps in large numbers under our military guard instead of S.S. troops. One is led to wonder whether the German people, seeing this, are not supposing that we are following or at least condoning Nazi policy.[17]

In Harrison's own opinion, he was proposing not to give these Jews any special privileges, but merely to restore them to a normal level. In both his journal and his letter to Truman, he identified one clear

---

[15] "Journal, May–July 1945," USHMM, Earl G. Harrison Papers (RG 10.088), fiche 1.
[16] "Report of Earl G. Harrison," CJH/YIVO, RG 294.1, folder 107; reproduced in Dinnerstein, *America and the Survivors*, appendix B.
[17] Ibid.

solution to the Jewish problem in postwar Europe: Palestine. Only by evacuating the Jews to Palestine could the American army be free of its burden and the Jewish DPs achieve satisfaction. To do nothing was inhumane.[18]

President Truman was surprised and appalled by Harrison's findings. On 31 August 1945, he wrote a letter to General Dwight Eisenhower, quoting the report and demanding better treatment for the Jews. Truman did not want the displaced persons to remain in the same camps where they had been incarcerated by the Nazis and demanded a wider program of requisitions from the German population. The president's tone was very strong:

I know you will agree with me that we have a particular responsibility toward these victims of persecution and tyranny who are in our zone. We must make clear to the German people that we thoroughly abhor the Nazi policies of hatred and persecution.[19]

He also wanted a Zionist solution: "I am communicating directly with the British Government in an effort to have the doors of Palestine opened to such of these displaced persons as wish to go there."[20] While Truman could give orders to the American army in Europe, his efforts to influence the British government on this point would be in vain. Despite Truman's failure, the Harrison report succeeded in bringing attention to Palestine as the best possible solution to the Jewish refugee question in Germany, and Harrison himself continued to spread his message through lectures around the United States.[21]

The War Department learned of the contents of Harrison's report in early August and took action soon thereafter. By late August, headquarters of the U.S. Forces, European Theater, had ordered the creation of special assembly centers for Jewish displaced persons with superior accommodations, even at the expense of the German population, a move vigorously opposed by some American

[18] Ibid.
[19] Letter from Harry Truman to Dwight Eisenhower, 31 August 1945, Harry S. Truman Library, Truman Papers, White House Central File, Office File, Series 127. On-line version available via www.nara.gov/nara/searchnail.html, ARC identifier 201125.
[20] Ibid.
[21] Among other places, Harrison spoke before the Phi Beta Kappa association of Philadelphia (October 1945), the United Jewish Appeal (December 1945), and B'nai B'rith district 6 (July 1946). USHMM, RG 10.088, fiche 3. For more information on the impact of Harrison's report, see Dinnerstein, *America and the Survivors*, 39–72, and Mankowitz, *Life between Memory and Hope*, 53–63.

army officers, including George Patton.[22] UNRRA would need military help to operate the centers, and Eisenhower himself repeated this claim in a letter he sent to all subordinate commanders on 20 September. He reiterated the duties of all persons who dealt with the former Nazi victims and demanded full cooperation with civilian authorities for their care. However, he saw this burden fundamentally as a German one:

> The burden of providing the means for caring properly for these people must be to the greatest possible extent thrown upon the German population. There will be no hesitancy in requisitioning houses, grounds, or other facilities useful to displaced persons except as limited by essential considerations of practical administration. While the need for general concentration of displaced groups is recognized, this necessity must be met in such a way that excessive overcrowding in displaced persons installations is avoided.[23]

Eisenhower wanted displaced persons to receive priority in employment over Germans and to police themselves without arms, a policy that remained controversial for many years.[24]

Stung by Harrison's criticism, however, Eisenhower went to great pains to reply to Truman. He had the occupation army's Civil Affairs Division draft his response to the president.[25] Since Harrison's visit, conditions had improved, he wrote in October. He defended the health care, nutrition, and housing provided for the displaced persons by UNRRA and the Joint Distribution Committee. The displaced persons needed to remain congregated to facilitate the distribution of medical supplies and food, and any Jews still in concentration camps at the time of Harrison's report had been too ill to move. "It has always been our practice, not just our policy, to remove these victims with the utmost speed from concentration camps." Eisenhower added that guards had to be posted because many of the liberated were engaging in banditry and drinking too much, which was injurious to their fragile health, but he wanted them to guard themselves to the degree possible.

[22] "Special Camps for State and Non-repatriables," 22 August 1945, USHMM, RG 19.024, fiche 1; Patton, *Patton Papers*, 2:743 and 2:751–752 inter alia.

[23] Letter from Dwight Eisenhower to all subordinate commanders, 20 September 1945, BAK, Z 45, 5/323-1/31.

[24] Ibid.

[25] Draft by Brigadier General C. L. Adcock, 14 September 1945, NARA, RG 338, European Theater of Operations, Assistant Chief of Staff, G-5, Decimal File-box 42, folder 387.7-3 (Jews). Hereafter abbreviated as NARA, RG 338, ETO, G-5.

In general, however, Eisenhower was indignant about much of Harrison's report and said as much to the president:

Mr. Harrison's report gives little regard to the problems faced, the real success attained in saving the lives of thousands of Jewish and other concentration camp victims and repatriating those who could and wished to be repatriated, and the progress made in two months to bring these unfortunates who remained under our jurisdiction from the depths of physical degeneration to a condition of health and essential comfort.[26]

Eisenhower insisted that the army had made real progress in the months since liberation to care for the displaced persons, particularly considering how unprepared it had been for the horrors that awaited its troops on entering Dachau and Buchenwald.[27]

Critical to the development of relations between the displaced persons and the American army was the appointment of a special adviser for Jewish affairs to serve directly under the theater commander. While this adviser technically served under UNRRA and received his salary from American Jewish organizations, he carried weight with the U.S. army. Eisenhower and his successors, particularly General Joseph McNarney, supported him and listened to his counsel on matters relating to the Jewish refugees. As early as 24 August, the first adviser, American military chaplain Major Judah Nadich, received his appointment on a provisional basis. On the conclusion of his thirty-day tour, Nadich surveyed the situation in the Jewish DP camps and wrote that despite modest improvements, the camps were still overcrowded and suffered from a chronic lack of clothing, furniture, fuel, and food. Nadich pleaded for an expansion of work programs and leisure activities because the displaced persons had little or no structure to their lives in the camps. He called for more cooperation between the army and the Joint Distribution Committee:

Many situations could be alleviated if greater facilities were extended to the American Joint Distribution Committee. Some army officers still look upon the Joint Distribution Committee workers as "intruders" or

---

[26] Letter from Dwight Eisenhower to Harry Truman, 8 October 1945, BAK, Z 45, 5/323-1/31; Harry S. Truman Library, Truman Papers, White House Central File, Office File, Series 127a. On-line version available via www.nara.gov/nara/searchnail.html, ARC identifier 201126.
[27] Ibid.

as a "pressure group" instead of an efficient agency prepared to help in relief and rehabilitation.[28]

The American army continued to have a rocky relationship with UNRRA and the Jewish voluntary organizations throughout the occupation period. However, by the end of 1945, the army could report that the Jews enjoyed a higher status than all other so-called United Nations displaced persons, and Jews helped to administer and guard their own camps. On the other hand, as later critics have noted, the Jewish camps were already becoming increasingly crowded as a result of migration from Eastern Europe. Driven by antisemitism or motivated by Zionism, Jewish Holocaust survivors flocked to western Germany in the hope of moving to Palestine.[29]

As the issue of Jewish displaced persons became more pressing, the American army increasingly relied on its Jewish advisers, civilians whose records of public service drew them to the military.[30] On 3 October 1945, U.S. federal judge Simon Rifkind of New York accepted the position as Jewish adviser to the theater commander and held the post until May of the following year. He recognized that the displaced persons camps lacked the conditions for the newly liberated Jews to establish normal lives and urged their replacement with other forms of communal organization.[31] Moreover, the expulsion of ethnic Germans from Poland and Czechoslovakia soon added to the crowded conditions in the American occupation zone, but Rifkind requested that those persecuted by the Nazis on account of their race or religion be given preferential treatment over others entering the zone.[32]

[28] "Report on Conditions in Assembly Centers for Jewish Displaced Persons," 16 September 1945, BAK, Z 45, 5/323-1/31.

[29] "Care and Administration of Jewish Displaced Persons . . . ," 27 December 1945, NARA, RG 338, ETO, G-5, Decimal File-box 42, folder 387.7-3 (Jews); Dinnerstein, *America and the Survivors*, 109–112.

[30] Lucius Clay, *Decision in Germany* (Garden City, N.Y.: Doubleday, 1950), 234–235; Shlomo Shafir, *Ambiguous Relations: The American Jewish Community and Germany since 1945* (Detroit: Wayne State University Press, 1999), 56–58.

[31] "Final Memorandum," 7 March 1946; "Jewish Displaced and Stateless Persons," 1 November 1945; NARA, RG 338, ETO, G-5, Decimal File-box 42, folder 387.7-3 (Jews).

[32] "Draft Cable to AGWAR," undated, NARA, RG 338, ETO, G-5, Decimal File-box 38, folder Volume III Staff Studies 1945.

COLLUSION AND CONFLICT AS THE JEWS ORGANIZE

Despite the appointment of a Jewish adviser, the American army faced serious challenges regarding the DPs. Only coordinating the DPs and cooperation with them would yield effective action; however, organizing the Jews to deal with military occupation authorities was not easy. While representative committees easily sprang up in the camps, uniting the disparate groups in a single, zone-wide body proved a major task. The American army and charitable organizations already used the camp committees to distribute aid to the displaced persons efficiently, while the committees represented the displaced persons' political and economic interests. Regional and zonal committees eventually formed to agitate for emigration from Germany to Palestine and for greater civil rights for the displaced persons still in Germany. However, these groups served the Eastern European DPs and not the German Jewish community. A long legacy of tension separated the two groups, even as they needed each other.

Additionally, the community of Jewish displaced persons in Germany formed irregularly. While many DPs had been inmates of concentration camps in Germany such as Bergen-Belsen, Dachau, and Buchenwald, or had been survivors of the death marches, they were soon joined by more recent arrivals to Germany. After liberation by the Soviets or the flight of their German captors, many Eastern European Jews left Nazi camps in Poland and simply headed west, reckoning they had no homes to which to return. One survivor headed west was Norbert Wollheim, a forty-two-year-old native of Berlin and survivor of Auschwitz, who made his way to the former concentration camp of Bergen-Belsen via Schwerin in the Russian zone and Lübeck in the British zone. Belsen was the provisional locus of Jewish life in the British zone.

Under the leadership of Josef (or Yossel) Rosensaft, a Yiddish-speaking Jew from Poland, the displaced persons there founded an interim organizational committee almost immediately after liberation. However, stranded in the DP camps, the Jews felt "liberated but not free," and no one wanted to return to Eastern Europe, where most of them had lived before the war. As Wollheim noted, they saw their future in America or Palestine: "Europe is one big cemetery for us."[33] Belsen developed into a center of Zionist agitation and one of the most important Jewish communities in the British zone. The political divisions that had beset Jewish politics in prewar Poland replicated themselves to a large extent in the DP camps, but historian Hagit Lavsky has posited that the intensely Zionist politicization of life in the camps drew survivors into public life, fostered a renewed sense of belonging, and created an organic civil society that could be transferred to Palestine.[34] However, it also provided political and organizational training for those DPs who remained in Germany after the founding of Israel.

Additionally, the British zone did not have a monopoly on DP organization. Under the leadership of American chaplain Abraham Klausner and Polish-born Jewish displaced person Zalman Grinberg, representatives of the DP camps in Bavaria, in the American zone, met on 1 July 1945 to found an organization for liberated Jews in that state. A spirit of Zionism pervaded the meeting, attended by representatives of both the Jewish Brigade and the Zionist Organization. "In the shadow of the fire of the crematoria and gas chambers," the delegates resolved that the Jews should be allowed passage to Palestine, and the new Federation of Liberated Jews in Bavaria, led by a Central Committee, claimed the right to speak to the Allied governments in the name of the displaced persons.[35]

Even though the Bavarian regional Central Committee represented almost exclusively Eastern European Jews and had little harmonious contact with German Jews, it claimed to be the legal successor to all Jewish "communities, associations, and foundations, etc. in the region of Bavaria." Furthermore, it directed all its efforts toward a mass exodus of Jewry from Germany. By contrast, many German Jews wanted to resettle in their hometowns and rejected claims made by the Central Committee to speak for all Jews.[36]

---

[33] Norbert Wollheim, oral history interview, part II, 17 May 1991, USHMM, RG 50.030*0267, tape 2. For anecdotal accounts of the Jews' wish to immigrate to Palestine, see Gay, *Safe among the Germans*, 75–77.

[34] Lavsky, *New Beginnings*, 219.

[35] "Protokoll der vereinigten Juden. Zusammenkunft der Delegierten aus den einzelnen Lagern in Bayern," 1 July 1945, CJH/YIVO, RG 294.1, folder 135. The Palestine-based Jewish Brigade fought for the British during World War II and operated an underground railroad to Palestine for Holocaust survivors after the war.

[36] "Satzung des Verbandes der befreiten Juden in Bayern," 26 October 1946, CJH/YIVO, RG 294.1, folder 129. Regarding the German Jews, see chapter 2, also Königseder and Wetzel, *Lebensmut im Wartesaal*, 83–85.

In seeking representation and redress for concerns, German Jews and Eastern European Jews parted ways once again. The Eastern European Jews in refugee camps looked to the Allied occupiers, while the German Jews living in towns and cities looked to the local, German authorities.

Meanwhile, the ambitious Bavarian Central Committee attempted to unite most of the Jews in western Germany in a single organization. In conjunction with the Jewish Brigade, it arranged in July 1945 for representatives of the displaced persons in the American and British zones to meet in St. Ottilien, Bavaria, to discuss forming a single group. Further meetings were planned for October and November in Frankfurt. Despite some concrete plans, the talks came to naught. Josef Rosensaft, leader of the small Jewish refugee community in the British zone, feared losing influence if his group united with the large community in the American zone. Thus, personal considerations also influenced the chances of unification.[37]

Within the British zone, Eastern European Jews and German Jews enjoyed harmonious relations. Meeting in Belsen on 25–27 September 1945, they selected Rosensaft, a Polish Jew, as chairman and Wollheim, a native Berliner, as vice chairman of the Central Committee of Liberated Jews in the British Zone. Many years later, Wollheim recounted that "our origin – German Jews or East European Jews – played no role, not even in my election; we were all Jews and considered ourselves only as Jews. In the American occupation zone, the situation was completely different."[38] There, the German Jewish communities felt threatened by the massive size of the Eastern European Jewish population. In the British zone, by contrast, the two groups were of roughly equal size, which facilitated their interaction.

Political organization flourished. Each displaced persons camp had a committee subordinate to the new zonal Central Committee. They worked with the American Joint Distribution Committee and the Jewish Relief Unit in addressing their needs. They also cultivated ties to the World Jewish Congress and to Jews in Britain,

37 "Protokoll Nr. 5," 3 August 1945, "Protokoll Nr. 12," 7 October 1945, CJH/YIVO, RG 294.1, folder 135; Brenner, *After the Holocaust*, 35; Königseder and Wetzel, *Lebensmut im Wartesaal*, 85–87.
38 Norbert Wollheim, "Jewish Autonomy in the British Zone," interview by Michael Brenner, *After the Holocaust*, ed. Brenner, 97.

Figure 1. Franco-Polish Zionist activist Marc Jarblum addresses a crowd of DPs at a demonstration protesting the forced return to Europe of the *Exodus 1947* passengers. Josef Rosensaft stands behind Jarblum. Norbert Wollheim is in the crowd directly in front of Jarblum, third from left. The Yiddish text of the banner on the right reads: "Illegal immigrants from the Exodus we are with you! United in the struggle for free immigration!" *Source:* USHMM.

including some members of Parliament. Still, a general sense of despair prevailed at this time, as many Jewish refugees could not achieve their goal of emigration from Germany to Palestine.

Jewish displaced persons in the British zone had particular animus against the British occupiers whose government prevented their free emigration to Palestine. Furthermore, the British were unprepared logistically and psychologically for the task before them in Germany. One former internee later complained,

Colonel Jones, who was in charge of the camp [Belsen] . . . , was a typical product of the British nobility. People of this class regarded the DPs as scum; they didn't understand that among the people who had just been liberated from the concentration camp, there were also physicians and lawyers and professors, and such.[39]

Fearful of acknowledging the right of the Jews to a homeland in Palestine, British occupation authorities gave the Jewish displaced persons almost no special treatment, even long after the Americans had begun to do so. The British even forced ships illegally carrying DPs to Palestine to return to occupied Germany. The most infamous among these was the *Exodus 1947*, whose return triggered widespread protests (see Fig. 1). As a result of this policy, the number of displaced persons throughout the British zone did not exceed 15,000, and Belsen remained the focus of British Jewish policy.

In contrast, the American occupation government dealt with a vastly larger refugee population, which was slow to organize, doing so on a zone-wide basis four months later than in the British zone. On 27 January 1946 – exactly one year after the liberation of Auschwitz – the Federation of Liberated Jews in the American Occupation Zone was founded for the "legal-political representation of general claims in the interests" of the Jews vis-à-vis governmental bodies and the military. It also planned to organize the emigration of the Jews and to serve as a liaison for the voluntary organizations. Once the emigration of the Jews from Germany was achieved, it would disband. In the presence of prominent Zionist leaders such as David Ben-Gurion and Nahum Goldmann, the delegates elected a governing council and a central committee with Zalman Grinberg as chairman. The Federation also claimed to be the heir to all formerly Jewish-owned property in the American

[39] Ibid., 98.

zone, including any property administered by the former Reich Union of Jews in Germany.[40] However, not all Jews in Germany accepted the Federation. Stuttgart Jewish leader Josef Warscher wrote that the German Jewish communities in Munich, Nuremberg, Fürth, Würzburg, and Württemberg rejected the new group and any decisions it made. *They* claimed to be the heirs to the pre-1933 communities, rejecting the displaced persons' claims to Jewish assets in the American zone.[41]

THE SEARCH FOR SOLUTIONS TO THE DP PROBLEM

The camps had improved since May 1945, and the DPs' committees were functional, but a new influx of Jewish refugees to western Germany created new problems, taxing the Allies' resources and straining relations with the displaced persons' leadership. Many Jewish survivors of the Holocaust had initially returned to their homes in Poland in search of relatives or remnants of their prewar lives; however, finding nothing, and often greeted by antisemitism, they headed westward in the hope of starting a new life outside Europe. While they saw the Allied occupation zones in Germany as the first stop on their way to Palestine or America, leaving Germany proved much more difficult than entering it. Soon, several hundred thousand Eastern European Jews crowded into the various displaced persons camps, yearning to emigrate.[42]

The most obvious yet most elusive solution to the mounting problem was emigration from occupied Germany to the British mandate territory of Palestine. In September 1945, the first Congress of Liberated Jews in the British zone had issued a manifesto demanding a Jewish state and the transfer of control over entry to Palestine from Britain to the Jewish Agency. The displaced persons expressed their "sorrow and indignation that almost six months after liberation we still find ourselves in guarded camps on German soil soaked with blood of our people." They further declared that they would not go home to their former countries – the

---

[40] Untitled document, 27–29 January 1946, CJH/YIVO, RG 294.1, folder 112; "Satzung des Verbandes der befreiten Juden in der amerikanischen Besatzungszone," 27 January 1946, CJH/YIVO, RG 294.1, folder 129.

[41] Letter from Josef Warscher to Bavarian Central Committee, 26 January 1946, CJH/YIVO, RG 294.1, folder 112.

[42] Dinnerstein, *America and the Survivors*, 109–112.

solution the British had proposed.[43] Meanwhile, President Truman carried through on his promise to ask the British for greater Jewish immigration to Palestine, suggesting that 100,000 Jewish displaced persons be allowed into the mandate territory. British foreign minister Ernest Bevin completely refused any such concessions to the Jews, and Jewish displaced persons in the U.S. zone responded with letters of protest and even a one-day hunger strike.[44] Ever more Jews illegally entered the U.S. zone in the hope of continuing on to Palestine. While the British made it almost impossible to leave their zone, the Americans were not above turning a blind eye to Jewish emigration. They allowed Jews with seemingly valid visas for Bolivia to enter France, where they promptly disappeared with the intention of going to Palestine. The Americans also wanted to relieve overcrowding in their zone by sending Jewish DPs to Italy, from where, American officials surely knew, they would attempt to depart for Palestine.[45] The fewer Jewish refugees stranded in their zone, the better.

As overcrowding in the Jewish DP camps in the American zone grew critical, the army considered radical solutions. In November 1945, Lieutenant Colonel Harry Messec of the American military's Displaced Persons and POW Division sent letters to his superiors, asking their opinion on setting up exclusively Jewish enclaves

[43] "Resolution One" and "Resolution Two," CJH/YIVO, RG 294.2/MK 483, film 114, frame 1.
[44] Letter of protest from Landsberg DP camp, 15 November 1945, NARA, RG 338, ETO, G-5, Decimal File-box 42, folder 387.7-3 (Jews). While Bevin was under great pressure from the British Foreign Office not to exacerbate the unrest among the British mandate territory's Arab population, historians have long debated whether Bevin was also an antisemite. Allan Bullock defends Bevin against the often-heard charge of antisemitism, claiming that he was a supporter of Jewish interests before the war and that the Labour Party never wholeheartedly believed in the pro-Zionist planks of its party platform. As foreign minister, Bevin resented pressure from Zionists and disdained what he perceived as Truman's pandering to the Jewish constituency. These factors led him to take heavy-handed measures against the Zionists' goals. Allan Bullock, *Ernest Bevin: Foreign Minister, 1945–1951* (London: William Heinemann, 1983), 164–183. Peter Weiler thinks Bullock overlooks Bevin's long history of antipathy for both "Jewish finance" and "Jewish Communism." As foreign minister, he was notorious for his derisive remarks about "the Chosen People," but these did not shape his Palestine policy, Weiler writes. Peter Weiler, *Ernest Bevin* (Manchester: Manchester University Press, 1993), 170–171.
[45] Letter from Lieutenant Colonel Harry Messec to deputy military governor of OMGUS, 6 September 1946, NARA, RG 260, OMGUS, Records of the Executive Office, Office of the Adjutant General: General Correspondence and other records, Decimal File-box 21, folder 014.33 (4). Hereafter cited as NARA, RG 260, OMGUS, AG. "Proposed Jewish DP Settlement in Italy," 13 September 1946, NARA, RG 338, ETO, G-5, Decimal File-box 45, folder 387.7-3.

in rural areas; however, Major General M. C. Stayer objected to the erection of what he called "a modern Ghetto," which might even include German Jews. Additionally, by removing them from the wider Germany community, Germans could avoid their responsibility to treat them as equal citizens. He wanted to force the Germans to have contact with the former Nazi victims.[46] Another option was allowing the Jewish displaced persons to emigrate to America. American commander Lucius Clay wrote in his memoirs that the army favored admitting displaced persons to America, as they made good citizens.[47] Jacob Blaustein of the American Jewish Committee lobbied the secretary of state to make full use of immigration quotas to help the displaced persons, and on 22 December, Secretary Dean Acheson replied that the president had issued an order regarding the granting of additional visas.[48]

Meanwhile, relations between UNRRA and the American army deteriorated as voluntary relief organizations proved unwilling or unable to fulfill all the functions designated to it. The army's Jewish adviser Rifkind pejoratively referred to the organization as "a bunch of social workers."[49] Major General J. M. Bevans wrote on 17 December 1945 that "the functions left to UNRRA are very limited and its responsibilities are nil."[50] Even though Congress had allocated funds to this branch of the United Nations, the voluntary agency would not furnish the displaced persons with supplies, leaving the army to fill this role in the American zone. Finally in February 1946, UNRRA entered into a new agreement with the American occupiers, enshrining the new reality and specifying that the UN relief group would perform the functions, but the army would furnish the supplies. Additionally, the UN relief organization was to operate a records office and tracing bureau, provide

---

[46] Letter from Lieutenant Colonel Harry Messec to Internal Affairs and Welfare Division, 13 November 1945, letter from Major General M. C. Stayer to POW and DP Division, 19 November 1945, BAK, Z 45, 5/323-1/31; "Proposal to Establish an Enclave for Jewish Displaced Persons," 23 November 1945, NARA, RG 338, ETO, G-5, Decimal File-box 41, folder 387.7-4 (Jewish).

[47] Clay, *Decision in Germany*, 233.

[48] Letter from Dean Acheson to Jacob Blaustein, 25 January 1946, CJH/YIVO, RG 371.7.1, box 33. For information on Jewish emigration to America, see Dinnerstein, *America and the Survivors*.

[49] Quoted in Dinnerstein, *America and the Survivors*, 12.

[50] "Agreement as to Relationship of UNRRA and the Commanding General, USFET," 17 December 1945, NARA, RG 338, ETO, G-5, Decimal File-box 38, folder: Volume IV Staff Studies 1945.

medical services, and arrange for DP movement.[51] "This in fact retains UNRRA as an agent of the Army instead of placing the Army as an agent of UNRRA," Bevans wrote.[52]

In spring 1946, American and British Jewish leaders expressed growing concern about the plight of Eastern European Jews in the British zone, leading A. G. Brotman of the British Jewish Committee for Relief Abroad and Harry Viteles of the American Joint Distribution Committee to petition the Allied occupiers. Compared with the situation in the American zone, relatively few displaced persons wanted to enter the British zone, where relations between the zonal Central Committee and the occupation authority were generally poor. Moreover, the displaced persons claimed that the western powers did not consult them when making decisions regarding their fate, and they resented the volunteer agencies claiming to speak for them. Brotman and Viteles demanded more "respect and consideration" for the British zonal Central Committee, which had realized remarkable achievements in the camps.[53] These included the establishment of a kindergarten, a secondary school, a theater, and a newspaper for the refugees. While the displaced persons did not elect representatives to the governing boards of the local German Jewish congregations, they did send delegates to the 22nd Zionist Congress in Basel, reinforcing their division from the German Jews who did not receive recognition from international Zionist groups.[54] In general, the German Jews usually dealt with the local German government, whereas the displaced persons dealt exclusively with the Allied occupation authorities. As a result, for example, in Hanover the German community enjoyed official recognition, but the local displaced persons committee did not.[55]

Large as was the problem of Jewish displaced persons in the American zone, it reached tremendous proportions in the spring

---

[51] "Agreement as to the Relations of UNRRA to Commanding General, USFET in the US Zone of Germany," 19 February 1946, BAK, Z 45, 3/171-1/13.

[52] "Agreement as to Relationship of UNRRA to Commanding General, USFET," 17 December 1945, NARA, RG 338, ETO, G-5, Decimal File-box 38, folder: Volume IV Staff Studies 1945.

[53] "Survey of Conditions of Jews in the British Zone of Germany," March 1946, CJH/YIVO, RG 294.1, folder 496.

[54] "Juden wollen streiken," *Jüdisches Gemeindeblatt für die britische Zone*, 6 January 1947. On cultural activities in the displaced persons camps, especially in the American occupation zone, see Angelika Eder, "Kultur und Kulturveranstaltungen in den jüdischen DP-Lagern," in *Leben im Land der Täter*, ed. Schoeps.

[55] "Survey of Conditions of Jews in the British Zone of Germany," March 1946, CJH/YIVO, RG 294.1, folder 496.

and summer of 1946, straining even the largest transit camps, such as Landsberg and Föhrenwald in Bavaria. Antisemitic incidents in Eastern Europe, including the infamous Kielce pogrom in July 1946, induced a new wave of mass migration to western Germany. Jews in the East saw no future for themselves in Europe and regarded the American zone as their first way station on their journey to Palestine or America. As of 21 May 1946, the American occupiers' Civil Affairs Division reported that 1,500 Jewish displaced persons were entering the American zone each week. On 11 June, the Jewish adviser Rabbi Philip Bernstein claimed that 150,000 Jews wanted to enter the zone, predicted that 10,000 per month would do so, and requested preparations for the first 40,000. The Americans also knew that the Jewish Brigade was partly to blame for the influx of refugees.[56] Writing after the expiration of his appointment, Bernstein admitted that when he had come to Germany, he thought the displaced persons problem had been solved; instead, it had mushroomed during his tenure. Nonetheless, he did have positive words for the army's handling of the matter. "This favorable attitude [by U.S. generals] yielded results. Although DP life is essentially untenable, the actual realities within the framework of existing conditions were not unbearable." Both the health and the living situation of the DPs had stabilized, and they ran most of their own camps and operated rehabilitation projects. Still, Bernstein noted, standards of care were low because of lack of funds. He predicted that it would take three or four years to send all the Jews to Palestine and accused the British of latent antisemitism: "The British had no love for these people and showed it plainly. They gave them no better care than their recent enemies, the Germans."[57]

Harry Viteles elucidated some of the reasons Polish Jews chose the U.S. zone over the British zone as their place of refuge. The American occupiers, he noted, granted the recent arrivals the same status as the earlier displaced persons, unless they lived outside the camps. In the British zone, he claimed, they received no recognition and had to survive on the minimum of calories – 1,000 per day. Viteles directly commended the American army's policy

[56] "History of G-5 Division, 1 April–30 June 1946," NARA, RG 338, ETO, G-5, History-box 1.

[57] "Report by Rabbi Philip S. Bernstein, Adviser on Jewish Affairs, U.S. Zones, Europe," CJH/YIVO, RG 347.7.1, box 33.

and attacked that of the British. Even for officially recognized displaced persons living in camps, there was a disparity of care. In the American zone, all-Jewish camps were the norm, while the British were slow even to grant the Jews their own housing blocks within camps.[58]

Faced with the burgeoning refugee population, the American army struggled to come up with solutions.[59] On 15 August, McNarney cabled the War Department, pleading his inability to stop Jews from pouring into the zone from Poland and Berlin. At the same time, there was not enough winter housing in the U.S. zone of Germany for all the Jewish and non-Jewish refugees, and McNarney wanted to send the Jews to Italy. Britain protested against this proposal, fearing the migrants might continue on to Palestine. McNarney asked his Jewish adviser Philip Bernstein to lobby the British government as well as Pope Pius XII on behalf of his plan. UNRRA, pleading overstretch, opposed the plan, but ultimately consented to admitting 10,000 displaced persons. McNarney also proposed raising the Germans' daily calorie ration in the hope they might better bear the overcrowding.[60] By the end of August 1946, Bernstein requested ten more uniformed Jewish chaplains to act as mediators between the American military and the displaced persons, and the War Department asked the Jewish Welfare Board to find for it Yiddish-speaking war veterans, for Yiddish was still the everyday language of most Jewish displaced persons.[61]

TENSIONS BETWEEN THE REFUGEES AND THE AMERICAN ARMY

Despite the improvement in living conditions and the American authorities' generally lax attitude toward emigration from the zone, the displaced persons still had difficult relations with the

[58] "Report on Visit to Germany, January 6th to April 8th, 1946, by H. Viteles," 11 May 1946, CJH/YIVO, RG 294.1, folder 52.
[59] "History of G-5 Division, 1 July–31 December 1946, Part One," NARA, RG 338, ETO, G-5, History-box 1.
[60] "Proposed Jewish DP Settlement in Italy," 13 September 1946, NARA, RG 338, ETO, G-5, Decimal File-box 45, folder 387.7-3; "History of G-5 Division, 1 July–31 December 1946, Part One," NARA, RG 338, ETO, G-5, History-box 1.
[61] Letter from War Department to USFET, 3 October 1946, NARA, RG 338, ETO, G-5, History-box 1.

Americans. Virtually no single issue created more tension than the question of policing and security. Left without gainful employment, many refugees turned to black marketeering, and some smugglers stored their illegal goods in DP camps, creating a situation in which both German police and American military police felt compelled to search the camps. Naturally, these Holocaust survivors were mistrustful of police authority and completely disdainful of the German police. Citing numerous individual incidents, Zalman Grinberg, leader of the Jewish displaced persons in the American zone, petitioned UNRRA for redress in late March 1946.[62] American military headquarters in Europe knew that there had been accusations that the Jewish displaced persons had been subjected to unreasonable searches and had been deprived of due process in their dealings with the occupiers' judicial system. Additionally, defendants often lacked qualified interpreters.[63] Many Jews coming from Eastern Europe had no experience in dealing with American soldiers. Moreover, they were accustomed to the chaotic conditions created by war. Thus, as they readjusted to conditions of civil order, there were frequent misunderstandings with military officials and police.

The Seventh Army was at pains to find a policy regarding the policing of Jewish DP camps. Lieutenant General Geoffrey Keyes, commander of the Seventh Army, ordered that when looking for evidence, the German police could enter the camps only when escorted by American military police. Harry Lerner, acting director of UNRRA Team 502, amended this policy in January 1946, so that American police reported to the camp's Jewish police and worked with them – not the Germans – when conducting a search. Keyes was furious over this change and the effect it had when 200 armed German police tried to search a DP camp in Stuttgart on 29 March 1946. Believing that the German police had no right to enter their camp under any circumstances, the Jewish refugees started a riot. In the ensuing violence, one Jewish Holocaust survivor was killed. The displaced persons' press described the incident in terms appropriate for depicting a Nazi raid. As a result of

---

[62] Letter from Zalman Grinberg to General Frederick Morgan of UNRRA, 26 March 1946, CJH/YIVO, RG 294.1, folder 62.
[63] "Military Justice in Relation to Displaced Persons," composed by Major General H. R. Bull, 4 March 1946, NARA, RG 338, ETO, G-5, Decimal File-box 45, folder 387.7-3.

the furor, Keyes and McNarney issued new regulations for raids on Jewish DP camps.[64]

Despite this modification, the situation regarding the DPs and subordination to police authority grew only more dire. On 28 April, two Jewish schoolboys disappeared from their posts as school guards in the Landsberg DP camp. As rumor spread that Germans had kidnapped and murdered the boys, fighting broke out between Jews and local Germans. When American police tried to disperse the crowd, the displaced persons stoned the police, who arrested twenty-three people. The arrest and ensuing trial of Jews who had just been freed from Hitler's camps became a cause célèbre among American Jews, including Congressman Adolph Sabath of Chicago. Of the defendants who were brought to trial, one was found not guilty, and nineteen others received sentences ranging from three months to two years. As a result of the controversy, American military commander McNarney decided to allow only unarmed, well-supervised German police to enter Jewish DP camps.[65] Several officers complained that Henry Cohen, head of UNRRA Team 106 at the Föhrenwald camp, refused to turn over fugitives from military justice.[66] The records of the American occupation regime are replete with reports of black market activity and clashes with German police.[67] While the illegal business practices of many Jewish displaced persons have colored the way historians have viewed them, one should not forget how prevalent such activities were at that time of economic devastation among all groups, including Germans. In many places the black market was the only economic activity. Additionally, many American GIs profited heavily from their involvement with the black market. In November 1945, *Stars and Stripes* reported that "American soldiers sent home approximately $11 million more than they drew in salary."[68]

---

[64] "Command and Notice" and numerous letters, NARA, RG 260, OMGUS, AG, Decimal File-box 44, folder 250.1 (3). For documentation on the OMGUS investigation of the Stuttgart riot, see NARA, RG 260, OMGUS, AG, Decimal File-box 45, folder 250.1 (1); Stern, *Whitewashing of the Yellow Badge*, 109.

[65] For the relevant documentation, "History of G-5 Division, 1 April–30 June 1946" and "History of G-5 Division, 1 April–30 June 1946, Documents," NARA, RG 338, ETO, G-5, History-box 1.

[66] Assorted letters, May–July 1946, BAK, Z 45, 3/170-3/8.

[67] See NARA, RG 260, OMGUS, AG, Decimal File-box 44, folder 250.1 (3).

[68] Dinnerstein, *America and the Survivors*, 50.

In contrast to its role in economic and political affairs among the Jews, the American military tried to limit its involvement in Jewish religious life. Lucius Clay was of the opinion that the army's Religious Affairs Branch should not interfere in domestic religious disputes but help local clergy and lay leaders to solve them themselves.[69] On 15 April 1946, the Allied Control Authority issued a statement that the various German religious groups should be free to revise their own constitutions.[70] In March, President Truman had approved the idea of providing American Catholic, Protestant, and Jewish liaisons to the German religious groups, and Secretary of War Robert Patterson asked Rabbi Herbert Goldstein of the Synagogue Council of America to appoint a representative. On 10 May 1946, the military government received news that the Synagogue Council had nominated Rabbi Alexander Rosenberg, who had been in Germany with the Joint Distribution Committee.[71] Clay, however, had reservations about this position, writing that "representatives from [the] US can only become special pleaders."[72] Despite Clay's opposition, the War Department did name religious liaisons. While the military generally limited its involvement in German religious life, it considered a renewal of religious activity a means of reforming and rehabilitating Germany. The Americans praised Christian religious leaders for their opposition to the Nazis and funded religious institutions and publications in their zone.[73] The army also sent one German rabbi to America on an exchange program, and in October 1947, a group of Jewish chaplains arrived in Germany to work with the Jewish refugees.[74]

WORKING WITH THE DPS IN THE AMERICAN ZONE

Relations between the American army and the DPs had been strained, but soon, the obvious solution to the problem became

[69] Clay, *Decision in Germany*, 304.
[70] "Policy Recommendations on Religious Affairs," 15 April 1946, BAK, Z 45, 5/337-2/6.
[71] Letter from Robert Patterson to G. Bromley Oxnam, 21 March 1946, NARA, RG 260, OMGUS, AG, Decimal File-box 2, folder AG-000.3 (4); cable to OMGUS, 10 May 1946, NARA, RG 260, OMGUS, AG, Decimal File-box 2, folder AG-000.3 (1).
[72] Letter from Lucius Clay to Oliver Echols, 29 May 1946, NARA, RG 260, OMGUS, AG, Decimal File-box 2, folder AG-000.3 (1).
[73] "Report on the U.S. Occupation of Germany (Religious Affairs Program)," 23 September 1947, BAK, Z 45, 5/337-2/6.
[74] "Religious Affairs Branch," undated, BAK, Z 45, 5/337-2/6; letter from General Clarence R. Huebner to U.S. army Berlin, Austria, Bremerhaven, and 1st and 2nd Military Districts, 20 October 1947, BAK, Z 45, 3/174-1/20.

reality. The army would work with the Central Committee in its zone. With growing Jewish displaced persons communities looking to the zonal Central Committees for leadership, the committees organized the social, economic, and intellectual life of the DP camps. Such grass-roots legitimacy made collaborating with the committees advantageous for relief organizations. However, working with the refugees' ambitious and recalcitrant leadership could be trying.

The activities of the Central Committee in the American zone became more routinized in spring 1946, but the Joint Distribution Committee had less than ideal relations with displaced persons' representation. Although the AJDC provided 90 percent of the Central Committee's funds and had legal authority over the organization, its real control did not go very far. The AJDC simply did not have enough staff members to monitor the DPs' organization properly. The Central Committee did not maintain stringent bookkeeping, even after reorganization. It often purchased food and clothing locally, with no way to verify how it spent the money or how it distributed the goods. One Jewish leader carefully wrote on 5 May 1946, "The Central Committee engaged in some transactions, which, although financially advantageous, may prove to be undesirable from a legal point of view."[75]

The Joint Distribution Committee was torn between the demands of the American army and those of the displaced persons in dealing with the situation. When the State Department asked for the AJDC's help in limiting the member of refugees entering the zone, AJDC chairman Edward Warburg replied that in light of the Kielce pogrom, Eastern European Jews needed to move to safety.[76] Though his organization had nothing to do with migration, it would help Jewish refugees wherever they were. The American zonal Central Committee, however, was not particularly pleased with its ally, and on 5 July 1946, Zalman Grinberg wrote to Warburg that as of 15 July the Central Committee was no longer going to rely on AJDC resources. Grinberg complained, "During the past few weeks the representatives of the American Joint have taken a contrary stand. It reflects an attitude of distrust and disrespect of the people it is commissioned to aid." He called the refugee

---

[75] Letter from Ch. Briansky to Leo Schwarz, 5 May 1946, CJH/YIVO, RG 294.1, folder 112.
[76] Letter from Assistant Secretary of State John H. Hilldring to AJDC secretary Moses Leavitt, 31 July 1946; letter from Edward Warburg to State Department, 23 August 1946; CJH/YIVO, RG 294.1, folder 107.

leaders "far superior and far more capable than those sent to assist us." By that time, the displaced persons had established tracing bureaus, newspapers, cultural programs, and hospitals. Still, they were reliant on AJDC help. Grinberg had the temerity to write that the AJDC could continue to support the Central Committee's budget, but it would not be allowed to supervise its activities.[77]

At last, in September 1946, the legal position of the Central Committee in the American zone became more stable. Although volunteer organizations such as UNRRA and the Joint Distribution Committee recognized the Central Committee as a viable partner, the American army had not done so and considered the Central Committee's internal constitution and self-arrogations as problematic. By August, however, Bernstein had begun laying the groundwork for the U.S. army's recognition of the Central Committee in its zone.[78] To fulfill the army's requirements, the Central Committee submitted additional documentation on its functions, including maintenance of a medical staff, supervision of religious practice and compliance with kosher regulations, distribution of teaching materials, and legal assistance for the displaced persons. Still, the army was hesitant to grant the Central Committee recognition. Military officials objected to its pretensions to represent all Jews, its claims to Jewish property with no heirs, and its ill-defined democratic procedures. They wanted these problems rectified before granting legal recognition.[79] AJDC supervisor Leo Schwarz also argued that the democratic principle had not sunk in, claiming that many displaced persons were not working for the common good. He wrote, "My conclusion is that they are not yet capable of self-government but that the Committee as an advisory council and channel to the people is essential and may gradually win confidence and assume more work and responsibility."[80] Despite general reservations, on 6 September the American zonal Central Committee sent a constitution to the European headquarters

---

[77] Letter from Zalman Grinberg to Edward Warburg, 5 July 1947, CJH/YIVO, RG 294.1, folder 112. For more information on the cultural renaissance in the Jewish displaced persons camps, see Brenner, *After the Holocaust*, 18–30; Gay, *Safe among the Germans*, 55–69; and Lavsky, *New Beginnings*, 141–188.

[78] Letter from Philip Bernstein to Major General Clarence R. Huebner, 2 August 1946, BAK, Z 45, 5/323-1/31.

[79] Letter from Major General Clarence R. Huebner to Central Committee, 5 September 1946, BAK, Z 45, 5/323-1/31.

[80] Leo Schwarz, "The Trend in Germany," undated, CJH/YIVO, RG 294.1, folder 62.

of the U.S. military. The revised constitution, which largely reconfirmed the structure adopted in January, met McNarney's demands, and on 7 September he granted written approval of the body as an elected representative body for displaced persons in the U.S. zone. Its mission included advising the American army on the needs of the Jews and representing the Jews to the Army via liaison officer Colonel George Scithers.[81] Having received official recognition, the Central Committee in the American zone no longer worked underground, but rather acted in open partnership with UNRRA to help the displaced persons. In contrast, the Central Committee in the British zone would have to be satisfied with de facto recognition. The British were unwilling to do anything that might legitimate or signal approval of the Jews' political aspirations in Palestine.

Historians Angelika Königseder and Juliane Wetzel regard American recognition of the Central Committee as a major turning point in policy toward the Jews in occupied Germany. Although the Americans took care to limit the Central Committee's activities to social matters rather than political affairs, the organization's power grew, and it regarded itself as the "Jewish government" to which voluntary organizations were responsible. With its various departments, it often resembled a state within a state.[82] Despite its power, the Central Committee could do little for Jews outside the DP camps, and it had no influence over American army policy regarding infiltrators into western Germany.

DIFFICULTY UNITING THE COMMUNITIES
AND TROUBLE WITH THE DPS

The Jewish displaced persons had achieved a legally sanctioned representation; however, they were not the only Jewish group beginning to organize in Germany. While the Jewish displaced persons had been politically active, Germans Jews had also been organizing, slowly uniting into state associations to represent their interests, a practice common before 1933. And as was the case

---

[81] "History of G-5 Division, 1 July–31 December 1946, Part One," NARA, RG 338, ETO, G-5, History-box 1; letter from General Joseph T. McNarney, 7 September 1946, BAK, Z 45, 5/323-1/31; "Central Committee of Liberated Jews in the US Occupied Zone of Germany," 15 October 1946, CJH/YIVO, RG 294.1, folder 89.

[82] Königseder and Wetzel, *Lebensmut im Wartesaal*, 91.

before 1933, German Jews and Eastern European Jews did not co-operate easily. Unwilling to ally with the DP communities and considering themselves underrepresented vis-à-vis the western Allies' occupation administrations, they saw some form of collective representation as a necessity.

Historically, local communities, which administered many social and cultural aspects of a Jew's life, collaborated in statewide federations of Jewish communities, such as the Superior Council of Israelites in Baden (Oberrat der Israeliten Badens), founded in 1809, and the Prussian Federation of Jewish Communities (Preussischer Landesverband jüdischer Gemeinden), founded in 1922. Before 1933, the state federations in southern Germany had legal standing and supervisory power over the communities, participating in the regulation of religious matters as well as in cultural and social affairs.[83] Moreover, German Jews – excepting a small, but influential minority – had looked askance on their eastern brethren. To some degree, they considered traditional eastern Jews in Germany to be an embarrassment and hoped that they would acculturate to western European norms.[84]

In the postwar era, there was one notable exception to this trend of continued separation. In northern Germany, the German Jews and DPs maintained cordial relations. Siegfried Heimberg of Dortmund was among the first who sought to unite the Jewish communities of a single region. In January 1946, he invited displaced persons' leader Norbert Wollheim, along with representatives of several German Jewish communities, to attend the founding meeting of the so-called Jewish State Association of Westphalia (Landesverband Westfalen).[85] Other regional groups also sprang up, including the Working Alliance of Jewish Communities in the

---

[83] Max Gruenewald, "The Beginning of the 'Reichsvertretung,'" in Leo Baeck Institute, *Year Book* 1 (1956), ed. Robert Weltsch (London: East and West Library, 1956), 57; Michael A. Meyer, ed., *German-Jewish History in Modern Times*, vol. 2: *Emancipation and Acculturation 1780–1871*, by Michael Brenner, Stefi Jersch-Wenzel, and Michael A. Meyer (New York: Columbia University Press, 1997), 109; Meyer, ed., *German-Jewish History in Modern Times*, vol. 4: *Renewal and Destruction 1918–1945*, by Avraham Barkai and Paul Mendes-Flohr (New York: Columbia University Press), 83–84.

[84] Steven E. Aschheim, *Brothers and Strangers: The East European Jew in German and German Jewish Consciousness, 1800–1923* (Madison: University of Wisconsin Press, 1982), 184, 189, and 220.

[85] Letter from Dortmund Gemeinde to Norbert Wollheim, 16 January 1946, ZA, B.1/7, 230. He was unable to attend.

Northwestern German Area, organized by the leaders of the communities in Hamburg, Lübeck, Kiel, and Hanover on 16 May 1946. While remaining independent, the various regional associations planned to work together.[86]

Even with their efforts to organize, the communities' members needed significant help from the occupying powers with matters as basic as securing facilities and gaining access to their own funds. Julius Dreifuss of Düsseldorf regularly petitioned the British for assistance. In Berlin, Siegmund Weltlinger wanted help in procuring apartments and obtaining the release of frozen bank accounts as well as more rations for Jews. He also wanted Jews to be exempted from requisitions of property by the Allies.[87]

Despite these obstacles and feelings of helplessness, the situation of German Jews did improve on 15 April 1946 with the publication of the *Jüdisches Gemeindeblatt für die Nord-Rheinprovinz und Westfalen* (*Jewish Communal Leaflet for North Rhine Province and Westphalia*) under the direction of Karl Marx. Marx, who came to play an important role in the postwar community, had grown up in Saarland and Alsace before service in the First World War, for which he won an Iron Cross, second-class. During the Weimar Republic, he worked as a journalist and was active in the liberal German Democratic Party, where he met politicians Theodor Heuss and Ernst Lemmer. His newspaper gave the postwar Jewish community an important tool in its struggle for recognition and support.

Initially a small newspaper for the Jewish community in the area around Düsseldorf, Cologne, and Dortmund, it grew into a national newspaper of considerable reputation. Philipp Auerbach, leader of the German Jewish communities in North Rhine-Westphalia, wrote the introduction for the first issue, which came out just before Passover, a celebration of Jewish liberation. Demonstrating the relative unity of the Jews in the British zone, Auerbach thanked Rosensaft's zonal Central Committee, as well as various

---

[86] "Gründung der Arbeitsgemeinschaft der nord-westdeutschen Gemeinden," *Jüdisches Gemeindeblatt für die Nord-Rheinprovinz und Westfalen*, 24 May 1946.

[87] Correspondence between Julius Dreifuss and British authorities, March–December 1946, ZA, B.1/5, 83; "Die gegenwärtige Lage der Juden in Berlin," 13 February 1946, LAB, E Rep. 200–22. 38. Dreifuss's name also appears in documents as "Dreifuß" and "Dreyfuss."

foreign Jewish organizations, for their aid. The paper's inaugural edition also revealed its strongly Zionist orientation.[88] Even though German Jews managed the newspaper, it reported on events both in the German Jewish community and in the DP camps, as well as serving as a medium for public announcements such as the reconstitution of B'nai B'rith and of Jewish socialist political parties.[89]

As early as spring 1946, Jewish leaders in Germany tried to form a common front, but their efforts were largely in vain, stymied by the tense relationship between German Jews and Eastern European Jewish displaced persons, a legacy of the two groups' poor relations before 1933. Before World War I, the influx of Russian Jews to Germany, seeking refuge from czarist persecution, displeased many German Jews. German Jewish communal leaders instituted grandfather clauses and residency requirements to exclude the easterners from congregational elections, and Eastern European Jews frequently maintained their own prayer houses (while not seceding from the larger German-run Jewish community). Their differences were not just religious but stemmed from deep-seated cultural differences. The German Jews tried to ban certain Eastern European practices during religious services that they considered not to be decorous. Eastern Europeans Jews rejected the Protestant model of a religious service.[90] Thus, overcoming seventy-five years of mutual mistrust would not be easy.

Before 1933, the German Jews had formed the majority of the community, but after 1945, with the influx of eastern DPs, the situation was reversed. Given the choice of uniting with the Eastern Europeans after the war or going it alone for purposes of representation, German Jews chose the latter option. At a meeting of Jewish leaders from the three western occupation zones in April 1946, Hans Lamm, future leader of Munich Jewry, said,

An amalgamation of the Jewish communities in all Germany should take place. In which organization is still to be considered. The [DPs'] Central Committee in Munich represents the viewpoint that it represents the

---

[88] "Zum Geleit," *Jüdisches Gemeindeblatt*, 15 April 1945.
[89] "B'nai B'rith Loge" and "Zum 1. Mai," *Jüdisches Gemeindeblatt*, 6 May 1946.
[90] Aschheim, *Brothers and Strangers*, 33; Trude Maurer, *Ostjuden in Deutschland 1918–1933* (Hamburg: Hans Christians, 1986), 588–589, 605–606, and 610–644.

German Jews. We should let it be known whether we feel represented there.[91]

Voices from the audience responded "no." Still, the German Jews knew that they could lobby the western occupation authorities for reparations more effectively with a common voice, and Philipp Auerbach suggested a committee that would meet monthly to represent their interests. Three delegates from the U.S. zone, three from the British zone, and two from the French zone would sit on the board of this proposed Interest-Representation (Interessenvertretung).[92] While this body would be the first interzonal representative organization for the Jews in western Germany, its limited scope prevented it from achieving much.

Despite their small and fragmented constituencies, German Jewish organizations soon began to act as political pressure groups. The North Rhine state association had lobbied province *Oberpräsident* (and future federal interior minister) Robert Lehr for preferential treatment for Jewish community members petitioning the government, and on 4 February 1946 Lehr consented to the request.[93] In May, the Interest-Representation issued a statement to the state governments to express its bitterness and regret over how little had been done to reestablish the Jewish communities in Germany:

Even though a year has gone by, nothing has happened to restore our rights. Only some alms and advances [of funds] have been made. We reject alms and charitable support in any form, for we have a claim to rights. . . . Great fortunes were taken away from our communities by the state. Property and money. We demand them back. We want to help our own poor.[94]

In its desperation, the Düsseldorf community considered other solutions to the difficulties of Jewish life in Germany, hosting a meeting in May 1946 about emigration from Germany to Palestine. The meeting was such a success that the community planned more meetings with authorities on that subject.[95]

---

[91] "Protokoll über die Sitzung der Vetreter der Jüdischen Vereinigungen der britischen Zone, der französischen Zone Süd Badens, der amerikanischen Zone Nordenbadens, Württemberg, Nürnberg," 19 April 1946, ZA, B.1/13, A.412, 23.
[92] Ibid., 30.
[93] "Bevorzugte Behandlung der Juden," *Jüdisches Gemeindeblatt,* 6 May 1946.
[94] "An alle Länder-Regierungen Deutschlands!," 9 May 1946, ZA, B.1/13, A.412, 20.
[95] "Wiedergutmachung," *Jüdisches Gemeindeblatt,* 24 May 1946.

Under these dire circumstances, many Jews began to realize that they would have more influence if the DP communities and the German communities combined their efforts. Although it took years to merge the two groups in Frankfurt, as early as 20 June 1946, the local displaced persons committee raised the issue and appointed negotiators.[96] In July, the Jews in the British zone actually founded a zone-wide committee to help all Jews, with Auerbach as president and Herbert Lewin of Cologne, Harry Goldstein of Hamburg, and Carl Katz of Bremen as additional board members.[97] Other regional Jewish groups, however, hesitated to merge. By the summer of 1946, the Jews of Westphalia and North Rhine Province considered combining their two state associations. The Rhinelanders wanted a merger, but none took place. For the next three years, leaders of the two associations met periodically to discuss such a project.[98]

The long delay in uniting the two groups was typical of the problems facing Jewish organizations and leaders in postwar Germany. Local and regional particularism persisted, and leaders protected their fiefdoms. Even when groups did manage to work together, their differences were apparent. Having attended a meeting of the Interest-Representation on 14 July 1946, an American army officer commented on the tensions between the German Jews and the displaced persons. He noted that apart from the cultural and religious differences, the German Jews considered themselves legal successors to the prewar communities and were intensely interested in restitution, while the displaced persons wanted all efforts to be directed toward resettlement in Palestine.[99] Tensions between the two groups also manifested themselves in other ways. To prevent the Eastern European Jewish DPs from taking control of the Frankfurt community, in October and November 1946,

---

96 "Protokoll Nr. 5 über die Sitzung von 20. Juni 1946 des Jüdischen Stadtkomitees Frankfurt am Main," 20 June 1946, ZA, B.1/13, A.46, 57. For more information on the immediate postwar history of the Frankfurt community, see Tauber, "Die Entstehung der Jüdischen Nachkriegsgemeinde [Frankfurt am Main], 1945–1949," in *Wer ein Haus baut, will bleiben*, ed. Heuberger.

97 "Der Zonenausschuß," *Jüdisches Gemeindeblatt*, 10 July 1946.

98 Letter from Landesverband Nordrhein to Landesverband Westfalen, 24 July 1946; letter from Siegmund Heimberg to Landesverband Nordrhein, 2 January 1947; "Kurzprotokoll," 24 December 1947; letter from Landesverband Nordrhein to Heimberg, 12 December 1948; ZA, B.1/15, 190.

99 "Report on Meeting of Interessen Vereinigung of Jews of the 3 Western Zones," 17 July 1946, BAK, Z 45, 5/342-1/43.

German Jews instituted stringent requirements for board membership, demanding residency in Frankfurt for a full year and membership in a German community for three years. For voting rights in community elections, these requirements were six months and a year, respectively. Some even insisted that pre-1933 residency in Frankfurt be a requirement for board membership.[100] Communities throughout southern Germany, including those in Stuttgart and Munich, faced the same issue. The Jewish community in Augsburg did not overcome the German Jewish–DP split for nearly ten years.[101]

Immediately after the Allies' defeat of the Nazis, the largest Jewish presence in Germany was that of the displaced persons. Soon, refugees fleeing antisemitism in Eastern Europe augmented their numbers. As the American zone, in particular, grew overcrowded, the DPs' relations with the military government deteriorated. The American military had contributed greatly to the defeat of Nazi Germany's armies, but it was unprepared to deal with the social catastrophe created by Nazi policies. It had no choice but to rely on Jewish and international nonsectarian relief organizations to perform the bulk of the aid work. The American army's relationship with these groups was often tense. Yet, guided by its Jewish adviser, the army succeeded in helping the Jewish Holocaust survivors to restore their human dignity through programs operated by the zonal Central Committee.

The displaced persons' camp and zonal committees represented their interests and supervised the camps in conjunction with the military occupiers and relief agencies. In the American zone, in September 1946, the army hesitantly acknowledged the Central Committee as its partner in administering Jewish displaced persons' affairs. Not only did these bodies provide the Jewish refugees with a voice, they also gave the Eastern European Jews practical political experience, from which many profited after 1949/1950 as they, having joined with the German Jews, sought to work with the new government of West Germany.

---

[100] "Protokoll der am 29. Oktober 46 stattfindenden Vorstandssitzung der Jüdischen Gemeinde," 29 October 1946, ZA, B.1/13, A.1, 18–19; letter to the Frankfurt community membership, 21 November 1946, ZA, B.1/13, A.1, 9.

[101] Brenner, *After the Holocaust*, 46–47.

In contrast to the displaced persons and their relationship with the Americans, German Jewish survivors of the Nazi genocide either acted alone or relied on local German officials for help with their goal of reestablishing their religious communities and social institutions. Although pre-1933 German Jewry had a strong tradition of regional organization, the small and divided postwar communities were slow to unite, first making efforts toward this end on the state level and then on the intrazonal level in the winter and spring of 1946. Moreover, the German Jews' cool relations with the displaced persons in the American zone kept the Jewish community in western Germany divided, despite its small size and need for unity as it sought critical assistance.

CHAPTER 2

Two Communities Unite in West Germany

Several years after the war's end, the Jewish community in Germany remained divided. Longstanding cultural and religious differences as well as political differences separated Eastern European Jews and German Jews. Most German Jews intended to stay in Germany, while most Eastern European Jewish displaced persons intended to leave for Israel. Moreover, as the DPs had official ties to governing Allied occupation regimes, their views on Jewish life in Germany and the use of property formerly owned by Jews prevailed. However, that situation would not last. Soon, a unique confluence of extreme circumstances convinced Eastern European Jewish displaced persons and German Jews of the need to cooperate, and the two groups founded a common representative organization to promote their needs.

After the foundation of the State of Israel in 1948, the movement of Eastern European Jews to Germany slowed considerably, and most displaced persons already there left for the new Jewish state. However, a few decided to remain in Germany, the country where they had made their homes for three or four years. Around the same time, the Americans altered their policy regarding Jewish displaced persons, increasingly focusing on preparing the Jews for life after the end of military occupation. A major aspect of that preparation involved bringing the Eastern European Jewish and German Jewish communities together.

While the displaced persons had interacted primarily with the occupation authorities, German Jews, wishing to resume their pre-1933 lives as far as possible, generally looked to German officials for support. To air their concerns – including reparations, restitution of confiscated property, and compensation for property that could not be returned – German Jews founded loosely organized intrazonal representative bodies. However, external events induced more decisive actions. The Americans began to withdraw their commitment to the Jews in Germany, and the new West German federal government began to interfere in the internal affairs of the Jewish community. These two factors compelled German Jews and Eastern European Jews to unite formally for common representation despite continuing antagonism between the two groups.

INTENSIFICATION OF THE DP PROBLEM AND THE REGULATION OF RESTITUTION

Although the Central Committee of Liberated Jews, the chief representative body for Jewish displaced persons in the American zone, gained recognized legal status in September 1946, its relations with the U.S. army remained strained. Until displaced persons could emigrate freely to Palestine, the army would find the increasingly crowded DP camps difficult to administer. With no end to the impasse in sight, many Jews marooned in the American zone attempted hazardous, illegal journeys to Palestine via France, a development that soured relations between the Americans and the French. American commander Joseph McNarney wanted the military, UNRRA, and the zonal Central Committee to work together to discourage such movement.[1] Other Jews took advantage of rehabilitation programs and prepared for a future life in Palestine. The American occupiers pledged to support UNRRA rehabilitation programs and to try to acquire German farms and training schools for the displaced persons.[2] Many others, weary of life in the camps, opened businesses in Germany. While some launched legitimate economic ventures, others traded on the black market, drawing the ire of German officials.[3]

Relations between the American army and the displaced persons proved complicated, as noted by Philip Bernstein, the army's adviser for Jewish affairs from May 1946 through the summer of 1947. While he praised high-level military authorities, he noted that relations on the lowest level were not good, especially those

---

[1] Memorandum from General Joseph McNarney for Third Army, 31 October 1946, BAK, Z 45, 3/174-1/20.

[2] "Staff Study Prepared by UNRRA Jewish Council," in "History of G-5 Division, 1 July–31 December 1946, Appendices," NARA, RG 338, ETO, G-5, History, box 1.

[3] "Weekly Intelligence Report," 1 November 1946, NARA, RG 260, OMGUS, AG, Decimal File-box 92, folder 387.7 (3).

between displaced persons and military police. Field commanders continued to initiate raids on the camps for black market goods, and the local Central Committee was impatient with the army's bureaucracy. However, as the DP community in the American zone continued to grow, the American army was learning to accept the refugees' organization as part of the occupation apparatus.[4]

To cope with the huge Jewish displaced persons population, the American Joint Distribution Committee (AJDC) built up its resources in Germany. Beginning with only twenty staff members prepared to serve 29,000 displaced persons when it began operations in August 1945, it soon grew to over 300 employees, enough to deal with 150,000 displaced persons. Since Palestine was still officially closed, and few displaced persons left the camps, the AJDC's mission had changed from one that provided temporary care to one that offered rehabilitation. Although it coordinated activities with UNRRA and the American military, it worked directly with the Central Committee and camp committees.[5] The American military recognized that this independence would pay dividends when the UN withdrew care of displaced persons. Still, army officials resented the fact that the American relief agency had downplayed the critical role played by the American army and had given the world a slanted view of the displaced persons problem in Germany: "All too frequently such publicity is designed to present Jewish political aspirations disguised as welfare necessities."[6]

For the average Jewish refugee in Germany, emigration to Palestine remained the primary goal. At the second Congress of the Liberated Jews in the U.S. Zone, meeting 25–27 February 1947, advocacy of any program other than emigration to Palestine was "political suicide." The Congress resolved that no significant number of Jews would participate in the German economy, and Jewish groups focused increasingly on vocational training for

---

4 "Confidential Report on the Situation of Jewish Displaced Persons in U.S. Zones, Germany and Austria," 6 December 1946, CJH/YIVO, RG 294.1, folder 69; NARA, RG 347.7.1, box 33. The membership of the Central Committee in Frankfurt, for example, grew from 686 members in December 1946 to 789 members in May 1947. "Oganisations-optejlung," 9 December 1946, 27 April and 25 May 1947, ZA, B.1/13, A.525, 56–59.
5 "Summary Analysis of AJDC Program in the U.S. Zone of Occupation, Germany," 13 January 1947, CJH/YIVO, RG 294.1, folder 9.
6 "Summary Analysis of AJDC Program in the U.S. Zone of Occupation, Germany," 30 January 1947, BAK, Z 45, 3/172-3/22.

emigration. Be that as it may, vocational schools suffered from a chronic lack of materials, forcing the displaced persons to build their own machines or recondition disused German ones.[7] In fact, Zionist displaced persons neatly combined their program of preparation for life in Palestine with self-conscious isolation within the German economy and society by establishing factories, work-shops, and farms that had nothing to do with the surrounding Germans.

Despite the Herculean obstacles, the Americans began to manage the displaced persons problem by the spring of 1947 and even tried to scale down their commitment to the Jewish refugees. The army sealed its displaced persons camps. After 21 April, no one outside the American zone could qualify for admittance to a displaced persons camp, and those in the zone – but not in camps – could enter only under emergency circumstances.[8] American officials also wanted to close their DP camps in Berlin. These were a strain on the army's resources to supply food and other goods to the former German capital, now isolated within the Soviet occupation zone.[9] The army's European headquarters ordered commanders to conserve personnel by consolidating or closing small camps and those with substandard facilities.[10]

As UNRRA's planned cessation of activities approached in the summer of 1947, the American army worked out an agreement with its successor, the International Refugee Organization (IRO), which planned to begin operations on 1 September. In the American zone, the IRO would operate the camps and supervise the work of all volunteer agencies, including the AJDC. It would also provide medical care, arrange repatriation, and develop an employment program, while the military would provide facilities, transportation within the zone, basic supplies, and security.[11] In the British zone, the IRO reimbursed the British for administrative costs, and British officials ran the camps under IRO supervision. Clearly, the British

---

[7] "Report of Conference at Bad Reichenhall," 6 March 1947, BAK, Z 45, 3/173-1/29.
[8] "Denial of UN Care and Treatment to New Applicants after 21 April 1947," BAK, Z 45, 3/173-2/1.
[9] "Inadvisability of Maintaining Displaced Persons Assembly Centers in Berlin," 3 May 1947, BAK, Z 45, 3/173-2/1.
[10] Order from European Command to first and second military districts, 3 June 1947, BAK, Z 45, 3/173-2/1.
[11] "Proposed Agreement between IRO and the Commander-in-Chief, European Command," 20 June 1947, BAK, Z 45, 3/171-1/13.

were worried about the camps' permeability if they relinquished control.[12]

On 20–23 July 1947, nearly two years after the first Congress of Liberated Jews in the British Zone, another convention met under the leadership of Norbert Wollheim and Josef Rosensaft. They considered Germany to be "neither a homeland nor a land for definite settlement." Wollheim spoke of their ties to the *Yishuv* (the early Jewish settlement in Palestine), and Rosensaft regarded the displaced persons as citizens of a future Jewish homeland. Despite the shared Zionist ideology, the Jewish communities of the British and American zones qualitatively differed. Unlike their counterparts in the American zone, the German Jewish communities in the British zone, represented by the Council of Jewish Communities in the British Zone (Rat der Jüdischen Gemeinden der britischen Zone), cooperated with and planned a merger with the displaced persons' Central Committee. After the initial postwar displacements, Jewish migration into the British zone largely ceased. Profiting from these stable conditions – under the leadership of the local Central Committee – displaced persons and German Jews achieved much cultural work, setting up schools and theaters while waiting for emigration. They also restored cemeteries, set up orphanages, and operated rest homes, contributing considerably to the basis of Jewish life in northern Germany for those who did not emigrate.[13]

Cultural and social welfare achievements did not mitigate Rosensaft's frustration with political developments, and he railed against German indifference to growing antisemitism. He hoped that a united organization for all Jews in the British zone would be more effective in lobbying for a Jewish homeland in Palestine.[14] Some Jews could not wait for political change, and in early August 1947, American authorities arrested two for attempting to blow up a railroad line in the British zone. Both men were employees of the Central Committee in the U.S. zone, and there was some debate as to whether the two should receive legal counsel from this

[12] "Report of the Executive Secretary on the Status of the Organization," 11 July 1947, BAK, Z 45, 3/171-1/14.
[13] "Von ersten zum zweiten Kongress" and "Aufriß der inneren Arbeit," *Jüdisches Gemeindeblatt,* 20 July 1947.
[14] "Der Zweite Kongress der befreiten Juden in der britischen Zone," *Jüdisches Gemeindeblatt,* 20 July 1947.

organization or even from the Americans, who extradited them to the British zone. Often, the Americans turned a blind eye to obvious preparations for peaceful emigration, but this matter was more serious.[15]

In addition to the practical concerns of caring for the Jews, the American army faced the challenge of issuing and enforcing a law for restitution of formerly Jewish property. On 10 November 1947, the Americans issued military law no. 59 to codify the restitution process.[16] Four days later, the French military government regulated restitution to the small and divided Jewish community in its zone with decree no. 120, which was weaker than its American counterpart. Most Jews in the northern district of the French zone were German-born and lived in cities such as Koblenz, Mainz, and Trier. Addi Bernd, chairman of the Jewish State Association of Rhineland-Palatinate, acted as the Joint Distribution Committee's agent there. In contrast, displaced persons from Eastern Europe dominated the Jewish community of the French zone's southern district.[17] Two of the western Allies' zones had acted, but one had not. Noting the gap in the new legislation, leading reparations expert Hendrik George van Dam asked, "And when will the British zone follow?" It did not before July 1949.[18] Meanwhile, the Länderrat, the pre-1949 parliament of the western German states, was working on its own proposal when the Americans unilaterally acted with their military law no. 59.[19] The German plan, sent to the Allies for review and approval, languished in Washington from October 1946 to February 1947, when it finally went to the Allied Control Council. There, the British and the Soviets further delayed

---

[15] Assorted telegrams, August 1947, BAK, Z 45, 3/169-2/138.

[16] "Law No. 59: Restitution of Identifiable Property, Extract," 10 November 1947, BAK, Z 45, 17/261-2/1. For more on German reparations to the Jews, see Christian Pross, *Paying for the Past: The Struggle over Reparations for Surviving Victims of the Nazi Terror,* trans. Belinda Cooper (Baltimore: Johns Hopkins University Press, 1998), and Goschler, *Wiedergutmachung. Westdeutschland.*

[17] For the Jewish view on the French zonal law, see World Jewish Congress, *Unity in Dispersion: A History of the World Jewish Congress,* 2nd ed. (New York: Institute of Jewish Affairs of the World Jewish Congress, 1948), 282 and 288; "Report on the Situation of the Jews in the French Zone," 28 April 1947, CJH/YIVO, RG 294.1, folder 54.

[18] "Und wann folgt die britische Zone?," *Jüdisches Gemeindeblatt,* 30 November 1947; Sagi, *German Reparations,* 40.

[19] "Rückerstattung," *Jüdisches Gemeindeblatt,* 30 November 1947. The Bundestag replaced the Länderrat (Council of States) after the constitution of a West German federal government.

its passage. By October, the American occupiers wanted a restitution law for the American zone and issued one shortly thereafter.

Essential to the nature of restitution in the American and French zones, the military governments – not the German states – would name successor organizations to assume ownership of ownerless property. While the Germans favored either the Jewish communities in Germany or émigré organizations for German Jews abroad, the Americans were inclined to designate an American Jewish organization to fill this function – yielding vastly different results from what would have occurred under German administration. American Jews, opposed to Jewish resettlement in Germany, were unlikely to donate proceeds from the sale of formerly Jewish property to the communities in Germany. However, law no. 59 was designed to facilitate the return of confiscated property and allotted six months for the property's owner to make a claim. Only if no claim was filed by 31 December 1948, the designated successor organization would have the right to prosecute the claim and to liquidate the property as it saw fit. German Jews welcomed the new law despite its intricacies, and their representatives sent a letter of thanks to American commander Lucius Clay.[20]

Just as the legal situation of the Jews in the American zone improved and stabilized in December 1947, a new wave of Jewish migration began, this time from Romania. With the official, IRO-sanctioned displaced persons camps sealed, military officials feared that these new displaced persons would become their responsibility; however, the occupation government told its administrators that the Germans would have to regulate this new group.[21] Illegal entrants did not receive any housing priority, leading the American army's Jewish adviser, Judge Louis Levinthal of Philadelphia (in office from July 1947 to January 1948), to protest that these new displaced persons needed protection, too. Placing them in camps would minimize the burden on the German public, and they would receive food from the Joint Distribution Committee and International Refugee Organization.[22]

---

[20] Letter from Interessenvertretung to Lucius Clay and state prime ministers, 23 December 1947, ZA, B.1/13, A.411, 6.

[21] OMG-Hesse to OMGUS, PW & DP Division, 8 December 1947; OMGUS, PW & DP Division to OMG-Hesse, 9 December 1947; BAK, Z 45, 3/174-1/8.

[22] Letter from Louis Levinthal to USFET commander, 19 December 1947, CJH/YIVO, RG 294.1, folder 71.

ISOLATION AND UNITY OF THE GERMAN
JEWISH COMMUNITY

While displaced persons streamed into the American occupation zone hoping for a better life, German Jews lost most of their illusions about their future status in Germany. Operating the communities was more difficult than anyone had originally foreseen, and the Jews who remained in Germany needed both moral and material support, which was rarely forthcoming from the occupying powers and foreign Jewish groups, both of which usually sided with the displaced persons.

The weak and impoverished Jewish community no longer focused on the operation of schools, orphanages, hospitals, and rest homes, as it had before 1933. Its post-1945 priorities included caring for the large Jewish cemeteries and pressing for reparations legislation and aid from the governments, with which it had a rocky relationship. On at least one occasion, board members of the Frankfurt Jewish community, angry at the dilatory return of their communal property, did not want the mayor to attend a Jewish service.[23] Money and facilities were so tight for the congregation that they offered to let Jewish American troops have the use of a prayer room in the Westend Synagogue every Friday night if the American Jewish Welfare Board paid for its reconstruction.[24] The Hessian state government's office for the care of former Nazi victims funded most of the reconstruction of the synagogue's interior.[25]

In the months following their liberation from Nazi terror, most German Jews had high expectations regarding the victorious Allies' and the Germans' behavior, but the delayed implementation of restitution and lack of a public discourse among Germans on Jewish questions led to much bitterness. This sentiment found expression in "Wir, die deutschen Juden" ("We, the German Jews"), a widely circulated *Jüdisches Gemeindeblatt* article from 27 November

---

[23] "Protokoll über die Vorstandssitzung vom 24. September 1946," 24 September 1946, ZA, B.1/13, A.1, 24.

[24] "Protokoll über die Vorstandssitzung vom 8. Oktober 1946," 8 October 1946, ZA, B.1/13, A.1, 23.

[25] Letter from Ministerium für politische Befreiung to Regierungspräsident-Hauptbetreuungsstelle, 8 May 1948, ZA, B1/13, A.570, 24; "Protokoll der am 29. Oktober 46 stattfindenden Vorstandssitzung der Jüdischen Gemeinde," 29 October 1946, ZA, B.1/13, A.1, 18.

1946. Though the German Jews were the first victims of the Nazi regime, no one looked after their interests now. They considered themselves unwanted by the Germans as well as by the occupying powers, who seemed more concerned with the all-German question. The author called on the world to come to the aid of German Jews and added that, fortunately, enlightened men in state governments had announced that legislation for reparations must be passed.[26]

In fact, one German political leader had already addressed the issue of the Jews' relationship to postwar Germany. During a visit to London, Kurt Schumacher, leader of the Social Democratic Party, expressed dismay that more Jews had not returned to Germany. He even claimed that "for most Germans there never was a 'Jewish question.'"[27] This was clearly a controversial position. While it drew some applause, the émigré publication *Central European Observer* attacked Schumacher for his tactlessness and lack of understanding of Jewish sensibilities, claiming that no Jews "with real Jewish feeling" would ever return to this country where "any neighbor might be a murderer."[28] In fact, many German Jews did wish to return, but they needed both encouragement and assistance. Some approached Schumacher for help in overcoming bureaucratic obstacles to remigration, and Jewish Berlin politician Siegmund Weltlinger asked Berlin mayor Otto Ostrowski to issue a statement supporting the return of all those who had emigrated during the Third Reich.[29]

While some German Jews, including Hans-Erich Fabian, leader of the amalgamated Jewish community in Berlin, and Norbert Wollheim, co-leader in the British zone, saw Germany merely as a way station before going to Palestine or America, many others were defiantly proud of having returned. The *Jüdisches Gemeindeblatt für die Nord-Rheinprovinz und Westfalen*, the leading Jewish newspaper in Germany, reflected this pride. The 10 December 1946 issue featured a new name (*Jüdisches Gemeindeblatt für die britische Zone*) and

---

[26] "Wir, die deutschen Juden," *Jüdisches Gemeindeblatt*, 27 November 1946.
[27] "Meldung Nr. 147: Schumacher in London II," 29 November 1946, AdsD, Bestand Kurt Schumacher (Abt. II), 39.
[28] Letter from Arthur Strauss to Kurt Schumacher, 3 December 1946, AdsD, Bestand Kurt Schumacher (Abt. II), 69; *Central European Observer* article noted in "Juden in Deutschland," 7 March 1947, AdsD, Bestand Kurt Schumacher (Abt. II), 17.
[29] Letter from E. Weinberg to Kurt Schumacher, 5 January 1947, AdsD, Bestand Kurt Schumacher (Abt. II), 83; "Aktennotiz," 15 January 1947, LAB, E Rep. 200–22, 101.

a masthead with a prominent Star of David. The author of the lead editorial proclaimed, "I returned from emigration because I am one of those who believes himself to be obligated as a German Jew to contribute to the reconstruction of Jewish institutions and then to the construction of a truly democratic Germany."[30]

This attitude, however, found little support among Jewish groups abroad, and it came under attack at the second plenary assembly of the World Jewish Congress (WJC), held in Montreux, Switzerland, in the summer of 1948. The WJC declared "the determination of the Jewish people never again to settle on the bloodstained soil of Germany."[31] In a speech given later, WJC general secretary A. Leon Kubowitzki proclaimed it to be the most important duty of Jewish organizations to ensure the ultimate liquidation of organized Jewish life in Germany. Arguing that a Jewish presence in Germany excused the guilt of the Germans, he endorsed the notion of German collective guilt for the Holocaust, which embarrassed many German Jews and later proved a serious impediment to German-Jewish relations.[32] Even displaced persons leader Norbert Wollheim expressed thinly veiled disdain for those who chose to remain permanently. He renounced his ties to Germany, the land of his birth: "I didn't destroy Germany; I have no duty to build it up again. I can't."[33]

Many Jews around the world characterized the German Jewish community as a "liquidation community," and German Jews were literally unwelcome or ostracized at many international Jewish gatherings, including those of the Jewish Agency, the World Union of Jewish Students, and the International Council of Jewish

---

[30] "Kurzes Gedächtnis oder ...?," *Jüdisches Gemeindeblatt,* 10 December 1946.

[31] World Jewish Congress, "Germany," in *Resolutions Adopted by the Second Plenary Assembly of the World Jewish Congress, Montreaux, Switzerland, June 27th–July 6th, 1948* (London: Odhams Press, [1948]), 7. Interestingly, the WJC viewed Austria differently. The WJC was working for "the existence and rehabilitation of the Jewish community" in Austria. Moreover, it believed that the Austrians were "prepared to fight, in a unified front, together with the victims of Nazism, against a revival of Nazism." World Jewish Congress, "Jews in Austria," in *Resolutions,* 9.

[32] "Wir und Deutschland," undated [autumn 1950], BAK, B 122, 2083 (29); "Protokoll der Sitzung der vorläufigen Direktoriums des Zentralrates," 29 November 1950, ZA, B.1/7, 221.7; Shlomo Shafir, "Der Jüdische Weltkongreß und sein Verhältnis zu Nachkriegsdeutschland," in *Menora: Jahrbuch für deutsch-jüdische Geschichte* 3 (1992), ed. Julius H. Schoeps (Munich: Piper, 1992): 210–237; Y. Michal Bodemann, *Gedächtnistheater: Die jüdische Gemeinschaft und ihre deutsche Erfindung* (Hamburg: Rotbuch, 1996), 69–78.

[33] Norbert Wollheim, oral history interview, part II, 17 May 1991, USHMM, RG 50.030*0267, tape 3.

Women. Germans were simply not invited to these assemblies, or when they were, other delegates refrained from contact with the Jews from Germany. Occasionally, they were invited but not given voting rights. This stigmatization led to great distress, frustration, and indignation.[34] Moreover, this hostile attitude only fostered misunderstandings and outright disputes between those who wished to use unclaimed Jewish assets for the new Jewish communities in Germany and those who wished to sell them and use the proceeds for Israel.[35]

It is here that the issue of relations between German Jews and Jewish displaced persons often merged with the question of German reparations to Jews. As it seemed likely that the American occupation government would issue a restitution law, the German Jews' trizonal Interest-Representation met to discuss reparations matters. Fearing that the Americans might designate a foreign organization as the heir to ownerless Jewish property in Germany, they adopted a conciliatory tone. They expressed their willingness to share proceeds from restitution with the displaced persons and Jews abroad. Frankfurt Jewish leader Max Cahn said, "We are of the opinion that the [German] Jewish communities do not need the entire property. What they do not need they should place at the disposal of the [successor] organization."[36] While willing to share the proceeds of the liquidation of formerly Jewish property with the displaced persons, the German Jewish community in Frankfurt was hesitant to merge with the local displaced persons community so long as so many East European Jews remained in the American zone.[37] They considered many displaced persons to be black marketers.[38] The Augsburg community asked the local government to support its restitution claims against those of the designated successor organization, which it did.

---

34 Cohn, *Jews in Germany*, 93; Lilli Marx, "Renewal of the German-Jewish Press," in *After the Holocaust*, ed. Brenner, 127; Y. Michal Bodemann, "Staat und Ethnizität: Der Aufbau der jüdischen Gemeinden im Kalten Krieg," in *Jüdisches Leben*, ed. Brumlik et al., 58.
35 The leaders of the Jewish Restitution Successor Organization did not think that Jewish communities in Germany could or should survive and were reluctant to grant them financial support. Ruth Schreiber, "New Jewish Communities in Germany after World War II and the Successor Organizations in the Western Zones," *Journal of Israeli History* 18, nos. 2–3 (autumn 1997): 172.
36 "Protokoll," 2 March 1947, ZA, B.1/13, A.412, 8.
37 Letter from W. Stern to Curt Epstein, 6 January 1947, ZA, B.1/13, A.66, 45.
38 "Protokoll über die Sitzung des Vorstandes der Jüdischen Gemeinde in Frankfurt am Main," 11 June 1947, ZA, B.1/13, A.2, 59.

As awkward as the relationship between the displaced persons committees and American military could be on occasion, the Americans had a much closer relationship to the displaced persons than to the German Jews, who generally looked to their local governments for support. When the son of Rabbi Philip Bernstein, the U.S. army's Jewish adviser, had his bar mitzvah in Frankfurt on 25 January 1947, the Frankfurt displaced persons committee gave the boy a gift – a DP identification card as a souvenir of his time in Europe.[39] Reflecting on the estrangement of the German Jews from both the Germans and the Allied occupiers, Karl Marx wrote that they would soon have to decide whether it was worth the effort to remain in Germany.[40]

Faced with isolation, the German Jews responded by uniting into representative bodies. Although the western German Interest-Representation was one year old in April 1947, the long-awaited establishment of an all-German group occurred in June of that year as Jewish leaders from both western and eastern Germany met in Frankfurt. Instead of a single, strong body, however, their new Working Alliance of Jewish Communities in Germany (Arbeitsgemeinschaft jüdischer Gemeinden in Deutschland) was a loose confederation, and like every other German Jewish group, its main concern was reparations.[41] On 20 July, just weeks after the Working Alliance's founding, the Jews in the British zone formed a single representative group, encompassing both the German Jewish communities and displaced persons committees. Not only was this new group Zionist in orientation, but for purposes of international representation, it affiliated with British Jewry.[42] By choosing to associate with the Jewish community in Britain, rather than with the German Jews, the displaced persons in the British occupation zone underscored their intention to turn their backs on Germany as soon as they could. Such concerted action in

---

[39] Letter from Philip Bernstein to the Central Committee, 5 February 1947, ZA, B.1/13, A.46, 9–10.

[40] "Vor Entscheidungen?," *Jüdisches Gemeindeblatt*, 19 March 1947.

[41] "Drinnen und Draußen," *Jüdisches Gemeindeblatt*, 9 July 1947; "Die Frankfurter Tagung," *Der Weg*, 13 July 1947. Board members were Norbert Wollheim for the British zone, Julius Meyer for the Russian zone, Philipp Auerbach for the American zone, Nathan Rosenberger for the French zone, and Hans-Erich Fabian for Berlin.

[42] "Warum Einheit," *Jüdisches Gemeindeblatt*, 11 June 1947; "Die politische Resolution des zweiten Kongresses," *Jüdisches Gemeindeblatt*, 13 August 1947.

the British zone worried German Jewish leaders in the American zone.[43]

Meanwhile, the Working Alliance found itself alienating its own constituents and non-Jewish potential friends. In discussing the fight against antisemitism, it could be often overbearing and self-righteous. It also issued a controversial declaration forbidding Jews married to non-Jews to serve on community boards.[44] This proposal drew a sharp reaction from the Interest-Representation, many of whose delegates had non-Jewish wives. Faced with pressure, the group backpedaled. Karl Marx, whose wife was Jewish, claimed that the Working Alliance had only been reacting to pressure from Orthodox Jewry and that the proposal was merely a recommendation. Moreover, the issue of mixed marriages divided the more religious displaced persons from the assimilated German Jews.[45]

The German Jews did have a few allies in their struggle for recognition. Several state governments had special officials designated to handle aid to victims of Nazi persecution. In Hesse, Curt Epstein regulated restitution claims, certified Jewish credentials, and vetted Jewish requests on behalf of the state government. In July 1948, he led the fight for the Jews of Offenbach to regain possession of their synagogue, and later that summer the Hessian state association of Jewish communities protested vigorously against a plan to close his office.[46] In Bavaria, Philipp Auerbach was state commissar for victims of fascism, administering the state restitution agency in addition to holding a number of elected Jewish community offices. Siegmund Weltlinger served as adviser for Jewish affairs to the Berlin state government. Particularly through his cordial relationship with deputy mayor Ferdinand Friedensburg, Weltlinger won concessions for the Jews,

---

[43] Letter from the Israelitische Kultusvereinigung Württemberg to the Jewish communities in the American zone, 13 August 1947, ZA, B.1/13, A.411, 13.

[44] "Beschlüss der zweiten Tagung der Arbeitsgemeinschaft der Jüdischen Gemeinden in Deutschland," 19–22 October 1947, ZA, B.1/13, A.411, 16–23.

[45] "Protokoll der Sitzung der jüdischen Gemeinden der US-Zone," 21 December 1947, ZA, B.1/13, A.411, 2–5.

[46] "Protokoll über die Sitzung des Vorstandes der Jüdischen Gemeinde in Frankfurt am Main," 9 April 1947, ZA, B.1/13, A.2, 49; "Protokoll der Tagung des Landesverbandes der Jüdischen Gemeinden in Hessen," 27 July 1948, ZA, B.1/13, A.745, 28; letter from Landesverband Hessen to Christian Stock, 11 August 1948, ZA, B.1/13, A.745, 44.

including the right for Jewish state employees to have paid leave for Jewish holidays.[47]

BREAKTHROUGHS FOR THE DISPLACED PERSONS: A JEWISH STATE IN PALESTINE, A SUCCESSOR ORGANIZATION IN GERMANY

As 1947 ended, German Jews were frustrated by the situation regarding property, and they seemed stymied by their relations with other Jewish groups. The Eastern European Jewish displaced persons were frustrated with their inability to emigrate. The latter group's situation soon changed dramatically. In December 1947, the United Nations voted to create a Jewish state in Palestine. Displaced persons in Belsen staged a jubilant torchlight parade, and their colleagues in Munich sent telegrams to the leading Allied statesmen. All across Germany the pattern was the same.[48]

The displaced persons quickly moved to aid their future home. On 26 February 1948, the Central Committee in the British zone held a fundraiser for the Haganah, the Jewish Agency's militia in Palestine. By the spring of 1948, the displaced persons' attention and efforts were fully turned toward the Middle East, and the Central Committee in the American zone began transferring its treasury and archives to Israel. At the third and final Congress of Liberated Jews, held 30 March to 2 April 1948, Zionist candidates prevailed, but most left for Israel before their terms expired.[49]

For the American occupiers, the Jewish question in Germany was far from resolved. On 1 January 1948, the Joint Distribution Committee began to care for German Jews who were not immediately leaving Germany. In December 1947, William Haber, an economics professor at the University of Michigan, became the new Jewish adviser to Lucius Clay, the American commander. Clay expected the adviser "to act as a buffer between the displaced persons and the military" and claimed that "anti-Germanism among the Jewish displaced persons is, perhaps, far stronger than the anti-Semitism among the Germans." He thought the Central Committee in the

---

[47] Letter from Siegmund Weltlinger to Ferdinand Friedensburg, 1 September 1948; letter from Heinz Galinski to Siegmund Weltlinger, 3 August 1949; LAB, B Rep. 2, 4874.

[48] "Jubel und Freude," *Jüdisches Gemeindeblatt*, 17 December 1947.

[49] "An alle jüdische Gemeinden und Komitees in der brit. Zone," 26 February 1948, ZA, B.1/5, 76; Königseder and Wetzel, *Lebensmut im Wartesaal*, 94–96.

American zone was provocative in its stance and disagreed with the recognition of the group by his predecessor, Joseph McNarney, but it was too late. The Central Committee had acquired "too much authority and influence."[50]

Relations between the Jews and the occupying powers in western Germany remained strained over the Palestinian question, even after the historic UN vote. On 15 April, the third anniversary of their liberation, the Jews of Belsen staged a hunger strike to protest the world's indifference to the violence in Palestine.[51] In early June, the U.S. government and the IRO stopped giving Jews emigration assistance and stopped recognizing Israeli visas, pending the end of the Palestinian war. The State Department did not want Jewish displaced persons emigrating to Palestine or going to fight there; however, diplomats, including the American ambassador in Germany, Robert Murphy, regarded American policy on this matter as futile. They knew there was an underground railroad by which Jews continued to be smuggled to Palestine.[52] By August, American military headquarters in Europe had accredited the Jewish Agency as the representative of the provisional government of Israel, allowing this body to issue visas for travel to Israel, with one notable exception: "Able bodied men between the ages of 18 and 45 inclusive [i.e., of fighting age] will not be accorded exit documentation."[53] Emigrating to America was no easier for the displaced persons, who needed a sponsor in America and faced restrictive quotas.[54]

In summer 1948, the American army's designation of a successor organization to inherit ownerless Jewish property led to a severe deterioration of relations with the German Jews. The Jewish Restitution Successor Organization (JRSO), founded in New York by several leading Jewish bodies, was assigned this function. Jews

[50] "Notes on Session with General Lucius D. Clay in Frankfurt," 14–15 January 1948, CJH/YIVO, RG 347.7.1, box 33.
[51] "Protestkundgebung statt Befreiungsfeier," *Jüdisches Gemeindeblatt,* 28 April 1948.
[52] "Emigration of Jewish DPs to Palestine," 8 June 1948; letter from Robert Murphy to John Hickerson, 10 June 1948; NARA, RG 84, U.S. Political Advisor – Berlin, Top Secret General Correspondence, 1948-box 5, folder TS 840.1a (DPs General). For more on smuggling Jews to British Palestine, 1945–1948, see Yehuda Bauer, *Flight and Rescue: Brichah* (New York: Random House, 1970).
[53] Telegram from Chenard to state military governments, 9 August 1948, BAK, Z 45, 3/170-2/10.
[54] *Nachrichtenblatt,* nos. 2, 2a, and 3; ZA, B.1/15, 136. The AJDC recommended that German Jews register under the German quota so as not to fill the displaced persons quota.

Figure 2. Escorted by U.S. military officials, rabbis emigrate from Munich. *Source*: Preußischer Kulturbesitz Photoarchiv.

outside the displaced persons camps vigorously protested this designation, which took effect on 18 August 1948. They wanted their communities to be recognized as the successors of the prewar communities and resented the displaced persons' supposed influence with the American occupiers. They presumed that the anti-German, Zionist displaced persons had convinced the western occupation authorities that *all* the Jews in Germany planned to emigrate and there was thus no need to fund Jewish institutions in Germany.[55] German Jewish leaders such as Philipp Auerbach in Munich and Max Cahn in Frankfurt tried to rally support and to exert pressure, but it was futile.[56] In addition to pressure exerted by the Zionist displaced persons, foreign Jewish public sentiment was also largely against them.

The year 1948 brought a sea change in the displaced persons problem. When William Haber's tour of duty as Jewish adviser drew to a close in December of that year, he could report that the displaced persons population had shrunk, largely as a result of Israeli independence (see Fig. 2). In the American zone, the number of displaced persons contracted from 129,500 to 54,500; in the British zone, from 17,500 to 11,000; and in the French zone, from 2,700 to 1,200. Additionally, the flood of refugees entering Germany had stopped. The American army was able to move ahead with camp consolidation, sending displaced persons from Berlin to the U.S. zone. Israel claimed that it could absorb all the displaced persons by September 1949. Despite the wishes of the Israeli government and American Jewish groups, many displaced persons would stay in Germany, and over time they would join the German Jewish communities, forming the majority of the new Jewish community.

Haber understood that some Jews would remain in Germany, but even he did not foresee the precise nature of the situation. He wrote, "The DPs do not belong here. Their presence is an accident. They were brought here by force. Their status here is basically insecure and their life among the Germans is abnormal and artificial." He added, "These views should probably not be extended to include the German Jews in the several gemeinden [German communities]." He wrote that this group could not feel

55 "Weltlinger: Ausfürhungen auf der Aussprache des Freien Rats der Berliner betreffend Antisemitismus und Probleme d. Wiedergutmachung," LAB, E. Rep. 200–22, 80.
56 Letter from Philipp Auerbach to Max Cahn, 31 August 1948, ZA, B.1/13, A.410, 13.

at home anywhere else. Thus, they "should be encouraged to leave Germany but should not be penalized for the failure to do so."[57] By March 1949, the American military reported that the Jewish population in the U.S. zone was reaching a stable core, with the largest communities in Berlin, Munich, Frankfurt, and Stuttgart. Only 20 to 30 percent had been born in Germany or been prewar German citizens.[58] In fact, a new and enduring German Jewish community was emerging.

AMERICAN DISENGAGEMENT FROM JEWISH AFFAIRS

For many, the exodus of so many Jewish refugees seemed to signal the end of the Jewish issue in Germany, but that would not be the case. The Americans, who had governed the largest Jewish population in Germany, reacted to the new reality, and their policy on Jewish affairs soon took a different direction. Their focus shifted from transient displaced persons to those who seemed likely to stay in Germany. General Clay told his new Jewish adviser, Baltimore lawyer Harry Greenstein, that his goals were the liquidation and consolidation of the displaced persons camps, working with the JRSO, fighting antisemitism, and working for a Jewish presence in Germany. Clay wanted the Jews to establish roots in Germany. Greenstein wrote, "It is his conviction that it is possible for Jews to build a future for themselves and their families in Germany and felt it would be a tragic mistake on the part of the Jews to make Germany 'Judenrein.'"[59] That same spring, the western German states founded the Federal Republic of Germany, and soon the Jewish problem would pass from the American military into German hands.

In the summer of 1949, the Office of the High Commissioner for Germany (HICOG) under civilian John J. McCloy prepared to assume the authority formerly held by the military occupation government. Under McCloy, the Americans adopted a different modus operandi regarding Jewish questions. Rather than taking

---

57 Report by William Haber, 20 December 1948, CJH/YIVO, RG 347.7.1, box 33.
58 7 March 1949, BAK, Z 45, 5/342-1/43. The sociologist Y. Michal Bodemann wrote that those who remained were "rarely of the intellectual or leadership type." Bodemann, "'How can one stand to live there as a Jew...': Paradoxes of Jewish Existence in Germany," in *Jews, Germans, Memory*, ed. Bodemann, 26.
59 Report by Harry Greenstein, 22 March 1949, CJH/YIVO, RG 347.7.1, box 33.

an active hand in matters dealing with Jews, they tried to influence West German institutions. In early August, the *Süddeutsche Zeitung*, Munich's leading newspaper, published an editorial condemning antisemitism. Numerous Germans replied with antisemitic letters to the editor, one of which was published. The following day, 1,000 Jews – mainly Eastern European DPs – protested in the streets of Munich. Their legally unauthorized demonstration degenerated into a clash with the police, who fired on them despite having no orders to use their weapons. Although the official inquiry did not attribute the police response to antisemitism, the tense atmosphere between the DPs and the Germans authorities was noted. McCloy chose not to intervene in the situation. Many voices in the German press condemned the *Süddeutsche Zeitung* editors' poor judgment regarding the letter, and for McCloy, that sufficed as punishment. He wrote,

It appears to me to be far better to allow the free democratic forces in Germany and the reaction of a vigorous public conscience to rebuff and combat Nazi and anti-Semitic sentiments wherever they appear, than to intervene with arbitrary Military Government action in every instance of this sort and thereby discourage the initiative and sense of responsibility of the German public.[60]

West German chancellor Konrad Adenauer's first major address, on 19 September 1949, drew disapprobation from both Jews and his political opposition for his weak handling of the Jewish question, causing Harry Greenstein to complain vigorously to McCloy that "no German leader had apparently considered it politically profitable to openly disavow Nazism."[61] This message was sent to Adenauer, and it prodded him to make more forthright remarks in his annual Rosh Hashanah greetings, a move that McCloy applauded.[62] While many Jews continued to look to the American occupation authorities for redress of their grievances, they were to be disappointed in doing so.[63] The Americans were losing interest

---

[60] Letter from John J. McCloy to Murray D. Van Wagoner, undated [August 1949], BAK, Z 45, 15/118-1/43. For more on the incident, see Stern, *Whitewashing of the Yellow Badge*, 337–339.

[61] "Final Report of Major Abraham S. Hyman," 30 January 1950, CJH/YIVO, RG 347.7.1, box 33.

[62] Telegram from John J. McCloy to Konrad Adenauer, 26 September 1949, PA-AA, B 10, 307 (Fiche A 2023), 1.

[63] Letter from Axis Victims League to HICOG, September 1951, PA-AA, B 10, 308 (Fiche A. 2028), 120.

in Jewish affairs, and the onus rested increasingly with the West German government.

Nonetheless, the American occupiers did not allow the reparations program to collapse during the HICOG era (1950–1955). McCloy appointed an official to make sure that the restitution law in the U.S. zone went through the review process quickly. Meanwhile, the German liberal party, the FDP, supporting a unified restitution law for all Germany, wanted to suspend all other versions until that end could be achieved. Major Abraham Hyman, Greenstein's successor as Jewish adviser, wrote that since the western zonal laws were almost alike, the FDP was probably trying to take a populist stand and to weaken the laws.[64] According to McCloy's records, as of 31 January 1950, only 138 JRSO claims had been settled; 11,565 were still before restitution agencies; and more than 15,000 were working their way through the system. As it seemed that the backlog would never be resolved, the Americans, the JRSO, and the Germans agreed to a bulk settlement totaling 22,859,000 marks.[65] In fact, the JRSO's rapacity had exacerbated the backlog of unresolved claims. Unable to ascertain exactly to which property it had legitimate claim, it claimed "whatever it could, intending to sort out the private claims" later.[66]

As it became clear in 1949 that the Americans were reducing their active participation in Jewish affairs, adviser Harry Greenstein took it upon himself to work for a merger of the residual displaced persons Jewish community with the German Jewish communities. Initially, regional associations strengthened themselves. Soon, leaders of the two Jewish groups met to discuss the future of Jewish life in Germany and to negotiate the establishment of a joint representative body. Moreover, the American occupation authorities let all the Jews in Germany know that they thought it was important for them to unite on a permanent basis. U.S. High Commissioner John J. McCloy strongly favored a central organization for all the Jews in Germany, and his staff consistently worked toward this end.[67] American pressure, if not coercion, was decisive in inducing the Jews in Germany to unify at last.

---

[64] "Report of Major Abraham S. Hyman, Acting Adviser on Jewish Affairs to the US Commands, Germany and Austria," 27 January 1950, CJH/YIVO, RG 347.7.1, box 33.

[65] Office of the U.S. High Commissioner for Germany, *Report on Germany: Sept. 21, 1949–July 31, 1952* (Cologne: Greven and Bechtold, 1952), 141.

[66] Schreiber, "New Jewish Communities in Germany," 171.

[67] Van Dam, "Die Juden in Deutschland nach 1945," 2:901.

Greenstein planned a series of conferences on the continuity of Jewish life in Germany. The first conference was held in Heidelberg on 13–14 March 1949. All the major foreign Jewish organizations active in Germany sent representatives, as did the German Jewish communities and the displaced persons' Central Committee in the American zone. While Jewish leaders in Stuttgart and Frankfurt planned for smaller, enduring communities whose members would originally hail both from Germany and Eastern Europe, not everyone shared this view. Displaced persons leader Pessach Piekatsch was blunt: "We feel no responsibility toward those DPs who choose to remain. By helping the Gemeinden to achieve permanence we encourage DPs to remain too." He wanted the displaced persons to leave or be abandoned by world Jewry. If there were no organized community, they would have to leave, he claimed. Alexander Easterman of the WJC's European Section disagreed. "If a Jew elects to stay in Germany or Austria his choice should be respected." That included the German Jewish communities. They should be encouraged to go to Israel but not forced to do so. Curt Epstein, opposing permanent Jewish settlement in Germany, called this view "generous but very dangerous."[68]

Greenstein arranged a second, more important conference for 31 July, attended by German Jewish and displaced persons leaders from all three western zones, as well as by representatives from the leading Jewish organizations in America.[69] (see Fig. 3). Greenstein organized an elaborate agenda of speakers and panels, which dissected almost every aspect of Jewish life in Germany and made major strides toward the establishment of a single representative body for all the Jews in western Germany.

The American Jewish adviser opened the conference with direct remarks about the future of the Jews in Germany. The conference participants needed to recognize that Jews would continue to live in Germany, and they should work to ameliorate the situation. He did

---

[68] "Report of Conference held in the Office of the Adviser on Jewish Affairs," 13–14 March 1949, CJH/YIVO, RG 294.1, folder 76.

[69] Notable leaders attending included Max Cahn (Frankfurt), Benno Ostertag and Josef Warscher (Stuttgart), Julius Spanier (Munich), Norbert Wollheim (Lübeck/Central Committee in the British zone), Otto Nachmann (Baden), Philipp Auerbach (Bavaria), Julius Dreifuss (Düsseldorf), and Curt Epstein (Hesse). Hendrik George van Dam participated as the legal adviser of the Jewish Committee for Relief Abroad. American groups included the AJC, AJDC, JRSO, WJC, B'nai B'rith, the Hebrew Immigrant Aid Society, and the Jewish Agency.

Figure 3. Conference on the future of the Jews in Germany, held in Heidelberg, July–August 1949. Pictured on the dais (*left to right*): John J. McCloy, Harry Greenstein, army chaplain Major Abraham Hyman, and Eugen Kogon. *Source:* ullstein bild Abraham Pisarek.

not wish to discuss the moral implications of Jews in Germany. "This conference has been planned on the premise that there are at the present time and there will continue to be Jewish communities in Germany." It was time to merge the German Jewish and displaced persons communities and to be "united in our aims and purposes." Additionally, he proclaimed the desirability of "setting up an over-all Jewish organization which will make it possible for us to plan together for *all* of the Jews in Germany."[70]

U.S. High Commissioner John J. McCloy, keynote speaker at the conference, regarded German attitudes on the Jews as a barome-ter of democratization in Germany. He called the development of the Jewish community "the test of Germany's progress toward the light," which the entire world would be watching. Although McCloy perfunctorily offered his help to the community and pledged to combat antisemitism, he oddly placed the onus on the Jews. West Germany was experiencing a rash of cemetery and synagogue des-ecrations. Police and politicians had their hands full combating the outbreak, but McCloy expected that it would be some time before the climate created by Nazi propaganda changed, and he claimed that the Jews could contribute greatly to the transfor-mation of German attitudes by comporting themselves with hon-esty and courage. To avoid generating anti-Jewish sentiment, they needed to make themselves seen less specifically as Jews: "[T]he success of those that remain will to a large extent depend on the extent to which that community becomes less a community in itself and merges with the general community." He considered it obvi-ous that a country as large and as prominent as Germany should have a substantial Jewish community, but he did not foresee the numerous obstacles to a normal Jewish life there.[71]

Most other observers acknowledged the hindrances, but some saw hope. Rabbi Joachim Prinz said that the Jews needed to plan for the future in Germany without set time limits. He knew that many Jews had criticized the composition of the Jewish community in Germany, noting that most German Jews were not religious and that many had non-Jewish wives. He denounced the attitude, ex-pressed by many at the conference, that they were dealing with the

[70] "Introductory Remarks by Harry Greenstein, Adviser on Jewish Affairs," in *Conference on "The Future of the Jews in Germany,"* ed. Office of Adviser on Jewish Affairs (Heidelberg: Office of Adviser on Jewish Affairs, [1949]), 5.
[71] "Remarks by John J. McCloy, High Commissioner US Zone, in Germany," in ibid., 20–22.

apathetic dregs of Jewry, observing that many famous Zionists had returned to Judaism after having led assimilated lives. German Jews should not be driven away from Judaism. Prinz's comments ruffled quite a few feathers, and his critics ascribed the supposed weakness of the Jewish community in Germany precisely to the reasons he cited.[72] Eliahu Livneh, the Israeli delegate at the conference, argued that intermarried Jews had already inwardly broken with Judaism and were of no use to a struggling community. He wanted Israel to salvage the remnants and to liquidate the Jewish community in Germany.[73]

Regardless of how Livneh or Piekatsch felt, Greenstein was right: Jews would stay in Germany. They needed to organize themselves, and now was the time to do so. As long as such a large Zionist, anti-German group had remained in Germany and wished to emigrate, there had been no point in uniting the two communities, nor would the displaced persons have submitted to German Jewish leadership. With the Jewish community in Germany reaching a consistent size – and most of those who were immediately going to emigrate having done so – the two groups could plan for a common future. Philipp Auerbach proposed a joint committee, preserving full autonomy for both the German Jews' communities and the displaced persons' organizations. Piekatsch and Rosensaft endorsed the idea, the latter stating that "the primary objective of the proposed organization should be to enlighten those who intend to remain here, that there is no place for them in Germany" – the exact opposite of the group's intended purpose.[74]

The delegates debated the organization's composition and appointed an organizing committee, which Greenstein asked to convene that same day. Josef Rosensaft, Pessah Piekatsch, and Chaskiel Eife represented the displaced persons, while the most prominent German Jews on the committee were Philipp Auerbach, Julius Dreifuss, Curt Epstein, Benno Ostertag, Nathan Rosenberger, and Norbert Wollheim. Ironically, Israeli consul Eliahu Livneh presided over the meeting. The delegates endorsed a common body for the Jews throughout Germany, representing preexisting groups, and Auerbach's office in Munich would be their temporary

---

[72] "Discussion," in ibid., 45–51. The German-born Prinz went on to become an associate of Martin Luther King, Jr., in the American civil rights movement.
[73] Ibid., 50–51.   [74] "Formation of a Dachkommittee," in ibid., 32–33.

seat. In the next three weeks, each group would propose its ideas for the organization, and they would meet again on 4 September 1949 to discuss these ideas. Meanwhile, there were to be no public discussions or press statements regarding their plans.[75]

As the various Jewish communities in Germany began to unite, what were these communities like? According to American military officials, there were 3,650 registered Jews in the U.S. zone, 3,400 in the British zone, and 7,000 in Berlin. However, they estimated another 7,000 neither registered with the communities nor living in displaced persons camps. Those displaced persons living in cities usually did not join the local congregation. The division between German Jews and Eastern European Jews was stark. Membership of Jewish communities such as Darmstadt, Heidelberg, and Wiesbaden was more than 60 percent Eastern European. Stuttgart was 76 percent Eastern European. The membership in Mannheim, Düsseldorf, Cologne, and Hamburg was more than 60 percent German Jewish. Berlin was 80 percent German Jewish. A clear division existed between northern Germany and southern Germany. As critics pointed out at the Heidelberg conference, most German Jews had non-Jewish spouses, while displaced persons' rates of intermarriage were very low. Most of the Jews were unemployed, and German Jews often lived from advances against future reparations. Somehow, the displaced persons managed a decent economic existence, and one observer euphemistically explained why: "The DP element in the Gemeinden [Jewish communities] takes fairly good care of itself by extra-legal [i.e., black-market] trading in the German economy."[76]

In August and September, the German Jews and the displaced persons began to plan their unified organization; however, the tensions between the two groups did not completely abate. German Jews continually noted that they had dissolved their old communities only under pressure by the Nazis and repeated their claims of continuity between the prewar communities and the postwar communities. Regardless of these claims, the occupation authorities had recognized foreign Jewish organizations devoted to the emigration of the Jews from Germany and their resettlement in Palestine as the legal successors. The German Jews'

---

[75] "Report of the Commission Appointed to Formulate Tentative Plans for the Establishment of the Dachkommittee," in ibid., 57.
[76] "Preliminary Survey of the Jewish Communities in Germany," in ibid., 6–13.

Interest-Representation also protested supposed attempts by the displaced persons' leaders to predetermine the composition of the future umbrella organization.[77] As the planning meeting set for 4 September approached, a representative of the Interest-Representation noted that "it will be very hard to work with" the Central Committee in the U.S. zone.[78]

THE NEW WEST GERMAN GOVERNMENT
AND THE JEWISH QUESTION

In his final report as Jewish adviser, Major Abraham Hyman blamed the Jewish community itself for the delay in establishing any central directorate, calling the community "impoverished from the standpoint of leadership . . . with the most articulate elements pulling in diametrically opposite directions."[79] Not only were the Americans disappointed with the delay, but German leaders in favor of a rapprochement with the Jews were becoming frustrated. The Jews' inability to speak with a single voice stymied German efforts to reach out to them. Uncertain of whom to address and seeing the example of Jewish advisers in the state governments and Allied military governments, by September 1949, German leaders on the federal level favored the establishment of a Jewish adviser's office in the federal government, according to Düsseldorf city councilman Peter Lütsches.[80]

The controversy over the establishment of such an office dominated German-Jewish dialogue for almost a year. While the Jewish leadership came to oppose the establishment of such an office, many individual Jewish leaders initially favored the idea and actively worked for its implementation. Archival evidence indicates that the idea might have originated with the Jewish side. On 15 September, Karl Marx wrote to President Theodor Heuss, introducing himself and reminding the president that they had met at youth rallies during the Weimar Republic. Moreover, he offered

---

[77] Resolution by the Interessenvertretung, 7 August 1949, ZA, B.1/13, A.409, 16; letter from the Interessenvertretung to the communities, 19 August 1949, ZA, B.1/13, A.409, 14.

[78] Letter from Interessenvertretung to Frankfurt Gemeinde, 28 August 1949, ZA, B.1/13, A.409, 11.

[79] "Final Report of Major Abraham S. Hyman," 30 January 1950, CJH/YIVO, RG 347.7.1, box 33.

[80] Letter from Peter Lütsches to Karl Marx, 20 September 1949, BAK, B 136, 5862.

his services to the government as an adviser for Jewish affairs, adding, "It seems to me that a clarification of all these [Jewish] questions is only possible if the federal government would decide to call in a Jewish adviser, at least for the first few years."[81] On 22 September 1949, Marx wrote Chancellor Adenauer, thanking him for his Rosh Hashanah greetings and again raising the idea of a Jewish adviser:

Today the federal president told me that he is passing on to you the suggestion I made, which has as its goal the establishment of an office for a Jewish adviser within the federal government. I am of the opinion that we would very quickly proceed in mutual interest if you would decide to establish this office and occupy it with a prominent German Jew.[82]

He requested that Adenauer meet with him and industrialist Siegfried Seelig and later requested an interview with the chancellor for his newspaper.

Despite his often harsh criticism of the government, Marx could take an unusually friendly approach in dealing with the politicians. In his newspaper, he continually questioned the Germans' efforts regarding antisemitism, but in private he praised the new president and related that the Jews in Germany were reassured by his election.[83] In his letter to Adenauer from 22 September, Marx praised the government's devotion to fighting antisemitism.[84] When Marx interviewed the chancellor in early November, Adenauer reviewed the questions in advance and had the opportunity to revise the manuscript before publication. He had every opportunity to make a good impression via Marx's article, which was critical, for during that interview, he officially unveiled his plan for a ministerial Department for Jewish Affairs.[85]

In the meantime, government officials worked out details of the proposed office, which one official in Adenauer's office characterized as desirable for domestic and foreign political reasons. The proposed department, within the Interior Ministry, not only would handle cultural questions, but also would represent "Jewish

---

[81] Letter from Karl Marx to Theodor Heuss, 15 September 1949, BAK, B 122, 2086 (29).
[82] Letter from Karl Marx to Konrad Adenauer, 22 September 1949, BAK, B 136, 5862.
[83] Letter from Karl Marx to Theodor Heuss, 15 September 1949, BAK, B 122, 2086 (29).
[84] Letter from Karl Marx to Konrad Adenauer, 22 September 1949, BAK, B 136, 5862.
[85] Draft of interview, BAK, B 136, 5862.

interests in the issuing of laws."[86] Adenauer considered Ernst G. Löwenthal, the Cologne-born director of the British Jewish Relief Unit, for the position. Meanwhile, Löwenthal expressed his willingness to accept the post if he could retain his British citizenship, which he had acquired as an exile during the Nazi era.[87]

The idea of the Jewish department within the West German federal government quickly encountered opposition from Jewish organizations. The Frankfurt Jewish community opposed the plan, as did the Interest-Representation. At the December meeting of the latter group, delegates resolved that on all "questions which affect the Jews in Germany," they wanted the government "to consult with the [Jews'] democratically elected representatives," that is, themselves. Moreover, they threatened sanctions against any Jew who took the office. Under the direction of Bruno Weil, a leader of Weimar-era German Jewry, the émigré organization Axis Victims League also protested Chancellor Adenauer's idea, noting that such a sub-ministerial department was no substitute for a proper Ministry or State Secretariat for Reparations.[88]

Despite widespread resistance from German Jewish groups, Karl Marx initially supported the proposal and worked for its implementation. In late December 1949, after the Interest-Representation's protest, he suggested that changing the office's name to "Department for Reparations" might make it more palatable to the Jews in Germany. Many state governments already had German Jews serving as commissioners for reparations, and Marx wanted the federal official to administer reparations, as well. Additionally, as Marx correctly noted, much of the opposition related to the fact that "under the previous German government [i.e., the Nazis] there was a Jewish department."[89]

As it became likely that Marx would not have the position for himself, he corresponded frequently with the government about who was to occupy the post. On 14 February 1950, he wrote to Rolf Pauls in Adenauer's office that the majority of the Jewish

---

[86] Letter from State Secretary of the Interior in the Federal Chancellery to Gustav Heinemann and Fritz Schäffer, 28 November 1949, BAK, B 136, 5862.

[87] Letter from Konrad Adenauer to Brian Robertson, 7 December 1949, BAK, B 136, 5862.

[88] "Protokoll über die Sitzung des Vorstandes der Jüdischen Gemeinde in Frankfurt am Main," 7 December 1949, ZA, B.1/13, A.4, 4; letter from Interessenvertretung to Konrad Adenauer, 16 December 1949, BAK B 136, 5862; letter from Axis Victims League to Konrad Adenauer, 21 December 1949, BAK, B 136, 5862.

[89] Letter from Karl Marx to Herbert Blankenhorn, 24 December 1949, BAK, B 136, 5862.

community in Germany was upset over the idea of Munich rabbi Aaron Ohrenstein occupying the position and added, "The mood in the communities is *agreed* for Dr. Löwenthal's candidacy." Moreover, in reporting on the issue, Pauls claimed that Marx had told him that Philipp Auerbach advocated Ohrenstein's receiving the position. It is not clear whether this assertion was disingenuous or not, but government officials believed it, adding to the confusion. In his letter to Pauls, Marx also wrote that Adenauer was no doubt aware of the backlash that had erupted in some quarters against the proposal, but he insisted that the leading Jews in Germany were for the idea. Many Jews opposed Ohrenstein, he claimed, because they felt the position should have more than purely religious functions, and he even cited Leo Baeck as supporting Löwenthal. Meanwhile, he asked the chancellor to meet with German Jews before making a final decision and regretted that there was no central Jewish group in Germany.[90] Had the Jews had a central organization at this time, it is entirely possible that they would have obviated this controversy, which engendered additional distrust between Germans and Jews. According to a government report, officials at the Interior Ministry felt that having no clear Jewish negotiating partner hindered the progress of German-Jewish dialogue.[91]

Both Karl Marx and Philipp Auerbach served as self-appointed interpreters of Jewish public opinion for the West German government. According to Luitpold Werz, one of President Heuss's top aides and a future ambassador, Marx told the president on 21 February that the greatest difficulty was with the position's nomenclature.[92] Philipp Auerbach wrote to officials in the chancellor's office in March 1950, repeating the protest of the Interest-Representation against the appointment of a Jewish expert. He demanded that the government should meet with the democratically chosen representatives of the Jews in Germany, who

[90] Letter from Karl Marx to Rolf Pauls, 14 February 1950, PA-AA, Bestand B 10, 307 (Fiche A 2023), 22, emphasis in original; "Bildung eines Referates für jüdische Angelegenheiten in Bundesministerium des Innern," 14 February 1950, "Aufzeichnung," 1 March 1950, BAK, B 136, 5862. Rolf Pauls, a highly decorated German army officer who lost an arm during the war, went on to serve as the first West German ambassador to Israel, ambassador the United States, and first West German ambassador to the People's Republic of China.
[91] "Bildung eines Referates für jüdische Angelegenheiten in Bundesministerium des Innern," 14 February 1950, BAK, B 136, 5862; "Aufzeichnung," 1 March 1950, BAK, B 136, 5862.
[92] "Aufzeichnung," 23 February 1950, BAK, B 122, 2083 (29) and BAK, B 136, 5862.

would send a delegation to Bonn. He did not mention that the Jews had failed to establish a single representative organization. Auerbach threatened that any Jew accepting the position as head of Adenauer's Jewish department would automatically be excluded from the Interest-Representation, a threat independently echoed by Rabbi Wilhelm Weinberg of Frankfurt. Considering Auerbach's vigorous opposition, chancellery chief of staff Hans Globke forwarded the letter to Adenauer, who asked, "What is the opinion of the Jews in the British and French zones?"[93] Writing years later, community leader Hendrik George van Dam commented that the German Jews feared Auerbach's growing power, and therefore they delayed establishing a central institution that he might dominate.[94] To the government's complaint that as of March 1950, the Jews still had no single organization, Auerbach replied that his Interest-Representation represented 90 percent of the Jews in West Germany.[95]

Adenauer was not completely convinced by Auerbach's protests, and he continued to seek Jewish support. On a visit to Berlin in April, he met with local Jewish leaders Siegmund Weltlinger and Heinz Galinski. After discussing antisemitism and reparations, he asked what they thought of his proposal for a governmental Jewish department, and they supported the idea. Weltlinger told the chancellor that a similar office had worked extremely well with the Berlin state government. Later, he recalled the meeting in a report:

I recommended the urgent establishment of a Jewish department in the Federal Republic despite, or rather exactly because of the protests from certain Jewish circles which fundamentally rejected cooperation with German officials and suffered from a fanatical hate psychosis.

Adenauer reacted very positively to this opinion and said he was determined to set up such an office, despite the opposition.[96]

In fact, this controversial proposal, which ultimately woke the divided community from its torpor, had significant Jewish support at times. Some Jewish protests, including Auerbach's, might have

---

93 Letter from Philipp Auerbach to Hans Globke and handwritten marginal commentary by Konrad Adenauer, 6 March 1950, BAK, B 136, 5862; on Weinberg, "A Congress Office," 16 April 1950, CJH/YIVO, RG 347.7.1, box 35.
94 Van Dam, "Die Juden in Deutschland nach 1945," 2:900.
95 Letter from Philipp Auerbach to Gustav Heinemann, 24 March 1950, BAK, B 136, 5862.
96 "Aktennotiz! Betr. Besuch Adenauer," 19 April 1950, LAB, B Rep. 2, 4866.

been self-interestedly motivated, and Karl Marx was already making his presence felt as a behind-the-scenes actor. Both his machinations and the opinions of others sent mixed signals to the West German government. That confusion encouraged Adenauer to press forward with his idea, which ignited strengthened opposition from the Jewish community and ultimately resulted in real unity.

THE NEW CENTRAL COUNCIL OF JEWS IN GERMANY

By 1950, the Jews in Germany had the desire to unite, but they still could not get the job done. Foreign Jewish groups, including the World Jewish Congress (WJC) and the American Jewish Committee (AJC), followed with great interest the German Jews' inability to unify. In spring 1950, the World Jewish Congress established offices in Germany under Gerhard Jacoby, giving the leading international Jewish body a greater role in Jewish affairs in that country. In contrast to many of his colleagues, WJC president Nahum Goldmann had long wanted the Jews in Germany to set up a single organization, but he had lacked the time to supervise such a project. Furthermore, as demonstrated by the continuing fiasco with the proposal for a Jewish department, "Jewish leaders in Germany were too busy stabbing each other in the back" to cooperate for serious work, according to the AJC's representative in West Germany. Jacoby and A. L. Easterman, European director of the WJC, called for a meeting on 8 July to resolve the outstanding issue of unified representation. As the date approached, tensions grew. The WJC's advocacy of the collective guilt thesis worried German Jews, and the displaced persons did not want an organization committed to a permanent community in Germany. Even Israeli consul Eliahu Livneh was jealous of the WJC's taking a leading role.[97]

The meeting was controversial and indicative of the unreligious nature of many leaders of German Jewry, beginning on Shabbat and providing nonkosher food to the participants. Philipp Auerbach and Julius Spanier arrived one day late from Munich, as did the attorney Josef Klibansky from Frankfurt. While many

---

[97] AJC report "WJC Woos German Jewry," 24 July 1950, CJH/YIVO, RG 347.7.1, box 35. The AJC had an observer in Germany who filed regular reports on the community there.

representatives from the British zone and Hesse attended, Galinski was the only delegate from eastern Germany. The AJC's observer in Germany reported that the delegates agreed, at Jacoby's insistence, to hold a decisive meeting on 19 July and that they would found a group patterned on the Interest-Representation.[98] At this same meeting, some delegates could not help but betray their anti-German sentiments and their feeling that there was no place for Zionist Jews in Germany. Wollheim demonstratively asked Jacoby to thank the WJC for recognizing German Jewry, and Jacoby ended the meeting by expressing his pleasure that the Jews in Germany wanted to found a unitary organization and to increase their ties to world Jewry.[99]

On 19 July 1950, twenty-five leading Jews met in Frankfurt to discuss the foundation of an umbrella organization for the Jews in Germany. Heinz Galinski proposed establishing a directorate of four delegates and four alternates supported by a council of fifteen representatives. Galinski, chairman of the Berlin Jewish community, showed himself to be a champion of East German Jewry from the start, a bias that nearly derailed the entire project.

He [Galinski] regretted that no representative of the German Democratic Republic had been invited. This absolutely should have happened. The Jews from the GDR [German Democratic Republic] must have a seat in the soon-to-be founded directorate.

Jacoby and Klibansky felt that Galinski could represent all of Berlin, assisted by a deputy from East Germany, but Galinski protested this notion.

Berlin and the East-Zone are different. He would represent both parts of Berlin, but not the GDR outside of Berlin. If the latter is not represented, the Berlin community will not be able to cooperate.

Epstein opposed East German involvement, but Auerbach proposed keeping a seat open for East Germany without labeling it as such. Others were worried about the independence of their own groups, and Wollheim wanted the state associations to retain powers over all regional questions.

Discussion then turned to the directorate's membership. Auerbach picked himself, Heinz Galinski, Norbert Wollheim,

---

[98] Ibid.
[99] "Eine Gesamtorganisation in Deutschland vor der Gründung," *Jüdisches Gemeindeblatt*, 14 July 1950.

and Pessah Piekatsch for the directorate; Benno Ostertag, Josef Rosensaft, Chaskiel Eife, and someone from the French Zone would serve as deputies. While at least one delegate saw this as a conflict of interest on Auerbach's part, Auerbach boasted that he could balance his obligations. Galinski managed to win a seat on both the directorate and the council for an eastern representative. He proposed a governing council with three seats for the communities in the American occupation zone, three for the British, one for French, three for Berlin, one for the Soviet zone/East Germany, one for the British zonal Central Committee, and three for the Central Committee in Munich, totaling fifteen. The delegates accepted Galinski's ideas. The council was to be independent of the directorate, but directorate members could vote in the council.

Unanimously, the delegates agreed to name the new body the Central Council of Jews in Germany (Zentralrat der Juden in Deutschland) with its seat in Frankfurt. Other than a levy of 100 marks per community per month, its chief source of funding was 500 marks per month from the American Joint Distribution Committee. Josef Klibansky said the Jewish Bank for Industry and Trade would make a one-time donation of 3,000 marks. Klibansky and Hendrik George van Dam, both jurists, were to work on bylaws.[100]

The two men could scarcely have been more different. Klibansky was a lightning rod for strong opinions. His leadership of the Jewish Bank for Industry and Trade caused many Jewish leaders to accuse him of unethical business practices. During the trial of Philipp Auerbach (see chapter 4), he was aggressive and confrontational, accusing the court and the press of antisemitic bias. His flamboyant and controversial comportment brought him into contempt of court and drew unwelcome attention to the Jewish leadership in West Germany. In contrast, van Dam was used to working within the system. His father had been court antiquarian to Kaiser Wilhelm II, his maternal grandfather a liberal Bremen city councilman. Van

---

[100] "Protokoll der am 19. Juli 1950 14 Uhr in Frankfurt a. M. Hebelstr. 17 stattgehabten Sitzung zum Zwecke der Konstituierung einer Gesamtvertretung der Juden in Deutschland," 19 July 1950, ZA, B.1/7, 221.1. In 1960, van Dam reported that the Central Council had a budget of 1,050 DM per month until January 1952, when this amount increased to 1,250 DM. 500 DM came from the AJDC and 500 DM from the communities in the British zone. Zentralrat der Juden in Deutschland, [H. G. van Dam], *10 Jahre Zentralrat der Juden in Deutschland 1960* (Düsseldorf: Zentralrat der Juden in Deutschland, 1960), 5.

Dam earned his doctorate in law in Basel in 1934 and spent the war years in England. After the war, he helped to rebuild the German judiciary in Oldenburg and worked for the Jewish Relief Unit in the British zone. Despite these differences, it fell to these men to lay the legal groundwork for the most important Jewish institution in postwar Germany.

Foreign reaction to the Central Council's founding varied. The American Jewish Committee's commentary was insightful and critical. While the directorate was to consist of the outstanding leaders of Jewry in Germany, the council contained "second-rank 'machers' [*sic*]." The AJC's unnamed commentator called Galinski "plodding" and "honest and diligent, no great intellectual." The same observer reported on the debate over the inclusion of East German Jewry, noting that its leader, Julius Meyer, was considered close to the Soviets but a hard worker "for Jewish causes in East Berlin and in the East Zone." Reporting on the possibility of Hendrik George van Dam's serving as the Central Council's administrator, he wrote, "an important consideration in post-war Jewish life – his integrity is beyond question." The same could not be said about Klibansky as a result of his involvement with the Jewish Bank for Industry and Trade and his professional conduct as an attorney. The AJC observer reported that Livneh and Klibansky had started a wide-ranging argument over integrity and alleged involvement in illegal activity. Concerned about the internal feuds, Sam Haber of the AJDC pledged the meeting's participants to secrecy.[101]

The Central Council's second meeting, held on 20 August in Munich, focused primarily on technical issues and on the group's mission. Delegates seemed undecided as to whether contact with the government or more practical work should be paramount.[102] When the Central Council met again on 6 September, it was in disarray. There was still no secretariat, but most members supported van Dam's taking the position, which he assumed on 15 October. The young Central Council was also already facing its first internal crisis. Wollheim and Marx bitterly clashed over Marx's attempts at reconciliation with former antisemitic entertainers Veit Harlan and Werner Kraus. While most delegates disagreed with Marx, they

---

[101] "Gesamtvertretung gegründet," *Allgemeine Wochenzeitung*, 28 July 1950; AJC report, "A 'Roof Organization' Is Born," 23 July 1950, CJH/YIVO, RG 347.7.1, box 35.

[102] "Protokoll des Zentralrates der Juden in Deutschland," 20 August 1950, ZA, B.1/7, 221.2.

wished to avoid any public disturbances and did not want any internal hearings on the matter. The Central Council's political activity was also a matter of discussion. The delegates debated whether or not they could participate in the festivities for the first West German national holiday and how they should communicate with the federal government.[103] Such issues frequently appeared on the Central Council's agenda and reflect the difficulty the group's leaders had in rebuilding a German Jewish identity.

Meeting a month later, the Central Council's directorate faced the issue that had indirectly led to its creation: Adenauer's desire to have a Department for Jewish Affairs in the Bonn government. On 10 September, the federal interior minister had asked the Central Council for its opinion on the nomination of Rabbi Aaron Ohrenstein to the controversial post. Ohrenstein seemed to want the appointment but would not accept it against the Central Council's wishes. The vast majority of delegates were against the proposal, fearing that the official would have no real responsibility for decisions but would take the blame when things went wrong. Several speakers characterized the precarious situation of such an appointee as that of a "whipping boy" (*Prügelknabe*). As a result of the discussion, they wrote a letter to the Interior Ministry, requesting that the government not appoint such an official.[104]

It was not surprising that the Central Council would oppose the appointment of an official bureau for Jewish affairs, as this office might have reduced its own influence or authority. On other issues, however, the Central Council was still making its voice heard. It was not yet well known to German and Allied authorities, and delegates were uncertain whether they would be able to get interzonal travel passes to attend a meeting in November in Berlin.[105] On the other hand, the Jewish Restitution Successor Organization was afraid that the West German Central Council would negotiate directly with the West German government for restitution of formerly Jewish property – relegating the

---

[103] Zentralrat der Juden in Deutschland [van Dam], *10 Jahre Zentralrat*, 5; "Sitzung des Zentralrates der Juden," 6 September 1950, ZA, B.1/7, 221.4. Harlan and Kraus had been involved in the making of viciously antisemitic films during the Nazi years. The most notable of these was *Jud Süss*.

[104] "Protokoll der Sitzung des Direktoriums des Zentralrates," 15–16 October 1950, ZA, B.1/7, 221.5.

[105] Ibid.

New York-based JRSO to irrelevancy.[106] In the words of one AJC observer, the Central Council wanted to "arrogate to itself the authority on all important matters affecting the Jews in Germany," but it still had little status.[107] In an effort to rectify this situation, members of the directorate, shepherded by Gerhard Jacoby and Sam Haber, met with American High Commissioner McCloy on 29 November 1950.[108]

As the Central Council was beginning to find its voice and presented itself as the sole voice for the Jews in Germany, the Central Committee in Munich was disintegrating (and ultimately disbanded in August 1951). The Central Council could now arrogate to itself the right to speak in the name of all Jews in Germany, and it jealously guarded this prerogative. Within Germany, it was gaining respect, and abroad it was strengthening its ties to world Jewry.[109] Because Hendrik George van Dam lived in Hamburg, he moved the group's offices there, and through his contacts with the British occupiers, he secured office space for the group. Hendrik George van Dam provided the Central Council with invaluable institutional leadership. In Düsseldorf, Karl Marx provided the moral mouthpiece of the new German Jewry through his newspaper.[110]

Establishing a single representative body for all the Jews in Germany had not been easy. While German Jews had quickly reorganized their communities and united in state-wide or regional associations, they were often loath to unite with the Jewish displaced persons' communities. Moreover, many displaced persons leaders, supported by Jewish groups abroad, firmly opposed a permanent Jewish presence in Germany. Foreign Jewish organizations, promoting Jewish emigration from Germany, isolated the German Jews. The displaced persons population was unstable, and only with the foundation of the State of Israel, when most of the

[106] Schreiber, "New Jewish Communities in Germany," 77.
[107] AJC report, "Shall Jews Remain in Germany?: An Observer's Report from Inside Germany," November 1950, CJH/YIVO, RG 347.7.1, box 33.
[108] "McCloy beriet mit Zentralrat," *Allgemeine Wochenzeitung*, 8 December 1950; "Besprechung von Mitgliedern des vorläufigen Direktoriums mit Mr. J McCloy," 29 November 1950, ZA, B.1/7, 221.6.
[109] "Summarisches Protokoll der Sitzung des Zentralrates," 7 January 1951, ZA, B.1/7, 221.9.
[110] Bodemann, "'How can one stand to live there as a Jew...,'" in *Jews, Germans, Memory*, ed. Bodemann, 32.

displaced persons left Germany, did the size of the Jewish community stabilize.

Despite the Americans' initial suggestion at the Heidelberg conference and their decreasing interest in administering Jewish affairs, the German government's proposal for an official Jewish adviser ultimately compelled the German Jews and the remaining displaced persons to form a single representative organization. As sociologist Y. Michal Bodemann has noted, "triple isolation and stigmatization of the Jewish communities in Germany" were the critical factors in inducing unity. Only in the face of abandonment by the American occupiers, isolation by world Jewry, and the imposition by the West German government of an official representative did they put aside their disputes and found the Central Council of Jews in Germany.[111] From now on, German politicians had a viable domestic partner for the German-Jewish dialogue, and the Jewish communities had a single institution to represent their demands for reparations and support.

Yet even with this important step, the Jews in Germany found themselves isolated among their coreligionists who did not recognize them or accept them at international meetings. The Central Council struggled to call attention to itself and to its message. Jewish issues were not at the top of the agenda for civil servants and legislators in the new Germany. Additionally, Jewish groups abroad continued to dominate Jewish representation in Germany as government passed from Allied hands to German ones, and as a new organization, the Central Council had to prove itself. These challenges would preoccupy the struggling community for many years.

[111] Bodemann, "Staat und Ethnizität," in *Jüdisches Leben*, ed. Brumlik et al., 59.

CHAPTER 3

The Challenge of Jewish Life under Soviet Occupation

Although most Jewish Holocaust survivors and émigrés who returned to Germany after 1945 went to western Germany, a significant number of Jews returned to Communist-dominated eastern
Germany either out of political conviction or simply because their
homes had been there before the years of Nazi dictatorship. This
group faced challenges very different from those of their coreligionists in the West. For them, attempts to refound and to coordinate Jewish life would largely depend on their relations with
the Soviet military occupation administration and their German
Communist protégés.

Like the Jews in the occupation zones of western Germany, eastern German Jewry quickly moved to refound their disbanded communities. Soon thereafter, they established a central organization
to represent their interests to the Soviets and to the local German
administration. However, even in advocating Jewish interests, this
group's room to maneuver was limited. Not only were the Jews
asking for special recognition in a society whose very existence
was predicated on radical equality, they also – unintentionally –
challenged an important aspect of the ruling Communists' self-
conception.[1] In governing eastern Germany after the Nazi era, the
Party of Socialist Unity (Sozialistische Einheitspartei Deutschlands,
or SED), the Marxists' vehicle for rule, touted its anti-Nazi credentials and the history of persecution of the Communists under the
Nazis as justification for the party's rule. It viewed itself as the very
antithesis of National Socialism, and as such, it deserved to govern the new, post-Nazi Germany, SED leaders reasoned. Moreover,

---

[1] In the egalitarian society of eastern Germany, "*All* areas of life were observed, manipu-
lated, controlled, in the interest of the alleged greater good of the whole." Mary Fulbrook,
Anatomy of a Dictatorship: Inside the GDR, 1949–1969 (Oxford: Oxford University Press,
1995), 19.

as an anti-Nazi party that had suffered persecution, it claimed to bear no legal or moral responsibility for reparations for the Nazis' crimes. This logic became part of the East German state mythology.

However, SED leaders – many of whom were antisemitic – seemed to feel threatened by claims of greater Nazi victimization posited by Jewish groups. Jewish groups did not accept the Communists' claim to owe nothing to those persecuted by the Nazis on account of their religion or ethnicity. The Jewish community looked to the Soviet occupation regime and the post-1945 state governments in eastern Germany, led by the SED, for support and reparations. Additionally, many SED leaders feared that if non-Jewish Germans accepted that the Communists had not been the Nazis' primary targets, and thus were not the very antithesis of National Socialism, the SED's claim to have the right to govern might lose resonance. Trifling with such important aspects of national ideology in an increasingly authoritarian society entailed tremendous risks for those persons and groups advocating Jewish needs, including reparations.

INITIAL COMMUNAL ORGANIZATION AND ITS CHALLENGES

Attempts to coordinate Jewish life in eastern Germany on the local level began as soon as the war ended, and in eastern Germany, as in western Germany, Jewish organizations arose on the local level first. Hard as it was to found Jewish groups amid the physical and social destruction wrought by the war, there was another, political obstacle to organization: Communist obstruction. Any new organization founded after the war in eastern Germany needed to have the approval of local German administrators, and these were ordinarily Communists. As such, they were deeply suspicious of independent or semi-independent organizations. As a result, they often declined to authorize the formation of new groups, including Jewish communities. Many of the administrators were antisemitic, and others were simply hostile to organized religion and had no desire to grant the Jews any recognition.[2]

---

[2] Catherine Epstein claims the pre-1933 Communist Party was not antisemitic but rather disinterested in Jewish issues as most German Jews were bourgeois. However, she does characterize the party as antisemitic by 1946. Epstein, *Last Revolutionaries*, 25 and 127.

Prior to the war, Berlin had the most prominent and the most vibrant Jewish life in Germany. A single, unitary Jewish Community of Berlin (Jüdische Gemeinde zu Berlin) maintained numerous Jewish institutions – including schools, hospitals, orphanages, libraries, and ornate synagogues. After the war, unity remained elusive, and each city district (*Bezirk*) formed its own Jewish community. Only after public transportation in the city had resumed service were neighborhood Jewish leaders able to meet to found a community for the entire city, and even then politics complicated unification. Among the most successful local communities, at least in the short term, was that of northwestern Berlin, which had both practical and political origins.[3]

In seeking support for their renascent community, Berlin Jews naturally approached the Soviet Military Administration – a problematic proposition. For in addition to their erratic and frequently corrupt comportment, Soviet occupiers used their position to discriminate against Social Democrats. However, in other cases they allowed former Nazis and Nazi sympathizers to continue to occupy important municipal posts. As historian Norman Naimark has shown, the Soviets neither were prepared to occupy eastern Germany nor did they have long-term goals in mind. Their primary preoccupation was to serve the Soviet Union's perceived economic and political goals.[4]

Despite the Soviets' undependable administration, the Jews of Berlin had little choice but to deal with the occupiers. Until July 1945, the victorious Soviets were the only Allied power represented in the capital, and after the division of the erstwhile capital, they retained control of central and eastern Berlin. In late May 1945, Fritz Hirschfeld, chief doctor of the Jewish hospital, corresponded with the Soviet commander in Berlin, Nikolai Besarin,

---

Thomas Haury feels that only Germany's particular history restrained Communist antisemitism from manifesting itself in even more dangerous ways. Thomas Haury, *Antisemitismus von links. Kommunistische Ideologie, Nationalismus und Antizionismus in der frühen DDR* (Hamburg: Hamburger Edition, 2002).

3 Hermann Simon, "Die Jüdische Gemeinde Nordwest: Eine Episode aus der Zeit des Neubeginns jüdisches Lebens in Berlin nach 1945," in *Aufbau nach dem Untergang. Deutsch-jüdische Geschichte nach 1945*, ed. Andreas Nachama and Julius H. Schoeps (Berlin: Argon, 1992).

4 Norman Naimark, *The Russians in Germany: A History of the Soviet Zone of Occupation, 1945–1949* (Cambridge: Harvard University Press, 1995), 15–16 and 465.

about the needs of concentration camp survivors.[5] Meanwhile, the Jews of the community of North Berlin telegraphed Stalin to express their thanks for their liberation. Despite this effort to curry favor, the Soviet Military Administration, acting on the recommendation of German Communist and deputy mayor of Berlin Karl Maron, rejected the Jews' application for a representative organization.[6]

In postwar Berlin, even finding suitable persons to establish a unitary Jewish community was difficult. Leaders of the Reich Union of Jews in Germany (Reichsvereinigung der Juden in Deutschland), the central administrative organization initially formed in February 1939 and strictly regulated by Nazi fiat from July 1939, made the first attempt. Despite an Allied order in the summer of 1945 dissolving all organizations established by the Nazis, the organization did not automatically disband. On 15 June 1945, Walter Lustig, leader of the Reich Union since 1943, wrote to the Soviet military authorities to register a new Jewish community and to renounce the organization's status, as per the terms of the Soviets' order no. 2, issued on 10 June. Lustig and his colleagues chose the appellation "Jüdische Gemeinde zu Berlin," the same name used by the Jews of Berlin before the Nazi era. Of his eleven co-signatories, none would have leadership positions five years later, and many ended up in Soviet prisons.[7] Siegmund Weltlinger, adviser for religious affairs in the Berlin-Mitte district government, wrote that the Reich Union "can in no way count as untainted" or

---

[5] Letter from Fritz Hirschfeld to Nikolai Besarin, 25 May 1945, LAB, B Rep. 2, 4617. The Russians later arrested Hirschfeld and in 1950 sentenced him to a twenty-year prison term for violating Control Council law no. 10, originally intended as an instrument of denazification. Erika Siesler to Julius Meyer, 16 December 1951, CJA, 5 B 1, 2, 395.

[6] Olaf Groehler, "Antifaschismus und jüdische Problematik in der SBZ und der frühen DDR," in *Die SED-Politik, der Antifaschismus und die Juden in der SBZ und frühen DDR*, by Mario Keßler and Olaf Groehler (Berlin: Gesellschaftswissenschaftliches Forum, 1995), 8. Maron had spent the war in Moscow and shared the anti-Jewish bias of many of his fellow Moscow émigrés.

[7] Letter from Walter Lustig to Soviet Military Administration, 15 June 1945, LAB, B Rep. 2, 4617; Ulrike Offenberg, *"Seid vorsichtig gegen die Machthaber,"* 17 and 21. Although many scholars have preferred to call the post–June 1943, Gestapo-supervised incarnation the "Rest-Reichsvereinigung," the group itself did not change its appellation. In 1968, a West German court ruled that the group had never been legally dissolved. See Esriel Hildesheimer, *Jüdische Selbstverwaltung unter dem NS-Regime. Der Existenzkampf der Reichsvertretung und Reichsvereinigung der Juden in Deutschland* (Tübingen: Mohr, 1994), 125 and 233–234.

have the trust of Berlin Jewry, and, as mentioned above, Jews in the British sector of Berlin set up their own, autonomous community.[8] In the eyes of the Soviets and other independent Jewish groups, the wartime leadership of the Jewish community was discredited for its collaboration with the Gestapo. In fact, the Soviets arrested and tried Lustig, who was never seen again.[9]

With help from the Berlin city government's office for religious affairs under Pastor Peter Buchholz, a rival group under Erich Nelhans and Fritz Katten more successfully established a Jewish administration in the old communal headquarters in East Berlin's Oranienburger Straße in June 1945. The community eventually regained its prewar legal status as a *Körperschaft des öffentlichen Rechts* (incorporated body under public law), guaranteeing its autonomous administration and allowing it to collect taxes from its members with assistance from the authorities.[10] However, throughout the summer of 1945, Nelhans wrote to the Berlin city government complaining about the Red Army's misuse of Jewish property, including its quartering of horses in the Weißensee cemetery. In airing his grievances, the Jewish leader made himself very unpopular. In 1948, the NKVD, the Soviet secret police, arrested him for allegedly aiding Jewish deserters from the Red Army and had him sentenced to fifteen years' hard labor, which he presumably did not survive.[11]

To help with the immense tasks facing the newly reestablished Jewish community, the Berlin city government established the office of adviser for Jewish affairs. As early as 16 June, Buchholz tapped Siegmund Weltlinger for the position, which he held

[8] "Bericht," 7 June 1945, LAB, E Rep. 200–22, 41; letter from Adolf Schwersenz to Pastor Peter Buchholz, 19 June 1945, LAB, B Rep. 2, 4617; Simon, "Die Jüdische Gemeinde Nordwest," in *Aufbau nach dem Untergang*, ed. Nachama and Schoeps. For more information on the rival groups involved in the reestablishment of the Berlin Jewish community and Jewish life in Berlin in general, see Gay, *Safe among the Germans*, 144–201, esp. 153–161, and Offenberg, "Die jüdische Gemeinde zu Berlin 1945–1953," in *Leben im Land der Täter*, ed. Schoeps.

[9] Hildesheimer, *Jüdische Selbstverwaltung*, 125 and 234 n. 99. Ruth Gay even provides a date for his execution. Gay, *Safe among the Germans*, 155.

[10] "Bericht über die Neubildung der Jüdischen Gemeinden in Berlin," 13 November 1946, LAB, E Rep. 200–22, 38; letter from Peter Buchholz, 21 June 1945, LAB, B Rep. 2, 4617; "Bericht (16. November 1945): Wiederaufbau der Jüdischen Gemeinde in Berlin," 16 November 1945, LAB, E Rep. 200–22, 41; "Die Lage der Jüdischen Gemeinde zu Berlin und ihrer Mitglieder," undated [April 1946], LAB, B Rep. 2, 26065.

[11] Letter from Erich Nelhans to Peter Buchholz, 27 July 1945, LAB, B Rep. 2, 4866; Offenberg, *"Seid vorsichtig gegen die Machthaber,"* 37.

from September 1945 until 1957 (after 1948 in West Berlin).[12] A survivor of Sachsenhausen concentration camp, Weltlinger functioned as a pivotal intermediary between Berlin Jewry, the municipal government, and the Christian Democratic party, of which he was a member.

Once Weltlinger and his colleagues had formally reestablished the community, attempts to reconstitute patterns of prewar Jewish life in Berlin began. In late September 1945, city officials met with Jewish leaders to discuss the community's development. Seeing the need for an administration to handle religious services, schools, and a home for the elderly, Weltlinger wanted the Jewish community to hold early elections for a representative body. Moreover, protective of the Jews' public image, he insisted that his office should vet all press releases and that Jewish community officials should serve without remuneration.[13] With 5,000 registered Jews and 2,000 more unregistered persons of Jewish heritage, according to the U.S. military, Berlin could claim the largest community in postwar Germany, and the army's representative claimed that three Berlin synagogues held Rosh Hashanah services in 1945.[14]

The dominant figure in Berlin Jewish life from the immediate postwar years until the early 1990s was Heinz Galinski, a West Prussian Jew who first came to Berlin in 1938. After surviving Auschwitz, where he lost his parents and first wife, and the death march to Bergen-Belsen, Galinski returned to Berlin in July 1945. Like so many Holocaust survivors, he wanted to emigrate to America, but his plans fell through when his daughter was born prematurely.[15] He would remain in Germany and, as he later explained, became determined that there would be Jewish life there:

I have always represented the point of view that the Wannsee Conference cannot be the last word in the life of the Jewish community in Germany. Therefore, I participated with a few others to restore the Jewish community in Berlin. I have never been one of those who considered the

---

[12] "Bericht (26. Juni 1945)," 26 June 1945, LAB, E Rep. 200–22, 38.
[13] "Protokoll," 26 September 1945, LAB, E Rep. 200–22, 41.
[14] Letter from Sergeant Abraham Aaroni to Major M. M. Knappen, 12 September 1945, BAK, Z 45, 5/342-1/43. The three synagogues were Rykestraße, Joachimsthaler Straße, and Pestalozzistraße. Cf. Gay, *Safe among the Germans*, 161.
[15] Andreas Nachama, "Der Mann in der Fasanenstraße," in *Aufbau nach dem Untergang*, ed. Nachama and Schoeps.

community here as a liquidation community, but rather I have endeavored to give back to the survivors the belief in a restored, new life.[16]

After serving on the community board under the leadership of Hans-Erich Fabian, Galinski became chairman in April 1949 and held this position for forty-three years.

Despite the administrative obstacles, organized Jewish communities sprang up throughout the Soviet occupation zone. The Jews in Leipzig and Magdeburg founded communities almost immediately after the war's end, their coreligionists in Dresden did so in June, and those in Chemnitz and Erfurt did so later that summer. Halle's Jewry organized itself in 1947, and the Jews of Mecklenburg founded an organized community in the summer of the same year, although their small organization did not receive legal recognition until June 1948.[17] As the largest Jewish community and the one with the closest contact with the Soviets and with the German administrators, the Berlin Jewish community remained a focal point for East German Jewry.

DEBATES ON VICTIMHOOD

Almost immediately after liberation from the concentration camps, debate on the hierarchy of victimhood began. In May 1945, future Communist Party central committee member Franz Dahlem spoke to the former prisoners of Mauthausen on the need for unity between the Jewish victims and Communist victims of Nazi persecution. Dahlem could not forget the persecution of the Jews, but as a thoroughgoing Communist, Dahlem also politicized the memory of the persecution:

One needs only to think about how broad is the class of those who enriched themselves through the expropriation and extermination of the Jews, who profited from the Aryanization of business, shops, apartments, etc.[18]

---

[16] Heinz Galinski, "New Beginnning of Jewish Life in Berlin," interview by Michael Brenner, *After the Holocaust*, ed. Brenner, 101. At the Wannsee Conference of January 1942, the Nazis formally planned the organized mass extermination of European Jewry.

[17] "Fragebogen für den Almanach Die Juden in Deutschland 1950/51-5711," CJA, 5 B 1, 2; cf. Offenberg, *"Seid vorsichtig gegen die Machthaber,"* 50–63.

[18] Franz Dahlem, "Einige Probleme unserer künftigen Arbeit in Deutschland, Rede vor ehemaligen Häftlingen des KZ Mauthausen, Mai 1945," in *Ausgewählte Reden und Aufsätze, 1919–1979: Zur Geschichte der Arbeiterbewegung* (Berlin: Dietz, 1980), 254.

He seemed to equate the Nazi extermination of the Jews with the murder of political and military enemies of the Nazi state:

Millions of people were exploited in the most varied ways, tortured, and exterminated in concentration camps in Germany and in the occupied countries, whereby the Jews of Europe alone were exterminated in the millions. For years, we ourselves were impotent witnesses as each Jew was beaten to death in Mauthausen concentration camp or chased into the electric wire or the cordon, how week after week, the Russian officer prisoners of war and especially the political officers were rifled down or eliminated by a shot in the neck according to plan. We experienced the planned extermination of the intelligentsia of Poland and Czechoslovakia [and] the communist cadre of various lands, the imprisoned partisans and men of the resistance movements from Yugoslavia, Greece, from France, Belgium, Italy, who were hanged, injected, poisoned, or were killed through simple starvation or allowed to freeze to death.[19]

He noted that Germany would have to prove that it was worthy of the trust of other nations, and a precondition was the acceptance of German collective guilt for the crimes committed under the Nazis.[20]

Naturally, Dahlem mentioned the persecution suffered by Communists and their allies, but the fact that he singled out the Jews for special mention as the equals of political persecutees is remarkable in light of the political line soon taken by East German Communists. His narrative of the past included the Nazi persecution of the Jews alongside the Communist orthodoxy in which the Nazis fought a fascist, imperialist war against the Communists and the international working class.

However, the ownership of the legacy of the Holocaust soon gained tremendous importance in the Communists' world-view and self-identity, and they would not let another group stake a claim to this heritage more prominent than theirs. In the developing public discourse over the Holocaust and the hierarchy of victimhood, it was not clear exactly how those persecuted by the Nazis for their religious beliefs or ethnic origins, especially Jews, stood in relation to victims of political persecution, especially Communists.

In the new East German society, built on the ruins of Nazi Germany, one's relationship to the Nazi past had great significance. Because the architects and leaders of the new Germany had been

[19] Ibid., 254–255.   [20] Ibid., 256–262.

victims of National Socialist persecution (as they frequently reminded postwar society), bearing the official designation of "victim of fascism" (*Opfer des Faschismus*) gave one particular standing in the new society.[21] Soon, special interest groups known as "mass organizations" (*Massenorganisationen*) facilitated the supervision of society, including the regulation of the status of "victim-of-fascism," with all the advantages that came from having such a designation in a country where housing, food, and clothing were distributed on a rationed basis. In the highly politicized atmosphere of eastern Germany, the right to victim-of-fascism status became a source of fierce debate. Many political persecutees did not wish to grant the designation to the Jews, who, they claimed, had not done anything to combat fascism and therefore bore some blame for their fate. These political opponents argued that Jewish passivity was tantamount to complicity and rendered them undeserving of the coveted status.

In October 1945, as the various local committees charged with regulating victim-of-fascism status met in Berlin with the goal of standardizing the criteria for receiving such status, it became clear that vast differences existed between the groups. Communist leader Karl Raddatz stressed that the coveted status applied to those whom "we characterize as having acted out of political conviction, thus completely the illegal fighters of the antifascist parties [who were in concentration camps] ... and also functionaries of the workers' movement known from before."[22] Others qualifying included political émigrés, Spanish civil war veterans, underground fighters, and the anti-Hitler plotters of 20 July 1944. However, Raddatz did not overlook the status of so-called racial persecutees, a common euphemism for Jews. In Berlin, where he administered the committee, they would create a new status above victim-of-fascism status. Political resisters would have the word "fighter" ("Kämpfer") stamped on their official identity cards.[23] Creating

---

[21] The Communist leadership of East Germany and the eastern bloc continually referred to National Socialism as "fascism." They later applied this vague term to their non-Communist adversaries in the West, cynically casting their opposition to the liberal, American-led bloc in the same light as their earlier opposition to the Nazis.

[22] "Konferenz der Ausschüsse 'Opfer des Faschismus' am Sonnabend, 27. Oktober und Sonntag, dem 28. Oktober 1945 im Walter-Albrecht-Haus in Leipzig," 27 October 1945, BAB (SAPMO), DY 54/V 277/1, 1, 36.

[23] Ibid., 37–38; cf. Herf, *Divided Memory*, 82. Raddatz did not mention the Jews by name, euphemistically calling them simply "racial persecutees," rather than religious or ethnic

this new status was his compromise to get the regional committees to grant some recognition to "mere" victims and not just resistance fighters.

At the same conference, Heinz Brandt of the cultural division of the central coordinating committee for victim-of-fascism matters noted that it would be impossible not to award the Jews victim-of-fascism status after all that had befallen them. It was impossible to discuss the Holocaust without considering the Jews as victims of fascism, and it would be impossible to build the new, enlightened Germany "if we, on the other hand, pursue such a policy regarding the Jews." He endorsed the compromise whereby resistance fighters would receive a stamp on their identification cards, but all victims of the Nuremberg Laws would receive victim-of-fascism status.[24] For Brandt, the political persecutees would be first among equals, but they would not omit the Jews.

Granting the Jews victim-of-fascism status was not popular with many Communists. Jenny Matern of the Saxon delegation and wife of prominent Communist inquisitor Hermann Matern regarded the category as a political one, merited only by members of political parties that had opposed the Nazis and that now stood in the postwar coalition. She did not want all Jews to receive a status that would place them on par with the Communists in the hierarchy of victimhood. Moreover, a crass antisemitism, tied to anticapitalism, permeated her speech. She opposed financial aid to the Jews and claimed that Jewish victims were interested only in money. "The question of financial support – and I want to say this completely openly and to express it honestly – plays a particular role in those [Jewish] circles which is often very unfortunate." To justify her low opinion of Jewish victims, she claimed to know German Jews who gleefully aided in the persecution of their own people in the camps.[25] While she opposed granting blanket victim-of-fascism status to Jews, she did support it for other oppressed religious groups. She also denied that the status was, in fact, politicized or tied to Communist Party membership.[26]

---

persecutees. The dubious nomenclature "racial persecutees" was popular with the Nazis and remained current after their defeat.

[24] "Konferenz der Ausschüsse 'Opfer des Faschismus' am Sonnabend, 27. Oktober und Sonntag, dem 28. Oktober 1945 im Walter-Albrecht-Haus in Leipzig," 28 October 1945, BAB (SAPMO), DY 54/V 277/1, 1, 41–43.

[25] Ibid., 77–79 and 82.   [26] Ibid., 80.

Offering an alternative view were Jewish representatives Julius Meyer from Berlin and Leon Löwenkopf from Dresden, both Marxists. Not only did they demand victim-of-fascism status, they also demanded that they have a voice in evaluating petitions for the status.[27] Löwenkopf, a survivor of Auschwitz and Sachsenhausen, sardonically asked his comrades whether they had not seen the brutal persecution of the Jews:

I don't know if these gentlemen were flying around somewhere in the air as angels and weren't on earth at that time. Didn't they see what took place in Germany, and weren't they in the concentration camps, and didn't they see how the Jew was beaten not only by SS-men and professional criminals but also by people who now wear the red triangle [i.e., Communists]?[28]

At this point, a voice from the audience shouted out, "Also by Jews themselves!" Löwenkopf admitted that some Jews had colluded with the Nazis, but the majority of Jews should not suffer further for it. He added that Jews did not need this assembly to designate them as victims-of-fascism to be regarded as such. All over the world, people considered the Jews to be victims of Nazi oppression. "What would the world say – which has recognized the Jews as victims of fascism – if we say 'No, we don't recognize you.' Everyone would laugh at that ... We would make ourselves the joke of the world."[29] Löwenkopf's remarks indicated just how far out of touch with reality the Communist Party had become only a few months after the war's end. In the end, even Communists such as Jenny Matern had to admit that the Jews were victims of fascism, and in July 1946, in official documentation, she enumerated them among qualifying groups. However, of Matern's eighteen categories of qualifiers – including underground fighters, resisters from religious groups, 20 July 1944 conspirators, political émigrés, those who served long prison terms for listening to foreign broadcasts, and those who would not commit war crimes in the field – the very last named were "all victims of the Nuremberg Laws," including "wearers of the [yellow] star," that is, Jews.[30]

Despite this seeming resolution, the issue of special status for victims of Nazi persecution remained both controversial, particularly as the Communists maintained a particular investment in it. The

[27] Ibid., 93.   [28] Ibid., 94.   [29] Ibid., 95.
[30] Report sent by Jenny Matern to Belke, 29 July 1946, BAB (SAPMO), DY 30/IV 2/2.027, 29, 73–75.

Victim-of-Fascism committees remained small, and problems with the standardization of qualification for the status persisted. A new representative organization was needed. Thus, in February 1947, delegates in the Soviet zone met to found a branch of the Association of Victims of the Nazi Regime (Vereinigung der Verfolgten des Naziregimes, or VVN). This new organization officially represented the interests of all former Nazi victims in eastern Germany, and it would review and judge "victim-of-fascism" status. Although the association claimed to be a nonparty organization, the SED dominated the central board for the Soviet zone as well as the boards for each of the five states in eastern Germany as these began operations in the course of 1947.[31] The VVN also provided a new, allegedly neutral arena of debate over victimhood. In a society that was ostensibly politically diverse and that was still finding its way on many sensitive issues, the VVN had the potential to be an important voice for the recognition of Jewish victimhood, if not for the primacy of Jewish victimhood.

Franz Dahlem, who had addressed the Jewish question immediately after liberation, again addressed the issue at the East German VVN's founding conference. In a speech principally focused on other matters, he attacked a new wave of antisemitism and recalled the shame of German culpability for the deaths of six million Jews.[32] Karl Raddatz also addressed the Jewish question in his remarks at the VVN's opening meeting. He called for reparations for the "victimized nations" within the "framework of the possible." He made it clear, however, that "We are not for a capitalist [i.e., non-Communist-led or overly pro-Jewish] reparation, but we are of the opinion that the beneficiaries of stolen Jewish property should be held legally responsible. Also, the contemporary state should consider that political prisoners spent years of unpaid labor building roads and railroads and cultivating moors." He wanted VVN membership to be contingent on completion of a comprehensive questionnaire that would allow them to weed out "criminal elements."[33]

[31] Elke Reuter and Detlef Hansel, *Das kurze Leben der VVN von 1947 bis 1953. Die Geschichte der Vereinigung der Verfolgten des Naziregimes in der sowjetischen Besatzungszone und in der DDR* (Berlin: edition ost, 1997), 124–135.
[32] Franz Dahlem and Karl Raddatz, *Die Aufgaben der VVN: 2 Referate gehalten auf der Zonendelegiertenkonferenz am 22./23. Februar 1947 in Berlin* (Berlin: Neues Deutschland, 1947), 8.
[33] Ibid., 25–27.

Figure 4. VVN demonstration in Berlin, 1950. The banner at left reads, "The fight against antisemitism is the fight for peace and understanding among the nations." *Source:* Bildarchiv Preußischer Kulturbesitz.

The VVN soon established itself as an organization with prominent members and an effective internal organization. Communist
Ottomar Geschke became chairman, and Karl Raddatz general
secretary. Membership in the VVN was open to holders of victim-
of-fascism identification cards, to active resisters against the Nazi
regime, and to those persecuted for their world-view, religion, or
race.[34]

VVN activities were not just limited to the provinces (see Fig. 4).
Berliners met in January 1948 at a Jewish communal building in
the western neighborhood of Charlottenburg to found a separate
VVN branch for their as-yet undivided city. A sense of nonpartisanship pervaded the meeting, and the organization presented itself
as an institution "above parties, however not above politics." Communist Walter Bartel was elected chairman. Berlin's most prominent Jewish leaders were his deputies. Heinz Galinski, who was
not politically affiliated, became first vice president, and Jeanette
Wolff of the SPD was second vice president. While nonpartisanship
was initially observed in Berlin and soon became a serious issue,
within the Soviet occupation zone, it was little more than a formal-
ity. Considering the potential for making trouble regarding the
issue of victimhood, the SED was loath to allow anyone else to run
the mass organization, reserving that task for loyal Communists.[35]
SED leaders considered Communist victims of the Nazis unques-
tionably to be first among equals, and party leader Walter Ulbricht
did not hesitate to ask the Soviets for help in exerting control over
the victims' organization.[36]

Despite Jewish prominence in the new VVN and the discussions at the victim-of-fascism conference held in Leipzig in
October 1945, debate over equality between political and religious persecutees continued to smolder within the Victim-of-
Fascism committees. Julius Meyer wanted them to stop differ-
entiating between the two groups and raised the issue at a
meeting of the Victim-of-Fascism central board in April 1947.
Geschke had no objections and set up a committee to deal

[34] "Sonderrundschreiben," March 1947, BAB (SAPMO), DY 55/V 278/2, 4.
[35] "Berliner Vereinigung der Verfolgten des Naziregimes: Organisationsbericht des
Hauptvorstandes zur Gross-Berliner Delegierten-Konferenz," BAB (SAPMO), DY 55/V
278/1, 1, 3. Other delegates included Marion Yorck von Wartenburg, Pastor Heinrich
Grüber, and Ottomar Geschke. Reuter and Hansel, *Das kurze Leben der VVN*, 182–184.
[36] Naimark, *Russians in Germany*, 286.

with the matter.[37] On the other hand, the German administration of the Soviet zone reviewed the issue and saw no reason to revise the regulations governing victim-of-fascism status.[38]
The Jews continued to have second-class status as victims of
Nazi persecution in the government's eyes, despite the large Jewish membership in the VVN and strong Jewish support for the
organization.[39]

Even within VVN circles, the Jews did not enjoy the same prestige
as Communists. In April 1948, some 3,000 delegates from all over
Germany met in Weimar under the banner "Fighters against Fascism, Fighters for Freedom." Of those present, 800 came from the
western zones, 500 from Berlin, 1,500 from the Soviet zone, and
200 from abroad. Allusions to the Jews were few and far between
in the speakers' remarks. While VVN official Stefan Heymann paid
homage to the victims of the Holocaust in his comments, the Jews
did not figure prominently among them:

> We salute the 55,000 victims of the concentration camp Buchenwald. We
> salute the 4 million murdered Jews and Poles from Auschwitz. We salute
> the millions murdered in other concentration camps, and we salute the
> tens of thousands who bravely ended their lives on the scaffold.[40]

While historian Jeffrey Herf finds it notable that Heymann included the Jews in "this circle of remembrance, victimization, and
martyrdom," Heymann mentioned the Jews in the most off-handed
manner possible, particularly considering that 90 percent of those
killed at Auschwitz were Jews. The Nazis built the camp explicitly
to kill Jews, not to kill non-Jewish Polish civilians.[41]

In fact, during the entire conference, attended by high-ranking
Soviet occupation officials, the only ones to address Jewish issues
directly were Jews. This silence about the Jews as victims of the

[37] "Protokoll der Sitzung des Hauptausschusses 'Opfer des Faschismus,'" 15 April 1947,
BAB (SAPMO), DY 54/V 277/1, 45, 43.
[38] "Richtlinien für die Anerkennung und Ausgabe der Ausweise an 'Kämpfer gegen den
Faschismus' und an 'Opfer des Faschismus' in der sowjetischen Besatzungszone Deutschlands," 21 April 1947, BAB (SAPMO), DY 30/IV 2/2.027, 30, 63.
[39] A strong indication of Jewish support for the VVN is a request made by Julius Meyer of
Carl Katz, chairman of the Bremen Jewish community, that he support the VVN there as
strongly as the Berlin Jews supported their local VVN. Letter from Julius Meyer to Carl
Katz, 4 December 1947, CJA 5 B 1, 1, 65.
[40] VVN-Verlag, *Befreiungstag Buchenwald: 9. bis 11. April 1948* (Berlin: VVN-Verlag,
1948), 4.
[41] Cf. Herf, *Divided Memory*, 96.

Nazis spawned criticism from Jewish delegates. Heinz Galinski, representing the Berlin VVN, stated that when the Jews left the camps, they were ready to rebuild Germany, but their offer was not accepted. They were also surprised by the cool reception that greeted the idea of reparations. Galinksi expressed his disappointment with renewed antisemitism in Germany but tempered his criticism with words of praise for eastern German governments' steps to combat this phenomenon.[42] Julius Meyer spoke as the representative of Jewish persecutees. Without mentioning Israel by name, he compared the Jewish struggle for a homeland, a government, and a just peace in the Middle East with the Communist struggle in Germany.[43] He ended his speech, "In conclusion, I would like to say only one sentence: Joint struggle, joint cause for justice and no empty promises like they gave us in those days."[44] He was determined to remind the Communists what they owed to the Jews as victims of the Nazis. These critiques did not go unnoticed. In his concluding speech, organizer Walter Bartel addressed the concerns of Galinski and Meyer directly:

In the discussion, there were a few questions which were not sufficiently stressed by me in my speech. I completely accept this critique and only personally would like to stress once what our comrades Galinski and Meyer said – how far we are in the democratic development of Germany can be measured exactly by antisemitism. Every manifestation of antisemitism contradicts democratic development.[45]

The goal of this development was a unified, democratic republic. Therefore, they needed to fight any manifestation of antisemitism, in his opinion: "Anyone who attacks our Jewish comrades attacks us."[46]

Despite these assurances, prominent Jews soon quit the VVN. Jeanette Wolff, a founder of the Berlin VVN and a Berlin city councilwoman, resigned twice. In February 1948 she quit, alleging that the VVN had become a Communist front organization. Unable to offer concrete proof, she withdrew her resignation. In June, she resigned again. In November 1948, Heinz Galinski resigned.[47] Despite protests and claims of multiparty representation, the VVN

[42] VVN-Verlag, *Befreiungstag Buchenwald*, 39–40. [43] Ibid., 42. [44] Ibid., 43.
[45] Ibid., 59. [46] Ibid., 60.
[47] "Berliner Vereinigung der Verfolgten des Naziregimes: Organisationsbericht des Hauptvorstandes zur Gross-Berliner Delegierten-Konferenz," 4–5 February 1949, BAB (SAPMO), DY 55/V 278/1, 1, 5.

was, in fact, becoming a Communist organization. According to a report in Otto Grotewohl's papers, the VVN supported the government of SED member Friedrich Ebert as the city of Berlin became divided into two distinct halves.[48] Rather than lead an open and honest discussion on the nature of Nazi persecution and recognition of its victims, the VVN relegated the Jews to second-class status and sanctioned the SED's self-serving stance on the matter.

COORDINATING EAST GERMAN JEWRY

There was more to Jewish life in eastern Germany than congresses and the struggle for political recognition of victimhood. There was the practical matter of coordinating the community. In fact, successful accomplishment of the latter task had implications for the former. Despite the urgency of the matter and the relatively quick establishment of local Jewish communities, over a year passed before the Jews in the Soviet occupation zone founded an umbrella organization for all Jewish groups in eastern Germany. Several local Jewish leaders, including Leon Löwenkopf from Dresden and Julius Meyer and Heinz Galinski from Berlin, undertook to speak in the name of eastern German Jewry at conferences and political rallies, though they had no real authority to do so. However, as issues of concern to the Jews became more acute, the community needed to form a collective representative organ. This organization would coordinate care for the impoverished eastern German, Jewish survivors of the Holocaust, lead efforts for the restoration of Jewish ownership of confiscated property, and curry favor for compensatory reparations.

At last, delegates from Jewish groups throughout the Soviet zone met in the East Berlin Rykestraße synagogue on 10 November 1946. They founded a representative organization provisionally named the Association of Jewish Communities in the Russian Occupation Zone (Verband jüdischer Gemeinden in der russischen Okkupationszone). Founding communities were Bernburg, Chemnitz, Dresden, Eisenach, Erfurt, Halle, Leipzig, Magdeburg, and Berlin.[49] The new group had a governing board and an

---

[48] Report on the VVN, 26 July 1949, BAB (SAPMO), NY 4090, 522, 2.

[49] "Protokoll über die am 10.11.1946 am 1500 Uhr in der Rykestrasse tagende Versammlung zum vorbereitenden Ausschuss für den Verband jüdischer Gemeinden in der russischen Okkupationszone," CJA, 5 B 1, 30, 61; cf. Gay, *Safe among the Germans*, 209.

assembly that was to meet once a year to ratify and to regulate decisions. Jewish communities with more than 100 members had two votes on the board.[50] Meeting as infrequently as the assembly did, the board had disproportionate power. Auschwitz survivor and Communist Julius Meyer took charge of the organization as acting chairman and was soon elected its president. Although at the initial meeting he disclaimed any political goals, stressing economic ones, Meyer was an unwavering advocate of equal rights and specific benefits for Jewish victims of Nazi persecution, and his election was to have repercussions for the future of Jewish communal life in eastern Germany. Meanwhile, the State Association, like the local Jewish communities before it, needed official authorization. The Soviet Military Administration, showing no great enthusiasm for the project, delayed granting the new organization official permission or recognition.[51] Gaining attention and aid from a government preoccupied with building a new society would not be easy.

Initially, the State Association's mission was not obvious and became the subject of discussion among Jewish leaders. While the bylaws of the organization stipulated that its goals were the cultural, social, and economic care of its members, and the organization did distribute imported groceries and held events for youth and the elderly, it also assumed a political advocacy role that necessarily brought it into public view.[52] The State Association supported local Jewish communities in their dealings with the regime regarding synagogues, cemeteries, and reparations. By December 1946, the State Association began the work of hammering out its duties more precisely. Meyer wanted the group to provide care for non-Jewish spouses of Jews and for those of mixed parentage. He also made arrangements for the Jews in the Soviet zone to receive care packages from the American Joint Distribution Committee via Switzerland and Czechoslovakia. Even though these packages provided much-needed food for the Jews, their provenance would later have serious political ramifications. To save costs, Meyer also

[50] "Satzung für den Verband der Jüdischen Gemeinden der Deutschen Demokratischen Republik," undated, CJA, 5 B 1, 59, 59.
[51] "Protokoll über die am 19.12.1946 am 10 Uhr im Zoo-Restaurant zu Leipzig abgehaltenen zweiten Tagung des vorbereitenden Ausschusses für den Landesverband jüdischer Gemeinden in der sowjetrussischen Zone," CJA, 5 B 1, 30, 52.
[52] "Satzung für den Verband der Jüdischen Gemeinden der Deutschen Demokratischen Republik," undated, CJA, 5 B 1, 59, 59.

proposed to keep staff at a minimum and to provide no honoraria for the officers.[53] Though all legally binding decisions had to be approved by two of seven board members, the president, Julius Meyer, and the hired general secretary, Leo Eisenstaedt, made most of the decisions, bypassing the assembly and board. As a result, they had a disproportionate amount of power and bore a disproportionate amount of responsibility.

What role did Berlin Jewry play in this new organization? Even though Berlin was an enclave in the Soviet occupation zone, it had special administrative status under the Allied Four Power administration of Berlin. At the time of the State Association's founding, it was not clear whether the Berlin Jewish community could belong to a group in the Soviet zone. Even though Berlin Jewry would not belong to the State Association for much of that organization's existence, Berlin Jews did help to found the organization and to guide it early on. Hans-Erich Fabian of Berlin was the first general secretary, and Heinz Galinski participated in State Association meetings starting in December 1946.[54] Despite Berlin's special occupation status, the Berlin Jewish community saw itself as part of East German Jewry.

The Jewish community in the Soviet occupation zone soon came to the attention of the SED. In January 1947, Politburo member Paul Merker asked his aide Kurt Netball to supply him with information about the Jewish community. Specifically, Merker wanted to know about rations and housing for the Jews, restitution of confiscated property, whether they were in any administrative positions, and how they viewed the state's ongoing campaign against antisemitism. One month later, Netball supplied the desired information. He counted 9,000 Jews in Berlin and the Soviet zone combined. Most received normal rations, except those with official victim-of-fascism status, which came with special privileges. According to Netball, the Jews were disappointed with the fight against

---

53 "Protokoll über die am 19.12.1946 am 10 Uhr im Zoo-Restaurant zu Leipzig abgehaltenen zweiten Tagung des vorbereitenden Ausschusses für den Landesverband jüdischer Gemeinden in der sowjetrussischen Zone," 19 December 1946, CJA, 5 B 1, 30, 52.
54 "Protokoll über die am 10.11.1946 am 1500 Uhr in der Rykestrasse tagende Versammlung zum vorbereitenden Ausschuss für den Verband jüdischer Gemeinden in der russischen Okkupationszone," CJA, 5 B 1, 30, 61; "Protokoll über die am 19.12.1946 am 10 Uhr im Zoo-Restaurant zu Leipzig abgehaltenen zweiten Tagung des vorbereitenden Ausschusses für den Landesverband jüdischer Gemeinden in der sowjetrussischen Zone," CJA, 5 B 1, 30, 51–52.

antisemitism and felt that denazification had ended too early. While some Jews were Zionists and wanted to leave Germany, many others wanted to rebuild the new, democratic (i.e., communist) Germany.[55] These Jews were the State Association's constituency.

THE JEWISH COMMUNITY AND POLITICS

The period of Soviet occupation was one of transition for both the Jews and the wider political community. Faced with the task of building a new society after the near total destruction of civil society, the idea of political unity appealed to many in eastern Germany, and under Soviet pressure, the two political parties of the Marxist left merged. While this new party quickly lost its independence from the Soviets, Soviet positions on a number of issues of importance remained unsettled as the nascent Cold War slowly developed. Meanwhile, the Jewish leadership's dealings with the regime were tentative and exploratory. With a lack of official direction, the Jewish community and the State Association chose their own path, advocating political positions that became unacceptable after the establishment of the German Democratic Republic and the hardening of Cold War alliances.

In the first year after the defeat of Nazi Germany, a number of political groups emerged or reemerged, including the two most prominent political parties of the left, the Social Democratic Party (SPD) and the Communist Party (KPD). Although they did largely compete for the same working-class and leftist intellectual constituency, some within both groups felt that their vicious rivalry in the early 1930s had unnecessarily fractured the political left and rendered it incapable of resisting the rise of Hitler. As a result, the two groups began discussions regarding the unification of the political left. The Communists had another reason for desiring a merger with the much larger Social Democratic Party. They seemed very unlikely to defeat the SPD at the polls if they ran separate candidates. However, by cooperating or uniting with the Social Democrats, they formed the largest electoral bloc in eastern Germany. While many Social Democrats in eastern Germany favored unity, the western German SPD, under the leadership of

---

[55] Letter from Paul Merker to Kurt Nettball, 25 January 1947; report by Kurt Nettball, 28 February 1947; BAB (SAPMO), DY 30/IV 2/2.027, 20, 39–42.

Kurt Schumacher, resolutely opposed the merger. It was clear that any such fusion would be possible only in the Soviet occupation zone. Additionally, the Soviets, backed by the presence of soldiers and political officers, aggressively pressed the two parties to unite. Under these circumstances, in late April 1946, the eastern German branches of the Social Democratic Party and the Community Party merged to form the SED, disabling the most important non-Communist loci of political debate in the Soviet zone of occupation.

As a result of this merger, many Social Democratic Jews found themselves confronted with the choice of joining the SED or facing expulsion from the party. Concentration camp survivor and Berlin politician Jeanette Wolff refused to endorse the merger. Future Dresden community board member Helmut Eschwege, who had spent the war years in Palestine, returned to Germany shortly after the merger and enthusiastically welcomed the new antifascist grouping.[56] As the leading party in eastern Germany, the SED exercised critical control over policy formation, including that over reparations and relations with religious groups. Moreover, the new party followed the Soviet line, and the Soviet occupiers were not shy about exercising decisive influence over party policy, as historian Norman Naimark has shown.[57]

The occupation years 1945 to 1949 formed a transitional phase, and some doctrinal or political fluidity existed in eastern Germany. In caring for the Jews of the Soviet zone, the State Association had extensive contact with American organizations. At a meeting in November 1947, considering the poor state of the Jewish community, State Association delegates wanted more aid from the American Joint Distribution Committee; in particular, they concentrated on the distribution of food and clothes. AJDC Director Fink wanted the Jews to administer more of the Americans' projects themselves and planned to erect a clothing warehouse in the American sector of Berlin. Julius Meyer would mediate for

---

[56] Willy Albrecht, "Jeanette Wolff – Jakob Altmaier – Peter Blachstein. Die drei Abgeordneten jüdischer Herkunft des Deutschen Bundestages in den 50er und zu Beginn der 60er Jahre," in *Menora: Jahrbuch für deutsch-jüdische Geschichte* 6 (1995), ed. Julius H. Schoeps et al. (Munich: Piper, 1995), 270; Helmut Eschwege, *Fremd unter meinesgleichen: Erinnerungen eines Dresdner Juden* (Berlin: Ch. Links, 1991), 50 and 53. Eschwege encountered difficulties with the SED for promoting the uniqueness of Jewish persecution under the Nazis. Eschwege, *Fremd unter meinesgleichen*, 184–227.

[57] Naimark, *Russians in Germany*, 284–292.

the individual Jewish communities.[58] While this plan was more efficient, it also gave Meyer more power and put him in close, regular contact with Americans, on whose aid many eastern German Jews relied. Later, some Communists alleged that the Jews in East Germany were necessarily beholden to the Americans and represented a potentially disloyal body.[59] Economic necessity in the late 1940s became a political liability in the early 1950s.

The State Association also had amicable ties to the new state of Israel. In December 1947, the organization wrote to the Jewish Agency to offer its congratulations on the UN resolution in favor of establishing a Jewish homeland, and in June 1948, during the Israeli war of independence, the organization sent congratulatory telegrams to the government of Israel, praising the army's exploits.[60] In 1948, a pro-Israeli position was not incompatible with loyalty to the SED and to the Soviets. The USSR was among the first countries to recognize Israeli independence, and the new state received aid from Soviet bloc states. At this time, the SED stressed its support for the Zionists, portraying the western, imperialist powers as supporting Arab interests. In his memoirs, the East German historian Helmut Eschwege noted that the SED issued a pro-Israeli pamphlet on 12 June 1948. Future East German president Wilhelm Pieck stated:

The democratic forces of Germany welcome the decision of the UN to divide Palestine into an Arab and a Jewish state. We regard the establishment of a Jewish state as a significant contribution enabling thousands of people, for whom Hitler-fascism brought the deepest suffering, to build a new life.[61]

Future prime minister Otto Grotewohl reportedly favored formal relations with Israel and said that "we are ready to help, but only after we have the unity of Germany."[62] Innocuous in 1947–1948

---

[58] "Kurz-Protokoll, Sitzung am 22.10.1947," 25 November 1947, CJA, 5 B 1, 30, 36. No first name for Fink is provided in the files.

[59] "Lehren aus dem Prozeß gegen das Verschwörerzentrum Slansky," Sozialistische Einheitspartei Deutschlands (Zentralkomittee der SED), *Dokumente der Sozialistischen Einheitspartei Deutschlands*, vol. 4 (Berlin: Dietz, 1954), 208.

[60] Letter from State Association to Jewish Agency for Palestine, 2 December 1947, CJA, 5 B 1, 1, 251; telegram from Julius Meyer and Fritz Grunsfeld to Israeli prime minister and cabinet, 11 June 1948, CJA, 5 B 1, 30, 28.

[61] Eschwege, *Fremd unter meinesgleichen*, 63–64.

[62] "Aussprache mit dem Genossen Julius Meyer, Präsident der jüdischen Gemeinde am 6.1.53," BAB (SAPMO), DY 30/IV 2/4, 404, 34.

and conforming to Soviet policy at the time, the State Association's ties would have severe consequences in the 1950s when Israel came to be seen as an American ally in the Cold War, and antisemitism, cloaked as fervent anti-Zionism, swept the eastern bloc.

DEBATES ON EAST GERMAN REPARATIONS TO HOLOCAUST SURVIVORS

Support for Israel was not the only issue that later had negative consequences for the community. Advocacy for reparations, one of the issues most central to Jewish life in postwar Germany, also entailed risks for the community. At varying times the SED seemed receptive to the idea of reparations to the Jews; at other times, the issue was virtually taboo. Moreover, it developed into a source of conflict between Communist Party members who had spent the war in Moscow, most notably Walter Ulbricht, and party members who had spent the war in exile in western countries, including Paul Merker. In this sense, the debate was about more than just the Jewish community per se and became a tool in a power struggle within the party.[63]

As was the case in western Germany, the initial impetus for reparations to victims of the Holocaust in eastern Germany came from the states. In September 1945, the state of Thuringia passed a law for restitution of property, one of the first states and the only East German state to do so.[64] Some saw the Thuringian law as a potential model for states in western Germany, and Walter Cappel, the restitution administrator in Eisenach and a former resident of Düsseldorf, corresponded with the chairman of the Jewish community in Düsseldorf regarding the matter.[65] The reparations debate

---

[63] For more information on the power struggle between the Moscow exiles and the Mexico City exiles and the instrumentalization of the reparations debate, see Herf, *Divided Memory*, 106–161.

[64] For more information on the Thuringian law, see Mertens, *Davidstern unter Hammer und Zirkel*, 229–237; Jan Philipp Spannuth, "Rückerstattung Ost. Der Umgang der DDR mit dem 'arisierten' Vermögen der Juden und die Gestaltung der Rückerstattung in der wiedervereinigten Deutschland," in *"Arisierung" und Restitution. Die Rückerstattung jüdischen Eigentums in Deutschland und Österreich nach 1945 und 1989,* ed. Constantin Goschler and Jürgen Lillteicher (Göttingen: Wallstein, 2002), 242; and Jan Philipp Spannuth, "Rückerstattung Ost. Der Umgang der DDR mit dem 'arisierten' und enteigneten jüdischen Eigentum und die Gestaltung der Rückerstattung im wiedervereinigten Deutschland," Dr. phil. diss., Universität Freiburg, 2001.

[65] Letter from Walter Cappel to Julius Dreifuss, 27 January 1947; letter from Julius Dreifuss to Walter Cappel, 28 February 1947; ZA, B.1/5, 76.

soon spread to other states in eastern Germany, and the Liberal Democratic Party in Saxony planned to propose a bill for restitution of Jewish property in the spring of 1947. In May, Leon Löwenkopf, an SED leader in Saxony – and a Jew – telegraphed SED leaders that formerly Jewish property that had come into possession of the state would not be exempt.[66] Less than one week later, Paul Merker, who worked closely with Lehmann, wrote to SED chairman Walter Ulbricht and central committee member Max Fechner that he had long tried to get the Victim-of-Fascism committees to propose a law for Jewish restitution. Now that another party was making a proposal, Merker offered his help in resolving this difficult question.[67] In fact, Merker would soon become the primary supporter within the SED for reparation for the Jews.

By early 1948, a core of support within the SED for reparations had developed. In January, Merker and Lehmann met in Berlin and drafted a reparations law. Each German state would have an office, directly under the state premier, staffed by recognized victims-of-fascism, to administer reparations for victims of Nazi persecution. Furthermore, according to their plan, political persecutees and Jews would have the same status.[68] For the proposal, Merker also enlisted the aid of prominent Jewish Communist Leo Zuckermann, whom he had known in Mexican exile.[69] Merker and Lehmann were deft at exploiting the growing east-west conflict to gain attention for their proposal. In the preface to their proposal, they wrote that because state legislatures in the western occupation zones were considering reparations laws, the SED should send this proposal to the eastern state legislatures as soon as possible.[70] Merker and Zuckermann also discussed reparations with representatives of the Jewish community, including the

[66] Letter from central secretariat of the SED, Abt. Arbeit und Sozialfürsorge [spring 1947], BAB (SAPMO), DY 30/IV 2/2.027, 30, 87.

[67] Letter from Paul Merker to Walter Ulbricht and Max Fechner, 4 June 1947, BAB (SAPMO), DY 30/IV 2/2.027, 30, 88.

[68] "Entwurf: Gesetz über die Betreuung für Verfolgte des Naziregimes und die Vorbereitung für Wiedergutmachung," 5 January 1948, BAB (SAPMO), DY 30/IV 2/2.027, 31, 3.

[69] Letter from Paul Merker to Leo Zuckermann, 13 January 1948, BAB (SAPMO), DY 30/IV 2/2.027, 31, 14.

[70] "Vorlage an die Mitglieder des Zentralsekretariats," 19 January 1948, BAB (SAPMO), DY 30/IV 2/2.027, 18.

State Association, meeting on 15 March 1948 in the West Berlin neighborhood of Kreuzberg.[71]

While the SED debated its reparations proposal, the Soviet occupation authority issued its own, weaker restitution order. In accordance with the terms of Soviet Military Administration order no. 82 from April 1948, all property, mobile and immobile, that the Nazis had confiscated from democratic organizations was to be returned to those democratic organizations, parties, and unions approved by the Soviets. If the former owner were no longer alive or able to make a claim, a similar, existing organization was allowed to assume ownership of the property. The order explicitly mentioned property formerly belonging to humanitarian and religious organizations. However, any property in use by the occupation authority, that had been divided up in accordance with land reform, or that had military value would not be returned. Additionally, the Soviets required state premiers to form committees comprised of the political parties, unions, and other organizations to administer the order and to return the property by 1 July 1948.[72] Interestingly, at the time of its issue, the German Economics Commission (Deutsche Wirtschaftskommission), the East German proto-government, did not publish Soviet order no. 82. According to the State Association, it appeared initially in the newsletter of the government of the state of Mecklenburg.[73] Reparations and restitution for the Jews did not occupy a prominent place on the SED's agenda.

Considering the importance of the VVN in pressuring for a reparations statute, Leo Zuckermann began lobbying within the organization for the Merker/Lehmann proposal that he had helped to draft. To this end, he published a short piece on reparations in the leftist intellectual journal *Die Weltbühne* on 27 April 1948.[74] Zuckermann wrote that while there was dialogue within the VVN on reparations, this group needed to achieve more clarity on the issue. Not only did he defend the equality of political and religious

[71] "Sitzung des Landesverbandes der Jüdischen Gemeinden in der Deutschen Demokratischen Republik vom 15.3.1948," 8 January 1953, BAB (SAPMO), DY 30/IV 2/4, 404, 46.

[72] "Befehl des Obersten Chefs der sowjetischen Militärverwaltung und des Oberbefehlhabers der Gruppe sowjetischer Besatzungstruppe in Deutschland," 29 April 1948, CJA, 5 B 1, 107, 37.

[73] Letter from State Association to Otto Nuschke, 2 April 1951, CJA, 5 B 1, 107, 11.

[74] Leo Zuckermann, "Restitution und Wiedergutmachung," *Die Weltbühne* 3, no. 17 (27 April 1948): 430–432.

persecutees, he intimated that the Jews had a greater claim to reparations than did the Communists. The political resister under the Nazis chose his path; the Jew could not avoid persecution. In fact, "[t]he Nazi state declared war against the entire Jewish people. It did not have to do with the removal of a domestic political enemy but rather the extermination of a national minority."[75] Zuckermann's line of reasoning flew in the face of official ideology. While it was certainly true that the Nazis had singled out the Jews for persecution, to consider the Jews a national minority violated the official party line on the minority question as articulated by Stalin as early as 1913. Nonetheless, Zuckermann endorsed individual reparations only for Jews living in Germany. Giving reparations to those abroad would not benefit the German economy, and returning their factories would place German institutions at the service of foreign economic interests. He proclaimed that the Jewish people decried misusing claims for imperialistic purposes. He added that Israel could represent world Jewry in negotiations for a collective settlement at a later date.[76] Zuckermann supported reparations for the Jews, but he also knew that only an SED-sponsored proposal had a chance of passage. Thus, he tailored his arguments to fit his audience, the SED and the VVN. He also received support from the Jewish Communists Leon Löwenkopf and Julius Meyer, who did not want state-run enterprises to be exempted from restitution to Jewish owners.[77]

Zuckermann's article drew an angry response from the Jewish Communist and Spanish Civil War veteran Götz Berger. Berger wrote that only those who had fought against fascism deserved payment, but he also adopted a line of reasoning that one might have reasonably expected to hear in western Germany, not eastern Germany. He claimed that it was unjust to favor only the Jews when all those who had lived through the war in Germany had suffered large material losses, regardless of political or religious affiliation. He even claimed, "The victims of fascism, who belong to the best representatives of the German people, cannot and should not want to stand out among the general people." They wanted to share the fate of the entire German people because

---

[75] Ibid., 431.   [76] Ibid., 431–432.
[77] Letter from Schäfermeyer to Walter Ulbricht, 25 May 1948, BAB (SAPMO), DY 30/IV 2/2.027, 31, 194.

they were German, he wrote.[78] Berger could not have been more wrong. While some Jewish Communists did not feel an affinity for their coreligionists, most Jews in eastern Germany knew that they were different and knew that they had suffered extraordinary persecution under the Nazis. Berger claimed that singling out the Jews for preferential financial treatment would encourage renewed antisemitism, and he contacted SED leaders Walter Ulbricht and Max Fechner to attack Zuckermann's ideas. Berger wrote that the party must not allow reparations to flow to Jewish capitalists or to burden the state's budget in any way. He also attacked the proposal "from the socialist standpoint." Reparations would, he claimed, "form a strong burden for our party and for the entire new order."[79]

Both Zuckermann's original article and Berger's response found their way to the files of the Central Party Control Commission (Zentrale Parteikontrollkommission, or ZPKK), the SED's internal review board for ideological uniformity led by Hermann Matern. On 7 January 1953, at the height of an antisemitic purge that enveloped the SED and threatened Zuckermann's career, if not his life, Berger sent Matern a handwritten report on Zuckermann and his wife, and he probably attached copies of the *Weltbühne* article and the response.[80] Zuckermann's argumentation in 1948, made during an ideologically flexible period, had severe repercussions five years later.

Merker, co-author of the reparations proposal, continued to lobby for his proposal in the face of opposition or indifference. In a letter written to Wilhelm Pieck in May 1948, he denied that he wanted to return property to "large Jewish capitalists," but he did want the Jewish communities and individual Jews living in eastern Germany to receive all confiscated property not in state possession.[81] According to Kurt Netball, Merker's assistant, some VVN groups had accepted the proposal, while others, including that

---

[78] "Wiedergutmachung – eine politische Frage," 8 May 1948, BAB (SAPMO), DY 30/IV 2/4, file 124, 240–245.

[79] Letter from Götz Berger to Walter Ulbricht and Max Fechner, 14 May 1948, BAB (SAPMO), DY 30/IV 2/2.027, 31, 189.

[80] Letter from Götz Berger to Hermann Matern, BAB (SAPMO), DY 30/IV 2/2.027, 31, 240–245.

[81] Letter from Paul Merker to Wilhelm Pieck, 4 May 1948, BAB (SAPMO), DY 30/IV 2/4, 124, 139.

in Saxony-Anhalt, continued to reject it.[82] Meanwhile, the SED wanted its representatives in state legislatures to bring the bill to the floor as soon as possible. Nettball could sense the bill's fate: "The law has been discussed for over a year already and if the discussion and modifications so continue, there will be no end in sight."[83] As state representatives of the SED continued to propose changes to the original proposal, Netball found the situation nearly intolerable and suggested to Merker that the SED central committee intervene.[84] The ongoing debate over Merker's proposal for a reparations law reflected the disinterest within the SED on this question. Furthermore, the VVN, the mass organization devoted to promoting the interests of former Nazi persecutees, could not even unify to support the idea.

In light of the unending discussions, the Jewish State Association weighed in on reparations. At a meeting of the State Association in June 1948, Fritz Grunsfeld, the State Association's legal expert on reparations, attacked the proposal as too narrow in scope. Zuckermann, also present, replied that he did not want to exclude German (or formerly German) Jews, but reparations to Jews abroad would have to wait until after the signing of a final peace treaty (i.e., until the German question was resolved). Karl Raddatz of the VVN tried to stress the difficulty of winning acceptance for the proposal within the SED and VVN. The State Association did profit from Soviet order no. 82, as they noted, and this step was a good start.[85] The day after the meeting, Meyer and three Thuringian Jewish leaders wrote to Zuckermann about the need for a reparations law comparable to the one enacted in Thuringia.[86]

One year after Merker, Lehmann, and Zuckermann had proposed a reparations law, the debate dragged on, seemingly making no progress. By mid-May 1949, Lehmann had given up on the state legislatures, and he wanted the central administration

---

[82] Letter from Kurt Netball to Paul Merker, 11 May 1948, BAB (SAPMO), DY30/IV 2/2.027, 31, 160.

[83] Ibid.

[84] Letter from Kurt Netball to Paul Merker, 26 June 1948, BAB (SAPMO), DY 30/IV 2/2.027, 31, 206.

[85] "Protokoll, Sitzung des Landesverbandes Jüdischer Gemeinden in der Russischen Okkupationszone am 10. und 11. Juni 1948," 10 June 1948, CJA, 5 B 1, 30, 24–26.

[86] Letter from State Association to Leo Zuckermann, 11 June 1948, BAB (SAPMO), DY 30/IV 2/2.027, 31, 201.

simply to enact the law by decree.[87] In late July, Lehmann wrote to Zuckermann and Netball. His tone had changed, as if he seemed to know that the proposal would never pass. Nonetheless, he wanted to do something for so-called racial victims of Nazi persecution.[88] On 5 October 1949, two days before the establishment of the German Democratic Republic, the government of the Soviet occupation zone issued a law guaranteeing care for victims of Nazi persecution. It granted no reparations to the Jews, provided for no restitution of confiscated property, and enshrined the difference between Communist "fighters" and Jews, who were mere "victims." Moreover, political loyalty to the regime was a precondition for receiving any benefits.[89]

THE SPECTER OF COMMUNIST ANTISEMITISM
AND THE JEWISH RESPONSE

Although Communists and Jews had suffered side by side in Hitler's concentration camps, some German Communists could not accept the victimhood of German Jewry and were unwilling to grant the Jews any special status – even one granted to other victims of Nazi persecution. While Merker and Lehmann were receptive to Jewish problems, many Communist officials, motivated by either antisemitism or opportunism, hindered the Jewish community's efforts to reestablish itself and to resume possession of property confiscated by the Nazi regime. The State Association, led by Julius Meyer, responded by continually pressing its claims and seeking allies within the ruling caste.

Communist obstructionism, particularly on a local level, forced the State Association to petition the SED central committee. In April 1948, State Association administrator Leo Eisenstaedt forwarded to central committee member Franz Dahlem a letter by

---

[87] Letter from Helmut Lehmann to Hauptverwaltung Arbeit und Sozialfürsorge in der Deutschen Wirtschaftkommission, 15 May 1949, BAB (SAPMO), DY 30/IV 2/2.027, 32, 15.

[88] Letter from Helmut Lehmann to Leo Zuckermann and Kurt Netball, 26 July 1949, BAB (SAPMO), DY 30/IV 2/2.027, 32, 95.

[89] Germany (Territory under Allied Occupation, 1945–1955: Russian Zone), Deutsche Justizverwaltung der sowjetischen Besatzungszone in Deutschland, *Zentralverordnungsblatt. Amtliches Organ der Deutschen Wirtschaftskommission und ihrer Hauptverwaltungen, sowie der Deutschen Verwaltungen für Gesundheitswesen, Inneres, Justiz u. Volksbildung* (Berlin: Deutscher Zentralverlag, 1949), 765; Herf, *Divided Memory*, 95.

Kurt Friedländer, a Jewish leader in Schwerin. The state government in Schwerin would not grant the Jews permission to found a legally recognized community. The Mecklenburg state minister responsible for such matters, Gottfried Grünberg, called the Jews a special interest group and expressed himself in extremely antisemitic terms: "You aren't a Jewish community, but rather an organization for receiving American bacon [i.e., care] packages." This ironically unkosher epithet reveals both chauvinistic xenophobia and Communist antisemitism. Grünberg had spent the war in Moscow and would later become the chief political officer in the East German army. Friedländer also observed that even in the VVN, "one can recognize the appearance of antisemitism, which shouldn't, however, exist within SED membership circles. It is absolutely the duty of the party to intervene here."[90] Friedländer had stumbled across one of the facts of life in eastern Germany. The SED was riddled with antagonism to organized religion, including latent and increasingly overt antisemitism, making the Jews' struggle even more difficult. Jewish groups came to rely on those few SED leaders who were sensitive to Jewish concerns.

The State Association was now serving as the general advocate for Jewish interests in eastern Germany. Over the next five years, Meyer incessantly petitioned government offices to secure special requests for Jews.[91] Even Victor Klemperer, who was not a practicing Jew and who had a non-Jewish wife, turned to the State Association for help with a reparations claim.[92] Meyer helped to arrange for travel visas, clothes, employment, and kosher food for individual Jews. Every year before Passover, the State Association ensured that even the most isolated Jews in eastern Germany had wine and matzo.[93] The organization also agitated for legislation against racial hatred or incitement to hatred. In early 1948, the Saxon government had considered such a law, but rather than simply having the state legislature approve it, the politicians passed it on to the German Justice Administration, the proto-Ministry of Justice in Berlin, which considered a similar law for the entire

---

[90] Letter from Kurt Friedländer to Franz Dahlem, 12 March 1948, BAB (SAPMO), DY 30/IV 2/2.027, 31, 114–116. On 12 May 1948, Paul Merker wrote to the Mecklenburg SED concerning Friedländer's letter, demanding that it assign a Jewish SED member to investigate the situation.

[91] CJA, 5 B 1, 1.

[92] Letter from Leo Eisenstaedt to Victor Klemperer, 21 May 1951, CJA, 5 B 1, 2, 497.

[93] Various correspondence and delivery requests, CJA, 5 B 1, 21.

Soviet zone. Rather than acting swiftly on the measure, the central administration sent its proposal back to the state governments for approval, effectively ending any chance for expeditious passage.[94]

As popular antisemitism became more prevalent, even the SED politburo saw the need for a public pronouncement on the matter. In February 1949, it delegated Leo Zuckermann to make such a statement.[95] Zuckermann formed a commission to spearhead a campaign against antisemitism – that is, western German antisemitism. The SED secretariat, including Walter Ulbricht, wanted Zuckermann to give a radio address and to publish an article in *Neues Deutschland* on the topic.[96] Furthermore, the secretariat issued a statement protesting against purported antisemitism in the British occupation zone. In particular, the SED focused on the suppression of protests against the release of the film *Oliver Twist* with its negative portrayal of the Jewish character Fagin. The SED also claimed the British had issued press licenses to openly antisemitic newspapers. The wording of the protest shows that for the Communists, invoking purported West German antisemitism had more to do with the nascent Cold War than with any actual Jews: "Antisemitism, racial hatred, and incitement to hatred have always been the methods of Reaction for the subjugation of the working class and the destruction of its progressive powers."[97] It is true that western Germany was experiencing a rash of cemetery desecrations and vandalism of Jewish businesses, not to mention antisemitic attitudes manifesting themselves in everyday comportment and speech, but eastern Germany was not immune from antisemitism, either.

In fact, antisemitism was becoming part of the Communist political landscape in eastern Germany. In March 1949, the Soviet press attacked "cosmopolitans without a fatherland," a thinly veiled reference to Jews. Moreover, by this time, the SED had undergone a process of Stalinization, which rendered it an imitation of the Soviet Communist Party, ending any multiplicity of political

94 Letter from Johannes Dieckmann to Jüdische Gemeinde Dresden, 17 December 1948, CJA, 5 B 1, 31, 92.
95 "Protokoll Nr. 5 der Sitzung des Politbüros am 22. Februar 1949," 22 February 1949, BAB (SAPMO), DY 30/IV 2/2, 5, 3.
96 "Protokoll Nr. 8 der Sitzung des Kleinen Sekretariats am 28. Februar 1949," 28 February 1949, BAB (SAPMO), DY 30/J IV 2/3, 8, 1.
97 "Anlage Nr. 2 zum Protokoll Nr. 8 vom 28. Februar 1949: Entwurf, Entschließung gegen die antisemitische Propaganda," 28 February 1949, BAB (SAPMO), DY 30/J IV 2/3, 8, 11.

opinion on issues of import and signifying a hardening of Cold War stances. Although the Western press was quick to perceive the threat that the Soviet article might portend, Zuckermann attacked that same press, writing an article entitled "We Will Never Fight against the Liberators of Maidanek and Auschwitz."[98] Leading Communists, including Jews, conveniently ignored antisemitism in the eastern bloc, concentrating on that in western Germany.

As the Jewish community faced an indifferent or increasingly hostile regime, Communist Julius Meyer's power within the State Association remained as solid as ever. In July 1949, in the presence of Soviet Major Olympiew, the State Association assembly reelected Meyer to another term as president. Leon Löwenkopf thanked Meyer for all his work in ensuring that the Jews would receive the care due to them. Rather than suggesting increased distance from the Soviets and Communist officials, Meyer encouraged closer ties and thanked the Soviets for supporting the return of Jewish property. One assembly member even suggested changing the group's name to Zonal Association (Zonenverband), and other assembly delegates wanted to ask the Soviets for permission to change the name. Though Jewish leaders had cultivated a good relationship with the Soviet occupation authority, the situation was not as stable as it seemed. One State Association member alleged that the state governments did not always treat the Jewish community with the same respect as they did the Christian religious communities.[99] The state of Brandenburg did not want to give the Jewish community its former property back because the Jews had missed the deadline for submitting their claims, and the State Association appealed directly to the Soviet Military Administration for redress.[100] In this time of structural change in East Germany, the State Association invested much power in a single person – namely, Julius Meyer – as a way to maintain its status vis-à-vis the various state and party institutions. These institutions were, however, reluctant to grant concessions to the Jews.

Not only was the State Association hard-pressed to master the political balancing act, it also faced a more banal challenge to its survival. It had almost no money. While the organization had received a building, it needed funding to hire a staff. Each of the

---

[98] Herf, *Divided Memory*, 102.
[99] Untitled protocol, 31 July 1949, CJA, 5 B 1, 31, 127–135.
[100] Letter from State Association to Soviet Military Administration, Finanzverwaltung, Abt. Vermögenskontrolle, 22 August 1949, CJA, 5 B 1, 107, 60.

communities was obliged to contribute money to the State Association's coffers, and many leading Jews in the Soviet occupation zone
gave large sums privately. Between the communities and a few generous board members, the State Association raised 35,000 reichs-
marks on 10 June 1948.[101] This arrangement was only a stop-gap
measure. Only the routinization of funding from the East German
state would ensure the State Association's financial stability, but
how could the Jews' organization receive official support from a
state dominated by a political party hostile to its existence?

Leaders of the Jewish community in eastern Germany faced a
largely unexpected challenge to their efforts to gain recognition
of the needs of Jewish Holocaust victims. The Communists, who
had suffered alongside the Jews in many concentration camps, refused to accept Jewish claims to victimhood as equal or superior to
their own. In some cases, their claims received no recognition at
any level. As the Party of Socialist Unity, the Communists' vehicle
for rule, attempted to justify its increasingly comprehensive control over eastern German society, it relied on its claim to be the
principal anti-Nazi resister and principal target of Nazi persecution. Not only did Jewish claims distract or detract from their own
claims, but Jewish insistence on reparations from the administration of eastern Germany signaled a rejection of Communist claims
that their government was in no way responsible for the recent
Germany past and owed nothing to the Nazi victims.

To help the Jewish community lobby for support and to coordinate its efforts, the different Jewish groups united in the State
Association, led by politically active Communist Julius Meyer. Additionally, the Jews had allies within the SED, most notably Paul
Merker and Leo Zuckermann. These two prominent Communists
drafted a law that would have provided for reparations to Jewish victims of Nazi persecution. Both the law and the mere idea of Jewish
uniqueness meriting recognition became the subject of intense debate in former victims' associations, which were increasingly dominated by minions of the SED. As the SED moved to constitute
an East German state in 1949, the position of East German Jewry
seemed particularly precarious.

---

[101] "Protokoll, Sitzung des Landesverbandes Jüdischer Gemeinden in der Russischen
Okkupationszone am 10. und 11. Juni 1948," 10–11 June 1948, CJA, 5 B 1, 30, 26.

CHAPTER 4

Politicians and Political Parties before 1950

While increasing political centralization limited the options available to the Jewish community of East Germany as it sought support, the case was different in West Germany, where political variegation both complicated the resolution of Jewish issues and offered a spectrum of potential allies for the community. Additionally, the two Germanys dealt with the legacy of the Holocaust in different manners. East Germany gradually suppressed debate on victimization and reparations, and the view of history represented by the SED became the predominant one, if not the only politically acceptable one. In West Germany, where a profusion of competing political parties greeted the establishment of democracy, there was an opportunity for genuine public discourse on the past.

For many politically active Germans, the hallmark of the Nazi era was the persecution of the Jews, and consequently postwar Germany's treatment of the Jews and handling of Jewish-related issues would reflect on the new state's relationship with its own past. Compared with pre-1933 Germany, very few Jews lived in Germany after 1949, and their potential as a voting block was minimal. Invoking Jewish-related issues had more symbolic importance than actual value. The manner in which each segment of the politically active population dealt with Jewish questions reflected how it viewed the past. In some ways, Germans' positions on the Jews living in Germany and on Holocaust survivors in general had little to do with the Jews themselves.

Although the murderous persecution of the Jews had resulted from an authoritarian dictatorship, the reestablishment of electoral democracy actually complicated the handling of Jewish-related issues. Postwar Germany was pervaded by an atmosphere of competing interpretations of German history and competing demands for state support. As mentioned in the introduction, a number of social groups claimed to be victims based on their economic or social circumstances after 1945. In fact, many Germans, with little consideration of who had originally started the war, conceived of themselves as victims of what they considered to be an unjust Allied occupation. As a result, the recent German past became a politically volatile issue in the postwar democracy.

Some groups representing themselves as victims, including millions of Germans expelled from Eastern Europe after the war, offered potentially significant support at the polls. However, the issue transcended competing claims to victimhood. It also involved competing interpretations of the past. Some eight million Germans had been members of the Nazi Party, and millions more had willingly supported the regime at home or in battle. Since this group was also a potential constituency, postwar politicians often had to decide whether to appeal to these voters through a strategy of downplaying the past or to risk alienating them by stressing atonement for the National Socialist past. An additional factor was the persistence of antisemitism, which frequently manifested itself in cemetery desecrations, attacks on Jewish-owned shops, and overtly anti-Jewish utterances.[1]

For the Jewish community of West Germany, the attitude of the various political parties and politicians was critical. As it became clear that the community could not rely on support from Jewish groups abroad, the Jews in Germany became politicized and looked to their own federal and state governments for assistance, enabling their organizations to survive. However, German Jewish political affinities after 1945 did not always mirror political affiliations before 1933. Additionally, Jewish groups outside Germany evinced a clear interest in that country's democratization and atonement.

THE SOCIAL DEMOCRATS AND THE JEWS

In the years immediately following the war, the Social Democratic Party of Germany (Sozialdemokratische Partei Deutschlands, or

---

[1] In December 1946, demographers classified 61 percent of Germans in the American occupation zone as racists, antisemites, or intense antisemites. By April 1948 this had diminished only slightly to 59 percent. Office of Military Government of the United States (OMGUS), "Anti-Semitism in the American Zone" and "Prejudice and Anti-Semitism," in *Public Opinion in Germany: The OMGUS Surveys, 1945–1949*, ed. Anna J. Merritt and Richard L. Merritt (Urbana: University of Illinois Press, 1970), 146–148 and 239–240.

SPD) emerged as the strongest proponent of Jewish issues in Germany. Advocacy of these issues marked both an overt break with the country's Nazi past and an identification with the Jews' persecution at the hands of fellow Germans. However, this support was not without precedent. In fact, by 1945, the SPD could look back on a long history of struggle for equal rights for Jewish Germans and rejection of antisemitism.

In the pre–World War I German Empire, the Social Democrats were the primary defenders of Jewish civil rights. Party leader August Bebel called antisemitism "the socialism of the stupid." For the most part, German Social Democracy regarded antisemitism merely as a misguided manifestation of anticapitalism that could be curbed under its beneficent supervision. Over time, this view matured, and under Bebel's leadership, the Social Democrats were the primary obstacle to antisemitic legislation before 1918. Despite their support for equal rights for Jews, the Social Democrats were not proponents of religion, which the nineteenth-century socialist theorist Karl Marx had called "the opiate of the masses." Although few SPD officials of any faith were devout, most Germans were nominally religious at this time, and the SPD officially regarded religion as a private matter.[2]

During the Weimar Republic, as the party found itself governing Germany for the first time, it continued to demand equal status and equal treatment before the law for German Jews. The party also worked behind the scenes with Jewish organizations. In the Weimar system, the Jews' enemies were usually democracy's enemies, and the SPD was democracy's strongest defender. However, many Social Democrats regarded antisemitism largely as a ruse by right-wing forces to overthrow the republic, underestimating the sincerity of right-wing Judeophobia. At the time, few truly thought that a Nazi takeover would lead to extreme anti-Jewish measures. As a result, denunciations of antisemitism played a minor role in the Social Democratic fight against the growing Nazi threat in the early 1930s. Despite its failure, the SPD proved to be the most dedicated and most courageous champion of equal rights for Jewish Germans before the Nazi assumption of power in

---

[2] Richard S. Levy, *The Downfall of the Anti-Semitic Political Parties in Imperial Germany* (New Haven: Yale University Press, 1975), 174–178; Hans-Gerd Henke, *Der "Jude" als Kollektivsymbol in der deutschen Sozialdemokratie 1890–1914* (Mainz: Decaton, 1994).

January 1933.[3] In the final free Reichstag elections, held in 1932, many Jews voted for the SPD as the republic's last hope.[4]

After the Nazi era, the SPD continued to regard itself as the party of the fight against antisemitism.[5] For one of the earliest editions of the newspaper *Jüdisches Gemeindeblatt für die Nord-Rheinprovinz und Westfalen*, the editors asked each political party to contribute an article on its position vis-à-vis the Jews. Writing for the Social Democrats, Alfred Dobbert noted that many Jews had joined the SPD as the party of freedom and that its enemies often attacked it as being "Jew-friendly." Denunciations of Jewish intellectuals as unproductive members of society were mere manifestations of economic jealousy. Despite his vigorous condemnation of anti-semitism and what he saw as its economic origins, Dobbert could not help but link the resolution of the problem of antisemitism with the supposed crisis of capitalist competition. Resolving the capital-ist problem and organizing society along socialist lines would, he maintained, solve the Jewish question.[6] Thus, shortly after the war, capitalism and antisemitism remained naively linked in the SPD's narrative of the Nazi years and the struggle against fascism.

In the early postwar years, Kurt Schumacher was both the leader of German Social Democracy and its principal spokesman on the Jewish question. Before the war, Schumacher had ties to many Jews. In West Prussia, where he had grown up, German Protes-tants and German Jews presented a united cultural front against the majority Polish Catholic population. From his Jewish boyhood friends, Schumacher had also acquired an unusual fondness for Jewish argot and traditional Jewish foods, according to one biog-rapher.[7] Within the SPD, which he joined in 1918 after the loss of an arm ended his World War I service, he came to know many Jewish socialists.[8] After having been in the Reichstag for only three

3 Donald Niewyk, *Socialist, Anti-Semite, and Jew: German Social Democracy Confronts the Problem of Anti-Semitism, 1918–1933* (Baton Rouge: Louisiana State University Press, 1971).
4 Ernest Hamburger and Peter Pulzer, "Jews as Voters in the Weimar Republic," in Leo Baeck Institute, *Year Book* 30 (1985), ed. Arnold Paucker and Robert Weltsch (London: Secker and Warburg, 1985): 55–58.
5 Niewyk, *Socialist, Anti-Semite, and Jew*, 220.
6 "Die Parteien und Wir: Sozialdemokratie und Judentum," *Jüdisches Gemeindeblatt*, 25 June 1946.
7 Lewis Edinger, *Kurt Schumacher: A Study in Personality and Political Behavior* (Stanford: Stanford University Press, 1965), 11–12. Edinger claims that this philosemitism went so far that Schumacher preferred Jewish landlords.
8 Shafir, "Das Verhältnis Kurt Schumachers," 168–169.

years when Hitler came to power, he spent most of the National Socialist era in concentration camps and lost a leg as a result of his treatment there. While many of his Jewish fellow-prisoners remained incredulous that their beloved Germany could treat them so poorly, Schumacher recognized the depth of Nazi hatred for them, as he recalled in 1947, and he would not forget the shared legacy of persecution.[9]

Schumacher was one of the first German politicians to address the atrocities committed against the Jews. On 6 May 1945, only a few weeks after his release from incarceration, he addressed leading Social Democrats in Hanover. He attacked antisemitism, which, he claimed, stemmed from fear of Jewish competition. While Schumacher recognized the Nazi animus against the Jews, he did not note its centrality to Nazi ideology.[10] It is possible that like many earlier socialist theorists, he saw socialism and the removal of economic competition as the best means of eliminating antisemitism. Although Schumacher linked antisemitism with antisocialism, he continually integrated the Jewish question into postwar political discourse. In May 1946, at the SPD's first postwar party congress, he reminded his audience of the victims of fascism, namely nations oppressed under occupation; victims of bombings, hunger, and disease; and the Jews. Though not placing the Jews first on his list, he did not overlook them or simply make veiled references to them.[11] At his urging, the party congress endorsed German reparations as far as economically feasible.[12]

Schumacher clearly sought an honest confrontation with the past, and he wanted the Allies to do more to promote that goal. However, his statements were apparently not motivated by political calculations. The postwar Jewish electorate was minuscule and was inclined to vote Social Democratic at any rate. Schumacher's stance

---

[9] Kurt Schumacher, "Schumacher in einem Interview mit der New Yorker Zeitung 'Aufbau': Der Antisemitismus in Deutschland," beginning October 1947, in *Reden – Schriften – Korrespondenzen 1945–1952*, ed. Willy Albrecht (Berlin: J. H. W. Dietz Nachfolger, 1985), 989.

[10] Kurt Schumacher, "Wir verzweifeln nicht!," 6 May 1945, in ibid., 205.

[11] Kurt Schumacher, "Eröffnung des Parteitages und 'Ehrung der Opfer des Faschismus' durch Schumacher," in ibid., 386.

[12] Kurt Schumacher, *Grundsätze sozialistischer Politik* (Hamburg: Phoenix, 1946), 46; "Kundgebung der Sozialdemokratischen Partei Deutschlands. Beschlossen auf dem Parteitag in Hannover am 11. Mai 1946," 11 May 1946, in *Die SPD unter Kurt Schumacher und Erich Ollenhauer 1946–1963: Sitzungsprotokolle der Spitzengremien*, vol. 1: *1946–1948*, ed. Willy Albrecht (Bonn: J. H. W. Dietz Nachfolger, 2000), 9.

seems to have rested purely on principle, for it was unlikely to endear his party to the millions of potential voters who had joined the Nazi Party or were sympathetic to it before 1945.[13] In the first West German federal election, held in August 1949, the SPD won barely 29 percent of the overall vote, yielding 131 seats in the new Bundestag.

Kurt Schumacher also addressed the Jewish community directly. On 17 February 1947, he gave an interview to Jewish journalist Karl Marx, which the Social Democratic news agency Sopade Informationsdienst regarded as so important, particularly to former German Social Democrats in exile, that it republished the article in March 1947. Schumacher pledged his party's unequivocal support for reparations, which would be most effective in a united Germany unhampered by the Allied Control Council. Thus, he tied together two of his main political themes: the need for a new, morally reformed Germany after the Nazis and the need for an independent, unified Germany without the Allies.[14] Reparations would serve as a symbol of the break with the past and mark Schumacher's independence from the Allies who did not push for reparations. At any rate, such early and active advocacy of reparations set his party apart from others.

In the same interview, Schumacher repeated his call for Jews to return to Germany. "I am of the opinion that it lies in the interest of the emigrated Jews, as well as that of the German people, to promote cooperation in all areas." He regretted the loss of the Jewish contribution to Germany's spiritual, cultural, and economic life.[15] Schumacher's comments were not without resonance. Both he and his aide Fritz Heine carried on a lively correspondence with pre-1933 Jewish Social Democrats living in exile. Heine also worked tirelessly to preserve the SPD's link to its Jewish former members.[16]

---

[13] Herf, *Divided Memory*, 252–253.

[14] "Interview Dr. Schumachers über die Frage des jüdischen Neu-Einbaues in Deutschland," 17 February 1947 (Sopade Informationsdienst no. 115, 4 March 1947), AdsD, Bestand Kurt Schumacher (Abt. II), 40.

[15] Ibid.

[16] For Fritz Heine's work in saving Jews from Nazi extermination, including many prominent Social Democrats, Heinz Putzrath, a Jewish-born, high-ranking official in the SPD, raised money to have a tree planted in Heine's honor along the Path of the Righteous at Yad Vashem in Jerusalem. Open letter from Putzrath, 4 October 1985, AdsD, Nachlass Heinz Putzrath (Abt. I), 53.

Schumacher repeated his comments to his own party colleagues. At a party congress in Nuremberg in June 1947, he chided the Allies for having failed the Jews on reparations. In his words, "It is surprising that even regarding the unitary treatment of and reparations to the Jews on German soil the victor powers have not yet found a common formula." He also stressed the Germans' responsibility for the Holocaust: "The Third Reich attempted to exterminate Jewry in Europe. The German people are obligated to reparations and compensation." He railed against antisemitism and demanded more legal protection for the Jews, but he also tied antisemitism to capitalism and economic exploitation.[17]

In the autumn of 1947, Schumacher, accompanied by Fritz Heine, traveled to the United States where he repeated the same message to an American Federation of Labor conference in San Francisco (see Fig. 5). Throughout his trip, Schumacher stressed the ties between the SPD and the American labor movement. Although the legacy of the Nazi past burdened Schumacher's task, his honesty and personal integrity did much to foster an atmosphere of respect and mutual understanding.[18]

American Jewish leaders looked with hope to the SPD. During Schumacher's visit, they relied on him for information about conditions in Germany and even considered financial aid to the SPD. American Jewish Committee leaders John Slawson and Milton Himmelfarb corresponded regarding this issue, with Slawson writing, "One question that should be raised is whether the Social Democratic Party would be willing for us to produce for them such printed materials as they need in their work against anti-Semitism."[19] Schumacher considered developing this kind of relationship with the AJC, and he and Heine met with AJC representatives. They asked Schumacher about many issues, including resurgent antisemitism, reparations, and the Christian Democrats. He wanted the AJC to use its influence to have the American occupation regime release more newsprint to SPD newspapers in

---

[17] Kurt Schumacher, "Grundsatzreferat Schumachers auf dem Nürnberger Parteitag der SPD: 'Deutschland und Europa,'" 29 June 1947, in *Reden – Schriften – Korrespondenzen*, 508–509.

[18] Kurt Schumacher, "Rede Schumachers auf dem Jahreskongreß des AFL in San Francisco," 14 October 1947, in ibid., 562–569. For more on Schumacher's American trip, see Herf, *Divided Memory*, 256–260.

[19] Letter from John Slawson to Milton Himmelfarb, 24 October 1947, CJH/YIVO, RG 347.7.1, box 34.

Figure 5. Kurt Schumacher at Berlin Tempelhof Airport before departing for America, 21 September 1947. *Source*: AdsD of the Friedrich-Ebert-Stiftung.

Germany and to secure private Jewish funds for SPD work. He also wanted AJC advisers to help with SPD campaign work. Schumacher denied that the party would be hurt if this secret arrangement became public. Slawson had his doubts, however, fearing a backlash or negative reaction from the State Department or the Office of the Military Government.[20]

During the struggle for reparations to Israel and international Jewish groups, Schumacher proved himself tireless in his efforts. Only months before his death in 1952, he continued to lobby Chancellor Konrad Adenauer on the issue.[21] Long afterward, Jews in Germany fondly remembered Schumacher's support. Hendrik George van Dam wrote that the late Social Democratic leader had stood for "a just reparation on the federal level. That, too, should not be forgotten."[22]

The Social Democrats' pronouncements on the Jews and anti-semitism found resonance among German Jews, and many leaders of the Jewish community in Germany joined or sympathized with the party. Fritz Heine, one of Schumacher's closest aides and a member of the SPD board, considered it obvious that the German Jews would become involved in Social Democratic politics once again.[23] A small number of German Jews were active in the SPD leadership, and some held seats in the Bundestag. Jakob Altmaier, the first professing Jew elected to the Bundestag, helped Chancellor Konrad Adenauer to commence reparations negotiations with Israel in 1951. Other Jewish Social Democrats, including the Schleswig-Holstein minister of justice (and later deputy chief justice of the West German constitutional court), Rudolf Katz, and the Hessian attorney general, Fritz Bauer, used their influence to prosecute antisemitic libelers and alleged war criminals. Many leaders of Jewish communities also joined the SPD or looked to it for support. Jeanette Wolff was a leader of both the Berlin SPD

[20] Letter from John Slawson to Paul Jacobs, 29 October 1947, CJH/YIVO, RG 347.7.1, box 34.
[21] Letter from Kurt Schumacher to Konrad Adenauer, 10 May 1952, in *Reden – Schriften – Korrespondenzen*, 1005–1006.
[22] "Der 10. September," *Jüdischer Presse Dienst*, [September] 1972. While most scholarship on Schumacher and the Jews characterizes the Social Democratic leader's attitude as very positive, some critics have alleged that he was given to making occasional antisemitic statements. Cf. comments by Katrin Kusch, "Diskussion nach den Referaten von Maxwell, Shafir und Hartwig," in *Kurt Schumacher*, ed. Albrecht, 214.
[23] Fritz Heine, letter to author, 7 April 1999.

and the Berlin Jewish community. Düsseldorf community chairman Philipp Auerbach was active in the SPD, and his successor, Julius Dreifuss, had close ties to the party.[24] Karl Marx, editor of the leading Jewish newspaper in Germany, also joined the party. While Marx occasionally publicly criticized the SPD, in private he referred to the SPD as "the party which stands closest to us."[25] In 1957, in thanking party chairman Erich Ollenhauer for a birthday gift, Marx wrote,

> You know that among them [Marx's supporters] was our Kurt Schumacher, who died too early and who always spoke to me in uncertain situations and gave me much along his way. You know how bound I am to our party, and I will never break my loyalty to it, even when evil tongues think that is the case.[26]

The SPD's profile on Jewish questions gave it a long-enduring reputation as the political party for Jews in the Federal Republic.

While the SPD was the party most attractive to Jews in Germany, it was not immune from the taint of antisemitism. In June 1946, party board member Robert Göhrlinger announced that the Jews in Germany were receiving foreign aid not commensurate with their numbers and demanded that they share with Germans.[27] In September 1949, the city council of Offenbach, an SPD electoral stronghold, appointed Herbert Lewin, a renowned physician and leader of the Jewish community in Cologne, to serve as chief of the gynecology department at the municipal hospital. At the urging

---

[24] Albrecht, "Jeanette Wolff – Jakob Altmaier – Peter Blachstein," 267–300; Christoph Moß, *Jakob Altmaier. Ein jüdischer Sozialdemokrat in Deutschland (1889–1963)* (Cologne: Bohlau, 2003); letter from Rudolf Katz to Jakob Altmaier, 3 January 1950, AdsD, Nachlass Jakob Altmaier (Abt. I), 4; Birgit Seemann, *Jeanette Wolff. Politkerin und engagierte Demokratin (1888–1976)* (Frankfurt: Campus, 2000); Bernd Faulenbach, ed., *"Habt den Mut zu menschlichem Tun". Die Jüdin und Demokratin Jeanette Wolff in ihrer Zeit (1888–1976)* (Essen: Klartext, 2002); correspondence between Philipp Auerbach and Walter Auerbach, 26 January 1947, 9 October 1948, 18 October 1948, 21 October 1948, 29 November 1948, AdsD, Nachlass Walter Auerbach (Abt. I), 2:31; letter from Düsseldorf SPD to Jüdische Gemeinde Düsseldorf, 24 January 1946, ZA, B. 1/5, 86; letter from Julius Dreifuss to *Rhein-Echo*, 27 January, Alfred Dobbert to Julius Dreifuss, 30 January 1948, ZA, B. 1/5, 85.

[25] "Nach den Wahlen," *Jüdisches Gemeindeblatt*, 30 April 1947; letter from Karl Marx to Kurt Schumacher, 10 February 1947, AdsD, Bestand Kurt Schumacher (Abt. II), 79.

[26] Letter from Karl Marx to Erich Ollenhauer, 22 May 1957, AdsD, Bestand Erich Ollenhauer (Abt. II), 218. In the years since his death, Marx's family has denied that Marx had a political affiliation, seeking to protect him from the accusation of being a "court Jew." Lilli Marx, "Renewal of the German Jewish Press," in *After the Holocaust*, ed. Brenner, 128; Lilli Marx, interview by author, Düsseldorf, 14 April 1999.

[27] "Sitzung des Parteivorstandes am 4. Juni 1946 in Hannover," 4 June 1946, in *Die SPD unter Kurt Schumacher und Erich Ollenhauer 1946–1963*, 1:12.

of Christian Democratic deputy mayor Karl Kasperkowitz, Social Democratic mayor Johannes Rebholz revoked the appointment. Kasperkowitz had claimed that Offenbach's women could not be entrusted to a Jewish Holocaust survivor. Moreover, he claimed that after years of reading the viciously antisemitic newspaper *Der Stürmer*, with its lurid fabricated tales of lustful Jews attacking German maidens, ordinary Germans were not ready to accept a Jewish gynecologist.[28] When Rebholz agreed with Kasperkowitz, Lewin protested the mayor's decision, and his case became a cause célèbre. Jewish Social Democrats Jakob Altmaier and Peter Blachstein protested to party leader Schumacher, who replied that the SPD would not tolerate such discrimination and that ethnic heritage was not to be a criterion for the selection of government employees or candidates for office.[29] The South Hesse SPD appointed a committee to investigate the matter, and the SPD's central board attacked the conduct of the mayor and Social Democratic city government officials. The board further declared that if the committee's findings matched the rumors surrounding the case, expulsions from the party would be warranted. The controversy embarrassed the party, and in reporting on it, the party organ placed the story deep inside its official newspaper – not on page one.[30] In 1950, Lewin received the post, which he held for seventeen years. Rebholz resigned, presumably to avoid the embarrassment of party discipline and dismissal. Charges brought against him for slander were dropped when he endorsed Lewin's candidacy.

Despite the Lewin affair, the SPD had a strong record on Jewish affairs. In many ways, the SPD was the most progressive of the political parties in terms of its relationship with the Jews. It understood that reconciliation was both a part of the rehabilitation of Germany and an indicator of a break with the past. Moreover, the SPD shared with the Jews a legacy of persecution under the Nazis.

[28] Letter from Karl Kasperkowitz to Theodor Heuss, December 1949, BAK, B 122, 2083 (29). Caricatures in *Der Stürmer*, published by the ardent Nazi Julius Streicher, routinely portrayed Jews as bloodthirsty fiends raping and grotesquely murdering innocent German girls. In his letter to the West German president, Kasperkowitz drew attention to his pro-Jewish credentials, citing his childhood contact with Jews and attaching numerous letters of recommendation. He later faced charges for slander.

[29] Kurt Schumacher, "Schumacher an Peter Blachstein über die Gefahren eines Neoantisemitismus," 26 November 1949, in *Reden – Schriften – Korrespondenzen*, 990–991.

[30] "Parteivorstand zum Offenbacher 'Fall Lewin,'" *Neuer Vorwärts*, 24 September 1949.

THE CHRISTIAN DEMOCRATS AND THE JEWS

While the Social Democratic Party had a long heritage and a strong internal party structure dating back more than seventy years, the other leading political force in postwar Germany was totally new and had no legacy regarding Jewish issues. However, that very same party would soon become the leading political movement in the country and the governing party. Thus, its stance regarding the Jews and Jewish issues became particularly important.

Founded largely by former members of the pre-1933, Catholic-oriented Center Party, the Christian Democratic Union (Christlich-Demokratische Union, or CDU) considered itself to be the protector of Western, Christian values. However, unlike the Center Party, the CDU did not explicitly affiliate with any one faith, and Germans of varying religious and professional backgrounds joined the new party and assumed leadership positions within it. Many economic liberals and moderate conservatives, drawing lessons from the bourgeois parties' disunity in the face of the National Socialist threat in the early 1930s, rallied behind the new CDU and its smaller Bavarian sister party, the Christian Social Union (Christlich-Soziale Union, or CSU). Together, they garnered 31 percent of the vote cast in the first West German federal election in 1949. Only four years later, the party had increased its strength to over 45 percent of the vote.

Konrad Adenauer, a strict Catholic and a morally upright man, dominated the party until his death in 1967, but he could not control every facet of party life nor could he always change members' long-held opinions. As a result, the CDU and CSU developed a mixed record on Jewish affairs, with noticeable differences among members and even regions of the party.

During the Weimar Republic, the Center Party, led by Wilhelm Marx, did enjoy some Jewish support. Despite the Center's religiously Catholic nature – or perhaps because of it – Orthodox Jews regularly supported the party, whose advocacy of public religious education and moral social codes appealed to them.[31] The party did not capitalize on this sentiment, however, and no Jew ran for office as a Center Party candidate until 1930. After the decline of

[31] Donald L. Niewyk, *The Jews in Weimar Germany* (Baton Rouge: Louisiana State University Press, 1980), 28; Hamburger and Pulzer, "Jews as Voters in the Weimar Republic," 28–29.

the moderate, middle-class parties during the Great Depression, growing numbers of Jews, including Zionists and liberals, voted for the Center Party. These groups considered the Center Party to be the last hope in the fight against right-wing antisemitism.[32] While members of other Weimar political parties joined the postwar CDU, Jewish support for these parties had varied from considerable (the left liberals) to minuscule (the archconservative nationalists).[33]

Christian Democratic political groups sprang up across Germany in 1945. Each group had a different identity. Some had a humanistic, Catholic orientation; others – often Protestant – regarded themselves as a middle-class bulwark against socialism. The early CDU even had a prominent Christian social wing. In Berlin, under Jakob Kaiser, the party maintained ties to both trade unions and conservative Protestant politicians. The party's interconfessional coalition was often fragile, but it maintained its stance as the champion of occidental, Christian values.[34]

Party chairman Konrad Adenauer served as West German chancellor from 1949 to 1963, leaving an indelible imprint on politics and society in the Federal Republic of Germany, including on German-Jewish dialogue. He largely set the tone for any pro-Jewish discourse emanating from the party, and as chancellor, Adenauer was largely responsible for West German reparations to Israel and to international Jewish organizations. However, in order to appeal to the largest possible segment of the German electorate, he also discouraged a comprehensive purge of Nazi fellow travelers from West German public life.

While Adenauer's party was new after the war and had no track record on Jewish issues, Adenauer had long been engaged with Jewish politicians and the Jewish community. Even before becoming mayor of Cologne in 1917, he had amicable dealings with local Jews, including a number of his National Liberal counterparts on the Cologne city council, who regarded him as "a tolerant, candid,

---

32 Ronald Ross, *Beleaguered Tower: The Dilemma of Political Catholicism in Wilhelmine Germany* (Notre Dame: University of Notre Dame Press, 1973), 38; Hamburger and Pulzer, "Jews as Voters in the Weimar Republic," 55–59.

33 See Hamburger and Pulzer, "Jews as Voters in the Weimar Republic," 8–31. For more information on Jewish support for Weimar liberal parties, see section on "The Liberals and Jewish Issues" below.

34 Hans-Otto Kleinmann, *Geschichte der CDU 1945–1982*, ed. Günter Buchstab (Stuttgart: Deutsche Verlags-Anstalt, 1993), 15–48 and 80.

and progressive man."[35] In 1927, he wrote an overtly Zionist open letter in which he expressed his support for a Jewish homeland in Palestine.[36] As an opponent of the Nazi regime, he was forced from his position by the Nazis in 1933. After the war's end, he served again as mayor until the British occupiers dismissed him from that office in October 1945. As postwar mayor, he helped to renew Cologne's Jewish community. Using the influence of his office, he expedited the return of Jews to Cologne from Theresienstadt concentration camp.[37] The Cologne Jewish community recognized Adenauer and political Catholicism as allies. In August 1946, it sent condolences on the occasion of the death of Wilhelm Marx, former leader of the Center Party, Reich chancellor, and presidential candidate. Adenauer sent a warm note of acknowledgment.[38] In April 1947, as chairman of the CDU in the British zone, he wrote to the Cologne Jewish community, expressing his wish that Jewish émigrés who had survived the war years safely abroad would return to Germany. He also asserted that Jewish congregations deserved help as far as public means allowed.[39]

It is important to note that Adenauer was a deeply religious man. Throughout his life, he attended church regularly and observed Lent, even when traveling on state business. He absorbed Church teachings regarding human fallibility, sin, and divine justice, and his piety surely informed his politics.[40] Moreover, the environment in which Adenauer was raised shaped his Catholicism and contributed to his desire for moral reconciliation in later years. The Catholicism of his hometown of Cologne was known for its cosmopolitanism and was seen as corrective to the materialism of late nineteenth-century capitalism. The social wing of the Center Party

---

[35] Hans-Peter Schwarz, *Adenauer*, vol. 1: *Der Aufstieg, 1876–1952* (Stuttgart: Deutsche Verlags-Anstalt, 1986), 171. Louis Hagen, Catholic power-broker of the Cologne Liberals before 1919, had been born Jewish as Louis Heymann Levy. The leader of the Liberals in the city council, Bernhard Falk, was a member of the local Jewish community. Schwarz, *Adenauer*, 1:159–161.

[36] Letter from Konrad Adenauer to Count Johann Bernstorff, 22 November 1927, Deutsches Komitee Pro Palästina zur Förderung der jüdischen Palästinasiedlung, *Tagung in Köln am 22. November 1927* (Berlin: Siegfried Scholem, [1927]), 7–8.

[37] Letter from Konrad Adenauer to the Czech Authorities, 8 August 1945; certificate for Dr. Herbert Lewin, 11 August 1945; *Briefe 1945–1947*, 69 and 72.

[38] Letter from Konrad Adenauer to Jüdische Gemeinde Köln, 9 August 1946, *Briefe 1945–1947*, 306.

[39] Letter from Konrad Adenauer to the Synagogengemeinde Köln, 25 April 1947, *Briefe 1945–1947*, 474.

[40] Schwarz, *Adenauer*, 1:73–74.

was unusually strong in Cologne. Additionally, Jewish alumni of Adenauer's Catholic high school fondly remembered its religious tolerance and classical humanistic tradition.[41]

Adenauer's faith affected his relations with the postwar Jewish community in tangible ways. In an interview with journalist Karl Marx, Adenauer denied that the new Christian Democratic Union was anti-Jewish. He saw it instead as inspired by the spirit of the Christian West and dedicated to the restoration of Christian respect for morality and rights abolished in Nazi Germany. The new Germany would protect basic human rights and fight antisemitism, including the desecration of Jewish cemeteries.[42] Unlike many Social Democratic leaders who defended the right to be religious but were not observant themselves, Adenauer could establish a rapport with devout people of different faiths. In April 1949, Adenauer wrote to the Cologne Jewish community to express his congratulations on the consecration of a new synagogue. His brief note had a marked tone of religiosity.[43] Postwar Christian Democratic politicians, including Adenauer, believed that under the Nazis, without the presence of faith in public life, Germany had lost its moral compass.

Additionally, one of Adenauer's closest friends, Dannie Heineman, was a Jew.[44] The two first met in 1907, when Adenauer was still a Cologne city official conducting municipal business. Their friendship grew, and after Adenauer lost his position as mayor in 1933, Heineman supported him financially. Heineman, who was neither a religious Jew nor a Zionist, also repeatedly aided

[41] Ibid., 1:38–39 and 1:80. Despite his devotion to the Catholic Church, he blamed Christian clergy, in part, for what had transpired in the Nazi years. Writing in February 1946 to a pastor in Bonn, he leveled particular invective at the German bishops who had failed to protest. Adenauer also obliquely criticized Pope Pius XII for his inactivity, whereas Pope Pius XI, in his opinion, would have taken action. Letter from Konrad Adenauer to Bernhard Custodis, 23 February 1946, *Briefe 1945–1947*, 172.

[42] "Bekenntnis zur Verpflichtung," *Allgemeine Wochenzeitung*, 25 November 1949; AJC report, "The Adenauer Interview," November 1949, CJH/YIVO, RG 347.7.1, box 34. On the early CDU's attempts to invent a space for itself within the political spectrum based on an antimaterialist, Christian philosophy, see Maria Mitchell, "Materialism and Secularism: CDU Politicians and National Socialism, 1945–1949," *Journal of Modern History* 67, no. 2 (June 1995).

[43] Letter from Konrad Adenauer to the chairman of the Synagogen-Gemeinde Köln, 5 April 1949, Konrad Adenauer, *Briefe 1947–1949*, ed. Hans Peter Mensing, Rhöndorfer Ausgabe, ed. Rudolf Morsey and Hans-Peter Schwarz (Berlin: Siedler, 1984), 435.

[44] Heineman (1872–1962) was born in Charlotte, North Carolina. His widowed mother, a German Jew, raised her son in Hanover. Trained as an electrical engineer, Heineman worked for AEG before becoming an executive for the Belgian firm SOFINA.

Jewish refugees during the Nazi era.[45] The absence of any mention of the plight of Jewish Holocaust survivors among Heineman's correspondence with Adenauer from the period under examination is striking. Even after the West German reparations to Israel began, Heineman was reluctant to bring up such issues with his influential German friend. One can only imagine that Heineman considered the topic too sensitive.[46] However, considering the strength of their friendship, Adenauer's opposition to the Nazis, and Heineman's aid to Adenauer during the Nazi era, German-Jewish relations could not have been far from Adenauer's mind.

By the 1960s, legacy of the Nazi years and Jewish topics became more present in West German public discourse. In fact, in 1958 and 1959, West Germany experienced a rash of antisemitic outbursts, including the infamous desecration of a synagogue in Cologne on New Year's Eve, 1959–1960. Under these circumstances, as many foreign observers cast aspersions on West German democracy and democrats, Adenauer increased his engagement with Jewish affairs and Israel, even though he did not open formal diplomatic relations with the Jewish state.[47] Through the efforts of Max Adenauer, the chancellor's son, and Dannie Heineman, Konrad Adenauer became a patron of the Weizmann Institute in Israel, and his influence enabled Israeli scientists to establish contacts with West German scientists.[48] Long after his retirement, Adenauer traveled to Israel where he met former prime minister David Ben-Gurion and received an honorary degree from the Weizmann Institute.[49]

Despite Adenauer's strong sense of moral rectitude and obligation, he could not ignore the practical concerns of rebuilding German democracy. After twelve years of Nazi dictatorship, most

[45] Hans-Peter Schwarz, "Dannie N. Heineman und Konrad Adenauer im Dialog (1907–1962)," in *Staat und Parteien. Festschrift für Rudolf Morsey zum 65. Geburtstag*, ed. Karl Dietrich Bracher et al. (Berlin: Dubker und Humblot, 1992), 805.

[46] Herf, *Divided Memory*, 269; letters from Dannie Heineman to Konrad Adenauer, 24 January and 24 March 1959, Stiftung Bundeskanzler-Adenauer-Haus, Privatbestände H: D. Heineman, Band 4/2.

[47] Detlef Siegfried, "Zwischen Aufarbeitung und Schlußstreich. Der Umgang mit der NS-Vergangenheit in den beiden deutschen Staaten 1958 bis 1969," in *Dynamische Zeiten. Die 60er Jahre in den beiden deutschen Gesellschaften*, ed. Axel Schildt, Detlef Siegfried, and Karl Christian Lammers (Hamburg: Hans Christians, 2000), 78–91.

[48] Letter from Dannie Heineman to Konrad Adenauer, 24 March 1959, StBKAH, Privatbestände H: D. Heineman, Band, 4/2.

[49] Weizmann Institute of Science, *Konrad Adenauer Ehrenmitglied des Weizmann-Instituts: Ein denkwürdiger Tag in Rehovoth* (Zurich: European Committee of the Weizmann Institute of Science Rehovoth, [1966]).

observers expected the Social Democrats to assume the reins of government. To forestall this electoral victory, Adenauer's CDU needed the support of some politically compromised voters. At a meeting of the CDU in March 1946, Adenauer tried courting them while denouncing the Nazi past. He condemned National Socialism and demanded the removal from office of "active National Socialists and active militarists" who were responsible for the war and its prolongation. Despite his energetic attack on leading Nazis, he did not seek punishment for "fellow travelers who did not oppress others" and who did not commit any crimes. Adenauer noted that soldiers who had done their duty and nothing else were not militarists, and even those former soldiers with mildly questionable pasts were welcome to join the CDU, though they were excluded from internal party-leadership positions.[50] Adenauer did not want to see these voters supporting parties further to the right.[51] Confronting the Nazi past, particularly discrimination against the Jews, had potentially negative consequences for Adenauer. One German Jewish journalist quoted Adenauer's adviser Herbert Blankenhorn as saying,

For years Dr. Adenauer said nothing on the topic of Jews because he wanted to win over the entire German people for democracy. If in 1949 Adenauer had said what we did in the past, the German people would have been against him.[52]

In contrast to Social Democratic leader Schumacher's method of confrontation with the past, Adenauer sought compromise, and he clearly reaped tangible political benefits from this course.

Just as Adenauer was largely motivated by a sense of Christian tradition, many of the CDU's strongest proponents of German-Jewish reconciliation were deeply involved in Christian religious organizations, including lay Catholic groups and the Protestant Church of Germany. Local co-chairmen of the confessionally organized Society for Christian-Jewish Cooperation were often CDU

---

[50] Konrad Adenauer, "Grundsatzrede des 1. Vorsitzenden der Christlich-Demokratischen Union für die Britische Zone in der Aula der Kölner Universität," 24 March 1946, in *Reden 1917–1967: Eine Auswahl*, ed. Hans-Peter Schwarz (Stuttgart: Deutsche Verlags-Anstalt, 1975), 86 and 92.

[51] Frei, *Vergangenheitspolitik*, 19.

[52] Inge Deutschkron, "Das Verhalten der bundesrepublikanischen Politiker ist eine Schweinerei gegenüber NS-Opfern," in *Blick zurück ohne Haß: Juden aus Israel erinnern sich an Deutschland*, ed. Dieter Bednarz and Michael Lüders (Cologne: Bund, 1981), 62.

members. In Berlin, all three chairmen were CDU members with prominent public positions. Catholic Heinrich Vockel was the West German government's representative in Berlin; Protestant Joachim Tibertius was a Berlin state cabinet member; and Jewish chairman Siegmund Weltlinger also held a state government position.[53] Franz Böhm, who led the Society in Frankfurt, gained fame for negotiating the West German reparations agreement with Israel. As a Bundestag deputy, he was a watchdog against antisemitism and a guardian of reparations.[54] Speaker of the Bundestag Eugen Gerstenmaier had studied theology before the war and during Adenauer's chancellorship was one of the chief CDU advocates for reparations. He was the first German governmental official to address a session of the World Jewish Congress.[55]

While the name alone – *Christian* Democratic Union – alienated some Jews, many others were active in the party. Lilli Marx, widow of Karl Marx, said "it was impossible for us [to join] with the word 'Christian' in the title."[56] Other Jews did not share these hesitations. After 1945, the classical liberal party, the former political home of German Jewry, had a strong nationalist orientation. As a result, the CDU became the catch-all party for many nonsocialists. For Jews who could not or would not join the SPD because it stood too far to the left, the CDU was the natural choice, and it welcomed members of all faiths.[57]

The Berlin CDU enjoyed a particularly good relationship with the Jewish community. Notably, in Berlin the party originally bore the name "Democratic Union," belatedly adding the

---

53 "Interkonfessionelle Zusammenarbeit," 25 April 1951, LAB, E Rep. 200–22, 54; Josef Foschepoth, *Im Schatten der Vergangenheit. Die Anfänge der Gesellschaften für Christlich-Jüdische Zusammenarbeit* (Göttingen: Vandenhoeck und Ruprecht, 1993), 109, 214, and 245.

54 Felix Shinnar, *Bericht eines Beauftragten: Die deutsch-israelischen Beziehungen 1951–1966* (Tübingen: Rainer Wunderlich, 1967), 36; BAK, N 1351, 16–17 (Sonderakte Israel); ACDP, I-200, esp. 001/1, 001/3, 004/7, 004/8, 006/2, 006/4, 006/5, 044/4, and 044/5.

55 "Entwurf," 25 February 1953, ACDP, I-210, 067/2; "Unser jüdischer Mitbürger gehört in unsere Mitte!," 14 October 1963, ACDP, I-210, 078/1; "Zur Aussprache bereit, Rede vor dem Jüdischen Weltkongreß in Brüssel," 4 August 1966, ACDP, I-210, 081/2.

56 Lilli Marx, interview by author, Düsseldorf, 14 April 1999. She noted that many Jews of the next generation did join the party, including Michel Friedman, who at various times served as a member of the CDU's national board, a Frankfurt city councilman, and a member of the presidium of the Central Council of Jews in Germany.

57 The postwar liberal party, the FDP, was becoming a "party of a right-wing national[ist] clientele," according to Norbert Frei. Frei, *Vergangenheitspolitik*, 19. Therefore, many Weimar liberals, including some Jews, united with moderate conservatives in the Christian Democratic Union to found a nonsocialist, democratic bloc.

"Christian."[58] Richard Kantorowicz, a Jewish veterinarian and neighbor of the Stauffenberg family, cofounded the Berlin CDU.[59] Siegmund Weltlinger, a banker and stockbroker before the war, also joined the party. He served as Jewish adviser to Berlin state government and co-chairman of the Berlin Society for Christian-Jewish Cooperation. Within the Berlin CDU, Weltlinger remained the de facto expert on reparations. In October 1947, on behalf of the Christian Democratic deputies in the local legislature, he drafted a proposal for a reparations law.[60] Weltlinger claimed that from its founding, the CDU had opposed antisemitism, and in public addresses, he repeatedly stressed the CDU's roots as a party based on faith, but also one committed to interconfessional relations.[61]

The fact that Berlin Jewry was represented in the CDU and that the CDU worked with the community was no accident. Many Christian Democratic politicians in Berlin had a close relationship with the Jewish community, often reaching back to their Weimar Republic–era membership in the German Democratic Party, the party with the most Jewish members. When Weltlinger needed to petition the Berlin government, he usually went through Deputy Mayor Ferdinand Friedensburg, a cofounder of the Berlin CDU and a former member of the German Democratic Party. Before the Nazis dismissed him, Friedensburg was a rising star in the Prussian civil service, and despite choosing the path of "internal emigration," he spent some time in Gestapo prisons.[62] Ernst Lemmer, another cofounder of the Berlin CDU and a former member

---

[58] Arnold Heidenheimer, *Adenauer and the CDU: The Rise of the Leader and the Integration of the Party* (The Hague: Martinus Nijhoff, 1960), 35.

[59] Brigitte Kaff and staff (Archiv für Christlich-Demokratische Politik), letter to author, including dossier on Richard Kantorowicz, 7 December 2000; "Sondermaterial Nr. 5: Unionspolitik in 130 Stichworten," p. 73, ACDP, LV-Westfalen, III-002–024/1; Kurt Witt, "Wie die Union entstanden ist," in *Politisches Jahrbuch der CDU/CSU* 1, ed. Bruno Dörpinghaus and Kurt Witt (Frankfurt: K. G. Lohse, 1950), 188.

[60] To Weltlinger's dismay, no action was taken on the proposal. "Notizen für ein Wiedergutmachungsgesetz der CDU," October 1947 and April 1949, LAB, B Rep. 2, 4874.

[61] "Politik und die Kirche," 21 September 1948, LAB, E Rep. 200–22, 80; "Interkonfessionelle Zusammenarbeit," 25 April 1951, LAB, E Rep. 200–22, 54.

[62] For example, the two men corresponded regarding paid leave on Jewish holidays for Jewish city employees. Friedensburg also attended Jewish functions as the government's representative and sent greetings on Rosh Hashanah. Letters from Ferdinand Friedensburg to Siegmund Weltlinger, 1 September 1948 and 7 September 1949; letter from Ferdinand Friedensburg to board of Jüdische Gemeinde zu Berlin, 22 September 1949; LAB, B Rep. 2, 4874.

of the Reichstag for the German Democratic Party, also enjoyed close ties to many Jews, including Karl Marx and Heinz Galinski. When the *Jüdisches Gemeindeblatt* ran a series on the political parties and the Jews, the CDU asked Lemmer to write on its behalf. He reminded the newspaper's readers that the Berlin CDU had expressly opened its doors to Jewish membership and wanted Jewish help in the reconstruction of "a better Germany."[63] In 1953, all five CDU Bundestag deputies from Berlin, including Lemmer and Friedensburg, voted for reparations to Israel, the only such unified bloc within the CDU.[64]

Despite philosemitic elements within the CDU, many Christian Democrats were indifferent or hostile to Jewish-related issues. Siegmund Weltlinger often had to goad his party into taking action on topics important to the Jews. He was aware that the CDU was not automatically a pro-Jewish entity, and the SPD still had the reputation of being the most progressive party on Jewish questions. Even on issues seemingly as innocuous as preserving the right to kosher butchery, an easy and frequent target of antisemites (masquerading as animal rights activists), the CDU showed little enthusiasm.[65] Karl Kasperkowitz, the deputy mayor of Offenbach who began the Lewin affair, was a Christian Democrat, and one-third of the Christian Democratic Bundestag deputies did not support reparations to Israel. In an atmosphere marked by competing claims to victimhood, many Christian Democratic constituents complained bitterly about reparations. They claimed that they, whose country had been impoverished by the war, could not afford to pay restitution to the heirs of those murdered by the Nazis. One CDU politician even told Adenauer that paying reparations would awaken resentment that would lead to renewed antisemitism.[66]

---

[63] Correspondence with Karl Marx and Heinz Galinski, inter alia, ACDP, I-280, 017/1, 030/1, and 118/1; "Die Parteien und Wir: Die CDU," *Jüdisches Gemeindeblatt,* 25 June 1946. As a member of the last Reichstag, Lemmer had the dubious distinction of voting for the Enabling Law that ultimately gave semi-legal santion to the Nazi dictatorship.

[64] "254. Sitzung," 18 March 1953, Germany (West), Bundestag, *Verhandlungen des Deutschen Bundestages, I. Wahlperiode 1949,* vol. 15: *Stenographische Berichte von der 250. Sitzung am 25. Februar 1953 bis zur 262. Sitzung am 29. April 1953* (Bonn: Bonner Universitäts-Buchdruckerei, 1953), 12293.

[65] Letter from Siegmund Weltlinger to Berlin deputy mayor Walter Schreiber, 3 September 1951, LAB, B Rep. 2, 4874.

[66] Letters from Jakob Diel to Konrad Adenauer, 4 April and 13 November 1952, ACDP, I-139, 022/6.

Many civil servants who had faithfully served the Nazi government acquired positions of influence under Konrad Adenauer. Most of them became CDU members. The most famous servant of the Nazi state to achieve high standing in the early CDU and West German government was Hans Globke, whom Adenauer chose as chief of staff in the chancellor's office. As an official in the Nazi-era Interior Ministry, but not a member of the Nazi Party, Globke wrote an official interpretation of the Nuremberg Laws, which defined Jewish identity for discriminatory purposes.[67] Allowing a man with Globke's past to serve the West German state in such a sensitive position left Adenauer open to criticism from both the Jewish community and the SPD.[68] For nearly a generation, the issue of activities during the Nazi era continued to plague CDU politicians, including president Heinrich Lübke and Baden-Württemberg prime minister Hans Filbinger. Even if a CDU member's behavior during the Nazi era was above reproach, any postwar statements that smacked of antisemitism incurred great criticism – often from CDU liberal Franz Böhm, who made it his mission to defend reparations to the Jews and to further the German-Jewish reconciliation.[69]

The Christian Democratic movement was not a monolithic force, and in Bavaria, it was represented by the Christian Social Union (CSU). This party, which had strongly Bavarian particularist elements and which was more conservative than the mainstream CDU, encountered serious problems with antisemitism or suspicion of antisemitism. In many ways, the difference between the sister parties only underscored regional differences in

---

[67] Ulrich von Hehl, "Der Beamte im Reichsministerium: Die Beurteilung Globkes in der Diskussion der Nachkriegszeit, Eine Dokumentation," in *Der Staatssekretär Adenauers. Persönlichkiet und politisches Wirken Hans Globkes*, ed. Klaus Gotto (Stuttgart: Klett-Cotta, 1980). Throughout his later career, Globke claimed that he had interpreted the law as narrowly as possible, so as to omit many so-called partial Jews from official classification.

[68] "Eine Frage, Herr Dr. Globke!," *Allgemeine Wochenzeitung*, 8 December 1950; "Mitteilung an die Presse," 13 July 1950, letter from Erich Ollenhauer to Theodor Heuss, 14 July 1950, letter from Theodor Heuss to Erich Ollenhauer, 29 July 1950, AdsD, Nachlass Adolf Arndt (Abteilung I), 322.

[69] More than once, Böhm started intraparty controversies over perceived antisemitism. Two particular objects of his criticism were Bundestag deputy Jakob Diel and federal finance minister, later justice minister, Fritz Schäffer. On Diel: AdsD, Nachlass Adolf Arndt (Abteilung I), 5. On Schäffer: letter from Robert Pferdmenges to Fritz Schäffer and Franz Böhm, 1 July 1958, BAK, N 1168, 48; "Antisemitismus," [1958], ACDP, I-200, 044/5; "Ehrengericht," [1958], ACDP, I-200, 006/4.

Germany regarding Jewish issues. While Berlin had historically been cosmopolitan, and Düsseldorf had long been known for Jewish-Christian interaction, Bavaria had traditionally been a hotbed of antisemitic sentiment. For instance, Munich had been the so-called capital of the Nazi movement, and Julius Streicher, the fanatically virulent antisemitic Nazi publisher, had his base in Nuremberg. After the war, many Bavarians resented the large Jewish refugee population living in their state under American protection.

Dealing with antisemitism, even on a theoretical plane, was difficult for the CSU. In October 1946, CSU delegates met to formulate the party platform. Hermann Strathmann, a CSU Bavarian state legislator, revealed the bias within the CSU when he claimed that there was such a thing as legitimate racial theory. Science had proven that different races had different characteristics with varying values; this fact, however, did not legitimize racial hatred, he noted.[70] The CSU long wrestled with what it meant to be a Christian political party. CSU board member August Haußleiter denounced antisemitism as anti-Christian and wanted the party platform to feature an explicit condemnation, phrased, "Therefore we reject with determination any form of racial hatred, and in particular antisemitic [hatred], as an ignominious relapse into an overpowering barbarism." Many CSU leaders rejected this proposal, however. Echoing ongoing debates about historical memory and responsibility for the past, one CSU delegate demanded the condemnation be stricken from the platform, claiming, "We are not guilty, and we do not need to excuse ourselves." While Jews should stay in Germany, he said, denouncing racial hatred sounded too "trendy" ("nach Zeitgeschmack"). He cautioned, "There can be a time when other things are once again fashionable." Another delegate demanded that the phrase "an ignominious relapse into an overpowering barbarism" be stricken. While Haußleiter consented to this change, CSU chairman Josef Müller suggested they be "prudent" and adopt simply the wording, "We reject any form of racial hatred" with no explicit reference to Jews. The delegates

[70] "Sitzung des Landesausschusses der Christlich-Sozialen Union am 4. Oktober 1946 in München," 4 October 1946, Christlich-Soziale Union, *Die CSU 1945–1948: Protokolle und Materialien zur Frühgeschichte der Christlich-Sozialen Union*, vol. 1: *Protokolle 1945–1946*, ed. Barbara Fait and Alf Mintzel, vol. 4 of Texte und Materialien zur Zeitgeschichte (Munich: R. Oldenbourg, 1993), 638.

accepted his idea by acclamation.[71] The party, which probably had little appeal to Jewish Germans, made a politically expedient decision to gloss over the legacy of the Nazi years, even as it tried to build a new Germany.

In fact, some members of the CSU still cherished old myths about Jewry. At a meeting of young CSU politicians held in March 1947, Bavarian agricultural minister Josef Baumgartner made disparaging remarks about the Jews. When one participant at the meeting claimed that the American occupiers were primarily freemasons and Jews, Baumgartner cautioned the man not to make such reckless remarks. "Without the Jews, and especially without the Jewish businessman in the USA and throughout the world," Germany would never overcome its difficult economic situation. Baumgartner had no qualms, however, about condemning the Eastern European Jewish displaced persons in Bavaria. He regretted that he had been forced to attend the Second Congress of Liberated Jews. He claimed that the only enjoyment he had at the meeting resulted from the refugees' proclamation of their wish to leave Germany. This remark drew laughter from his listeners.[72] While some Bavarian politicians found comments of this nature amusing, the Allied occupiers did not. Elements of the American military government in Bavaria regarded the CSU as "federalistic and narrow-minded."[73]

Accusations of antisemitism continually plagued CSU leader and federal finance minister Fritz Schäffer, an opponent of reparations to Israel. Though historian Christian Pross has claimed that Schäffer had made antisemitic statements in the 1920s, the general consensus is that Schäffer was not antisemitic.[74] As federal finance minister, he acquired the reputation of a "pedantic, petty bean counter, a miserly politician."[75] Schäffer maintained that as guardian of the postwar West German economy, which was his job,

---

[71] "Sitzung des Landesausschusses der Christlich-Sozialen Union am 31. Oktober 1946 in München," 31 October 1946, *Die CSU 1945–1948*, 1:711 and 1:740–741.

[72] "Dienstag-Club am 4. März 1947," 4 March 1947, Christlich-Soziale Union, *Lehrjahre der CSU: Eine Nachkriegspartei im Spiegel vertraulicher Berichte an die Militärregierung*, ed. Klaus-Dietmar Henke and Hans Woller (Stuttgart: Deutsche Verlags-Anstalt, 1984), 122.

[73] "Report on Present Inter-Faith Relations," 26 April 1949, BAK, Z 45, 5/338–2/8.

[74] Cf. Pross, *Paying for the Past*, 8; Michael Wolffsohn, "Globalentschädigung für Israel und die Juden? Adenauer und die Opposition in der Bundesregierung," in *Wiedergutmachung*, ed. Herbst and Goschler, 161.

[75] Pross, *Paying for the Past*, 8.

he could not permit something as financially frivolous as reparations. Others – including Franz Böhm – claimed that Schäffer's opposition to the Nazis masked his latent antisemitism.[76] In fact, Schäffer's motivations remain unclear, and the suspicion of antisemitism continues to haunt his memory.

THE LIBERALS AND JEWISH ISSUES

While the bourgeois Christian Democratic movement had no established record on Jewish issues before 1945, bourgeois liberalism in Germany did. Historically, the various liberal groups had been regarded as the Jews' closest allies, and with the rebirth of German liberalism after 1945, one might have expected the new liberal parties to continue the policies of their political predecessors and to attract Jewish participation. In fact, of the three major political parties in West Germany, the liberal Free Democratic Party (Freie Demokratische Partei, or FDP) exhibited the most complicated relationship with Jewish issues.

Soon after the destruction of the centralized Nazi regime, liberals throughout Germany founded regional political organizations. Many were wary of the Christian socialist tendencies within the CDU, and in December 1948 they organized the Free Democratic Party as an antisocialist political party. This dedication to secular free-market principles drew committed liberal democrats, but it also attracted antisocialist nationalists, some of whom had been Nazis or Nazi fellow travelers. Nonetheless, the FDP quickly established itself as the third political force in West Germany, winning almost 12 percent of the vote in 1949 and over 9 percent of the vote in 1953.

However, the two wings of the FDP often opposed each other. The left liberals, led by Theodor Heuss, found their principal support in southwestern Germany and the Hanseatic cities. The national liberals, led by Franz Blücher, and overt nationalists, led by Friedrich Middelhauve, found their strongest support in the states of northern Germany.[77] Discord between these two factions limited the FDP's ability to form coalitions in state governments and

---

[76] "Ehrengericht," undated [1958], ACDP, I-200, 006/4.

[77] Dieter Hein, "Der Weg nach Heppenheim 1945–1948," in *Verantwortung für die Freiheit, 40 Jahre F. D. P.*, ed. Wolfgang Mischnik (Stuttgart: Deutsche Verlags-Anstalt, 1989); Fritz Fliszar, "Mit der FDP regieren: Ein Gespräch mit Erich Mende," in ibid., 128.

to follow a single line on controversial issues, and no single issue divided the liberals more than Germany's responsibility for and relationship to the Nazi past.[78] Debates on atonement and memory of the past divided society, but in the case of the FDP, it threatened to split the party.

This division had historic roots. During the Weimar Republic, two parties competed for the votes of liberals: the German Democratic Party (Deutsche Demokratische Partei, or DDP) and the German People's Party (Deutsche Volkspartei, or DVP). The Democratic Party enjoyed the electoral support of most German Jews, and many Jews became party members, including scientist Albert Einstein and Hugo Preuss, father of the Weimar constitution. The Democrats were committed to equal rights and denounced antisemitism. However, the Democratic Party's leadership feared being seen as the party of the Jews, and the DDP was considerably more timid than the Social Democrats about running Jewish candidates for office.[79] Irrespective of its tentativeness, the party remained the first choice of most German Jews until the liberal parties disintegrated during the Great Depression.

The other predecessor of the FDP did not have the same Jewish following. The opposition to antisemitism by the center-right German People's Party was tepid at best, and it did less than the DDP to combat anti-Jewish sentiment or to attract Jewish voters. The DVP's leader, Gustav Stresemann, did not endorse antisemitism, but he probably did share the popular dislike of Eastern European Jewry. Many of Stresemann's party colleagues were overt antisemites, and the People's Party never nominated a practicing Jew for national or statewide office. German Jews maintained a hesitant relationship with the DVP. While many wealthy and nationalistic Jews were inclined to support the party, its ambivalence about antisemitism, even within its own ranks, alienated other Jews. After Stresemann's death in 1929, the party drifted to the right, causing virtually all of its Jewish support to evaporate.[80]

---

[78] Heino Kaack, "Die FDP im politischen System der Bundesrepublik Deutschland," in ibid., 22–23.

[79] Hamburger and Pulzer, "Jews as Voters in the Weimar Republic," 10–13; Bruce Frye, *Liberal Democrats in the Weimar Republic: The History of the German Democratic Party and the German State Party* (Carbondale: Southern Illinois University Press, 1985), 3.

[80] Hamburger and Pulzer, "Jews as Voters in the Weimar Republic," 15–16 and 20–21; Niewyk, *Jews in Weimar Germany*, 73–74; Jonathan Wright, *Gustav Stresemann: Weimar's Greatest Statesman* (Oxford: Oxford University Press, 2002), 136-138 and 204.

The FDP combined elements of both of these parties, initially under Theodor Heuss, who had lifelong attachments to German Jewry. Like Social Democratic leader Kurt Schumacher, who grew up around Jews and befriended leftist Jewish intellectuals through his work, Theodor Heuss had a social circle and professional life that brought him into close contact with the pre-1933 German Jewish bourgeoisie. As a student, journalist, political science professor, and liberal democratic politician, Heuss counted innumerable Jews as friends and colleagues. Four and a half years after the war, looking back on his youth, Heuss said, "When I think of the four or five closest friends in my life, those who have accompanied me and helped build my life, two or three of them were Jews." He noted, however, that their religious heritage played no role in their friendship.[81] Religious or national differences never dictated who his friends were, and he pleaded for postwar Germans to transcend these distinctions in their own lives, judging each man on his character alone.[82]

As an academic and journalist before 1933, Heuss became an observer of the so-called German-Jewish symbiosis. He honored and analyzed aspects of this phenomenon by writing about its leading exponents. In 1906, on the fiftieth anniversary of Heinrich Heine's death, Heuss wrote of the "misfortune to be a baptized Jew," subjected to the criticisms of German nationalists.[83] Heuss wrote obituaries for the painter Joseph Israels, the parliamentarian Ludwig Frank, and the German foreign minister Walther Rathenau. He investigated the lives of the socialist revolutionary Gustav Landauer, the German nationalist Max Naumann, and the liberal democratic Reichstag deputy Ludwig Haas.[84] Through his involvement in the German Democratic Party, Heuss came into frequent contact with Jewish supporters of the party, including journalist Karl Marx.[85]

---

[81] Theodor Heuss, "Mut zur Liebe," *Die grossen Reden. Der Staatsmann* (Tübingen: Rainer Wunderlich, 1965), 102.

[82] Ibid., 103.

[83] Theodor Heuss, "Zum 17. Februar 1906," 18 February 1906, from *Die Hilfe*, reprinted in *An und über Juden*, 24.

[84] Theodor Heuss, "Joseph Israels†," 1911, from *Die Hilfe*; "Ludwig Frank†," 17 September 1914, from *Die Hilfe*; "Rathenau," July 1922, from *Die Deutsche Nation*; "Landauers politischer Nachlass," 15 June 1919, from *Das literarische Echo*; "Naumann, 'Der Nationaldeutsche Jude,'" 10 December 1921, from *Deutsche Politik*; "Dr. Ludwig Haas: Seine Persönlichkeit und sein Wirken," 7 August 1930, from *Israelitisches Familienblatt*; reprinted in *An und über Juden*, 41, 43, 62, 56, 61, and 65.

[85] Letter from Karl Marx to Theodor Heuss, 15 September 1949, BAK, B 122, 2086 (29).

After 1945, he maintained an extensive correspondence with German Jewish émigrés living in America and Israel.[86] Even after the war, he seemed to continue to conceive of the Jewish community in Germany in terms of its prewar existence: upper- and middle-class, intellectual, and proudly German and Jewish.[87]

In 1932, long before most, Heuss recognized that the Nazis were manipulating democratic processes and using pseudo-legal means to destroy German democracy. In his book *Hitlers Weg: Eine historisch-politische Studie über den Nationalsozialismus* (Hitler's Path: A Historical-Political Study of National Socialism), he exposed the methods used by the Nazis in their antisemitic campaign. The Nazis, he claimed, were hypocrites, denying German Jews their civic freedoms while defending the rights of ethnic Germans living scattered throughout Eastern Europe.[88] Heuss pointed out that the Nazi Party, acknowledging the influence and prestige of the churches in Germany, tried to take a neutral position on religion. However, the Nazis classified Judaism not as a religion but as race in order to deprive the Jews of their rights as German citizens.[89] He noted that the Nazis misused anthropological research to create a politicized racial theory, culminating in an obsession with "the Jew" and the idea of the subhuman (*Untermensch*).[90] Despite his prescient analysis of National Socialism, Heuss, as a liberal democratic Reichstag deputy, ostensibly bowed to party discipline and voted for the Enabling Act of 23 March 1933, granting Hitler unlimited powers. This decision, which Heuss later regretted, tainted his anti-Nazi credentials and cast a shadow over his later political career.[91] Additionally, Heuss, who saw the Nazis' violent antisemitism, did not resist their government in any tangible way. He withdrew from public life, going into so-called internal emigration.

---

[86] In 1958, Heuss received an honorary doctorate from the New School, now called New School University. Chartered in 1934, German Jews fleeing Hitler made up much of the institution's faculty.

[87] Heuss, "Mut zur Liebe," in *Die grossen Reden*, 103–106; Rosh Hashanah greetings, 2 August 1956, BAK, B 122, 2083 (29).

[88] Theodor Heuss, *Hitlers Weg. Eine historisch-politische Studie über den Nationalsozialismus* (Stuttgart: Union Deutsche Verlagsgesellschaft, 1932), 46.

[89] Ibid., 105–106.

[90] Ibid., 31–32 and 38.

[91] Theodor Heuss, *Die Machtergreifung und das Ermächtigungsgesetz. Zwei nachgelassene Kapitel der Erinnerungen, 1905–1933*, ed. Eberhard Pikart (Tübingen: Rainer Wunderlich, 1967), 23–25.

After 1949, as West German president, Heuss began to make up for his and other Germans' failings regarding their Jewish fellow citizens. He became the moral compass for many Germans in dealing with the Jewish question and enjoyed the respect and affection of Jews around the world. Karl Marx developed a close relationship with Heuss, and the Central Council considered him its principal ally in the government.[92] World Jewish Congress president Nahum Goldmann later described Heuss as the ideal representative of the new, antiauthoritarian, democratic Germany.[93]

While Theodor Heuss inspired great confidence, during the Federal Republic's early years, the national liberal wing of the FDP alienated many observers. Its relationship to the National Socialist past, including opposition to denazification, won many right-wing supporters. American Jewish observers feared the FDP's right wing, especially in northern Germany. North Rhine-Westphalian FDP leader Friedrich Middelhauve was the object of particular concern.[94] In his "German Program," written in July 1952, he argued that postwar liberals, raised during the Nazi dictatorship, not during the Weimar Republic, could not pick up where their parents had left off in 1933.[95] More troubling was the case of Werner Naumann, whom the British occupation authority accused of heading a neo-Nazi conspiracy.[96] While Naumann was not convicted of the charges, the investigation uncovered considerable neo-Nazi influence within the FDP, particularly in North Rhine-Westphalia and in Lower Saxony. Although the investigation implicated no high-ranking FDP leader, the party's reputation suffered considerably. After recovering from the scandal, however, the FDP was never again subject to such internal pressure for a radical turn to the right.[97] The party did, however, appeal to former German army officers, and Erich Mende, a highly decorated career army officer, represented the so-called war generation within the

---

[92] Theodor Heuss, "Vor einer schweren Aufgabe," undated [December 1956], BAK, B 122, 2065; "Protokoll des Zentralrates der Juden in Deutschland," 29–30 April 1951, ZA, B.1/7, 221.13.

[93] Goldmann, *Mein Leben als deutscher Jude*, 427.

[94] AJC report, 13 December 1952, CJH/YIVO, RG 347.7.1, box 38.

[95] Dieter Hein, "Der Weg nach Heppenheim," in *Verantwortung für die Freiheit*, ed. Mischnik, 57; Frei, *Vergangenheitspolitik*, 365.

[96] See Frei, *Vergangenheitspolitik*, 361–396.

[97] Theo Rütten, "Von der Plattform-Partei zur Partei des liberalen Programms 1949–1957," in *Verantwortung für die Freiheit*, ed. Mischnik, 73–74.

FDP.[98] Evaluating the party in 1952, the American Jewish Committee concluded that the FDP had given up its liberal heritage to appeal to rightist voters.[99]

While Middelhauve was on the far right of the party and unlikely to achieve national power, federal justice minister Thomas Dehler was a more realistic object of Jewish concern in the postwar era. A non-Jew, Dehler had enjoyed close ties to German Jewry before the war. His wife, law partners, and political mentors in the German Democratic Party were Jews. During the Third Reich, Dehler defended Jewish clients against charges leveled by the Nazis.[100] Following the war, he reentered politics, holding local and state offices before Konrad Adenauer named him federal minister of justice in 1949. After his rise to national prominence, however, Jewish observers became fearful of Dehler's rightward drift. While his behavior under the Third Reich had been "beyond reproach," he displayed an increasingly nationalist outlook, according to Arthur Meyer, chairman of the AJC's committee on Germany.[101] When attacked for indifference toward Jewish concerns, Dehler protested that Jewish issues were necessarily important to him, citing his Jewish wife as evidence.[102] Moreover, within the FDP, Dehler had a reputation for moderation and liberalism, in contrast to Middelhauve.[103] Some FDP leaders saw Dehler's Jewish wife as an encumbrance to the party's success. Wolfgang Döring, chief administrator of the North Rhine-Westphalian FDP, allegedly said, "Dehler must go. He has a Jew for a wife."[104] Ironically, Dehler's rise within the

---

98 Erich Mende, *Die FDP: Daten, Fakten, Hintergründe* (Stuttgart: Seewald, 1972), 24 and 29–30. As a young parliamentary deputy, concern for POWs and care for "war victims" – Germans who had suffered because of the war – were his chief interests.

99 AJC report, 7 July 1952, CJH/YIVO, RG 347.7.1, box 38.

100 Udo Wengst, *Thomas Dehler 1897–1967: Eine politische Biographie* (Munich: R. Oldenbourg, 1997), 43–45, 58, and 62. Dehler spent some time in jail after Kristallnacht, and he worked as a forced laborer as the war was ending.

101 "Memorandum," 28 March 1950, CJH/YIVO, RG 347.7.1, box 26.

102 "Bundesminister der Justiz antwortet Dr. Schumacher," *Allgemeine Wochenzeitung,* 17 November 1950.

103 Fliszar, "Mit der FDP regieren," in *Verantwortung für die Freiheit,* ed. Mischnik, 129.

104 This comment, allegedly made during a meeting of the local FDP in Düsseldorf, was recalled by Willi Weyer during a meeting of the FDP's federal board. "7.6.1953: Sitzung des Bundesvorstandes," 7 June 1953, Freie Demokratische Partei, Bundesvorstand, *FDP-Bundesvorstand: Die Liberalen unter dem Vorsitz von Theodor Heuss und Franz Blücher: Sitzungsprotokolle 1949–1954,* half-vol. 2: 27.-43. Sitzung 1953/54, ed. Udo Wengst, Quellen zur Geschichte des Parlamentarismus und der politischen Parteien, 4th series: Deutschland seit 1945, ed. Karl Dietrich Bracher, Rudolf Morsey, and Hans-Peter Schwarz, vol. 7/I (Düsseldorf: Droste, 1990), 1061 n. 25.

FDP and the West German government both worried Jewish observers and disappointed right-wing supporters of the FDP.

Despite a long tradition of support for equal rights for Jewish Germans, not to mention significant Jewish membership before 1933, the postwar reincarnation of the Weimar liberal parties, the Free Democratic Party, did not establish itself as the most philosemitic party. Even though some members, most notably Theodor Heuss, were overt advocates of Jewish interests, the party was, at best, ambivalent about German responsibility to the Jews after the Nazi years.

SPLINTER PARTIES OF THE RIGHT AND THE LEFT

In addition to the three major parties, a multiplicity of smaller political groups emerged once the Allies allowed the restoration of party politics, most notably in the American zone of occupation. Virtually every shade of political opinion, excepting outright National Socialism, manifested itself and competed to some degree in the public arena.[105] This situation persisted, and splinter parties held 20 percent of the seats in the first Bundestag (1949–1953). Although none of these parties was still represented in the Bundestag by 1958, they had a parliamentary presence as West Germany struggled to renew the German-Jewish political relationship. The most established of the minor parties was the Communist Party of Germany (Kommunistische Partei Deutschlands, or KPD), originally founded after World War I. Although the KPD exerted no influence over government policy formation, its mere presence in the Bundestag required that its voice be heard. Larger than the KPD were the German Party (Deutsche Partei, or DP) and the Bavarian Party (Bayernpartei, or BP). Even though the DP served in the governing coalition, it brought pressure to bear on the CDU from the right of the political spectrum. After 1950, another powerful splinter party exerted considerable influence in Bonn. The new Refugee Party (Block der Heimatvertriebenen und Entrechteten, or BHE) appealed specifically to Germans who had been expelled from their homes in Eastern and Central Europe.

---

[105] On Allied policy toward these splinter parties, see Daniel E. Rogers, "Transforming the German Party System: The United States and the Origins of Political Moderation, 1945–1949," *Journal of Modern History* 65, no. 3 (September 1993).

Although technically an interest-group party, this faction, represented in the governing coalition, exerted pressure on Adenauer's CDU, rendering that party increasingly conservative.

Under Hitler, the Communists suffered more than any other political party, and this experience shaped their postwar policy on reparations and the state's relationship to the Nazi past. It is believed that half the members of the KPD were persecuted under the Nazis, and in the Ruhr, a Communist electoral stronghold in the Weimar Republic, that figure reached 60 to 70 percent by 1940.[106] While many of the party's founders were Jewish intellectuals, in 1925–1926, under the leadership of Ernst Thälmann, the party adopted an anti-intellectual attitude. This new stance alienated many Jews on the political left.[107]

In the late 1940s and 1950s, the West German Communist Party maintained close, covert ties to the Soviet-dominated, Communist SED in East Germany. It elected representatives to the SED party executive and received instructions and funding from the SED politburo.[108] The KPD used its representation in the Bundestag not to effect change, but rather to obstruct legislation, and party members did not vote for West Germany's provisional constitution.[109] In the Bundestag, the party uniformly supported policies endorsed by Moscow and East Berlin, and this stance informed its view of the Jewish question. It could not transcend its rigid view of class conflict in commenting on the Holocaust. For a series in the *Jüdisches Gemeindeblatt* on the subject of political parties and the Jews, Louis Gymnich of the KPD wrote that in the concentration camps, Jewish capitalists were incapable of resistance, but Jews without means fought bravely. He added, "We must never forget how much the rich Jews contributed to the graves of Auschwitz and Maidanek by supporting Hindenburg."[110] For the Communists, even the murderous persecution of the Jews reflected a fixation on class conflict. The party opposed the reparations agreement

---

[106] Patrick Major, *The Death of the KPD: Communism and Anti-Communism in West Germany, 1945–1956* (Oxford: Clarendon, 1997), 29.

[107] Hamburger and Pulzer, "Jews as Voters in the Weimar Republic," 43–44.

[108] Major, *Death of the KPD*, 60–73.

[109] Ibid., 106–108.

[110] "Die Parteien und Wir: Deutsche ohne Antisemitismus," *Jüdisches Gemeindeblatt*, 25 June 1946. Gymnich was second deputy mayor of Cologne. In this quote he referred to Jewish support for conservative retired general Paul von Hindenburg in the German presidential election of 1932. Hindenburg's two opponents in the election were Adolf Hitler and Communist Party leader Ernst Thälmann.

with Israel, which it saw as enriching Jewish industrialists and serving American foreign-policy goals in the Middle East rather than aiding individual Holocaust survivors.[111]

Communists formed the majority of the Association of Victims of the Nazi Regime, which was technically a nonpartisan organization. The association wanted compensation for all victims of Nazi persecution – political and religious. Considering the group's sizable Jewish membership in West Germany, it is likely that some Jews were members of the party; however, most prewar Communists of Jewish ancestry who settled in Germany after the war chose to live in the Soviet zone and later East Germany. Moreover, anti-Communism was becoming more prevalent in western Germany, and in 1948 the SPD barred its members – including Jews – from belonging to the Communist-dominated organization. Although the West German government's attempts to ban the group in 1951 miscarried and provoked an international outcry, they did help to isolate it within West German political life.[112]

In 1947, after the dissolution of the Prussian state, Lower Saxon and Hannoverian nationalists founded the German Party (DP), and throughout its existence, that party's core constituency lay in northern Germany. Although highly conservative, it was not National Socialist, and some of its supporters had opposed the Nazis from the political right. The party, opposing socialization of the economy and critical of denazification, participated in the governing federal coalition, even though it disapproved of the West German constitution.[113] Its most prominent member was Hans-Christoph Seebohm, Adenauer's transportation minister and a conservative nationalist. Not adverse to invoking the Nazi past, Seebohm was a favorite of the DP's right wing.[114] For the purpose

---

[111] "Ratifizierung im Deutschen Bundestag," 18 March 1953, *Der deutsch-israelische Dialog: Dokumentation eines erregenden Kapitels deutscher Außenpolitik*, Part I: *Politik*, vol. 1, ed. Rolf Vogel (Munich: K. G. Saur, 1987), 114–116.

[112] Major, *Death of the KPD*, 216–217. For more information on Jewish Communists in the Soviet zone and East Germany, see Lothar Mertens, *Davidstern unter Hammer und Zirkel*, and Mario Keßler, *Die SED und die Juden*.

[113] Dennis Bark and David Gress, *A History of West Germany*, vol. 1: *From Shadow to Substance 1945–1963*, 2nd ed. (Oxford: Blackwell, 1993), 239; Hermann Meyn, *Die Deutsche Partei: Entwicklung und Problematik einer national-konservativen Rechtspartei nach 1945* (Düsseldorf: Droste, 1965), 21–30.

[114] See chapter 4. "Stenographische Niederschrift der Tonbandaufnahme von der Rede des Bundesministers Dr. Seebohm," 2 December 1951, BAK, N 1178, 22, 42–45; Meyn, *Die Deutsche Partei*, 33–36.

of restitution to the Jews, he did not want any German-owned property to be confiscated. He wanted all property in Germany to revert to its owners as of 8 May 1945. Furthermore, he explicitly equated the "injustices" suffered by Sudeten Germans with the crimes committed against the Jews by the Nazis.[115] Whether Seebohm was an antisemite remains unclear, but he seemed insensitive to the Jews' suffering and oblivious to the transgressions committed in the name of the German people. His party initially opposed reparations talks with Israel but soon endorsed them.[116] In fact, its Bundestag caucus divided evenly on the reparations to Israel, and Seebohm even opposed reparations to individual Jews, drawing an angry reaction from Jewish leaders.[117] German Party Bundestag deputy and former Nazi Wolfgang Hedler was prosecuted – and acquitted – for having made seemingly antisemitic comments in a newspaper interview about the mass murder of the Jews.[118] While the DP's state branches were replete with former Nazis, national chairman and federal cabinet minister Heinrich Hellwege insisted on drawing a clear line between his party and the Nazi Party. In the Hedler case, Hellwege did not even wait for the verdict before expelling Hedler from the party.[119] He did, however, resent the continued intervention of Allied occupation authorities in combating neo-Nazi political tendencies, and the party's policies generally appealed to former Nazi Party members.[120] Small parties such as the DP had a limited constituency and limited effectiveness. Over time, its voters and leaders joined either the CDU or the FDP as these parties co-opted much of the DP's program.[121]

The Bavarian Party (BP) remained exclusively regional in its appeal. Founded in the autumn of 1946 by Bavarian nationalists

---

[115] Letter from Hans-Christoph Seebohm to Hendrik George van Dam, 8 June 1953, forwarded to Theodor Heuss by Karl Marx, BAK, B 122, 2080 (26).

[116] "Eine destruktive Polemik," *Allgemeine Wochenzeitung*, 21 September 1951; Gardner Feldman, *Special Relationship*, 58.

[117] Five for reparations, five against, and ten abstentions. "Namentliche Abstimmungen," during "262. Sitzung," 18 March 1953, *Verhandlungen des Deutschen Bundestages, I. Wahlperiode 1949*, 15:12292; "Die Deutschen und die anderen," *Allgemeine Wochenzeitung*, 5 June 1953.

[118] Frei, *Vergangenheitspolitik*, 309–325; AJC report "The Adenauer Interview," 15 December 1949, CJH/YIVO, RG 347.7.1, box 34.

[119] Frei, *Vergangenheitspolitik*, 312; Meyn, *Die Deutsche Partei*, 32.

[120] Frei, *Vergangenheitspolitik*, 372; Meyn, *Die Deutsche Partei*, 27. The German Party favored reinstatement of former Nazi civil servants dismissed in 1945 and the equation of former Waffen SS members with regular army soldiers for purposes of pensions and legal status.

[121] Meyn, *Die Deutsche Partei*, 43 and 58–59.

and disaffected members of the CSU, it had precedent in a similar political faction during the Weimar Republic. It combined confederational sentiment with Bavarian monarchism, and the state of Bavaria never properly ratified the West German constitution.[122] Bavaria teemed with Germans deported from the Sudetenland and Silesia, Jewish Holocaust survivors, and Germans who had come to rural Bavaria to avoid Allied bomb attacks on north German cities. According to the 1946 census, nearly one-quarter of the population had not lived in Bavaria before 1 September 1939.[123] Some scholars have seen the BP's success, in part, as a protest vote by local residents against the refugees.[124] As a special-interest group and opposition party in the Bundestag, the BP rarely dealt with questions concerning the Jews or German-Jewish relations. In 1953, the BP's Bundestag caucus, by then called the Federalist Union, accepted reparations to the Jews in theory but rejected the agreement with Israel signed in September 1952, claiming that collective reparations would preclude reparations to individual victims. In fact, three deputies voted for the treaty, while thirteen abstained. Purely a protest party, the BP soon lost its rasion d'être and ceased to be a factor in national or Bavarian politics.

Although the Refugee Party (BHE) claimed to be neither on the right nor the left, it exerted a decidedly conservative influence on the governing coalition. The party's platform proclaimed, "The BHE is not a capitalist or a workers' party. It is neither 'left' nor 'center' nor 'right,' but rather the party of law, of human rights, and of international law."[125] In 1952, party leader Waldemar Kraft

[122] Ilsa Unger, *Die Bayernpartei. Geschichte und Struktur 1945–1957*, Studien zur Zeitgeschichte, vol. 16 (Stuttgart: Deutsche Verlags-Anstalt, 1979), 138–154. The late Weimar-era Bavarian People's Party had a record of antisemitism, but in Bavaria at that time the only other effective electoral option was the Nazi Party, and many Jews voted for the lesser evil. Hamburger and Pulzer, "Jews as Voters in the Weimar Republic," 16 and 29–30.

[123] Unger, *Die Bayernpartei*, 16.

[124] Werner Kaltefleiter, *Wirtschaft und Politik in Deutschland. Konjunktur als Bestimmungsfaktor des Parteiensystems* (Cologne: Westdeutscher, 1966), 130–131. Unger notes the positive correlation between a large refugee population and BP success in electoral districts but disputes the necessary cause and effect. Unger, *Die Bayernpartei*, 109.

[125] "Kieler Programm," 8 January 1950, quoted in York R. Winkler, *Flüchtlingsorganisationen in Hessen 1945–1954. BHE – Flüchtlingsverbände – Landsmannschaften* (Wiesbaden: Historische Kommission für Nassau, 1998), 356; Pertti Tapio Ahonen, "The Expellee Organizations and West German Ostpolitik, 1949–1969," Ph.D. diss., Yale University, 1999.

justified his interest party's existence by claiming that the Allied occupiers had created the existing political parties from the remnants of discredited Weimar-era groups, acting as if the intervening years had not existed.[126] Founded in January 1950 as a reaction to the larger parties' unresponsiveness to German refugees' demands, the BHE quickly made known its potential as a protest party. In state elections in Schleswig-Holstein in July 1950, it won over 23 percent of the vote, and in Lower Saxony in May 1951, it won 15 percent.[127] Adenauer took notice of this electoral force, and it participated in the federal government coalition from 1953 to 1956.[128] Although many of the BHE's leaders had been members of the Nazi Party and the party overtly recruited former Nazis, its leadership denounced extremist political activity and wholeheartedly supported the new West German republic.[129] The party strongly supported the Equalization of Burdens (*Lastenausgleich*) program, which heavily taxed those with property in order to aid those who were propertyless, including German refugees from the east. Jewish groups opposed the program. Just as impoverished Jews regained houses previously confiscated from them by the Nazi German government, they had to sell those properties simply to pay the equalization taxes.[130] On foreign policy, the BHE was highly conservative, most of its supporters having lost homes in the east. Some party members joined the Naumann circle, which had driven

126 Franz Neumann, *Block der Heimatvertriebenen und Entrechteten 1950–1960. Ein Beitrag zur Geschichte und Struktur einer politischen Interessenpartei* (Meisenheim: Anton Hain, 1968), 22–23.

127 Neumann, *Block der Heimatvertriebenen*, 20–27; Winkler, *Flüchtlingsorganisationen in Hessen*, 275; Ahonen, "The Expellee Organizations," 90–91; "Bis hierher und nicht weiter!," *Allgemeine Wochenzeitung*, 25 May 1951. As a result of party defections, the BHE gained four seats in the first Bundestag. Neumann, *Block der Heimatvertriebenen*, 47 and 64.

128 Neumann, *Block der Heimatvertriebenen*, 65, 92, and 96–113; Ahonen, "The Expellee Organizations," 106–114. In 1952, trying to widen its appeal, the BHE adopted the name Gesamtdeutscher Block/BHE. The GB/BHE received little more than 5 percent in the only federal election in which it participated (1953).

129 Neumann, *Block der Heimatvertriebenen*, 24–25, 66–67, and 325–334; Bark and Gress, *A History of West Germany*, 1:308–309. All three national party chairmen and five state party chairmen had been in the Nazi Party or in Nazi organizations.

130 Bark and Gress, *A History of West Germany*, 1:310; "Instrument einheitlicher Willensbildung," *Allgemeine Wochenzeitung*, 5 September 1952; letter from Karl Marx to Thomas Dehler, 11 November 1950, BAK, B 136, 5862. Approved in May 1952, the program taxed all property in West Germany at a rate of 50 percent of its value on 21 June 1948. Property owners had thirty years to pay, and most of the revenue went to compensate refugees for lost property in the east. For more information on this program to recreate the prewar distribution of property, see Hughes, *Shouldering the Burdens of Defeat*.

the FDP so far to the right.[131] By the late 1950s, Adenauer's CDU had absorbed most of the BHE's voters and adopted a decidedly conservative profile itself.[132]

The legacy of the Nazi years raised complicated and sensitive political issues integral to postwar German political identity. As competing claims to victimhood and debates on memory of the past enveloped West German politics, the issues of accountability for the Nazis' crimes and the place of Jews in postwar Germany loomed in the background. For the small and impoverished Jewish community, struggling for survival, these issues assumed critical importance. Facing isolation from their foreign coreligionists, the Jews in Germany needed support from the West German state. However, there was no consensus among political elites or politically active Germans regarding responsibility to the Jews.

Honest Germans could not deny the crimes committed against the Jews, but the nature of politics and society in postwar Germany precluded any swift and universally supported action in favor of the Jews. Many Germans, if not most, preferred to leave the past behind them without further reflection, while others still harbored antisemitic sentiments. Millions of former Nazi Party supporters had been left with no political home, and they represented a decisive constituency after 1945. The major political parties faced the dilemma of appealing to these voters or confronting Germany's moral debts.

The Social Democrats under Kurt Schumacher took a blunt and courageous stance in supporting renewed Jewish life in Germany and immediate reparations to Jews. As a result, some Jews entered Social Democratic politics, and many others voted for the party. Christian Democratic leader Adenauer took a more cautious stance, reflective of his political constituency. He supported the reestablishment of the Jewish community in West Germany, but he did not initially press the issue of German guilt for the Holocaust or German reparations to survivors of the Holocaust. Moreover, many within Adenauer's own political

---

[131] Letter from Karl Marx to Landesverband Nordrhein and British report, 22 February 1955, ZA, B.1/15, 296. On the BHE's effect on West German foreign policy under Adenauer, see Ahonen, "The Expellee Organizations," chaps. 4–6.

[132] Henry Ashby Turner, *Germany from Partition to Reunification* (New Haven: Yale University Press, 1992), 130; Bark and Gress, *A History of West Germany*, 1:308.

party had compromised pasts or showed outright hostility to Jewish issues. The liberal Free Democrats divided between left liberals, for whom civil rights and moral justice were imperative, and national liberals, who wanted to put the past behind them and who tried to exploit the electoral potential of former Nazi Party supporters.

CHAPTER 5

Jewish Organization between State and Party in East Germany

On 7 October 1949, four months after the foundation of a democratic West German state, the German Democratic Republic (GDR) came into being, and a Communist-dominated, German government took over administration of the Soviet occupation zone. During the era of Soviet occupation, with competing claims to victimhood and ideological fluidity, obtaining official support for the needs of the Jewish community had not been easy. However, the new government, dominated as it was by the SED, presented the Jewish community with a new and even more challenging situation. Myriad factors contributed to the increased difficulty. Chief among these were the basic Communist attitude to religion, an underlying miscomprehension of Judaism and the Jewish community, antisemitism, and Cold War tensions in a divided Germany.

The role of religion in a society dominated by an officially atheist political party was fraught with ambiguity, and this uncertainty extended to religious communities other than the Jewish one. Communist officials, for example, also feared the independence of the Protestant Church's hierarchy.[1] In making demands on the government, religious groups frequently invoked the GDR constitution, and SED officials debated their obligation to the churches.[2] While paragraph one of article 45 repealed all previously existing agreements with the religious communities, paragraph two stated:

The property as well as the other rights of the religious communities and religious associations regarding institutions, foundations, and

---

[1] Fulbrook, *Anatomy of a Dictatorship*, 93–94.
[2] Letter from Georgino (Finance Ministry) to Otto Grotewohl, 17 August 1951, BAB, DO 4, 2224.

miscellaneous wealth for their religious, educational, and welfare activities will be protected.[3]

Interpretation of this clause set up a fierce debate within the SED. The Finance Ministry did not wish to honor agreements made by previous German governments with religious organizations, but the government's Main Division for Ties to the Churches did.[4]

While the East German constitution protected freedom of religion and banned discrimination based on one's religion, five of the eight constitutional articles dealing with freedom of religion addressed freedom *from* religion, at least in part.[5] In July 1950, the SED drafted a law standardizing the procedure for withdrawing from a religious community.[6] The government went to great pains to ensure that religious dissenters and atheists found the most comfortable atmosphere possible. From the constitution one could have easily gained the impression that Germany had a long history of compulsory and oppressive church membership, when, in fact, persecution of the churches had been one of the most pressing issues in Germany's recent history.

While all religious groups faced certain fundamental difficulties from the East German regime, the Jewish community's situation was unique. Not only were SED party functionaries and the central police antagonistic to organized religious groups, more specifically, many of them knew next to nothing about Judaism or the Jews' needs. This fundamental ignorance engendered misunderstanding and distrust and certainly did not aid the Jews in their quest for support. Even those SED officials who were not openly antisemitic, including East Berlin mayor Friedrich Ebert, displayed hostility and a marked lack of sympathy to the concerns of the local Jewish community.[7] Organs of the state charged with knowing

---

3 Germany (East), *Gesetzblatt der Deutschen Demokratischen Republik: Jahrgang 1949* (Berlin: Deutscher Zentralverlag, 1949), 9.

4 Letter from Georgino (Finance Ministry) to Otto Grotewohl, 17 August 1951, BAB, DO 4, 2224.

5 Articles 42.2, 44.1, 46.1, 47.1, and 48.1 all guaranteed protection from religious compulsion and provided for self-determined legal withdrawal from religious communities, even for children as young as fifteen.

6 "Zweite Durchführungsbestimmung zu Verordnung über den Austritt aus Religionsgemeinschaften des öffentlichen Rechts vom 13.7.1950," 13 July 1950, BAB, DO 4, 307, 276 and 283.

7 Letter from Friedrich Ebert to small secretariat of the SED party board, 21 March 1950, BAB (SAPMO), DY 30/IV 2/14, 11, 81; letter from Benzmann to Alfred Neumann, 22 October 1953, BAB (SAPMO), DY 30/IV 2/14, 249, 47; letter from Hermann Baden

about all aspects of society failed to comprehend the situation of the Jews. Central police files evince misconceptions about Jewish religious practices: "During prayer hours they bind their hands and hang a prayer box of wood around the neck. Every Friday is a day of fasting. It is a religious requirement that one not cut meat with a knife." One internal police report claimed that the Jews' "world headquarters" was located in "Jerusalem/Palestine." The same report noted that gaining membership in the Jewish community was very difficult.[8] When Otto Grotewohl sent the community Rosh Hashanah greetings in 1951, his note focused less on the Jews themselves and more on the joint antifascist struggle for a democratic, independent Germany.[9] Both the rituals and the temperament of the Jewish community remained alien to SED leaders, and they made little effort in the early 1950s to inform themselves of the truth.

Additionally, the international political situation complicated the Jews' situation. As Israel drifted into America's political orbit, Communist policy regarding the Jewish state grew increasingly hostile. Attacks on Zionism in the eastern bloc were, to a large degree, a symbolic proxy attack on America. This factor, combined with antisemitic attitudes by Communist leaders, including Joseph Stalin's antisemitic paranoia, culminated in a wave of anti-Jewish persecution throughout Eastern Europe. Jewish Communists and Jewish communal officials were purged from their positions of power, placed on trial, and imprisoned or executed. Tragically, the GDR, where many Jews had hoped to build a new, tolerant, antifascist Germany was not exempt, and in 1953, the Jewish community there was decimated.

Considering these hostile conditions, how did the Jewish community manage to rebuild itself in the years before the purge? There was one factor working in the Jews' favor. Despite the SED's dominating position, the government of the German Democratic Republic did technically remain a multiparty coalition, which allowed the Jews a chance to receive a non-Communist, governmental hearing. The SED had a monopoly on power and used it to

to Otto Nuschke, 22 October 1953, CJA, 5 B 1, 8, 91; letter from Helmut Enke to Friedrich Ebert, 26 October 1953, CJA, 5 B 1, 8, 90. Friedrich Ebert bore the same name as his father, the first president of the Weimar Republic.

[8] "Jüdische Gemeinde," undated, BAB, DO 1/11.0, 864, 5–6.

[9] Letter from Otto Grotewohl to the State Association, 1 October 1951, CJA, 5 B 1, 11, 80.

imprison its perceived political enemies. However, in those aspects of policy where the SED did not exercise its dominance, including the day-to-day supervision of religious institutions, non-Communist administrators did have a degree of latitude. Even historians stressing the interconnectedness of party and state in the GDR recognize that "[l]ocal citizens, ... pastors and others might all find dealing with state functionaries, who could maintain a façade of some separation from the SED, more acceptable than dealing with the SED."[10] Such was the case with the Jewish leadership of eastern Germany.

NEW ALLIES IN A NEW STATE

With the formal establishment of an East German regime in the fall of 1949, the State Association had to look to the new government for support of Jewish interests, but Julius Meyer and the State Association benefited from the technical configuration of the East German republic. Meanwhile, Heinz Galinski, the leader of Berlin Jewry, remained in touch with the mayor of Greater Berlin (i.e., East Berlin), Friedrich Ebert. Because of Berlin's special political status under continuing four-power occupation, administration of the divided city did not technically fall under the purview of the either of the new German states. At that time, the office of the East Berlin mayor, not the government of the German Democratic Republic, remained responsible for supervision of the Jewish community in East Berlin.

On 23 February 1950, Galinski wrote Ebert asking for regular subsidies for the community. The community, which had been founded in 1945, now needed financial help. The currency reform of 30 June 1948 had left it practically broke. Ebert was firmly against state funding for the churches. On 21 March, he wrote to the SED leadership on this matter. He denied that the city had any responsibility toward the churches. That was a matter for the state government. In any event, the Berlin SED opposed any retroactive subsidies but left the question of future subsidies for the politburo to decide. In fact, Ebert wanted to create a financial situation that would humiliate the churches. If the state paid subsidies to the churches, he wanted them to be forced to make their finances

---

[10] Fulbrook, *Anatomy of a Dictatorship*, 44.

public so that everyone could see that the religious communities were unable to pay their debts, despite the church tax. He also did not want any East Berlin subsidies going to West Berlin churches.[11]

Concerning the German Democratic Republic proper, Julius Meyer wasted no time in addressing the new government with the community's concerns. The small communities had been tardy in pressing their claims for restitution or the return of communal property, and at least one state government did not wish to honor claims filed after the legal deadline. Faced with this petty intransigence, in November 1949, Meyer wrote to the Interior Ministry because some state governments were dilatory in returning Jewish property confiscated by the Nazis.[12] Throughout December 1949 and January 1950, the Jewish communities of East Germany communicated with Meyer, and Meyer and Eisenstaedt corresponded with the Interior Ministry's Office for the Protection of the People's Property (Amt zum Schutz des Volkseigentums) about reclaiming Jewish property throughout East Germany; the conflict would linger on into late 1951.[13] In an era when the Soviets and the East Germans were nationalizing property, the Jews had to proceed very carefully to regain the property they had lost.

Funding Jewish life preoccupied the State Association and drew the attention of the SED. In January 1950, Meyer contacted the Communist state secretary of finance to request funding totaling one million marks from the government for social welfare projects and religious functions. Moreover, Meyer urged the ministry to take into account the impact of the "extermination action of the fascist state" on the Jewish community. Invoking articles 43 and 45 of the GDR's constitution, Meyer repeated the request in September and October.[14] In the spring of 1950 the SED's Taskforce for Church Matters (Arbeitsgruppe Kirchenfragen) prepared a report on the Jews' financial situation.[15] In 1949 Jewish communal

---

[11] Letter from Heinz Galinski and A. Borchardt to Friedrich Ebert, 23 February 1950; letter from Friedrich Ebert to small secretariat of the SED party board, 21 March 1950; BAB (SAPMO), DY 30/IV 2/14, 11, 80–81.

[12] Letter from Julius Meyer to Interior Ministry, 19 November 1949, CJA, 5 B 1, 107, 42.

[13] Various correspondence, CJA, 5 B 1, 107, 1, 4, 7, 8, 19, 21, 23, 34, and 36.

[14] Letter from Julius Meyer to Willy Rumpf (Finance Ministry), 2 January 1950; letter from Julius Meyer to Otto Nuschke, 2 October 1950; letters from Julius Meyer to SKK Informationsdienst, 27 October and 6 November 1950; CJA, 5 B 1, 28, 144, 150, 152, and 154.

[15] "Vermerk," 26 April 1950, BAB (SAPMO), DY 30/IV 2/14, 11, 83.

groups had received 40,000 marks from the state and collected no church taxes. In 1950 Meyer wanted the state to furnish 80,000 marks for salaries, 250,000 marks for cemeteries, 125,000 marks for synagogue construction, 45,000 marks for general expenses, and 500,000 marks for maintenance of religious and cultural duties.[16] True independence for this autonomous organization was not feasible.

Official funding was critical for the survival of Jewish institutions, and they needed to find favor with the government if they were to have long-term viability. The principal government office responsible for the religious communities in East Germany was the Main Division for Ties to the Churches (Hauptabteilung Verbindung zu den Kirchen), established in January 1950 under deputy prime minister Otto Nuschke, a Christian Democrat. Otto Nuschke and his staff became the East German Jewish community's leading patrons.

Otto Nuschke was an atypical East German politician. An active liberal politician and party administrator in imperial Germany, he had been a Reichstag deputy for the left liberal German Democratic Party during the Weimar republic, and the Nazis arrested him repeatedly for his aid to persecuted Jews. After the war, he and Jakob Kaiser founded the Christian Democratic Union in eastern Germany, and Nuschke became head of the party after Kaiser's flight to the west in 1948. Nuschke served as deputy prime minister and head of the office for church matters from 1949 to 1957. Unlike SED members and many East German Christian Democrats, Nuschke did not initially advocate a pro-Soviet line, even on the questions of German reunification and unitary election lists.[17]

While the SED and its functionaries had a turbulent relationship with the Jews, Nuschke's office did not exhibit the antisemitism displayed by many SED officials. Despite occasional expressions of antisemitism, the eastern Christian Democratic Union had generally good relations with the Jews, unlike the SED.[18] The American

---

[16] Letter from Julius Meyer to SKK Informationsdienst, 27 October 1950, CJA, 5 B 1, 28, 150. All currency figures are in East German marks unless otherwise specified.

[17] Nuschke began supporting Soviet and SED policy on these critical issues only in the spring and summer of 1950. Michael Richter, *Die Ost-CDU 1948–1952. Zwischen Widerstand und Gleichschaltung* (Düsseldorf: Droste, 1990), 241–248 and 377–378.

[18] On eastern CDU antisemitism, see Richter, *Die Ost-CDU*, 178.

Jewish Committee called Nuschke "one of the few remaining relatively honest democrats in the Soviet Zone puppet government."[19] In June 1950, the State Association wrote the CDU to congratulate it on its party congress. Arnold Gohr, chairman of the East Berlin CDU and later deputy mayor of East Berlin, wrote back to thank the Jews, adding, "We will always strive to join in representing your interests in Berlin to the utmost."[20] Even if Gohr was neither overtly philosemitic nor politically close to Nuschke, he had warm relations with the Jewish community, and over the years, the community maintained a friendly correspondence with him.[21] Another prominent CDU member was Heinz Fried, the Jewish director of Berlin's water works. The allegedly pro-Communist Fried was active in VVN affairs on behalf of the eastern CDU.[22] The Berlin CDU's party publications also paid attention to Jewish affairs.[23] Despite Communist antisemitism, for many years the Jews benefited from having a non-Communist sympathizer in the East German government.

In January 1950, the deputy prime minister's office set up the Main Division for Ties to the Churches based on the former Prussian Education and Art Ministry's bureaus for church matters, and the State Association immediately looked to Nuschke and his staff to mediate conflicts with the East German authorities. In March 1950, Meyer lobbied Nuschke to allow Jewish prison inmates to have visits from a rabbi as previously promised by GDR president Wilhelm Pieck.[24] In April, Nuschke's office contacted the central administration of the People's Police because police authorities in Dresden did not accept the recognition granted the local Jewish community by the Soviet occupiers, and the Jewish community refused to subject itself to the vagaries of the administrative

---

[19] AJC report, CJH/YIVO, RG 347.7.1 (AJC, FAD 1), box 35.
[20] Letter from Arnold Gohr to State Association, 14 June 1950, CJA, 5 B 1, 4, 49. Julius Meyer's well-wishing to the CDU might not have been merely a matter of State Association business. Meyer was an SED member, and at the eastern CDU's party congress in September 1950, the Christian Democrats drew markedly closer to the Communists. Richter, *Die Ost-CDU,* 289.
[21] Letter from Arnold Gohr to Julius Meyer, 30 December 1952, CJA, 5 B 1, 11, 2. Nuschke felt Gohr was pro-Soviet and tried to prevent him from becoming head of the East Berlin CDU. Richter, *Die Ost-CDU,* 154.
[22] Letter from Heinz Fried to Julius Meyer, 19 June 1950, CJA, 5 B 1, 4, 128. On his pro-Communist sympathies, see Richter, *Die Ost-CDU,* 211.
[23] BAB, DO 4, 2128.
[24] Letter from Julius Meyer to Otto Nuschke, 3 March 1950, CJA, 5 B 1, 1, 3.

process by reapplying. By early May, the Dresden police had withdrawn the demand.[25]

Soon after its establishment, the Main Division for Ties to the Churches strengthened its link to the Jewish community by appointing a specialist for Jewish affairs. On 19 April 1950, Main Division director Kurt Grünbaum notified Nuschke that Albert Hirsch, an SED member and concentration camp survivor, had received the post, and by autumn Nuschke's closest aides were praising Hirsch's work.[26] Hirsch administered funding for State Association activities and the reconstruction of Jewish institutions, as well as reviewed requests made by Jewish communal officials for travel outside East Germany.[27] Nuschke preferred to fund the individual Jewish communities centrally through the State Association. However, the communities preferred to deal directly with Nuschke's office.[28] When the State Association felt that Jewish interests were threatened, its leadership turned to Nuschke's staff for help. During the summer of 1951, the East Berlin municipal abattoir forbade kosher slaughtering. Meyer wrote to Hirsch, asking for help and accusing the slaughterhouse's veterinary experts of antisemitism. Hirsch investigated the matter, rejected their claim to be upholding a 1935 law for the protection of animals, and resolved it to the Jews' satisfaction.[29] Limited by the regime's view of autonomous organizations and pervasive antisemitism, the State Association needed the support of key individuals, such as Nuschke and Hirsch, if it were to achieve its goals.

In contrast to many SED party members, Nuschke and his lieutenants were sensitive to the Jewish community's material and moral needs. On 28 September 1951, Nuschke sent the State Association a letter expressing his best wishes for Rosh Hashanah and acknowledging the necessity of healing the wounds of racial

[25] Letter from *Oberreferent* Leibau to Hauptverwaltung Deutsche Volkspolizei, 11 April 1950; letter from Dr.h.c. Fischer to Otto Nuschke, 3 May 1950; BAB, DO 1/11.0, 864, 1 and 4.

[26] "Referats-Verteilung, Hauptabteilung Verbindung zu den Kirchen," 19 April 1950; letter from Kurt Grünbaum to Otto Nuschke, 26 September 1950; "Gewährung von Leistungszulagen," 10 October 1950; BAB, DC 20, 956, 1, 14, and 20.

[27] "Stellenplan für die Hauptabteilung Verbindung zu den Kirchen ab 1. Januaur 1951," 20 September 1950, BAB, DC 20, 956, 13.

[28] Letter from the State Association to Otto Nuschke, 23 July 1951, BAB, DO 4, 2128. While some communities wanted funding for new construction, others wanted support for the preservation of cemeteries.

[29] Letter from Julius Meyer to Albert Hirsch, 14 August 1951; report by Albert Hirsch, 17 August 1951; CJA, 5 B 1, 6, 527 and 531–532.

hatred.[30] Hirsch kept the deputy prime minister apprised of the Jewish community's condition. Touring the country that autumn, Hirsch saw the poverty of the Jewish communities. In particular, he cited the community of Magdeburg, which remained impoverished and unable to support itself, even though the community had received a building in accordance with Soviet military order no. 82.[31] The Jewish communities of East Germany relied heavily on state funding, but there were limits on the use of government funds, which Grünbaum described to the State Association on 19 December 1951. The Jews could use funds from Nuschke's office for the construction of synagogues and the restoration of cemeteries, "in so far as it concerns a singular arrangement. The fund cannot be used for running maintenance."[32] The East German government wanted to correct the disgrace of the Nazi era by helping to rebuild and to restore Jewish institutions that all could see. The government was less interested in covering a religious community's overhead.

Despite these reservations, Otto Nuschke's office was generous in the dispensation of funds to Jewish groups, and they knew it. Nuschke's correspondence shows that the office continued to fund some communities even after they had exceeded their allotments. While Hirsch was worried that the communities would misuse the funds, he did understand the Jews' difficult situation.[33] Meyer frequently praised Nuschke. At a meeting of the State Association on 15 June 1952, he remarked that "Mr. Otto Nuschke regards us benevolently in every way, and we can count on him any time."[34] The files of the State Secretariat for Church Matters reveal just how generous Nuschke's office was to the Jewish communities. In 1951, he put 200,000 marks at their disposal, and in 1952 they were granted 300,000 marks. His office even made at least 1,250 marks available to the Jewish community in Dresden to buy an organ.[35]

[30] Letter from Otto Nuschke to the State Association, 28 September 1951, CJA, 5 B 1, 11, 78.
[31] Report by Albert Hirsch, 2 November 1951, BAB, DO 4, 2126.
[32] Letter from Kurt Grünbaum to State Association, 19 December 1951, CJA, 5 B 1, 28, 46.
[33] "Ergebnis der Überprüfung des Verwendungsnachweises über die Bauhilfe 1951 für die Synagoge-Gemeinde zu Magdeburg," 22 January 1952, BAB, DO 4, 2126.
[34] "Protokoll über die am 15.6.52 stattgefundene Tagung des Landesverbandes der Jüdischen Gemeinden in der Deutschen Demokratischen Republik," 24 June 1952, CJA, 5 B 1, 31, 33.
[35] "Zur Veröffentlichung im Weg," 24 June 1952, CJA, 5 B 1, 31, 25; letter from Albert Hirsch to the State Association, 30 August 1951, BAB, DO 4, 2128; handwritten annotation from

STORM CLOUDS GATHER OVER THE STATE ASSOCIATION

Beginning in 1951, the Jews of Eastern Europe, particularly Jewish Communists, had reason to be nervous. Within both East Germany and Eastern Europe, antisemitism reared its ugly head, often with deadly consequences. Jewish communists fell under suspicion all across the Soviet bloc, and in East Germany, where the communal leaders were often Communists, any fall from favor had potentially negative consequences for the Jewish community as a whole.

With the goal of rooting out so-called cosmopolitanism, the SED central committee instituted a review of party members. On 1 June 1951, a special review board of the Saxon SED pressured Helmut Eschwege to renounce "Jewish" as his nationality and to claim he was "German" by ethnicity. In his memoirs, Eschwege noted that the Sorbs, a small Slavic group in far eastern Germany, did not receive pressure to renounce their heritage. In fact, many assimilated Sorbs were forced to accept Sorbian nationality status rather than German. Only the Jews had to renounce their heritage.[36]

In September 1951, the position of Jewish communists took a turn for the worse. As part of a thoroughgoing purge of Jews from leadership positions in Czechoslovakia, the central committee of the Czechoslovak Communist Party removed Rudolf Slánský, a Jew, from his position as first secretary of the party.[37] Although reassigned to serve as deputy prime minister, the removal signaled the start of Slánský's persecution. He was initially charged with encouraging American imperialism and fostering Titoism, a cardinal sin against Stalinist communism, and during his trial, the Czech press linked him with Zionism.[38] The accusations and

7 July 1952 on a letter from Jüdische Gemeinde Dresden to Albert Hirsch, 26 June 1952, BAB, DO 4, 2128. For more information on this office, established later to supplant the Hauptabteilung Verbindung zu den Kirchen, see Offenberg, *"Seid vorsichtig gegen die Machthaber,"* 130–149.

36 Eschwege, *Fremd unter meinesgleichen*, 66–67. For a more comprehensive comparison of East German policy toward Sorbs and Jews, see Cora Ann Granata, "Celebration and Suspicion: Sorbs and Jews in the Soviet Occupied Zone and German Democratic Republic, 1945–1989," Ph.D. diss., University of North Carolina, Chapel Hill, 2001.

37 "Report on the Sitting of the Central Committee of the Communist Party of Czechoslovakia," 6 September 1951, in Josefa Slánská, *Report on My Husband*, trans. Edith Pargeter (New York: Atheneum, 1969), 10–12.

38 "The People Demand Extreme Punishment for the Accomplices of the Imperialist Murderers. Let the Traitors Hear the Stern Verdict of the People," 24 November 1952, in ibid., 28.

investigation, which veered into overt antisemitism, culminated in a show trial of fourteen defendants, eleven of whom were Jewish. Ultimately, the court condemned three non-Jews and eight Jews to death, including Slánský.[39]

If Julius Meyer, an SED member, needed any reminder of the need to curry favor with Communist authorities, the purge of Slánský served as such. In fact, Meyer was occasionally willing to do the party's bidding – even if it brought him into conflict with other Jewish groups. He often protested against the anti-SED tone of the independent Berlin Jewish newspaper *Der Weg*. On one occasion, he appealed to the Joint Distribution Committee about a supposed anti-East Berlin bias, adding, "with that, we have taken the first decisive step toward splitting the Jewish community of Berlin."[40] Meyer not only served as a front man for the regime within Germany, but also commended it to foreign Jews. On 7 February 1952, at the behest of Otto Grotewohl's personal secretary, he sent a letter on increasing antisemitism in West Germany to Joseph Amitay, an Israeli socialist who had inquired about conditions in Germany. Moreover, Meyer contrasted purported West German silence about antisemitism with East German legislation against incitement to religious or racial hatred. Amitay was convinced, calling the West Germans "murders" and "fascist scoundrels" while praising the progressive situation in East Germany.[41] The American Jewish Committee praised Meyer for his "good work for Jewish causes" but worried that he was too close to the Soviets. One commentator indicated that "he is considered their agent" and that his presence in meetings with West German Jews would cause uneasiness.[42] During State Association meetings, Meyer argued for more rather than less cooperation with the SED to realize the organization's goals. State Association members also recognized the importance of Leo Zuckermann, president Wilhelm Pieck's chief of staff and the most prominent Jew in the SED. Meyer stressed Zuckermann's friendship with Pieck

---

[39] "Record of the Court," in ibid., 34–39.

[40] Letter from Julius Meyer to Sam Haber, 7 September 1951, CJA, 5 B 1, 6, 660.

[41] Letter from Elli Barczatis to Julius Meyer, 7 February 1952, letter from Julius Meyer to Joseph Amitay, undated, CJA 5 B 1, 2, 14–17; letter from Joseph Amitay to Julius Meyer, 15 June 1952, CJA, 5 B 1, 7, 26.

[42] AJC report, "A 'Roof Organization' Is Born," 23 July 1950, CJH/YIVO, RG 347.7.1 (AJC, FAD 1), box 35.

and Grotewohl and his loyalty to the Jewish community.[43] The organization was walking a fine line between duty and deference, and personal ties to the SED and the government were consequently critical. When these personal ties began to loosen in late 1952 and 1953, its autonomous status – if not its very existence – became threatened.

Increasing antisemitism within the SED made the State Association's task more difficult. In late 1952, as the antisemitic show trial of Rudolf Slánský in Czechoslovakia gathered international attention, the SED began the first steps toward a purge of its own ranks. The Central Party Control Commission (Zentrale Parteikontrollkommission, or ZPKK) led this purge.

Paul Merker, the non-Jewish, Communist advocate for reparations to the Jews, quickly became the German Slánský. On 26 November 1952, as the German press linked him to the defendants in the trial in Prague, Merker wrote to Wilhelm Pieck to defend himself against these charges. He stressed his credentials as a loyal follower of the Soviet Union in the anti-imperialist struggle and tried to refute the three occasions during the Slánský trial on which he was mentioned. No reply to Merker's five-page letter appears in his file. On 30 November, Merker wrote again to proclaim his innocence.[44] A few days later he was arrested.

The symbolic high point of the purge came on 20 December 1952. After weeks of preparation, and with Walter Ulbricht's approval, the SED published its official justification for the purge: an article entitled "Lehren aus dem Prozeß gegen das Verschwörerzentrum Slánský" ("Lessons from the Trial against the Slánský Conspirators Center"). It was a work of virulently antisemitic invective and factual distortions, if not fabrications, designed to link and to incriminate the ruling clique's perceived enemies.

The author, ZPKK leader Hermann Matern, identified Paul Merker as the primary enemy of the party and accused him of being an imperialist Zionist agent – the same absurd charge leveled against Slánský. He claimed that the Czechoslovak defendants

---

[43] "Protokoll über die am 15.6.52 stattgefundene Tagung des Landesverbandes der Jüdischen Gemeinden in der Deutschen Demokratischen Republik," 15 June 1952, CJA, 5 B 1, 31, 32–34.

[44] Letters from Paul Merker to Wilhelm Pieck, 26 and 30 November 1952, BAB (SAPMO), NY 4102, 27, 10 and 15.

served pernicious American agents who camouflaged themselves as Zionist organizations "sailing under a Jewish nationalist flag" and as "diplomats of the American vassal government of Israel." Matern anticipated the charge of antisemitism by turning the issue around. The working class, he claimed, did not tolerate antisemitism and felt solidarity with persecuted Jews, but the Prague defendants tried "to discredit vigilant, progressive comrades through the accusation of antisemitism." In fact, according to Matern, Zionism was the real enemy:

> The Zionist movement has nothing in common with the goals of human-itarianism [*Humanität*] and true humanity [*Menschlichkeit*]. It is directed, guided, and commanded by USA-imperialism, serves its interests and the interests of Jewish capitalists.[45]

The antisemitic tone of his rhetoric was unmistakable. He accused Slánský of having "attempted to infect the workers with the poison of chauvinism and cosmopolitanism, with the most reactionary bourgeois ideology."[46] As Jeffrey Herf notes, Matern's very phraseology and vocabulary, particularly words such as "infect," "poison," and "cosmopolitanism," echoed Nazi rhetoric. Less than eight years after the Holocaust, representatives of a German government were invoking the bogeyman of an unseen Jewish conspiracy tainting the German nation.[47]

Merker's wartime and postwar activities on behalf of German Jewry became a source of condemnation. During the immediate postwar years, Merker had encouraged his Jewish comrades to register with the Jewish community so as to be eligible for care packages from the Jewish-administered American Joint Distribution Committee. The AJDC, which had helped indigent Jews all across Europe with care packages, became a special target of Communist criticism. The organization and all those associated with it fell under the suspicion of being imperialist Zionist agents in the employ of Israel and the CIA. Matern even accused Merker of trying to trick his "comrades of Jewish heritage" into being indebted to the AJDC, supposedly a well-known foreign espionage agency. Merker himself was characterized as a servant of "Zionist monopoly capitalists." Moreover, Merker had violated a tenet of Stalinist ideology by having recognized the Jews as a

---

45 "Lehren aus dem Prozeß gegen das Verschwörerzentrum Slánský," in *Dokumente*, 4:202.
46 Ibid., 204.   47 Herf, *Divided Memory*, 127.

national minority.[48] On one hand, Merker had led his comrades into the arms of the capitalist enemy. On the other hand, his efforts for recognition of Jewish suffering during the Holocaust awakened the worst impulses in Matern and his associates. With the "Lehren" article, Matern had revived the controversy over hierarchy of victimhood, but in Matern's incorrect characterization of Merker's policy, recognition of Jewish claims meant exclusion of Communist claims, which was patently unacceptable.[49]

Matern's diatribe placed the East German Jewish community and all Jewish Communists under a cloud of suspicion. After concentrating on Merker, the ZPKK's attention shifted to Julius Meyer, the head of the State Association, a loyal Communist SED member, and a member of the East German parliament. Unlike Merker, who had spent the war safely in exile, Meyer had faced death in Hitler's concentration camps. Moreover, he had not been friendly with the Slánský trial defendants. Attacking him served little purpose other than expressing antisemitic malice and undermining the State Association, an organization loyal to the regime but not under its complete control.

On 6 January 1953, two ZPKK officials interrogated Meyer. They intended to portray him as being Zionist and as having had ties to Slánský. When asked about his support for "Palestine" (i.e., Israel), Meyer criticized Israeli cooperatives as dependent on American capitalism. He also denied having met government officials during his trip to the Jewish state in 1948. Unbeknownst to Meyer, on 23 December 1952, SED member Josef Triebe had written a statement for the ZPKK in which he mentioned exactly such contacts: "Com[rade] Meier [*sic*] related that in Palestine he spoke to members of the government and deputies, also with the Jewish organization. He did not name names."[50] Wanting more information on Merker and Zuckermann, the ZPKK demanded that Meyer write a report on the State Association's meeting on 15 March 1948, attended by Merker, Zuckermann, and Hendrik George van Dam.[51] Anxious to connect Meyer to the Slánský defendants, his interrogators asked whether he had ever been to Prague, which he had on

---

[48] "Lehren aus dem Prozeß gegen das Verschwörerzentrum Slánský," in *Dokumente*, 4: 206–207.

[49] Herf, *Divided Memory*, 129.

[50] Report on the interrogation of Julius Meyer, 9 January 1953, BAB (SAPMO), DY 30/IV 2/4, 397, 194. The "Jewish organization" is presumably the Jewish Agency.

[51] Report by Julius Meyer, 8 January 1953, BAB (SAPMO), DY 30/IV 2/4, 404, 46.

several occasions. When asked whether he had read "Lehren aus dem Prozeß gegen das Verschwörerzentrum Slánský," Meyer gave an answer in line with the party orthodoxy. He had studied the article in detail and followed the trial closely. He added the following: "Personally, it is clear to me that there really is no race question for us. For me there is only a class question. For me there are no Jews, only traitors and comrades."[52] While a faithful Communist, Meyer had steadily worked for the Jews' interests vis-à-vis the SED and East German bureaucracy. Now, under duress, he renounced his earlier beliefs.

On 3 January 1953, even before Meyer's arrest, but after the publication of Matern's article "Lehren aus dem Prozeß gegen das Verschwörerzentrum Slánský," the Berlin community turned to its erstwhile friends in the SED for help. Communal leaders wrote to Wilhelm Pieck congratulating him on his seventy-seventh birthday, but the letter contained a plea that was a subtle reference to the widening purge: "We know that your person guarantees that a new antisemitism could never break out in the state you lead."[53] Pieck had been an old friend of the Jewish community and even sympathetic to Israel. Now the community placed its fading hopes in him.

The antisemitic wave, which had been primarily an East-Central European phenomenon with Stalinist connivance, returned to Moscow on 12 January 1953. The Soviet news agency TASS announced the so-called doctors' plot, and the SED's organ *Neues Deutschland* carried the news on 14 January. The Soviet government alleged that Jewish doctors had been conspiring to murder Communist officials. The Communist antisemitism that had earlier manifested itself in Hungary and Czechoslovakia took a dangerous turn, causing Jews all through the eastern bloc to panic. Meyer, sensing that he was personally in danger, fled to West Berlin, and on 17 January the ZPKK revoked his SED membership. In the spring of 1954, he moved to Brazil, where he died in 1979.

Many important Jewish Communists soon fell under suspicion and were subject to arrest. Leon Löwenkopf was arrested in Dresden in early January 1953. Although Helmut Eschwege

---

[52] "Aussprache mit dem Genossen Julius Meyer, Präsident der jüdischen Gemeinde am 6.1.53," 6 January 1953, BAB (SAPMO), DY 30/IV 2/4, 404, 36 and 40–41.
[53] Letter from Jüdische Gemeinde zu Berlin to Wilhelm Pieck, 3 January 1953, CJA, 5 B 1, 11, 4.

worked for Löwenkopf's release, most of Löwenkopf's friends did not come to his aid. After his release, the Jewish community threw him a birthday party, but most of his old friends did not attend.[54] Leading SED official Leo Zuckermann soon had to flee abroad, but before doing so, he tried to win favor with the ZPKK by fingering Julius Meyer as an Israeli agent. He also tried to defend his record by reminding the East German leadership that it had maintained ties to Israeli representatives in 1948.[55] In fact, in the weeks to follow, the ZPKK received a flood of letters from Jewish Communists eager to distance themselves from those already discredited. Some letter writers even denounced others, particularly Leo Zuckermann and Bruno Goldhammer, in the hope of finding favor with the SED's inquisitors. Hilde and Gerhart Eisler, an official in the Office for Information and brother of Hanns Eisler, sent Matern a stack of letters they had received from tainted individuals.[56] Klaus Gysi, a future East German cabinet minister and father of Gregor Gysi, volunteered information on individuals and disowned his old friends.[57]

In the weeks to come, a flood of emigrants left East Germany. In early February 1953, the West German *Allgemeine Wochenzeitung der Juden in Deutschland* reported that 500 Jews had left East Germany, and that 1,500 to 2,000 non-Jews were fleeing to West Berlin every day.[58] Internal Jewish communal documents bear out the allegation concerning Jewish flight. Dresden's Jewish community decreased from 163 members in December 1952 to 116 in March 1953, and Erfurt's went from 217 to 97 during the same period.[59] *Neues Deutschland* vilified Meyer and several other Jewish communal leaders who fled to the West, including Leon Löwenkopf. The historian Helmut Eschwege lost his job at the

---

54 Eschwege, *Fremd unter meinesgleichen*, 68 and 70–71.
55 Letter from Leo Zuckermann to Herta Geffke, 7 December 1952, BAB (SAPMO), DY 30/IV 2/4, 124, 170.
56 Letters from Gerhart and Hilde Eisler to Hermann Matern, 21–22 January 1953, BAB (SAPMO), DY 30/IV 2/4, 124, 314–317. Hanns Eisler, possibly East Germany's most famous composer, wrote the state's national anthem.
57 Letters from Klaus Gysi to Hermann Matern, 22 January 1953, BAB (SAPMO), DY 30/IV 2/4, 124, 318. Gregor Gysi was the last head of the SED and the first chairman and driving force behind its post-reunification successor, the Party of Democratic Socialism.
58 "Mobilisierung des Weltgewissens," *Allgemeine Wochenzeitung der Juden in Deutschland*, 6 February 1953.
59 Surveys of the Jewish communities, CJA, 5 B 1, 33, 44–48 (Dresden), 91 (Erfurt), and 157 (both).

German Historical Museum, and the SED leadership expelled him from the party.[60] Leading Communist Leo Zuckermann fled, ultimately settling in Mexico City, site of his wartime exile, after debriefing by American military officials in West Germany.[61] Crucially for the State Association, Nuschke's Jewish expert Albert Hirsch also fled. The State Association and the Jewish communities had lost their biggest proponent within the government.[62]

POSTPURGE EAST GERMAN JEWRY

After Meyer's flight and the official purge, Jewish groups faced formidable challenges to their mere survival. Their leaders had fled abroad, and the very state that had supported them financially now seemed hostile to their existence. Meyer had monopolized the leadership of the State Association to such a degree that the new leaders could not even enumerate all of the group's assets.[63] Moreover, Meyer had been an active, independent-minded leader, bringing the Jewish community both needed support and occasionally unwanted attention. After his removal or flight, the East German regime ensured that the communal leaders would be of a very different ilk. It was not willing to countenance the same degree of autonomy.

With Meyer and most prepurge leaders gone, many of the individual Jewish communities were adrift and without protection from the vagaries of the SED administration. With almost no other choice, on 2 March 1953, Georg Heilbrunn and Willi Bendit of the East Berlin community visited the new government official responsible for the Jewish community. They needed to know the details of state funding for the Rykestraße synagogue. Even though Bendit, Heilbrunn, and Israel Rothmann were among the leaders of East Berlin Jewry in the post-Meyer era, and the latter two were loyal SED members, they did not know how much money the community had or how much the government had pledged.[64] As late as October 1953, the State Association and

---

[60] Eschwege, *Fremd unter meinesgleichen*, 73 and 76.
[61] Herf, *Divided Memory*, 126 and 134.
[62] Letter from Otto Nuschke to Fritz Geyer, 19 March 1953, BAB, DC 20, 956, 70.
[63] State Association financial records and inventories, CJA, 5 B 1, 34, 31–35 and 41–42.
[64] "Vermerk," 2 March 1953, BAB, DO 4, 2128.

the East Berlin community were still not in possession of all their property.[65]

Meyer's flight necessitated a reorganization of the State Association. Hermann Baden of Halle and Georg Kaethner of Magdeburg arranged a meeting in Berlin on 3 February, attended by Jewish leaders from throughout East Germany. The State Association's very existence was now in doubt. While some delegates considered the organization unnecessary, Max Cars of Erfurt felt that they needed the State Association more than ever. He proposed giving their organization a new name, reflecting its new status: "Association of Jewish Communities" (Verband der Jüdischen Gemeinden) instead of "State Association" (Landesverband).[66] The Association had its new seat in Halle. Not enjoying good relations with Hermann Baden, the East Berlin Jewish community remained a nonaffiliated group until 1960.[67] Having the Association's main office deep in the German Democratic Republic, not in divided Berlin, sent a clear message about the association's orientation.

Under the leadership of Baden, Cars, and Kaethner, the Association distanced itself from Meyer. Some representatives wanted them to repudiate debts accrued under Meyer.[68] The new leaders pledged to represent Jewish communal interests in the strictest sense and to avoid politics scrupulously – including any conflicts between the GDR and Israel. They had learned their lesson from Meyer's deep involvement with the regime, and they did not hesitate to denounce their erstwhile president in the strongest terms possible:

The association's former chairman administered his office without conscience in order to enrich himself. He has left the German Democratic

---

65 Letter from Hermann Baden to Otto Nuschke, 22 October 1953, CJA, 5 B 1, 8, 91; letter from Benzmann to Alfred Neumann, 22 October 1953, BAB (SAPMO), DY 30/IV 2/14, 249, 47–49.
66 Letter from Hermann Baden and Georg Kaethner to all Jewish communities in the GDR, 27 January 1953; "Tagung des Landesverbandes der Jüdischen Gemeinden in der Deutschen Demokratischen Republik am 3. Februar 1953," 3 February 1953; CJA, 5 B 1, 34, 51 and 4–5. "Landesverband" was the name usually given to Jewish groups in a single region or state, and these found representation in the all-German Central Council of Jews in Germany, which had its seat in West Germany.
67 Letter from Hermann Baden to Helmut Enke, 7 May 1953, BAB, DO 4, 2129; Offenberg, *"Seid vorsichtig gegen die Machthaber,"* 112–114.
68 "Tagung des Landesverbandes der Jüdischen Gemeinden in der Deutschen Demokratischen Republik am 3. Februar 1953," 3 February 1953, CJA, 5 B 1, 34, 6–7.

Republic and the democratic sector of Berlin [i.e., East Berlin] in order to place himself at the disposal of his fascist clients and some others. His goal was the destruction of the apparatus of the Jewish communities in the German Democratic Republic.[69]

Their condemnation of Meyer was unequivocal. In the wake of Meyer's flight and the State Association's humiliation, they were completely subservient to the SED party line.

The Jewish group's relationship with the regime was on a new basis. At a meeting with new Jewish leaders Baden and Cars on 11 February 1953, Helmut Enke, Nuschke's personal adviser, requested that all correspondence with the individual communities be handled via the Association. He wanted much stricter controls over the dispensation of government funds to the Jewish communities, and he would hold the Association accountable.[70] However, Enke continued to deal with the local communities on many issues despite his clearly expressed wish for centralization. In general, the government wanted to monitor, if not control, Jewish matters more efficiently.

The days of autonomy and political activity enjoyed under Julius Meyer were over, but the Jews were still reliant on Nuschke's aid and enjoyed cordial relations with him. His office gave great help to the various Jewish communities throughout eastern Germany with the restoration of their buildings.[71] In late April 1953, leaders of the East Berlin Jewish community wrote about the poor state of their building in the Oranienburger Straße and requested 45,000 marks to repair the famous building.[72] In August, Jewish leaders wrote to Nuschke to notify him that the renovations of the Rykestraße synagogue were complete, and Nuschke sent a representative to the reconsecration ceremony. He expressed his joy at the reconstruction of the house of worship after its destruction during "the days of the Nazi rule of violence" and noted that government funds helped to support the reconstruction of destroyed

---

[69] "Entwurf," undated [mid-February 1953], CJA, 5 B 1, 34, 26.

[70] "Vermerk," 11 February 1953, BAB, DO 4, 2129.

[71] "Baubeihilfen 1953 – Jüdische Gemeinden," undated, BAB, DO 4, 2129.

[72] Letter from the provisional board of the Jüdische Gemeinde Groß-Berlin to Otto Nuschke, 26 April 1953, BAB, DO 4, 2129. The subvention granted to the community by the government was insufficient to complete repairs on the building, which was partially demolished a few years later.

places of worship.[73] From 1951 through 1955, the Jews received up to 1,125,000 marks for the reconstruction and restoration of synagogues and cemeteries.[74] In addition to overt financial aid, Association chairman Hermann Baden relied on Nuschke and Enke to compel East Berlin mayor Friedrich Ebert to return the organization's property confiscated from Julius Meyer's apartment.[75] Naturally, the reliance on aid from the government meant a level of accountability, especially after the purge earlier in the year, and in October 1953, a representative of Nuschke's office personally inspected the Jewish communities.[76]

Officially, the Association of Jewish Communities in the GDR did not break its ties to the all-German Central Council of Jews in Germany. After the domestic situation calmed down, the Association renewed its affiliation with the Düsseldorf-based Jewish body. On 22 April 1953, Enke encouraged Hermann Baden to renew the connection, and on 27 May, Baden sent the Central Council a list of the new Association board members.[77] Association deputy chairman Max Cars also wanted Baden to encourage renewed ties.[78] Until 1963, the East Germans maintained an official membership in the Central Council, and that body offered financial aid to East German Jewry. In some cases, West Berlin Jewish leader Heinz Galinski led the effort. After 1963, contact between the two groups diminished as relations cooled considerably.[79] Moreover, the East German government worked to ensure that the East Berlin

---

[73] Letter from Georg Heilbrunn and Israel Rothmann to Otto Nuschke, 20 August 1953; "Hochverehrte Festgemeinde!" (speech delivered at Rykestrasse synagogue dedication ceremony), undated [30 August 1953]; BAB, DO 4, 2128.

[74] "Finanzielle Aufwendungen des Staates für die Kirchen," undated, BAB, DC 20, 1233, 8. (For the sake of comparison, the Protestant and Catholic churches received together 1,200,000 marks annually.)

[75] Letter from Hermann Baden to Otto Nuschke, 22 October 1953; letter from Helmut Enke to Friedrich Ebert, 26 October 1953; letter from Bierbauer to Hermann Baden, 4 November 1953; CJA, 5 B 1, 8, 88 and 90–91.

[76] Letter from Hermann Baden to the Jewish communities, 29 September 1953, CJA, 5 B 1, 29, 115.

[77] Letter from Helmut Enke to Hermann Baden, 22 April 1953; letter from Hermann Baden to Central Council, 27 May 1953; CJA, 5 B 1, 34, 11–12.

[78] Letter from Max Cars to Hermann Baden, 12 June 1953, CJA, 5 B 1, 29, 147.

[79] Mertens, *Davidstern unter Hammer und Zirkel*, 80–81; Erica Burgauer, *Zwischen Erinnerung und Verdrängung*, 161–162. Representatives of the Association attempted to attend the 1966 meeting of the World Jewish Congress in Brussels, but East German officials prevented them from doing so. That year, West German politician Eugen Gerstenmaier addressed the congress, the first non-Jewish German to do so after the war.

Figure 6. Heinz Galinski (*left*) and Julius Meyer (*right*) celebrate Hanukkah together three weeks before Meyer's arrest. *Source:* Stiftung "Neue Synagoge Berlin-Centrum Judaicum" Archiv, 5 B 1.

community did not consider rejoining with the West Berliners. Despite its efforts, in the 1950s many East Berliners continued to attend synagogues in West Berlin and sent their children to summer programs in the Federal Republic. West Berliners still made use of the Weißensee cemetery in East Berlin. Although there was little progress toward reunification, contacts between the East Berliners and West Berliners, led by Heinz Galinksi, continued through the 1950s. They would practically cease in August 1961 with the construction of the Berlin Wall.[80]

In the months immediately following the purge, Galinski was the staunchest defender of the new Association within the Central Council. During a meeting on 28 June 1953, he was emphatic that the East German association had never resigned from the Central Council, even if Julius Meyer had (see Fig. 6). Central Council board members voted to invite East German delegates to their next meeting, and Galinski vouched that East German Jewry's

[80] Offenberg, *"Seid vorsichtig gegen die Machthaber,"* 104–105.

leaders were not politically active.[81] In fact, this statement was not true.

The East Berlin Jewish leadership was demonstratively loyal to the regime. In his sermons, Rabbi Martin Riesenburger, often called "the red rabbi," repeatedly attacked the resurgence of antisemitism in West Germany and praised the GDR.[82] In their Rosh Hashanah greetings for 1953 (the Jewish year 5714), the lay leaders of the East Berlin community made very political statements, including denouncing the execution of (Jewish) Communist spies Ethel and Julius Rosenberg, obliquely equating it with the Holocaust. The East Berliners denied that there was any antisemitism involved in the Slánský trial and claimed that East Germany could not possibly be antisemitic: "For only where there is fascism, is there antisemitism. Already, visible expressions of antisemitism, like the daubing of swastikas and the distribution of incendiary publications, are tolerated there [in West Germany]."[83] Their rhetoric was completely in line with SED propaganda, and several of the community board members were SED members.

Even though the Association and the individual communities were quite complaisant, the government and the Communist Party kept them under strict observation and control. The regime required Jewish leaders to renounce the AJDC and to reject the agreement between West Germany and Israel for Holocaust reparations, according to one West German commentator.[84] A report from 22 December 1956 is indicative of the SED's interest in religious affairs after the purges. The unnamed author in the SED's office for religious affairs provided an analysis of each Jewish community leader's political reliability. The SED considered Baden, the long-serving chairman of the Association, as neutral or hostile to governmental policy. The Association itself also did not find favor with the SED: "[A]s representative of the Jewish communities in the GDR," it could "not in any way be regarded as a positive element for society."[85] Baden, Meyer's successor, was the focus of

[81] "Beschlussprotokoll der Direktoriumssitzung," 28 June 1953, ZA, B.1/7, 221.38.
[82] "1. Entwurf. Bericht über die Lage auf dem Gebiete der Religionsgemeinschaften," February 1954, BAB (SAPMO), DY 30/IV 2/14, 247, 111.
[83] Letter from the board of the Jüdische Gemeinde Groß-Berlin to members, undated [September 1953], BAB, DO 4, 2128.
[84] "Juden in der SZ," 10 February 1953, BAK, B 106, 40, 21–22.
[85] "Betrifft: Jüdische Gemeinde in der DDR," 22 December 1956, BAB (SAPMO), DY 30/IV 2/14, 249, 5.

particular vituperation, and the report's author criticized the Association for not supporting the state in public, in contrast to the communities in Magdeburg and East Berlin – both led by loyal SED men.[86] Furthermore, the author recommended isolating Baden "and creating a board, which is positive in the sense of working for our societal order. For the Jewish communities are not to be seen simply as a religious community, but rather as a political factor in society."[87] It was no longer enough to regulate the Association's activities and to have SED members within the organization. The SED wanted complete control of the organization from the top down, and it still felt threatened by any Jewish leader who might be too independent.

Political controversy and the loss of any ideological independence did not stop the work of coordinating religious life for the Jews of eastern Germany. In August 1953, the Association of Jewish Communities in the GDR planned to establish a committee for religious affairs.[88] Moreover, Hermann Baden made arrangements to hire a new cantor and teacher for the scattered Jewish communities.[89] The very same Rosh Hashanah newsletter that contained such a strong political message from the Berlin community also provided details on religious services, religious instruction for children, and synagogue construction.[90] With the high holidays approaching, the Jewish community of Mecklenburg asked for the Association's assistance in bringing the dispersed community together.[91] The Jews of East Germany, particularly those of East Berlin, were dedicated to the preservation of Jewish life, even if it meant accommodating the regime's political stance.

In attempting to secure assistance for Jewish Holocaust survivors, the State Association and its plucky leader, Julius Meyer, faced several formidable obstacles, the first of which was the indifference

---

[86] Ibid., 7–8.   [87] Ibid., 9.

[88] Letter from the board of the Jüdischer Landesverband Mecklenburg to the Association of Jewish Communities, 4 August 1953, CJA, 5 B 1, 36, 5.

[89] Letter from Hermann Baden to Werner Sander, 3 August 1953; letter from Werner Sander to the Association of Jewish Communities, 6 August 1953; letter from Hermann Baden to Werner Sander, 13 August 1953; CJA, 5 B 1, 36, 1–3.

[90] Letter from the board of the Jüdische Gemeinde Groß-Berlin to members, undated [September 1953], BAB, DO 4, 2128.

[91] Letter from the Jüdischer Landesverband Mecklenburg to Association of Jewish Communities, 18 July 1953, CJA, 5 B 1, 29, 130.

with which the ruling regime viewed organized religion. In the case of East Germany's Jews, indifference developed into hostility insofar as the Jewish community and its allies staked a claim to a heritage of unique persecution under the Nazis.

Without any real chance of gaining support from the leaders of the SED, the Jewish community sought allies elsewhere. Fortunately for the communities, the government of the German Democratic Republic was technically an antifascist, national front coalition. Moreover, the official responsible for governmental oversight of and relations with religious communities was a Christian Democrat, Otto Nuschke. Not only was Nuschke not a Communist, but during the Weimar Republic, he had been active in the German Democratic Party, which enjoyed considerable support from German Jewry. Given the extremely difficult circumstances under which the Jewish community of East Germany sought support, Nuschke and his aides served as allies and patrons.

The community's chief allies within the SED were perceived by party boss Walter Ulbricht as rivals. Although they, too, were orthodox Communists, comrades Paul Merker and Leo Zuckermann had spent the war years in exile in Mexico, not in Moscow in proximity to Stalin and Ulbricht. Thus, they were considered ideologically suspect. Incidentally, in Mexican exile, they had come to know many German Jewish émigrés and gained an appreciation for their struggle with National Socialism. Merker's advocacy of Jewish uniqueness only made him more suspect in the eyes of Ulbricht and company. Merker's courageous stance led to his removal from power by a leadership cadre that "never felt secure."[92] In their relations with the Jewish community, Communist leaders chose a "grotesque" path. Rather than reinforcing East Germany's antifascist credentials through cooperative efforts and engagement with Jewish victims of Nazi persecution, they persecuted Jewish leaders and repressed public memory of the Holocaust and specific Jewish suffering.[93]

In 1953, the Jewish community of eastern Germany lost its true independence, and its most notable leaders fled to the West. The regime made certain that, as far as possible, pro-Communist leaders replaced them. Even so, the regime felt compelled to monitor and to report on the internal development of the Jewish

[92] Fulbrook, *Anatomy of a Dictatorship*, 23.   [93] Herf, *Divided Memory*, 384.

community. By the mid-1950s, the SED's fear of other religious institutions and their autonomy had grown sufficiently for the state to establish a full-fledged Ministry for Church Affairs, later called the State Secretariat for Church Matters, which worked closely with both the SED and the secret police, the Stasi.[94]

[94] Fulbrook, *Anatomy of a Dictatorship*, 99.

CHAPTER 6

The Jewish Community and the West German Government before Reparations

Under the unique circumstances of postwar German Jewish life, relations with the government were critical. As seen, the organized Jewish community of East Germany had a troubled relationship with political elites nearly from the start, and only the nominal inclusion of non-Communists in the government prevented a collapse of the community from lack of support.

In West Germany, contact with government officials was no less vital to the success of organized Jewish life. After overcoming the fundamental disunity of the community in western Germany, building a relationship with political elites and state officials became a priority of the new Central Council of Jews in Germany. In fact, initially the group's limited contact to governmental officials reduced its influence and undermined its very reason for being. Over time, however, the organization cultivated a relationship with West German president Theodor Heuss and his staff, who supported Jewish interests. Meanwhile, Chancellor Adenauer, who made tentative and ill-planned attempts to bring about a German-Jewish reconciliation in 1949, waited more than two years before he broached the issue again in public.

Additionally, the Central Council's low standing in the international Jewish community complicated the situation. Because groups such as the World Jewish Congress often disregarded the interests of the Jewish community in Germany, the Central Council intentionally drew closer to the West German government. By the autumn of 1952, the Central Council had established a working relationship with government officials, and Konrad Adenauer had begun a policy of reparations to the Jewish people. The Central Council had become a success.

GOVERNMENT LEADERS FIRST ADDRESS
THE JEWISH QUESTION

The West German republic was founded in the shadow of two failed German states: the Weimar Republic, with its liberal, democratic tradition, and the Third Reich, with its total rejection of civil liberties and rule of law. Naturally, the founders of the Federal Republic had to deal with both of these legacies, and much of that heritage centered on relations between the state and the Jewish community. In September 1949, as the new government came into office, chancellor Konrad Adenauer had two opportunities to make important declarations on the legacy of the Holocaust and on the future of the Jewish community in postwar Germany. They were the first postwar *Regierungserklärung*, or formal policy address of the new cabinet, and the chancellor's annual Rosh Hashanah greetings to the Jewish community. In making his remarks, Adenauer chose his words carefully, based on his targeted audience.

In his long and comprehensive *Regierungserklärung* delivered to the Bundestag, Adenauer spoke of the tasks before his government and of his basic policy ideas. Despite the import of the occasion, he scarcely mentioned German guilt for the Nazis' crimes and brought up the Jews only once, in a very brief reference to antisemitism:

We consider it unworthy and unbelievable that after everything that happened in the National Socialist era there are still people in Germany who persecute or despise the Jews because they are Jews.[1]

This one sentence, without any explicit reference to the Holocaust, was his only reference to the plight of the Jews in Germany. He spent more time discussing the so-called excesses of denazification and the injustices done to ethnic Germans driven from their homes in Central and Eastern Europe.

This omission did not go unnoticed. The Social Democratic opposition criticized Adenauer's policy address and issued its own call for reparations and reconciliation with the Jews. Jewish Bundestag deputy Jakob Altmaier considered the chancellor's remarks dangerous for having omitted explicit reference to the

---

[1] Konrad Adenauer, "20. September 1949: Erste Regierungserklärung von Bundeskanzler Adenauer," 20 September 1949, in *Reden 1917–1967*, 163–164.

Nazis' victims.[2] On 21 September, Kurt Schumacher gave the opposition's official reply in the Bundestag, characterizing Adenauer's comments on the Nazi past and the Jews as "too feeble and weak." It was the duty of all "German patriots" to place the fate of the Jews in the foreground and to help them wherever they could. Schumacher saw latent antisemitism threatening to reisolate Germany. Noting the contributions that Jews had made to German culture and science before the war, he wanted the new Germany to take advantage of these skills again.[3] In Schumacher's Rosh Hashanah greetings to the Jewish community in Germany, the Social Democratic leader and concentration camp survivor acknowledged the Germans' guilt for the crimes committed against the Jews and proclaimed it their duty to help the Jews and to fight antisemitism, which was continuing to manifest itself though attacks on Jewish cemeteries and synagogues, as well as in everyday attitudes on the part of Germans. Schumacher noted, "The wounds that Nazism caused to Jewry have not yet healed, and it will require very much enlightening and education work to bring about a real reconciliation."[4]

While Adenauer's remarks in the Bundestag failed to address the issue of the recent German past, he did deal with the past in more detail when directly addressing the Jewish community in Germany. In his Rosh Hashanah message, issued one week later after the Bundestag address, Adenauer expressed his hope that the coming year would heal the wounds suffered by the Jewish people and that German Jewish émigrés would return so that they could contribute to the "spiritual, political, and social reconstruction of our land." He accepted the "duty" of reparations as far as they were possible for the Germans.[5] Afterward, John J. McCloy, U.S. high commissioner in Germany, congratulated Adenauer for

[2] "20.9.1949: Fraktionssitzung," 20 September 1949, Germany (West), Bundestag, Fraktion der SPD, *Die SPD-Fraktion im Deutschen Bundestag: Sitzungsprotokolle 1949–1957*, half-vol. 1: *1.–181. Sitzung 1949–1953*, ed. Petra Weber, Quellen zur Geschichte des Parlamentarismus und der politischen Parteien, fourth series: Deutschland seit 1945, ed. Karl Dietrich Bracher, Rudolf Morsey, and Hans-Peter Schwarz, no. 8/I (Düsseldorf: Droste, 1993), 11.

[3] Kurt Schumacher, "Kurt Schumachers Rede vor dem Deutschen Bundestag vom 21. September 1949," 21 September 1949, in *Der deutsch-israelische Dialog*, 1:40.

[4] "Glückwünsch an jüdische Gemeinden Deutschlands," 22 September 1949, AdsD, Bestand Kurt Schumacher (Abt. II), 48.

[5] "Glückwünsche zum Jahreswechsel," *Allgemeine Wochenzeitung*, 29 September 1949.

his "very good statement regarding the position of the Jews in Germany."[6]

A few weeks after Adenauer's tentative remarks in the Bundestag on the Jewish question, the chancellor made a public attempt to heal the wounds of the past. He and his adviser Herbert Blankenhorn had been discussing the Jewish question, and they sought to approach the subject so as to win "trust, respect, and believability."[7] Fortuitously, German Jewish journalist Karl Marx had requested an interview with the chancellor, providing him with another opportunity to address German-Jewish reconciliation.[8] On 11 November, Adenauer met with Marx and pledged his support for the reconstruction of Jewish sites in Germany. As an initial sign of good faith, he promised 10 million marks' worth of goods to help with the construction of Israel, even though the Jewish state and West Germany maintained no diplomatic relations at the time. He also proposed erecting an office for Jewish affairs within the federal Interior Ministry.[9] Reparations and governmental relations to the Jewish community had multiple purposes. Not only could they have improved the material lot of some Holocaust survivors, they highlighted Adenauer's wish for contrition. His postwar administration needed to signal Germany's break with the past and its desire to right injustices committed by the state. Thus, he wished to support Israel, which had received so many Holocaust survivors, and to grant the Jews in Germany a voice in domestic policy formation, at least on matters of direct concern to them.

While some German Jews endorsed both of these proposals at first, neither idea found significant or enduring support, and many American, British, and Israeli Jews attacked them outright. One of the few strong promoters of Adenauer's suggestion was Karl Marx himself, who suggested increasing the West German offer to 40 million marks and urged Israel to accept the proposal. American Jewish leaders, however, considered Marx's support naive.[10]

---

[6] Telegram from John J. McCloy to Konrad Adenauer, 26 September 1949, PA-AA, B 10, 307 (Fiche A 2023), 1.

[7] Report by Herbert Blankenhorn for Rolf Vogel, "Bevor der offizielle Teil der Geschichte beginnt...," in *Der deutsch-israelische Dialog*, 1:18.

[8] Correspondence between Karl Marx and Federal Chancellery, BAK, B 136, 5862.

[9] "Bekenntnis zur Verpflichtung," *Allgemeine Wochenzeitung*, 25 November 1949.

[10] Shafir, "Der Jüdische Weltkongreß und sein Verhältnis zu Nachkriegsdeutschland (1945–1967)," 218; "Final Report of Major Abraham S. Hyman," 30 January 1950, CJH/YIVO, RG 347.7.1, box 33; letter from Karl Marx to Herbert Blankenhorn, 23 December

As seen in chapter 2, the proposal to nominate an official adviser for Jewish affairs in the federal government drew some support, despite intense opposition from Jewish representatives throughout Germany, and led to the establishment of the Central Council.

Even after the Central Council's formation, the issue of a government adviser lingered on. The Interior Ministry in Bonn, continuing to plan for a federal office, considered appointing Munich rabbi Aaron Ohrenstein and asked the new Central Council to confirm this controversial nomination, but the Central Council voted in October 1950 to oppose any such appointment.[11] The federal government could not ignore this opposition. In December, interior minister Robert Lehr advised the chancellery to let the matter drop, and in January 1951, Hans Globke, Adenauer's chief of staff, agreed, effectively ending debate on the matter.[12] The position was never filled, creating a vacuum within the government. Ministerial officials remained uncertain as to who was responsible for relations with the Jewish community in West Germany.[13]

As seen, Chancellor Adenauer's initial attempts to deal with reparations and the renascent Jewish community did not succeed. As a result, Jewish leaders looked elsewhere for patronage within the government, and president Theodor Heuss became the focus of that attention. Like Adenauer and Schumacher, Heuss made annual remarks for Rosh Hashanah starting in 1949, and his first such message helped to establish him as the leading spokesman for German remorse for the crimes of the Nazi past. He exhibited great empathy for the Jews and unequivocally recognized the horror of the Nazi regime "from which no Jewish family . . . was protected." Although many Jews held bitter feelings toward the Germans, he urged a genuine German-Jewish reconciliation. For

---

1949, BAK, B 136, 5862; AJC report, "The Adenauer Interview," 15 December 1949, CJH/YIVO, RG 347.7.1, box 34; "Aufzeichnung," 23 February 1950, BAK, B 122, 2083 (29); cf. Lilli Marx, interview by author, 14 April 1999.

[11] Letter from Robert Lehr to Otto Lenz, 23 December 1950, BAK, B 136, 5862; "Protokoll der Sitzung des Direktoriums des Zentralrates," 15–16 October 1950, ZA, B.1/7, 221.5.

[12] Letter from Robert Lehr to Otto Lenz, 23 December 1950; letter from Hans Globke to Robert Lehr, 22 January 1951; BAK, B 136, 5862. Oddly, Globke later reopened the issue. In November 1951, after Adenauer had announced his desire for reparations to Israel, Globke decided that the time was right to appoint an adviser for Jewish affairs, even if the Central Council disagreed. The Jewish adviser could administer the reparations proposed by Adenauer. Letter from Hans Globke to Robert Lehr, 27 November 1951, BAK, B 136, 5862.

[13] "Vermerk," 27 July 1953, BAK, B 106, 21407.

Heuss, mere mutual tolerance was too little. He wanted Germans and Jews to realize that their fates were intertwined.[14] Jewish leaders, including Karl Marx and concentration camp survivor Philipp Auerbach, applauded the president.[15]

On 7 December 1949, Heuss firmly established himself as the federal government's leading moral authority on German-Jewish relations with a speech entitled "The Courage to Love" ("Mut zur Liebe"). In addressing the Wiesbaden chapter of the Society for Christian-Jewish Cooperation, he stated that there was no sense in avoiding the core issue: Did ordinary Germans share in the guilt for the atrocities committed against the Jews?[16] He rejected the notion of German collective guilt, which many Jews had popularized. In his opinion, assigning blame to all Germans simply because they were Germans was little different from the Nazis' having assigned blame to all Jews simply because they were Jews. He proposed a more precise description of the Germans' relationship to the Nazi period – one that engendered a sense of collective shame. Being a German in the postwar era, he noted, involved a heavy moral burden. "The worst thing Hitler did to us [Germans] – and he did many things to us – was this, that he forced us to be ashamed that we shared the name German with him and his henchmen." Heuss admonished his listeners that even if they were not directly accountable for the Nazis' crimes, they "must not forget the Nuremberg Laws, the [yellow] Jewish star [badge], the burning of synagogues, the deportation of Jews to the unknown, to misfortune, to death."[17]

The speech found great resonance with the American occupiers and the German Jewish community in exile. U.S. High Commissioner John J. McCloy was present at the Wiesbaden meeting and expressed his view that the address was excellent.[18] Heuss was also aware of the political potential of his comments, and he encouraged his German Jewish friends to help distribute the speech abroad.[19] Despite the speech's generally positive reception, the

[14] "Glückwünsche des Herrn Bundespräsidenten an die 'Allgemeine,'" 24 September 1949, BAK, B 122, 2086 (29); Heuss, *An und über Juden*, 113.
[15] Letter from Karl Marx to Theodor Heuss, 22 September 1949, BAK, B 122, 2086 (29); letter from Philipp Auerbach to Theodor Heuss, 6 October 1949, BAK, N 1221, 108.
[16] Heuss, "Mut zur Liebe," in *Die grossen Reden*, 100.
[17] Ibid., 101.
[18] "Aufzeichnung," undated, BAK, B 122, 2080 (26).
[19] Letters from Theodor Heuss to Anselm Kahn, 29 December 1949 and 15 March 1950, BAK, N 1221, 157.

Jewish press in Germany was disappointed that it did not become a starting point for broader German-Jewish dialogue.[20]

EARLY DEBATES ABOUT REPARATIONS AND DIALOGUE WITH THE GOVERNMENT

Despite early tentative attempts at a reconciliation made by Heuss and Adenauer, real dialogue was slow in developing. The political culture of early West Germany militated against a consensus in favor of helping the Jews, even as many Jewish survivors of the Holocaust and their communities in Germany remained very poor. The issue of reparations became paramount to them and served as their barometer of relations with politicians. After September 1949, they looked to the new West German federal government for help, but many politicians seemed disinclined to assist the Jewish communities.

The liberal Free Democratic Party was the first to address the issue in the Bundestag. On 4 November 1949, the Free Democrats called for a unitary West German restitution law, effectively supplanting any Allied statutes regulating the issue. In proposing such a law, they never once mentioned the words "Jews" or "Jewish."[21] For the FDP, justice for the primary victims of the Nazis was secondary to establishing West German sovereignty and standardizing state laws.[22] Federal minister of justice and FDP member Thomas Dehler wrote to Theodor Heuss that the Germans wanted to weaken existing state restitution laws as a condition for unifying them. Dehler predicted that the western Allies would prefer to have disparate laws regulating restitution rather than a single law weaker than the one that already applied in the U.S. occupation zone.[23] In accordance with the Occupation Statute, issued in 1949 by the western Allies to regulate their relations with the new West German state, the Bundestag could not pass a reparations law without American, British, and French approval. The

---

[20] "Fragen, die uns bewegen!," *Allgemeine Wochenzeitung*, 26 January 1951; "Mangelnde Versöhnungsbereitschaft," *Allgemeine Wochenzeitung*, 13 July 1951.

[21] "Drucksache Nr. 159," 4 November 1949, Germany (West), Bundestag, *Verhandlungen des Deutschen Bundestages, I. Wahlperiode 1949, Anlagen zu den stenographischen Berichte, Drucksachen Nr. 1 bis 350 (1. Teil)* (Bonn: Bonner Universitäts-Buchdruckerei, 1950).

[22] Herf, *Divided Memory*, 270–271. The FDP "represented a judiciary and civil service determined to avoid any more denazification proceedings" initiated by the Allies.

[23] Letter from Thomas Dehler to Theodor Heuss, 21 June 1950, BAK, B 122, 2076 (20).

Association of Victims of the Nazi Regime, the most prominent lobbying organization for former victims of National Socialism, attacked the FDP's proposal, claiming that it would require a review of all cases decided under American occupation law no. 59.[24] In fact, many officials within the FDP scarcely recognized the severity of the problem facing the Jews in Germany or the persistence of antisemitism. At the FDP party congress in the spring of 1950, one prominent speaker, claiming that there was significantly less anti-Jewish sentiment in Germany than in England, counseled party members not to make any strong statements against antisemitism, lest they give foreign observers the impression that Germany still had problems.[25]

While the FDP did not consider antisemitism to be a significant problem, the SPD did, and it took action against politically active antisemites. In a public speech in November 1949, Bundestag member Wolfgang Hedler, a member of the right-wing German Party and a former Nazi, called members of the anti-Nazi resistance "traitors." He attacked SPD chairman Schumacher for his characterization of Hitler's antisemitism as barbarism. Moreover, many of those attending the address reported that Hedler questioned whether the Nazi murder of Jews was such a bad thing.[26]

The Social Democrats did not let such calumny go unpunished. In January 1950, Rudolf Katz, a Jewish SPD member and justice minister of the state of Schleswig-Holstein, asked his party colleague and coreligionist Jakob Altmaier to initiate proceedings against Hedler. Hedler had his parliamentary immunity lifted, and many prominent Social Democrats and anti-Nazi resistance leaders took action against Hedler. However, Katz and other prosecutors considered it particularly important that a German Jew press charges.[27] Despite the outrageous nature of Hedler's comments, he was initially found not guilty of libel or incitement to violence. The exonerated Bundestag deputy was warmly feted by the political right after his acquittal. Incidentally, two of the three

---

[24] Letter from Vereinigung der Verfolgten des Naziregimes to Wilhelm Laforet, 23 December 1949, ACDP, I-122, 096/2.
[25] "Bundesparteitag," 29 April 1950, ADL, A 1, 11, 44.
[26] Untitled AJC report, 15 December 1949, CJH/YIVO, RG 347.7.1, box 34.
[27] Letter from Rudolf Katz to Jakob Altmaier, 3 January 1950, AdsD, Nachlass Jakob Altmaier (Abt. I), 4.

judges originally hearing the case were former Nazis, and the West German judiciary was filled with ex-Nazis at that time. Only in July 1951, seventeen months after the first tribunal, did Hedler receive a sentence of nine months' imprisonment. His appeal to the highest federal court failed, and he served six months of his sentence.[28]

The Hedler affair illustrated the public challenges faced by those Jews who returned to Germany. A seeming indifference or even hostility to their plight pervaded society. Although Altmaier had decided to return to Germany and successfully entered politics, he was bitter about lingering antisemitism in the country. In an article on Jewish life in contemporary Germany, he rhetorically asked, "Is there no future, no space for 30,000 among 62 million?" He perceived a climate of antisemitism pervading German life, and he believed that former Nazis controlled the administration of West Germany. Rather than accept responsibility for the Nazis' policies, they blamed the American occupiers for Germany's poor condition.[29] Altmaier continually fought for justice on behalf of those persecuted by the Nazis.

Meanwhile, Adolf Arndt, a non-Jew, became the SPD's watchdog for Nazis and Nazi sympathizers in the West German government. He made criticism of Hans Globke one of his highest priorities and refused to accept the Americans' approval of Globke's appointment as Adenauer's chief of staff.[30] The campaign against Globke brought Arndt the attention and support of the Jewish press.[31] Noting the inactivity of Adenauer's government on reparations and antisemitism, in May 1950, party chairman Kurt Schumacher proclaimed reparations and reconciliation with Jews around the world to be essential to the restoration of Germany's reputation abroad.[32] Schumacher, who wanted to improve relations with Jews

[28] For more information on the Hedler case, see Frei, *Vergangenheitspolitik*, 309–325. On former Nazis in the West German judiciary, see Marc von Miquel, "Juristen: Richter in eigener sache," in *Karrieren im Zwielicht*, ed. Frei, 181–236.

[29] Unpublished manuscript "Die Juden im heutigen Deutschland," [1949], AdsD, Nachlass Jakob Altmaier (Abt. I), 13.

[30] Press releases, 13 and 14 July 1950; letter from Erich Ollenhauer to Theodor Heuss, 14 July 1950; letter from Adolf Arndt to Gustav Heinemann, 19 July 1950; letter from Adolf Arndt to Wolfgang Mommsen, 31 October 1950; AdsD, Nachlass Adolf Arndt (Abt. I), 322.

[31] "Prüfstein des Vertrauens," *Allgemeine Wochenzeitung*, 21 July 1950.

[32] "Nationalismus=Antisemitismus," *Allgemeine Wochenzeitung*, 26 May 1950.

abroad, not just with Jews in Germany, had been in contact with American Jewish labor leaders in the late 1940s.[33]

Within the government, Theodor Heuss was the one high official who continually fostered close ties to the Jewish community in West Germany. Although he usually declined requests for letters and endorsements, he agreed to write a congratulatory letter for the fifth anniversary edition of the *Allgemeine Wochenzeitung der Juden in Deutschland*.[34] He also met with Jewish leaders on many occasions. On 19 January 1950, Heuss and his staff met with Norbert Wollheim, a Jewish leader in northern Germany, and the president expressed regret that there had been no official contact between his office and the Jewish groups.[35] Though he recognized the limits of his largely ceremonial office, he told Wollheim that his principal task was to speak the truth and to help the German people emerge from their "state of spiritual, political, and moral shock." Furthermore, he desired to open a dialogue between Jews and Germans in an effort to bridge the gaps between the two peoples.[36] Politically astute as well as morally upright, Heuss claimed to oppose Adenauer's offer of 10 million marks, which so many Jews found objectionable, and indicated his desire to meet with Jewish leader Nahum Goldmann.[37]

Despite their concurrence on many issues, Heuss and Wollheim could not agree on the immediate future of German-Jewish relations. When they met again on 20 March 1950 (before the founding of the Central Council), Heuss and his aide Luitpold Werz regretted that there was no single Jewish authority in Germany with whom they could speak. Although Wollheim downplayed the divisions in Jewish opinion and representation, he rather pointedly noted that Philipp Auerbach, who had attempted to found a single group, had no authority outside the U.S. zone. Wollheim inadvertently revealed just how divided the Jewish community was

---

[33] Kurt Schumacher, "Schumacher an Erich Ollenhauer aus San Francisco: Bericht über die ersten Wochen des USA-Besuches," 7 October 1947, in *Reden – Schriften – Korrespondenzen*, 559–560.

[34] Letter from Karl Marx to Theodor Heuss, 18 January 1950; letter from Luitpold Werz to Karl Marx, 23 January 1950; BAK, B 122, 2083 (29).

[35] "Gespräch zwischen Bundespräsident Theodor Heuss und Norbert Wollheim," 19 January 1950, *Zwischen Moral und Realpolitik. Deutsch-israelische Beziehungen, 1945–1965*, ed. Yeshayahu Jelinek (Gerlingen: Bleicher, 1997), 135. Wollheim blamed Heuss for the lack of contact.

[36] Ibid., 136.   [37] Ibid., 137–138.

before the formation of the Central Council.[38] Wollheim, active in the Central Committee of Liberated Jews in the British Zone, saw Israel as the future of the Jewish people and advised Heuss to initiate contact with Israeli officials.[39] Heuss believed, however, that it was not the right time to discuss Israeli-German relations, even though he did wish to open a private dialogue with Israeli officials.[40] Unbeknownst to Heuss, Wollheim sent reports on his meetings to the Israeli government via Shalom Adler-Rudel, director of the European section of the Jewish Agency.[41]

Norbert Wollheim faced a Jewish rival for Theodor Heuss's attentions: Karl Marx. In fact, Karl Marx was in steady contact with many government officials and drew the attention of numerous others. A particular target of Marx's efforts was the West German president. On 23 February 1950, Marx told Heuss that countless German Jews in exile still looked to Germany with longing, but that the West German government had not done enough to capitalize on these sentiments. That same day, he wrote Werz to discourage Heuss from meeting with Wollheim, preferring a united front of Jewish leaders in Germany to meet with government officials in Bonn. Two weeks later, Marx wrote Werz again to warn the presidential office that Wollheim did not represent the Israeli government, despite his recent trip to the Jewish state as a representative of the World Jewish Congress.[42] Marx had also been in contact with Adenauer's adviser Herbert Blankenhorn about a secret dialogue with Israeli representatives.[43] Not everyone appreciated Marx's

[38] "Brief von Norbert Wollheim an Shalom Adler-Rudel mit Bericht über das Treffen mit Bundespräsident Theodor Heuss," 4 April 1950, *Zwischen Moral und Realpolitik*, 145.

[39] Ibid.; "Aktenvermerk," 20 March 1950, BAK, B 122, 2084 (29). In particular, Wollheim had Eliahu Livneh in mind. Livneh was Israeli consul to the American occupation authority in Munich. The Israeli government did not accredit him to West Germany. Yeshayahu Jelinek, "Like an Oasis in the Desert: The Israeli Consulate in Munich, 1948–1953," *Studies in Zionism* 9, no. 1 (spring 1988).

[40] "Brief von Norbert Wollheim an Shalom Adler-Rudel mit Bericht über das Treffen mit Bundespräsident Theodor Heuss," 4 April 1950, *Zwischen Moral und Realpolitik*, 146; letter from Theodor Heuss to Sammy Gronemann, 14 February 1950, BAK, N 1221, 139.

[41] "Brief von Norbert Wollheim an Shalom Adler-Rudel mit Bericht über das Treffen mit Bundespräsident Theodor Heuss," 4 April 1950, *Zwischen Moral und Realpolitik*, 142. Adler-Rudel, then living in London, had worked as a Jewish welfare administrator in Berlin before 1934.

[42] "Aufzeichnung," 23 February 1950; letter from Karl Marx to Luitpold Werz, 23 February 1950; letter from Karl Marx to Luitpold Werz, 6 March 1950; BAK, B 122, 2083 (29).

[43] Letter from Karl Marx to Herbert Blankenhorn, 23 February 1950, PA-AA, B 10, 307 (Fiche A 2023), 20–21.

behind-the-scenes efforts. On 11 April 1950, Minister for Refugees Hans Lukaschek wrote Chancellor Adenauer to pass along a warning about the Jewish editor. While Lukaschek did not know Marx, he trusted the source of the warning, Max Schindler of the United Restitution Office in London. Schindler feared Marx's growing influence and accused him of being persona non grata in international Jewish circles.[44]

In the spring of 1950, Heuss also took practical steps toward healing the rift between Germans and Jews. He gave interviews with the foreign Jewish press and stressed the changes in postwar Germany, downplaying a recent spate of cemetery desecrations.[45] In reaction to these attacks, he also met with Everitt Clichy, leader of the American group National Conference of Christians and Jews, and Carl Zietlow, his liaison in Germany.[46] Despite Heuss's earlier reservations, he also made an effort to contact the Israeli consul in Munich, hoping that the Bavarian state government could arrange a meeting.[47]

Even though the West German federal government did not initiate any formal moves for reparations until late 1951, discussions on the issue took place behind closed doors in the spring and summer of 1950. Officials in the West German Finance Ministry were tabulating how much their government would need to pay in reparations and restitution. One official considered payments of 50 million marks per year to be reasonable, but American occupation administration officials overruled the Germans, insisting that West Germany's currency must stay in the country. Foreign Office officials wanted experts at the Finance Ministry to devise a plan for reparations in the form of goods and called on the Justice Ministry to work on the structure of a potential agreement with Israel.[48] Adenauer's deputy foreign minister, Walter Hallstein, contacted state legislators about standardizing state reparations laws, using U.S. zonal law as a model. Hallstein did not rule out federal subsidies to help the state governments, however.[49]

---

[44] Letter from Hans Lukaschek to Konrad Adenauer, 11 April 1950, ACDP, I-070, 52/3.

[45] "Aktenvermerk," 9 May 1950, BAK, B 122, 2083 (29).

[46] "Aktenvermerk," 16 May 1950, BAK, B 122, 2081 (27).

[47] "Vermerk," 9 May 1950, BAK, B 122, 506.

[48] "Vermerk über eine Ressort-Besprechung im Bundesfinanzministerium," 26 May 1950, PA-AA, B 10, 1665 (Fiche A 4512).

[49] Letter from Walter Hallstein to Werner Hofmeister, November 1951, PA-AA, B 10, 1665 (Fiche A 4512).

KARL MARX: JEWISH ADVOCATE AND WATCHDOG

As seen, the journalist Karl Marx was responsible for much of the dialogue between German and Jewish leaders. In fact, in the five years from 1945 to 1950, his *Allgemeine Wochenzeitung* grew from a local newspaper in Düsseldorf to the symbolic voice of the Jewish community throughout Germany. Under his editorial leadership, the newspaper did much more than report on the activities of the Jewish communities in western Germany. It became a forum for Jewish opinion on German and international affairs, and its editorials reflected the hopes and frustrations of the Jewish communal leadership. Although technically independent, the newspaper maintained close ties with the Central Council, and Marx became close friends with Central Council general secretary Hendrik George van Dam.[50] During the Weimar Republic, Karl Marx had been a freelance journalist. Therefore, shortly after his return to Germany from exile in England, the British licensing officer in Düsseldorf asked him to take over operations of a small information sheet, and he accepted.[51] His newspaper profited from the warm relations between German Jews and eastern Jewish displaced persons in the British zone, allowing it to gain wide acceptance among the Jews in northern Germany. It survived while competitors failed, and Marx took advantage of this situation to expand into southern Germany and Berlin. By 1950, the *Allgemeine Wochenzeitung* was unrivaled within the Jewish community in Germany.

As the editor of the only nationwide Jewish newspaper in Germany, Marx exerted considerable influence, and he courted politicians as much as they courted him. He repeatedly offered his services to the West German government as an adviser on Jewish affairs or as a middleman for contacts with Israel.[52] West German politicians, including Kurt Schumacher and Konrad Adenauer, also used Marx's newspaper as a vehicle to address the Jewish community in Germany.[53]

---

[50] Lilli Marx, "Renewal of the German-Jewish Press," in *After the Holocaust*, ed. Brenner, 128.
[51] Brenner, *After the Holocaust*, 125.
[52] Letter from Karl Marx to Theodor Heuss, 15 September 1949, BAK, B 122, 2086 (29); letter from Thomas Dehler to Robert Lehr, 5 March 1951, BAK, N 1244, 25; Dominique Trimbur, *De la Shoah à la réconciliation: La question des relations RFA-Israël [1949–1956]* (Paris: CNRS Éditions, 2000), 209–219.
[53] "Interview Dr. Schumachers über die Frage des jüdischen Neu-Einbaues in Deutschland," 17 February 1947, in *Sopade Informationsdienst* no. 115, 4 March 1947, AdsD, Bestand Kurt

Marx used his newspaper as an instrument of pressure on the West German government and as a watchdog against renewed antisemitism. The *Allgemeine Wochenzeitung* regularly reported on suspect statements by right-wing politicians, and particular targets of its attention during the early 1950s were the Socialist Reich Party (Sozialistische Reichspartei, or SRP) and the German Reich Party (Deutsche Reichspartei, or DRP), both on the far right of the political spectrum.[54] The former party held seats in several state legislatures, and the latter held seats in the Bundestag. Marx harried federal officials about the two parties. While he wanted aggressive steps taken against political extremism, federal interior minister Robert Lehr preferred a more cautious approach so as not arouse public ire. Lehr therefore focused on both the radical left and the radical right.[55] In fact, by November 1951 the federal government initiated steps to ban both the SRP and the Communist Party of Germany as inimical to West German democracy.[56]

The *Allgemeine Wochenzeitung* also criticized rightward trends within mainstream political parties, including the Free Democratic Party and the German Party, both members of the government coalition. The north German FDP, in particular, became the target of much criticism. In the summer of 1950, the *Allgemeine Wochenzeitung* reported, "Germany's Iron Cross-wearing 'front-line generation' was brought together by a drum beat. . . . The occasion was the election campaign in North Rhine-Westphalia, and the drummer was the FDP."[57] Marx feared that as the extreme right-wing parties lost influence, their members would join the FDP, and he accused the German Party of encouraging neo-fascism.[58]

Marx applied the same kind of pressure to government personnel. He frequently denounced Hans Globke and cast aspersions

---

Schumacher (Abt. II), 40; "Bekenntnis zur Verpflichtung," *Allgemeine Wochenzeitung*, 25 November 1949; "Die Zeit der Pogrome ist vorbei: Interview Dr. Schumachers mit der 'Allgemeinen,'" *Allgemeine Wochenzeitung*, 10 November 1950.

[54] "Zweierlei Epochen," *Allgemeine Wochenzeitung*, 2 June 1950; "Exemplarische Strafe für Hedler wegen Beleidigung der Juden," *Allgemeine Wochenzeitung*, 27 July 1951.

[55] Letter from Robert Lehr to Karl Marx, 10 May 1951, BAK, N 1244, 25.

[56] On the SRP's demise, see Kurt Tauber, *Beyond Eagle and Swastika: German Nationalism Since 1945*, vol. 1 (Middletown: Wesleyan University Press, 1967), esp. 713–714, and Frei, *Vergangenheitspolitik*, 326–360. On the KPD, see Major, *Death of the KPD*, 283–293.

[57] "Die Schlacht fand im Saale statt," *Allgemeine Wochenzeitung*, 16 June 1950.

[58] "DRP verliert Anhänger," *Allgemeine Wochenzeitung*, 13 October 1950; "DP wird immer deutlicher," *Allgemeine Wochenzeitung*, 24 November 1950.

on Adenauer's defense of Globke's objectivity.[59] Disappointed with the level of persistent antisemitic violence, Marx and his reporters attacked the West German judicial system for its ineffectual prosecution of synagogue arsonists and cemetery desecrators. Additionally, the *Allgemeine Wochenzeitung* reported almost weekly on former Nazis and Nazi fellow travelers in positions of authority.[60]

Despite his often sharp criticism in print, Marx cultivated good personal ties with leading West German politicians, including those with whom he had conflicts.[61] By the mid-1950s, he and his newspaper were in great demand. Marx's widow claimed that "people stood in line to meet Karl Marx and buy his name for their businesses." In her opinion, having him on a board of directors bestowed legitimacy during an era marked by business leaders and politicians with questionable pasts.[62] The West German government also valued Marx's role in furthering German-Jewish reconciliation, awarding him one of the Federal Republic's highest civilian decorations in 1953.[63]

THE SPD ON THE OFFENSIVE

The Social Democratic leadership unhesitatingly supported Jewish interests in Germany, and in an interview with a Jewish journalist in November 1950, Kurt Schumacher stressed the natural ties between the Jews and his party. He expressed little confidence in Adenauer's government, considering the average cabinet member to be "cool and passive" regarding the Jewish question.[64] The *Allgemeine Wochenzeitung* applauded Schumacher's statements and the political risk he took by standing for Jewish interests.[65]

---

59 Letter from Karl Marx to Thomas Dehler, 13 December 1950, ADL, N 1, 1068; "Eine Frage, Herr Dr. Globke!," *Allgemeine Wochenzeitung*, 8 December 1950; "Dr. Adenauer's treuester Beamter," *Allgemeine Wochenzeitung*, 8 June 1951.
60 For example, "Gesetz über Gerechtigkeit," *Allgemeine Wochenzeitung*, 4 May 1951, and "Das Zünglein an der Waage," *Allgemeine Wochenzeitung*, 9 June 1950.
61 Lilli Marx, interview by author, Düsseldorf, 14 April 1999.
62 Lilli Marx, "Renewal of the German-Jewish Press," in *After the Holocaust*, ed. Brenner, 128.
63 "Auszeichnung für Karl Marx," *Allgemeine Wochenzeitung*, 30 January 1953.
64 "Interview des Korrespondenten der New Yorker Tageszeitung 'Jewish Daily Forward' mit Schumacher über die Situation der Juden in Deutschland," in *Reden – Schriften – Korrespondenzen*, 999.
65 "Unsere Meinung: Mut zur Unpopularität," *Allgemeine Wochenzeitung*, 10 November 1950.

Schumacher's comments on the government's lack of concern for Jewish issues unleashed a controversy. Almost immediately after the publication of the interview, justice minister Thomas Dehler wrote to Karl Marx to protest Schumacher's characterization of the cabinet and to attack his harsh language. As Dehler often did in such situations, he noted that he had a Jewish wife and that before the war he had worked alongside numerous Jewish colleagues. Claiming to be greatly concerned with the fate of German Jewry, he bitterly wrote to Marx, "My life is evidence of my position. It has truly not changed as a result of my position as a member of the cabinet."[66] Cowed by the letter, Marx wrote to Dehler the next day that he had reprinted the Schumacher interview in the *Allgemeine Wochenzeitung* even though he knew Schumacher's statements were not entirely accurate. He claimed that he had wanted to force the government to take a position on Jewish issues as it had done little for the Jews, many of whom returned to Germany completely impoverished.[67] In the next issue of his newspaper, Marx printed both Dehler's letter and his own editorial, in which he repeated this assertion.[68] Soon, Chancellor Adenauer took note of the brewing controversy. He counseled Dehler to restrict the scope of his exchanges with Marx and to stick to generalities in defending himself.[69] Dehler disregarded this advice. In a long letter, he claimed that the government favored "a just reparation of National Socialist injustices within the limits of the financial abilities of the federation and the states" and pledged to do his utmost to assist victims of the Nazis. However, he cautioned Marx not to overestimate the influence of right-wing groups in Germany, intimating that Marx was harming West Germany by drawing attention to them.[70]

In early 1951, an SPD spokesman in the Bundestag raised the issue of reparations, elucidating his party's position and obliging other parties to respond to the proposal. On 24 January, the SPD proposed a standardization of reparations laws throughout West Germany. Moreover, it advocated the official recognition of Israel, rather than foreign Jewish successor organizations, as the heir of

---

[66] Letter from Thomas Dehler to Karl Marx, 10 November 1950, BAK, B 136, 5862.
[67] Letter from Karl Marx to Thomas Dehler, 11 November 1950, BAK, B 136, 5862.
[68] "Bundesminister der Justiz antwortet Dr. Schumacher," *Allgemeine Wochenzeitung*, 17 November 1950.
[69] Letter from Konrad Adenauer to Thomas Dehler, 1 December 1950, BAK, B 136, 5862.
[70] Letter from Thomas Dehler to Karl Marx, 8 December 1950, BAK, B 136, 5862.

all unclaimed property in Germany formerly owned by Jewish victims of the Nazis. Only by granting Israel this prerogative could West Germany help those Jews who had fled Germany and lived in poverty abroad.[71] Not only did the SPD take the move of proposing immediate aid to the Jews, it also took the radical step of publicly recognizing Israel as the legitimate representative of the murdered Jews. On 22 February, as debate began on the proposal, SPD deputy Carlo Schmid spoke of the need to pay reparations to the Jews and to all those who had resisted Hitler and suffered for it. In 1945, there had been a willingness to do so but not the means. Now, the Germans had the opportunity. While some critics worried about West Germany's ability to pay its foreign debts, Schmid would not compare these debts to the moral debt owed to the Jews. To him, it was irrelevant whether reparations were easy or not. No group had suffered more at the hands of the Nazis than the Jews, and Judeophobia had been at the center of Nazi ideology.[72]

Schmid's remarks drew a variety of responses and opened the public discourse on what practical steps should be taken to recompense the Jewish people for the Nazis' crimes. Speaking for the government, Alfred Hartmann of the Finance Ministry claimed that only an international agreement could regulate the matter.[73] In his response on behalf of the FDP, Fritz Oellers supported reparations in theory but feared new injustices would result from redistributing German property to Jewish claimants. Furthermore, Oellers did not recognize Israel as the representative of the world Jewish community.[74] Ultimately, the FDP leadership opposed the proposal, recognizing only the claims of individual Holocaust victims, not a collective payment to a Jewish organization.[75] The Free Democrats did not discuss who would press claims on behalf of the millions of murdered Jews. The Jewish press eagerly followed

---

[71] "Interpellation der Fraktion der SPD, Drucksache Nr. 1828," 24 January 1951, Germany (West), Bundestag, *Verhandlungen des Deutschen Bundestages, I. Wahlperiode 1949, Anlagen zu den stenographischen Berichte, Drucksachen Nr. 1801 bis 2000 (9. Teil)* (Bonn: Bonner Universitäts-Buchdruckerei, 1951).

[72] "120. Sitzung," 22 February 1951, Germany (West), Bundestag, *Verhandlungen des Deutschen Bundestages, I. Wahlperiode 1949,* vol. 6, *Stenographische Berichte, 109.–132. Sitzung, 1951* (Bonn: Bonner Universitäts-Buchdruckerei, 1951), 4590–4593.

[73] "Vereinheitlichung der Wiedergutmachung gefordert," *Allgemeine Wochenzeitung,* 2 March 1951.

[74] "120. Sitzung," 22 February 1951, *Verhandlungen des Deutschen Bundestages, I. Wahlperiode 1949,* 6:4594–4595.

[75] "Kurzprotokoll Nr. 23/50," 15 March 1951, ADL, A 40, 728, 22–23.

the issue, and the *Allgemeine Wochenzeitung* noted that federal finance minister Fritz Schäffer considered this whole issue to be a matter for the states, while the states claimed to be unable to pay reparations.[76] Schäffer, guardian of the state's finances, opposed any large-scale reparations to Jews on the grounds that such an outflow of cash would be injurious to the West German economy.[77] Carlo Schmid branded this so-called principled opposition to reparations to Jews "collective innocence." He warned that the renunciation of collective guilt would lead to a myth of collective innocence, which would induce confusion in the public's mind about right and wrong. Hendrik George van Dam wrote that a sense of collective nonresponsibility would develop from the sense of collective innocence, which would "torpedo reparations and restitution."[78]

RELATIONS WITH THE GOVERNMENT AND FOREIGN JEWRY ON THE EVE OF REPARATIONS, JANUARY–SEPTEMBER 1951

The debate over who would represent Jewish interests to the West German government naturally had an impact on the Jews living in Germany. German Jewish leaders, desiring greater influence, could not ignore the intervention of foreign Jewish groups in internal West German affairs. In January 1951, Heinz Galinski, leader of the Jewish community in Berlin, wrote an editorial in the *Allgemeine Wochenzeitung* on the need for Jews to remain in Germany. He criticized those Jewish organizations, presumably abroad, which claimed to represent the Jews in Germany without involvement in their social situation.[79] The Central Council, eager to establish the postwar communities as successors to those of the prewar period, founded a Jewish welfare agency in January and quickly sought government approval of the new institution. This office revived an institution originally founded in 1917 and dissolved by

---

76 "Unsere Meinung: Wiedergutmachungs-Interpellation," *Allgemeine Wochenzeitung,* 2 March 1951.

77 Pross, *Paying for the Past,* 8; Christoph Henzler, *Fritz Schäffer (1945–1967): Eine biographische Studie zum ersten bayerischen Nachkriegs-Ministerpräsidenten und ersten Finanzminister der Bundesrepublik Deutschland* (Munich: Hanns-Seidel-Stiftung, 1994), 421–442.

78 "Neuer Mythos des 20. Jahrhunderts: Kollektive Verantwortlosikeit," *Allgemeine Wochenzeitung,* 13 April 1951.

79 "Mahnruf zum gegenseitigen Verstehen!," *Allgemeine Wochenzeitung,* 12 January 1951.

the Nazis.[80] While the Interior Ministry recommended that the welfare agency be an independent institution – similar to the prominent pre-1933 Jewish beneficent foundation – and not a mere branch of the Central Council, the government was not prepared to offer formal legal recognition. This policy stood in contrast to the recognition granted the group's predecessor in 1926 by the German government.[81] By August 1951, the Central Council had finalized plans for the agency. The Central Welfare Office of Jews in Germany (Zentralwohlfahrtsstelle der Juden in Deutschland), based in Hamburg under the leadership of Berthold Simonsohn, aspired to assume duties theretofore assigned to foreign Jewish bodies operating in Germany, including caring for the displaced persons.[82]

Tensions between the Jews in Germany and foreign Jewish groups hindered progress on reparations. Benjamin Ferencz, director of the Jewish Restitution Successor Organization, vigorously protested against the SPD's plan for reparations. The SPD wanted to designate the Israeli state as the successor to Jewish property with no legal heirs, but Ferencz noted that the Allies had designated the JRSO (in the American zone) and the Jewish Trust Corporation (in the British and French zones) as the heirs. He wrote to Carlo Schmid that no one else was eligible for this designation and that no new legislation was needed. The JRSO would handle the matter until its completion.[83] His objection was typical of the attitude of many foreign Jewish groups toward West German politicians and the Jews in West Germany. They did not trust the Germans to maintain reparations as promulgated by the western occupation authorities, and they feared that the Central Council might become the primary Jewish partner for dialogue with the government. Nahum Goldmann, president of the World Jewish Congress, was more positive about relations between foreign Jewry and the Jews in Germany. Goldmann had been reared

---

[80] Letter from Norbert Wollheim to Hendrik George van Dam, 21 January 1951, ZA, B.1/7, 157.

[81] Letter from Hendrik George van Dam to Interior Ministry, 25 February 1951, letter from Interior Ministry to Hendrik George van Dam, 29 March 1951, ZA, B.1/7, 157; Leni Yahil, *The Holocaust: The Fate of European Jewry*, trans. Ina Friedman and Haya Galai (Oxford: Oxford University Press, 1990), 24.

[82] Letter from Central Welfare Office to AJDC, 27 June 1952, ZA, B.1/7, 157.

[83] Letters from Benjamin Ferencz to Carlo Schmid, 27 February and 6 March 1951, AdsD, Nachlass Carlo Schmid (Abt. I), 626.

and educated in Germany, and he welcomed the Central Council as a means whereby the Jewish community in Germany could consolidate itself. He hoped its ties to world Jewry would grow stronger.[84]

Even though the western occupation authorities had designated foreign groups, notably the JRSO, as the legal successors to the prewar community, postwar Jewish groups made arrangements with the state governments to settle their legal status. In March 1951, the Westphalian State Association of Jewish Communities petitioned the North Rhine-Westphalian government to grant it status as a *Körperschaft des öffentlichen Rechts*, which would allow it to levy taxes on its members. In March 1950, the state had passed a law granting the Jewish body this valued status, but the British occupation authority rejected the measure, which would have designated the postwar Jewish communities as the legal successors of prewar communities. Now, State Association leader Siegfried Hamburg felt that having the treasured legal status was more important than being recognized as the successor to prewar German Jewry, and he asked that a new law be drafted without the designation of legal succession. He did not, however, renounce the possibility of later receiving successor status.[85] In September, the Jewish community in Berlin had its status as a *Körperschaft des öffentlichen Rechts* restored by the Berlin senate.[86]

Seeking greater status, the Central Council wanted to establish a more solid relationship with the federal authorities, but there was little unity among board members as to how to proceed. Norbert Wollheim felt that meeting with Bundestag deputies, including Kurt Schumacher and Jakob Altmaier, would achieve nothing. He claimed that most Bundestag deputies were not familiar with the latest developments:"All together they have no idea about reparations. This is a dangerous situation for us." Wollheim characterized Altmaier as "useless because he knows nothing about Jewish problems, not even about Jewish organizations." Wollheim wanted them to approach Adenauer, but Stuttgart leader Benno

[84] "Heute latent, und morgen?," *Allgemeine Wochenzeitung*, 23 February 1951.
[85] Letter from Landesverband Westfalen to North Rhine-Westphalia Minister of Education and Culture, 14 March 1951, ZA, B.1/15, 190.
[86] Letter from Siegmund Weltlinger to Jüdische Gemeinde zu Berlin, 7 September 1951, LAB, E Rep. 200–22, 38.

Ostertag suggested they contact Theodor Heuss.[87] An American Jewish Committee representative at the meeting termed Heuss "more than a fair-weather friend of the Jewish people," in contrast to Adenauer.[88] The Jewish Agency's representative to the Central Council, W. Schwarz, opined that Adenauer was interested only in foreign affairs, and thus in foreign Jews. Heinz Galinski resented foreign Jewish groups' involvement with the West German government, but Karl Marx and Israeli consul Livneh encouraged cooperation with foreign Jewish groups. Ultimately, the delegates were disposed to open a dialogue with the government but disagreed as to whether they should adopt a quiet approach or make a public effort.[89] In fact, by late summer the government did take notice of the Jews' organization, and on 28 August the federal cabinet decided to invite the Central Council to send delegates to the official celebration of the West German national holiday in September.[90]

On 31 May 1951, the Central Council began campaigning for government recognition and appealed directly to President Heuss. Van Dam expressed his desire to end the state of nonrelations between the government and the Jews in Germany and thanked Heuss for his previous efforts.[91] Heuss's aide Luitpold Werz passed the request on to Interior Ministry officials, who bristled at the allegation that they had been ignoring the Jewish community. On 29 June, the Interior Ministry official responsible for Jewish-related issues replied directly to Werz. Citing the resolution of the Jewish adviser controversy and the foundation of the Central Welfare Office, he claimed that the government had long-standing ties to the Central Council and considered it the "legal representation of the Jews and Jewish religious communities within the area of the

---

[87] "Protokoll des Zentralrates der Juden in Deutschland," 29–30 April 1951, ZA, B.1/7, 221.13.

[88] AJC report, "The Jews of Germany Want to 'Recognize' Bonn," 21 May 1951, CJH/YIVO, RG 347.7.1, box 35.

[89] "Protokoll des Zentralrates der Juden in Deutschland," 29–30 April 1951, ZA, B.1/7, 221.13.

[90] "169. Kabinettssitzung," 28 August 1951, Germany (West), Bundesregierung, *Die Kabinettsprotokolle der Bundesregierung*, ed. Hans Booms, vol. 4, *1951*, ed. Ursula Hüllbüsch (Boppard: Harald Boldt, 1988), 625. The federal cabinet had designated 12 September, the day of the first election for the West German president, as the national holiday.

[91] Letter from Hendrik George van Dam to Theodor Heuss, 31 May 1951, BAK, B 106, 36, 51.

Federal Republic."[92] After this initial attempt, in July the Central Council decided to wait for a signal from President Heuss.[93]

Indecision over the location of the Central Council's permanent office reflected the debate on that organization's relationship with the government and with other Jewish groups in Germany. Galinski, stressing the group's function as a political pressure group, suggested establishing the office in Bonn, the West German capital. Benno Ostertag considered Frankfurt the best option, as it was both centrally located and had a sizable Jewish presence. The representatives of the American Joint Distribution Committee, the Jewish Agency, and the Israeli government wanted the German Jews to set up their base in Munich. Sam Haber of the AJDC observed that Munich had the largest Jewish population and that many foreign Jewish groups maintained their German offices there. W. Schwarz of the Jewish Agency noted that the Jewish displaced persons had their headquarters in Munich, and relations with the DPs were as important as ties to the government in Bonn. Both men were short-sighted in their analyses. Munich had the largest Jewish population and the most Jewish institutions because of the large displaced persons presence in Bavaria, but, as Ostertag noted, the DPs were leaving Germany.[94] They were not casting their lot with the Jews who remained in Germany, whom the Central Council represented.

In spite of their shared goals, deep divisions and personal conflicts among the leaders of the Jewish community often hindered progress. Wollheim had criticized Karl Marx's efforts to rehabilitate film director Veit Harlan, director of the antisemitic film *Jud Süss*, made in 1940, and coordinated his attacks on Marx with Julius Dreifuss of Düsseldorf.[95] Dreifuss complained about van Dam's ties to Karl Marx.[96] Additionally, relations among Jewish groups in Germany were poor. After the dissolution of the Central Committee of Liberated Jews, Eastern European Jews in Munich, feeling

[92] Letter from Interior Ministry to Luitpold Werz, 29 June 1951, BAK, B 106, 36, 52; and BAK, B 136, 5862.
[93] "Beschlussprotokoll der Direktoriumssitzung," 9 July 1951, ZA, B.1/7, 221.14.
[94] "Protokoll des Zentralrates der Juden in Deutschland," 29–30 April 1951, ZA, B.1/7, 221.13.
[95] Letter from Norbert Wollheim to Julius Dreifuss, 11 October 1950, ZA, B.1/7, 230; letter from Karl Marx to Landesverband Nordrhein, 9 September 1950, letter from Karl Marx to Julius Dreifuss, 26 October 1950, ZA, B.1/15, 296.
[96] Letter from Julius Dreifuss to Norbert Wollheim, 19 March 1951, ZA, B.1/7, 230.

unrepresented in the Central Council, wanted their own representative organization. The Central Council, anxious to avoid a split
in the newly united Jewish community, sent a delegation to negotiate.[97] Writing in 1965, van Dam recognized that for its first five
years of existence, the Central Council had been riven with internal conflicts.[98] In fact, one of van Dam's principal functions was
representing the Jewish community in Germany to the German
public and foreign Jews on daily basis. He struggled to keep the
Central Council nonpartisan. This posture was important not only
in dealing with various West German political institutions, but
also because the Central Council officially represented the Jews
in Communist-ruled East Germany.[99]

In September 1951, German-Jewish relations were about to enter a new phase. Unbeknownst to the Central Council and to
most Jews in Germany, chancellor Konrad Adenauer had been in
touch with Nahum Goldmann, Jakob Altmaier, and Israeli officials
about declaring West Germany's intention to pay reparations to
the Jewish people.[100] Additionally, the displaced persons' Central Committee in the British Zone was ceasing operations.[101]
Norbert Wollheim, co-leader of the Jewish refugees in the British
zone, left Germany for America in September 1951. However, just
before leaving Germany for good, he acknowledged the contribution made by Jakob Altmaier in bringing Adenauer and international Jewish leaders together.[102] Even though progress in
German-Jewish reconciliation had begun, Wollheim chose not
to stay in Germany. In his public farewell speech, Wollheim
said, "We are on the eve of a Nazi restoration in Germany." He

---

[97] "Protokoll des Zentralrates der Juden in Deutschland," 30 April 1951, ZA, B.1/7,
221.13; "Protokoll des Zentralrates der Juden in Deutschland," 9 July 1951, ZA, B.1/7,
221.14.

[98] Van Dam, "Die Juden in Deutschland nach 1945," in *Judentum*, 2:904–905.

[99] "Bericht des Generalsekretärs für die Periode Januar-August 1951," August 1951, ZA,
B.1/7, 246.

[100] "Meine Arbeit und Mitwirkung am 'Israel-Vertrag,'" 5 May 1959, AdsD, Nachlass Jakob
Altmaier (Abt. I.), 7; Nahum Goldmann, *The Autobiography of Nahum Goldmann: Sixty
Years of Jewish Life*, trans. Helen Sebba (New York: Holt, Rinehart and Winston, 1969),
256.

[101] "Erfolgreiches Ende einer Zusammenarbeit," *Allgemeine Wochenzeitung*, 31 August 1951.

[102] Letter from Norbert Wollheim to Jakob Altmaier, 24 September 1951, AdsD, Nachlass
Jakob Altmaier (Abt. I), 5. In 1952, as German-Jewish relations improved, Karl Marx
and Jakob Altmaier feuded over who had done more to bring the Jews closer to the
government. Letter from Karl Marx to Jakob Altmaier, 14 January 1952, AdsD, Nachlass
Jakob Altmaier (Abt. I), 4.

counseled his coreligionists to maintain their close ties with world Jewry.[103]

Not long after the Central Council brought direction and stability to Jewish life in Germany, the Jewish community faced a crisis that embarrassed it and reawakened fears of resurgent antisemitism. Philipp Auerbach, leader of the Jewish community in Bavaria, Social Democratic politician, and middleman between the German Jews and eastern Jews, was at the center of the storm.[104]

Since 1946, Auerbach had served in the Bavarian government as administrator for reparations to former Nazi victims. As a German Jew helping primarily eastern Jews, he bridged the gulf between the two groups, eventually becoming president of the Jewish community in Bavaria and a member of the Central Council board, as well as Bavarian state commissar representing the interests of former Nazi persecutees – a clear conflict of interest. Moreover, he operated a slush fund so he could help those in need without recourse to the Bavarian state bureaucracy. His aid to former victims included support for students, private stocks of groceries and furniture, and private rest homes. The entire operation hinged on Auerbach personally.[105]

Auerbach was an intensely political man, and his machinations earned him the enmity of Germans as disparate as leading Communists in Bavaria and Josef Müller, deputy chairman of the CSU. By January 1951, various German groups were collecting evidence against Auerbach, and the American occupation authority prepared to investigate him. To prevent the Americans from taking the initiative, the Bavarian government decided to act first.[106] On 27 January, Bavarian police entered the State Compensation Office, headed by Auerbach, and seized its records to investigate allegations of fraudulent reparations claims. The Bavarian Justice

[103] "Undemokratische Behandlung in Deutschland," *Allgemeine Wochenzeitung*, 20 July 1951.
[104] Constantin Goschler, "Der Fall Phlipp Auerbach. Wiedergutmachung in Bayern," in *Wiedergutmachung*, ed. Herbst and Goschler, 77–98; Wolfgang Kraushaar, "Die Auerbach-Affäre," in *Leben im Land der Täter*, ed. Schoeps. For a more critical view of the Bavarian government in the Auerbach affair, see Pross, *Paying for the Past*, 33–36.
[105] Goschler, "Der Fall Phlipp Auerbach," in *Wiedergutmachung*, ed. Herbst and Goschler, 82–84.
[106] Ibid., 94–95.

Ministry, led by Josef Müller, accused Auerbach of having falsified reparations claims of at least 1.3 million marks in value. Many were patently false, and others had been antedated to favor the Jewish claimant. Auerbach described the allegations as "a frontal attack on reparation[s] and on Jewry."[107] The Central Council called for a thorough and fair investigation, but it denounced the incendiary attacks being made on the Jews as a result of the affair. It was already clear that the Auerbach affair had opened a Pandora's box of antisemitism and recriminations.[108]

At that time, Bavaria claimed the largest Jewish population in Germany, and this interruption in the reparations process quickly drew the attention of German Jewish groups. As early as 29 January, Auerbach complained that the closure of his office was directed against him personally, and he requested the Central Council's intervention.[109] However, cautiously guarding their public image, leaders of the Jewish community in Germany distanced themselves from Auerbach virtually from the start of the affair. Hendrik George van Dam admonished his colleagues, "Do you think it is wise to let yourselves be represented by functionaries against whom the Americans ordered an investigation?" He called on Auerbach to take responsibility, to spare the Jewish community embarrassment, and to resign his communal offices.[110] After some cajoling, Auerbach did consent to relinquish his seat on the Central Council board for the duration of the investigation. Even though they were cutting him loose, his fellow board members wanted to avoid the impression of stabbing him in the back.[111] Not long after Auerbach's initial arrest, investigators brought additional charges against him, including more cases of fraud and falsification of a doctorate.[112] In April 1951, Auerbach's colleagues in the American zonal Interest-Representation removed him from all his offices in the U.S. zone and criticized the Jews in Bavaria for not having

---

[107] "Die Vorgänge im Landesentschädigungsamt," *Allgemeine Wochenzeitung*, 16 February 1951.

[108] "Erklärung," 25 February 1951; letter from Karl Marx to Robert Lehr, 28 February 1951; BAK, N 1244, 25.

[109] "Protokoll," 29 January 1951, ZA, B.1/7, 221.11.

[110] "Ausführung von Dr. van Dam auf der Sitzung der Interessengemeinschaft der Jüdischen Gemeinden der US Zone," 11 February 1951, AdsD, Nachlass Jakob Altmaier (Abt. I), 8.

[111] "Protokoll der Sitzung des Direktoriums des Zentralrates," 25 February 1951, ZA, B.1/7, 221.12.

[112] "Unsere Meinung: Dr. Auerbach und die bayerische Justiz," *Allgemeine Wochenzeitung*, 27 April 1951.

done so earlier.[113] While the Central Council distanced itself from Auerbach, many other Jews supported the beleaguered reparations administrator. In German Jewish émigré circles, far removed from the actual investigation and its fallout, his case became a cause célèbre.[114]

By the summer of 1951, the Auerbach affair threatened to derail the distribution of restitution in Bavaria. With the police continuing to occupy the State Compensation Office, many Jews did not receive their payments.[115] As a result of the ongoing investigation and Auerbach's central role in disbursing reparations in Bavaria, the office nearly collapsed, and van Dam's efforts to restart its operations failed. Auerbach's near dominance of Jewish organizational life in Munich now had serious repercussions, and van Dam wanted the Central Council to intervene with the local Jewish communities.[116]

Auerbach's trial, which began at last in March 1952, proved to be sensational and controversial. Several of the prosecutors and judges handling the case had been members of the Nazi Party or Nazi organizations.[117] Rumors of bribery and missing evidence soon circulated, culminating in the resignation of Bavarian justice minister Müller.[118] Even though many Jewish groups had distanced themselves from Auerbach, they resented the proceedings' witchhunt atmosphere and feared renewed antisemitism.[119] The trial came to a tragic end in August 1952. After receiving a sentence of two-and-a-half years' imprisonment, Auerbach, unable to face incarceration after his time in concentration camps, committed suicide.[120]

---

[113] "Bericht über die Sitzung in Stuttgart," 8 April 1951, ZA, B.1/13, A.746, 4–5.

[114] Letters from Bruno Weil, spring 1952, ZA, B.1/13, 2631; "Unsere Meinung: Schwebendes Verfahren," *Allgemeine Wochenzeitung*, 11 May 1951.

[115] "Das blockierte Landesentschädigungsamt," *Allgemeine Wochenzeitung*, 13 July 1951.

[116] "Bericht des Generalsekretärs für die Periode Januar-August 1951," August 1951, ZA, B.1/7, 246.

[117] "Auerbach-Prozeß wiederum verschoben," *Allgemeine Wochenzeitung*, 4 April 1952; "Wir kommentieren: Im Dschungel des Auerbach-Prozesses," *Allgemeine Wochenzeitung*, 18 April 1952.

[118] "Auerbach-Akten verschwunden," *Allgemeine Wochenzeitung*, 9 May 1952; "Dr. Müller stellt Amt zur Verfügung," *Allgemeine Wochenzeitung*, 30 May 1952.

[119] "Affäre Dreyfus des IV. Reiches?" *Allgemeine Wochenzeitung*, 2 May 1952; van Dam, "Die Juden Deutschland nach 1945," 2:903; "Ehrengericht," undated [1958], ACDP, I-200, 006/4, 8.

[120] "Der Tod Philipp Auerbachs" and "Zweieinhalb Jahre Gefängnis," *Allgemeine Wochenzeitung*, 22 August 1952.

The Auerbach scandal was a searing experience for the Central Council and embarrassed the Jewish community. Central Council board members did not doubt that the trial fomented renewed antisemitism. As early June 1951, Karl Marx told Theodor Heuss that any more scandals might tarnish the Jews' reputation in Germany and that a thoroughgoing purge was necessary.[121] At a meeting of the Central Council leadership seven months after the affair began, Heinz Galinski suggested a revision of the Jewish leadership in Germany.[122]

HEIGHTENED TENSIONS AS REPARATIONS BECOME A
REALITY, SEPTEMBER 1951 TO SEPTEMBER 1952

After Konrad Adenauer announced his intention to approach Israel about Holocaust reparations, the Central Council grew increasingly conscious of its tenuous position between the West German government and foreign Jewish groups. Adenauer's declaration left the Jews in Germany stranded between those two poles. On 15 November 1951, van Dam wrote a letter to all Central Council directorate members emphasizing the need for ties to world Jewry. International support was critical, he reported, to the survival of a Jewish community in Germany. Concerned that the Central Council might become too close to the government, he wrote that "the existence of a Jewish community in Germany, even so small a one, provides a certain alibi for German democracy." For this reason, he feared, German authorities were taking an interest in Jewish groups out of all proportion to their numbers.[123]

The issue of how close the Central Council should be to the government in Bonn and to Jewish groups abroad was of primary concern in the autumn of 1951. The Central Council was in a bind. It was running a deficit, but its directors did not want to ask the federal government for money, fearing that any request might prejudice a future decision on reparations. They did, however, consider requesting financial aid from the two officially designated successor organizations, the Jewish Restitution Successor Organization

---

[121] "Vermerk," 23 June 1951, BAK, B 122, 2083 (29).
[122] "Beschlussprotokoll der Tagung des Zentralrates," 19–20 August 1951, ZA, B.1/7, 221.15.
[123] Letter from Hendrik George van Dam to Central Council directorate, 15 November 1951, ZA, B.1/7, 121.

and the Jewish Trust Corporation. Relations between the Central Council and the World Jewish Congress also remained a concern. Israeli consul Eliahu Livneh reported that Nahum Goldmann, president of the WJC, was working for closer ties between the two organizations. The Central Council board wanted to protect German Jewish interests abroad through the WJC, but it wished to reserve exclusive Jewish access to the West German government for itself.[124] It intended to ensure that West German officials recognize it as the sole legitimate voice of the Jews in Germany, and in the weeks after Adenauer announced his desire to approach Israel and international Jewish groups, both Hendrik George van Dam and Karl Marx reminded the federal ministries that the Central Council claimed sole right to represent Jewish interests in Germany.[125]

Even though Adenauer had initiated reconciliation between the West German government and Jews with his call for reparations, two members of his cabinet soon became embroiled in controversies about alleged antisemitic remarks: Transportation Minister Hans-Christoph Seebohm of the German Party and Justice Minister Thomas Dehler of the Free Democratic Party. The comments made by Seebohm had overtones of Nazism and drew international attention. Dehler's remarks offended the leadership of the German Jewish community, with whom he claimed to have a close relationship.

At a speech delivered in early December to the German Party, Seebohm seemed to support Nazi iconography. He said, "We are united in reverence for any symbol of our people – I expressly mean for any – for which Germans sacrificed their lives for the Fatherland."[126] Most critics interpreted this remark to mean the swastika. Seebohm also attacked Kurt Schumacher and the SPD for opposing the readoption of the *Deutschlandlied* (commonly known abroad as "Deutschland, Deutschland über alles") as the national anthem. For Seebohm and his nationalist party colleagues, it was more than a mere song; it was "a prayer we send to God for our

---

[124] "Protokoll der Tagung des Zentralrates," 18–19 November 1951, ZA, B.1/7, 221.18.

[125] Letter from Karl Marx to Brückner, 11 October 1951, PA-AA, B 10, 1665 (Fiche A 4512); letter from Hendrik George van Dam to Federal Chancellery, 12 October 1951, BAK, B 136, 5862.

[126] "Stenographische Niederschrift der Tonbandaufnahme von der Rede des Bundesministers Dr. Seebohm," 2 December 1951, BAK, N 1178, 22, 42.

people and our Fatherland."[127] In response to the international outcry over his speech, Seebohm claimed that he had not meant the swastika. He feebly explained that it was not a truly German symbol. It was an international symbol that one political party in Germany had happened to use as its party logo. The Allied occupation authorities, led by French High Commissioner André François-Poncet, protested the speech, and West Berlin mayor Ernst Reuter described Seebohm as undemocratic.[128] The SPD demanded his resignation, but Chancellor Adenauer defended him, claiming that no one in his cabinet could have Nazi sympathies.[129]

Thomas Dehler offended German Jewish sensibilities at a conference of Jewish jurists held in Düsseldorf on 15–16 December 1951. Reparations dominated the agenda, and two federal cabinet members, Thomas Dehler and Robert Lehr, gave keynote addresses. Dehler's remarks caused a stir, and the justice minister was later forced to defend himself and his record. At the conference, Dehler noted that it was a shame that German Jewish lawyers, feeling unwelcome among non-Jewish German lawyers, needed a separate professional organization. He blamed the Allies for having poisoned the atmosphere in Germany and having prevented an expeditious correction of the wrongs of the Nazi era. Dehler acknowledged the controversial nature of his remarks, but he excused himself, claiming he could speak frankly since he had a Jewish wife. Dehler could not understand why Israel did not open ties to a government made up of Germans such as he, who had opposed the Nazis. He also contended that the Germans were now being deprived of their wealth and welfare, not unlike the Jews under the Third Reich.[130]

His comments set off a firestorm among the Jewish jurists, who had seen Dehler as an ally. Their indignant communiqué and press reports compelled Dehler to respond. He claimed that his very presence at the conference indicated his concern for Jewish questions. While affirming the importance of reparations, he reiterated his opinion that Allied occupation policy had delayed the implementation of a reparations program. The following day, he

---

[127] Ibid., 43.
[128] Various clippings on Seebohm and the reaction to his speech, BAK, N 1178, 22.
[129] "SPD fordert Rücktritt Dr. Seebohms," *Allgemeine Wochenzeitung*, 25 January 1952.
[130] "Begrüssungsansprache des Bundesjustizministers Dr. Th. Dehler in der Eröffnungssitzung," 15 December 1951, BAK, B 106, 211.

met with a delegation of Jewish jurists to smooth things over.[131] Nonetheless, Dehler had opened a Pandora's box, and after his speech, he received innumerable letters from critics and supporters of reparations.[132] While Dehler was probably not an antisemite, his remarks evinced the deep rift between the Jews in Germany and those politically centrist or center-right Germans who regarded themselves as progressive and pro-Jewish. The two sides simply did not understand each other.

Despite frequent misunderstandings, the Central Council opened a direct relationship with the government in 1952. The *Allgemeine Wochenzeitung*, edited by Karl Marx, opined that the Jews in Germany had waited long enough to establish ties to the government in Bonn. The initiation of reparations negotiations between Israel and West Germany had removed a moral obstacle to relations with the government.[133] Hendrik George van Dam made arrangements to meet with interior minister Robert Lehr to discuss the legal status of former Jewish communal officials.[134] On 21 March 1952, a delegation from the Central Council met with Heuss, thanked him for his support, and asked the president for help in the fight against antisemitism. Heuss spoke of his longstanding ties to the Jews in Germany and expressed his pleasure that they now had a single representative organization.[135] The *Allgemeine Wochenzeitung* lauded the meeting as a great event for all Jews living in Germany.[136]

The meeting with West Germany's symbolic head of state inaugurated an era of new relations with the government. After having met with Heuss, the Central Council received an invitation to meet with Konrad Adenauer. Meeting with a delegation from the Central Council on 1 April, the chancellor expressed his satisfaction that the Jews in Germany had a unitary representation. He considered it important to combat antisemitism lest the world community think democracy was not taking hold in West Germany. The discussion then turned to financial matters. The

---

[131] "Der Dehler-Zwischenfall und seine Erledigung," 16–18 December 1951, ADL, N 1, 773; letter from Thomas Dehler to Arbeitstagung Jüdischer Juristen, 17 December 1951, BAK, B 136, 5862.

[132] Letters to Thomas Dehler, ADL, N 1, 774.

[133] "Rasch und zielbewußt handeln," *Allgemeine Wochenzeitung*, 15 February 1952.

[134] Letter from Hendrik George van Dam to Robert Lehr, 25 January 1952, BAK, N 1244, 25.

[135] "Aufzeichnung," 21 March 1952, BAK, B 122, 2080 (26).

[136] "Empfang bei Professor Heuss," *Allgemeine Wochenzeitung*, 28 March 1952.

Jewish delegates told Adenauer that their community was poor and needed state support to survive. Even though Adenauer made no concrete promises, the Jewish officials left the meeting with the impression that "in the federal chancellor we have a strong supporter of our wishes."[137] Berlin Jewish leader Heinz Galinski, however, did harbor great reservations about Adenauer's plan for West German rearmament and pledged opposition to federal funding for defense.[138] Despite these sentiments, the Jews' relationship with Adenauer's government was on a new basis. Frankfurt Jewish leader Leopold Goldschmidt noted that after these meetings the Central Council's goals should be "an orderly and pleasant relationship with the federal government" and "a clarification of the relationship of the Jews in Germany with Israel."[139]

As a largely ceremonial head of state, Theodor Heuss could not initiate negotiations for reparations; still, he could make important symbolic gestures to Jewish groups. A case in point is that of the Jewish community of Stuttgart, which invited Heuss to attend the opening of its new synagogue. While he was unable to attend the ceremony, he did donate the curtain for the ark, an important gift. Not wanting to encourage other groups to ask for donations, he asked the Jewish leaders to keep his name as donor of the item a secret.[140] He clearly had an affinity for the Jewish community in Germany and for the Jewish community in Stuttgart, where he had lived for some years. Heuss, active in the movement for Christian-Jewish reconciliation, agreed to lobby the government for funding for interconfessional projects, which the Central Council heartily endorsed.[141]

The group's new relationship with the West German government reopened the issue of whether it should move its base of operations from its provisional seat in Hamburg. President Heuss

---

[137] "Bericht über die Besprechung des Direktoriums des Zentralrates der Juden in Deutschland und dessen Generalsekretär mit dem Bundeskanzler Dr. Adenauer," 1 April 1952, ZA, B. 1/5, 213.

[138] "German Jews Bar Arms Aid," 15 February 1952, PA-AA, B 10, 1665 (Fiche A 4515).

[139] "Vorstandssitung der Jüdischen Gemeinde Frankfurt am Main," 3 April 1952, ZA, B.1/13, A.9, 42.

[140] Letter from Israelitische Kultusvereinigung von Württemberg-Hohenzollern to Theodor Heuss, 4 April 1952; letter from Luitpold Werz to Benno Ostertag, 29 April 1952; letter from Benno Ostertag to Luitpold Werz, 3 May 1952; letter from Theodor Heuss to Benno Ostertag, 7 May 1952; letter from Benno Ostertag to Theodor Heuss, 12 May 1952; BAK, B 122, 2084 (29).

[141] Letter from Luitpold Werz to Doerrbeck, 30 April 1952, BAK, B 122, 2081 (27); "Beschlussprotokoll der Direktoriumssitzung," 9 July 1951, ZA, B.1/7, 221.14.

saw the need for a Central Council bureau in Bonn, and the Central Council leadership met on 4 May 1952 to discuss the issue.[142] At a meeting of Central Council leaders, van Dam, who lived in Hamburg, argued that keeping the offices there would be least expensive. The Cologne community offered space in its building, and that city seemed to provide a good compromise. It was near enough to Bonn to obviate the need for a separate branch office in the provisional capital, and it had a sizable Jewish population. However, the board decided to move operations to Düsseldorf on 1 June. The North Rhine-Westphalian capital was near Cologne and a reasonable distance from Bonn.[143] Moreover, Düsseldorf had become a center for Jewish life in Germany. The *Allgemeine Wochenzeitung* had its offices there, and several other Jewish groups met there regularly.[144]

One major aspect of renewed Jewish communal life in western Germany was the foundation of the Central Welfare Office to coordinate Jewish charities in Germany and to represent their needs to the West German government, as well as to foreign Jewish organizations.[145] After its establishment by the Central Council, the Central Welfare Office proclaimed its independence but expressed a willingness to work with its founding organization, and the two bodies collaborated on all political questions.[146] The federal government gave the Central Welfare Office financial support, which the welfare agency then made available to the various Jewish communities through regional bodies.[147] In the first two years, it received 48,000 marks per year from the government and raised money by selling special stamps in cooperation with the West German postal service.[148] During the Auerbach affair, it helped to support the

[142] "Empfang bei Professor Heuss," *Allgemeine Wochenzeitung*, 28 March 1952.
[143] "Beschlussprotokoll der Sitzung des Direktoriums," 4 May 1952, ZA, B.1/7, 221.19.
[144] "Wir kommentieren: Düsseldorf-neues jüdisches Zentrum," *Allgemeine Wochenzeitung*, 6 June 1952.
[145] "Satzung (Entwurf) der Zentralwohlfahrtsstelle der Juden in Deutschland e.V.," B.1/11, 15 (Zugang 96/10).
[146] "Protokoll der Tagung des Vorstandes der Zentralwohlfahrtsstelle der Juden in Deutschland," 16 May 1952, ZA, B.1/15, 283. In fact, in 1953, the Central Welfare Office looked to the Central Council for guidance in revising its governing statutes. "Zentralwohlfahrtsstelle Rundschreiben Nr. 28," 5 August 1953, ZA, B.1/11, 218 (Zugang 93/01).
[147] Ibid.; "Rundschreiben Nr. 9," 1 December 1952, ZA, B.1/15, 283.
[148] "Aufstellung der Einnahmen und Aufwendungen," 1 January 1952–30 September 1953, ZA, B.1/11, 15 (Zugang 96/10); "Rundschreiben Nr. 2," 28 July 1952, ZA, B.1/11, 218 (Zugang 93/01).

Auerbach family, which had lost its source of income.[149] Although the Central Welfare Office helped to support indigent Jews in West Germany, it also aided Jewish refugees from Eastern Europe after they arrived in West Germany.[150]

The creation of the welfare office was a major step for the community, and new communities continued to spring up. Jewish life had returned to Germany despite the enormous practical and psychological obstacles. Nonetheless, prewar German Jewry existed primarily outside Germany. While some German Jews had prospered in other countries, many others remained poor. Hendrik George van Dam proposed using property formerly owned by Jewish victims of the Nazis to assist these exiled Jews, and he wanted the Central Council to help in administrating the property.[151] Meanwhile, the Jews living in Germany did not wish to alienate themselves from their foreign coreligionists.[152]

However, the various Jewish communities often clashed with foreign Jewish groups because of the legal power those organizations wielded over them. One case of disregard for the wishes of the Jewish community in Germany involved Jakob Altmaier. When the Jewish Restitution Successor Organization sold the Jewish cemetery in his hometown, Flörsheim near Frankfurt, in April 1952, the Jewish Bundestag deputy was irate. JRSO director Benjamin Ferencz dismissed the affair as a mistake by an employee who did not realize that the plot of land contained a cemetery. Altmaier did not believe the sale was a mistake. He noted that similar incidents had occurred elsewhere in the state of Hesse and claimed that JRSO had made no effort to verify whether prewar Jewish property was still in use by German Jewish groups.[153] The Berlin community resented that it depended on state subsidies for its existence, while the JRSO received indemnification and restitution payments for ownerless Jewish property in Berlin.[154] Even the Council of Jews

---

[149] Letter from B. Simonsohn to Central Welfare Office members, 10 June 1952, ZA, B.1/11, 218 (Zugang 93/01).
[150] "Rundschreiben Nr. 24," 22 June 1953; "Rundschreiben Nr. 43," 4 December 1953; ZA, B.1/13, 2121.
[151] "Das Erbe des deutschen Judentums," *Allgemeine Wochenzeitung*, 9 May 1952.
[152] "Protokoll des Verbandtages der Jüdischen Gemeinden Nordwestdeutschlands," 20 May 1952, ZA, B.1/15, 427.
[153] Letter from Benjamin Ferencz to Jakob Altmaier, 29 April 1952; letter from Jakob Altmaier to Benjamin Ferencz, 6 May 1952; AdsD, Nachlass Jakob Altmaier (Abt. I), 3.
[154] Letter from Heinz Galinski to Georg Dusedeau, 6 June 1952, LAB, B Rep. 2, 4866.

from Germany, a leading organization for German Jewish émigrés outside Germany, demanded that the proceeds from the sale of ownerless property be spent on Holocaust survivors in Germany.[155]

Beginning in mid-1950, faced with isolation by international Jewish organizations and disregard by German politicians, the Central Council struggled to establish itself as the sole representative of the Jewish community in West Germany. The Jewish community in Germany had a tense relationship with Jewish groups abroad. These tensions, beginning in the years of Allied occupation, stemmed from foreign Jewish control of ownerless property in Germany while the existing community there struggled financially. Jewish leaders in America, Britain, and Israel – backed by the Allies – wished to liquidate these formerly Jewish-owned assets and to use the proceeds to aid Israel. Under these circumstances, the Central Council turned to West German politicians.

It sought the government's attention without taking on the posture of a court Jew or token Jewish representative in official circles.[156] In pursuit of this goal, Jewish leaders, in particular Hendrik George van Dam, Karl Marx, and Norbert Wollheim, looked to federal president Theodor Heuss for support, his earlier remarks having established him as the authority within the government on Jewish issues and moral confrontation with the Nazi past. To achieve more practical goals, including the passage of a reparations law, the Jews in Germany looked to Kurt Schumacher and the Social Democratic Party. Eventually, Konrad Adenauer's government opened ties to the Central Council and broached the topic of reparations for crimes committed against the Jews during the Holocaust.

---

[155] "Eine gemeinschaftliche Aufgabe," *Allgemeine Wochenzeitung*, 6 June 1952.
[156] Van Dam, "Die Juden in Deutschland nach 1945," 2:904–905.

CHAPTER 7

West Germany and Reparations to Israel and World Jewry

In 1951, the official German-Jewish relationship entered a new phase as Konrad Adenauer, encouraged by German public figures, took steps to initiate reparations to the Jewish people. At first secret, his efforts became public in September 1951 with the announcement of the government's intention to negotiate with the Israeli government and with international Jewish groups. However, approaching Jewish representatives and achieving a settlement proved to be more difficult than the chancellor expected. He faced significant obstacles, including opposition from members of his own cabinet, but by the summer of 1952, a settlement, largely brokered by Adenauer and Nahum Goldmann personally, had been reached, leading to the Luxembourg Agreement for collective reparations.

While many scholars tend to consider the story of the Luxembourg Agreement as a straightforward German-Israeli one, it is important to recall its impact on the Central Council of Jews in Germany. West German reparations, which should have been a triumph for the Jewish community both in Germany and abroad, actually furthered damaged relations between the two groups. Despite their ideal mediating position, the Jews in Germany played a very limited role in negotiating the treaty. Instead, the Israeli government and a new group, the Conference on Jewish Material Claims against Germany, became the West German government's partners in the incipient German-Jewish reconciliation. Ultimately, as disagreements over distributing the reparations settlement developed between German Jews and their foreign coreligionists, the Central Council reexamined its relationship with Jewish groups around the world. As a result, it initiated an even closer relationship with German governmental authorities.

Negotiating a settlement was, indeed, arduous and represented a real step forward in German-Jewish relations. However, even after Adenauer had signed the Luxembourg Agreement, its parliamentary ratification remained uncertain. Between September 1952 and March 1953, the chancellor and his political allies defended the agreement and sought to win sufficient support to ensure ratification. While the votes of the opposition Social Democratic Party were never in doubt, Adenauer and his foreign policy adviser Walter Hallstein faced potential resistance from Bundestag deputies of the governing Christian Democratic Union and its Bavarian affiliate, the Christian Social Union. Attainment of a broad consensus on reparations, including the support of the primary governing party, bore great symbolic importance as West Germany sought entry into international organizations.

THE ROAD TO 27 SEPTEMBER 1951

For many years, Jewish groups had discussed the idea of German reparations for the crimes committed during the Holocaust. On one hand, they worked to establish a legal basis for such payments, and on the other, they pressured the West German government to take up the issue. Because there had been no Jewish state at the time of the Nazi transgressions and no Jewish entity participated in the military defeat of Germany, Israel needed to establish a legal justification for seeking reparation payments. As early as September 1945, Chaim Weizmann of the Jewish Agency for Palestine presented the Allies with a claim for reparations against Germany. He stressed compensation for the loss of material and financial assets and claimed that ownerless property formerly belonging to Jews in Axis countries should revert to collective Jewish ownership. Additionally, he requested that a portion of Germany's reparations to the Allies be applied to help Jewish Holocaust victims to resettle in Palestine. One month later, American Jewish groups formed a special committee to lobby in favor of these proposals.[1] In July 1950, in a memorandum addressing the concerns of Diaspora Jewry, Alexander Easterman of the World Jewish Congress executive in Europe also presented the Allies with reparations claims.[2]

---

[1] Sagi, *German Reparations*, 31–33.   [2] Ibid., 45–47.

At the same time, Jews in Germany worked for reparations in conjunction with Israel. The Israeli Finance Ministry asked Hendrik George van Dam – a noted expert on reparations law, legal adviser to the British Jewish Relief Unit, and future secretary general of the Central Council – for an analysis of the legal justification for reparations. In his report, submitted on 1 July 1950, van Dam likened Jewish claims against Germany to the demands made on the Central Powers by the so-called successor states after the First World War. Furthermore, van Dam considered the time ripe for an Israeli-German accord. With Israeli independence established, German aid sent to the former British mandate territory would not end up in British coffers. Moreover, van Dam believed that West Germans were increasingly uninterested in fulfilling any obligations beyond the letter of the Occupation Statute, which required the Federal Republic to retain legislation enacted by the occupation authorities and gave the western powers decisive control over matters of restitution, reparations, and care for displaced persons. He also felt that an agreement between Israel and Bonn would help to end the international Jewish isolation of Germany, thereby strengthening the position of Jewish organizations there.[3]

The government of Israel applied pressure for reparations, but rather than addressing the Bonn government, it approached the four victorious Allied powers with its demands. On 12 March 1951, the Israeli government insisted that future reparations funds be allocated to the resettlement of Jewish refugees within the new state. As the creation of Israel was itself an act of reparation, additional financial assistance was in order. Furthermore, Israel claimed the exclusive right to speak for all Jews, including the six million victims of the Nazis.[4] The Allies responded evasively and half-heartedly to these demands, leaving the decision in German hands.[5]

Without any prodding from the Allies, Konrad Adenauer had evinced an interest in the matter. Unbeknownst to all but a small circle of West German and Israeli officials, he had made tentative contact with representatives of the Israeli government in

---

[3] Hendrik George van Dam, "Das Problem der Reparation und Wiedergutmachung für Israel," 1 July 1950, *Der deutsch-israelische Dialog*, 1:21–22 and 24–25.
[4] "Die Note der Israelische Regierung zum 12. März 1951," *Der deutsch-israelische Dialog*, 1:37–38.
[5] For more information, see Sagi, *German Reparations*, chap. 4.

February 1951. During a session of the Bundestag Foreign Affairs Committee in February, Jakob Altmaier pressed Adenauer on the issue of reparations, and the following day, the chancellor asked the Social Democratic parliamentarian to approach Israeli diplomats on his behalf.[6] Throughout March and April, Altmaier and Israeli consul Eliahu Livneh conducted secret negotiations to arrange a meeting in Paris between Adenauer and Israeli envoys. Altmaier, acting without his own political party's consent or knowledge, considered it his duty as a German Jew to work for reconciliation between Germans and Jews.[7] While the secret meeting between Adenauer and the Israeli ambassador in Paris in April yielded no results, Adenauer remained in loose contact with the Israelis.[8] Israel's existence facilitated efforts for reparations and reconciliation by providing an internationally recognized collective representative for the Jews. Moreover, many German supporters of reparations, including the chancellor himself, justified the payments to Israel as compensation for the new state's having taken in so many European Jewish refugees.[9]

Reparations and German-Israeli relations were also the subject of discussions between West German cabinet members. Karl Marx had told Thomas Dehler, the federal justice minister, that Israel was willing to participate in a relationship, but that West Germany needed to make a symbolic gesture, such as the erection of an official memorial to the murdered Jews. On 5 March 1951, Dehler forwarded these ideas to Robert Lehr, the federal interior minister and a close associate of the chancellor. That same day, Lehr wrote to Adenauer with the suggestion and requested that he give Marx a message to pass on to officials in Israel during a forthcoming visit there. The Germans needed to win the trust of moderate Israeli politicians, Lehr mentioned, adding that efforts in that direction might even induce the Allies to lighten the burden of the

---

[6] "Meine Arbeit und Mitwirkung am 'Israel-Vertrag,' " 5 May 1959, AdsD, Nachlass Jakob Altmaier (Abt. I.), 7.

[7] Letter from Eliahu Livneh to Jakob Altmaier, 6 March 1951; letter from Jakob Altmaier to Eliahu Livneh, 8 April 1951; AdsD, Nachlass Jakob Altmaier (Abt. I.), 7.

[8] "Meine Arbeit und Mitwirkung am 'Israel-Vertrag,' " 5 May 1959, AdsD, Nachlass Jakob Altmaier (Abt. I.), 7; Sagi, *German Reparations*, 70. Altmaier blamed the Israelis for the meeting's failure.

[9] "Regierungserklärung zur jüdischen Frage und zur Wiedergutmachung," *Der deutsch-israelische Dialog*, 1:47.

Occupation Statute.[10] Vice Chancellor Franz Blücher of the Free Democratic Party also pressed for a resolution to the problem and consulted with German Jews about potential solutions. Karl Marx corresponded with Blücher about the issue, and in July, Blücher wrote to the chancellor to urge action. Adenauer responded that he was waiting for the right moment to issue a statement on the Jewish question.[11] Marx had suggested to Dehler that the forthcoming Jewish holidays would be the ideal time to make a statement, and Dehler passed this information on to Blücher, who in turn informed the chancellor.[12] In the political climate of competing claims to victimhood and debates about Germany's ability to pay seemingly massive foreign debts, President Heuss worried that public support for reparations might dissipate, and he wanted Adenauer to make a statement on the Jewish question soon. To this end, he suggested an address before the Bundestag on Rosh Hashanah.[13]

As Adenauer began to draft his statement in September, the president recommended that the coalition partners forgo their traditional responses on the floor of the Bundestag and allow Paul Löbe or Carlo Schmid of the SPD to speak on behalf of all the political parties represented in the parliament.[14] Paul Löbe's political pedigree was virtually unrivaled within postwar political circles. The oldest member of the Bundestag, Löbe had served in the Weimar constitutional convention in 1919 and had been president,

[10] Letter from Thomas Dehler to Robert Lehr, 5 March 1951; letter from Robert Lehr to Konrad Adenauer, 5 March 1951; BAK, N 1244, 25.

[11] "20.9.1951: Sitzung des Bundesvorstandes," 20 September 1951, Freie Demokratische Partei, Bundesvorstand, *FDP-Bundesvorstand: Die Liberalen unter dem Vorsitz von Theodor Heuss und Franz Blücher: Sitzungsprotokolle 1949–1954*, half-vol. 1: *1.-26. Sitzung 1949–1952*, ed. Udo Wengst, Quellen zur Geschichte des Parlamentarismus und der politischen Parteien, fourth series: Deutschland seit 1945, ed. Karl Dietrich Bracher, Rudolf Morsey, and Hans-Peter Schwarz, vol. 7/I (Düsseldorf: Droste, 1990), 280–281; letter from Franz Blücher to Konrad Adenauer, 6 July 1951, letter from Konrad Adenauer to Franz Blücher, 13 July 1951, BAK, N 1080, 79, 126–127 and 142; Konrad Adenauer, *Briefe 1951–1953*, ed. Hans Peter Mensing, Rhöndorfer Ausgabe, ed. Rudolf Morsey and Hans-Peter Schwarz (Berlin: Siedler, 1987), 82–83.

[12] Letter from Thomas Dehler to Franz Blücher, 30 August 1951; letter from Franz Blücher to Thomas Dehler, 4 September 1951; BAK, N 1080, 90.

[13] "Judenfragen," 24 August 1951, Konrad Adenauer and Theodor Heuss, *Unter vier Augen: Gespräche aus den Gründerjahren 1949–1959*, ed. Hans Peter Mensing (Berlin Siedler, 1987), 68.

[14] "Zur Behandlung der Erklärung zur Judenfrage," 4 September 1951, BAK, B 122, 2080 (26).

or speaker, of the Reichstag for almost twelve years before the Nazis came to power. Schmid, the son of a French mother and a German father, had been a judge and professor in the Weimar Republic. After the war, he joined the Social Democrats and contributed considerably to the writing of West Germany's provisional constitution, the Basic Law.

Extragovernmental pressure also mounted. Erich Lüth, press secretary of the Hamburg state government and a member of the Weimar-era Democratic Party, founded an organization called "Peace with Israel" to agitate for reparations and ties between the two countries. The group issued a manifesto in *Die Welt* on 31 August 1951, and Lüth and Norbert Wollheim issued an appeal on Hamburg radio. While they welcomed President Heuss's earlier formulation of German collective shame, they called for formal resolutions and concrete acts.[15] Lüth wrote that Germany should not expect the survivors of the concentration camps and torture chambers to break the ice. Rather, it was Germany's responsibility to approach Israel and the Jews.[16] Soon after, many leading Germans, including Willy Brandt, Hermann Hesse, Ernst Lemmer, and Ernst Reuter, joined the movement. On 10 September 1951, President Heuss wrote to Lüth to lend his support, and a copy of Heuss's letter found its way to the Central Council.[17] The Hamburg FDP and the Berlin CDU, on the progressive wings of their parties, supported "Peace with Israel," though many German politicians did not. The German Party, a member of Adenauer's governing coalition, attacked Lüth's efforts as a fight against antisemitic conditions that it claimed no longer existed.[18]

In addition to Adenauer's covert efforts, Bundestag and Knesset representatives met during a session of the Inter-Parliamentary Union held in Istanbul during August 1951. Initially, the Israeli delegation vigorously protested the presence of Germans at an international conference. The Israelis were unwilling to accept the reintegration of a German state – even a democratic one – into

[15] Erich Lüth on Aktion Friede mit Israel, *Der deutsch-israelische Dialog*, 1:31–32.
[16] "Gewährt uns Frieden," *Allgemeine Wochenzeitung*, 7 September 1951.
[17] Letter from Theodor Heuss to Erich Lüth, 10 September 1951, BAK, B 122, 2080 (26); and ZA, B.1/7, 96.
[18] "Damit auch Deutschland Frieden finde . . ." and "Eine destruktive Polemik," *Allgemeine Wochenzeitung*, 21 September 1951. At least one scholar has suggested that Adenauer used Lüth's movement to stir up support for a rapprochement with world Jewry. Gardner Feldman, *Special Relationship*, 58.

the international community.[19] Carlo Schmid, leading the West German delegation, quickly moved to defuse the situation with a speech in which he cited the thousands of non-Jewish Germans who had been consigned to Nazi concentration camps. He reminded his audience that the Inter-Parliamentary Union was not a tribunal and insisted that no one should declare the Germans collectively guilty or collectively innocent. Schmid also refused to side with the Arab delegations' denunciation of Israel. The Swiss delegate, Aymon de Senerclens, arranged a meeting between three Israelis and three Germans: Schmid, Robert Tillmanns, and Heinrich von Brentano, a close ally of Adenauer. Even though all three Israeli parliamentarians spoke German fluently, they insisted on conversing with the Germans in English.[20] The meeting's atmosphere remained particularly stilted until one of the Israelis mentioned, in German, that his dissertation adviser in Munich had been the famous economist Lujo Brentano – the German delegate's uncle. With the ice broken and a personal connection established, discussion continued in German. The Israelis agreed to raise the issue of negotiations with the Knesset, and they decided on Eliahu Livneh, the Israeli consul in Munich, and Jewish Bundestag member Jakob Altmaier as future mediators.[21]

As soon as the three Germans returned to Bonn, they met with Adenauer. Schmid later wrote of the Christian Democratic chancellor, "Since my first meeting with him, I knew reconciliation with the Jewish people was an important factor in his general political outlook." Schmid also conferred with his own party, the SPD, and Altmaier offered to go to Munich to meet with the Israeli consul there.[22] Brentano reported to his party, the CDU, on the talks, noting their long duration and cordial atmosphere.[23]

[19] Carlo Schmid, *Erinnerungen* (Bern: Scherz, 1979), 505–506; report by Carlo Schmid for Rolf Vogel, *Der deutsch-israelische Dialog*, 1:27. They had previously protested German membership in UNESCO.

[20] Schmid, *Erinnerungen*, 507–508; report by Carlo Schmid for Rolf Vogel, *Der deutsch-israelische Dialog*, 1:28.

[21] Report by Carlo Schmid for Rolf Vogel, *Der deutsch-israelische Dialog*, 1:29.

[22] Schmid, *Erinnerungen*, 510.

[23] "25.9.1951: Fraktionssitzung," 25 September 1951, Germany (West), Bundestag, Fraktion der CDU/CSU, *Die CDU/CSU-Fraktion im Deutschen Bundestag: Sitzungsprotokolle 1949–1953*, ed. Helge Heidemeyer, Quellen zur Geschichte des Parlamentarismus und der politischen Parteien, fourth series: Deutschland seit 1945, ed. Karl Dietrich Bracher, Rudolf Morsey, and Hans-Peter Schwarz, vol. 11/I. (Düsseldorf: Droste, 1998), 449.

After these promising developments, Adenauer could take the critical step of addressing the Jewish question and reparations in public. However, before making any official remarks in the Bundestag, he wanted Jewish approval of the text of his address. Notably, he turned to World Jewish Congress president Nahum Goldmann and Israeli authorities, not the Central Council, for advice. They, however, required several changes, and Goldmann refused to meet with the chancellor – even privately – before his address. Again, by seeking to broker a compromise on the text of the speech, Jakob Altmaier provided a critical link between German and Jewish groups.[24] Even after Adenauer adopted many of the proposed changes, the SPD considered the text too half-hearted and declined to join the other parties in a united response.[25] The federal cabinet, however, approved of the text with few alterations. President Heuss gave it his assent, too, despite his wish that certain aspects of it be made stronger. In particular, the president wished that the chancellor would not only acknowledge Germany's duty toward the Jews, but also clearly stress the desire to make reparations a reality. Heuss also wanted more shame to be expressed for the mistreatment of German Jews.[26] At any rate, with the approval of the cabinet and the president, Adenauer was in a position to open a new chapter in German-Jewish relations.

ADENAUER'S SPEECH AND ITS EFFECTS

On 27 September 1951, Chancellor Adenauer read to the Bundestag his government's official declaration on reparations. He knew that both Jewish and non-Jewish international opinion had recently focused on this topic, and many critics of the new state had accused West Germany of shirking its responsibility to promote "a new and healthy basis" for "the relationship of the Jews to the German people."[27] The chancellor stated that his government

---

[24] Goldmann, *Autobiography*, 256.
[25] "Meine Arbeit und Mitwirkung am 'Israel-Vertrag,'" 5 May 1959, AdsD, Nachlass Jakob Altmaier (Abt. I.), 7; "25.9.1951: Fraktionssitzung," 25 September 1951, *Die SPD-Fraktion im Deutschen Bundestag*, half-vol. 1:293.
[26] "175. Kabinettssitzung," 26 September 1951, Germany (West), Bundesregierung, *Die Kabinettsprotokolle der Bundesregierung*, ed. Hans Booms, vol. 4: *1951*, ed. Ursula Hüllbüsch (Boppard am Rhein: Harald Boldt, 1988), 662; "Bemerkung zu der Erklärung der Bundesregierung zur Juden-Frage," undated, BAK, B 122, 2080 (26).
[27] "Regierungserklärung zur jüdischen Frage und zur Wiedergutmachung," 21 September 1951, *Der deutsch-israelische Dialog*, 1:45.

was committed to civil rights and the fight against antisemitism. Yet only after discussing the new state's accomplishments did he address the Nazis' crimes against the Jews, proclaiming that the majority of the German people had not participated in the crimes. Still, in the name of the German people, unspeakable crimes had occurred, thereby committing the Germans to moral and material reparations.[28] For the purposes of reparations negotiations, West Germany would, he announced, speak with representatives of the State of Israel, which had to care for many Jewish refugees. Adenauer added this comment to justify paying reparations to a state not extant at the time of the crimes committed. He ended his speech forcefully: "The spirit of true humanity must be alive and fruitful once again. The federal government regards serving this spirit with all its power as the most distinguished duty of the German people."[29]

After Adenauer's address, the political parties represented in Bundestag replied, beginning with the opposition Social Democrats, who had for so long promoted reparations and a relationship with the Jewish people. Speaking for the Social Democrats was Paul Löbe. He welcomed the government's intentions and pledged to support them, though he regretted the government's tardiness in taking this step.[30] One by one, spokesmen of other significant parties in the Bundestag, including the Christian Democrats, the Free Democrats, the German Party, the Center Party, and the Bavarian Party, endorsed the chancellor's declaration. Notably, neither representatives of the Communists nor those of the fringe right-wing parties spoke.[31]

Jewish groups greeted Adenauer's declaration with enthusiasm. The Central Council applauded the government's desire to restore Germany's lost honor, although it criticized the government for having taken so long to address the Jewish question, obliquely noting that "no reconciliation is needed" with those Germans whom the Central Council deemed "the bearers of progress," presumably the Social Democrats.[32] Moreover, as the self-proclaimed sole representative of the Jews in Germany, the Central Council demanded

---

[28] Ibid., 1:46.   [29] Ibid., 1:47.   [30] Ibid., 1:47–48.   [31] Ibid., 1:48–49.
[32] "Zentralrat in Deutschland: 'Reinigung der Atmosphäre,'" October 1951, Germany (West), Presse- und Informationsamt der Bundesregierung, *Deutschland und das Judentum* (Bonn: Deutscher Bundes-Verlag, 1951), 11; "Stellungsnahme des Direktoriums des Zentralrat in Deutschland der Juden in Deutschland zu den Bonner Erklärungen," 8 October 1951, ZA, B.1/7, 221.17.

that it have the right to vet any concrete government proposal.[33] From his exile in London, Leo Baeck, former chief rabbi of Berlin and a close ally of the Central Council, welcomed the declaration and proclaimed his willingness to help with negotiations.[34] The American Jewish Committee regarded Adenauer's address as the first step toward West Germany's acceptance into the community of democratic states and helped to circulate the text of Adenauer's speech in the United States.[35]

Israel's initial reaction to Adenauer's address was guarded. An official spokesman noted Adenauer's acknowledgment of the crimes committed by the Nazis in the name of the German people but added that his government would study the declaration and "in due course make its attitude known."[36] According to the *Allgemeine Wochenzeitung der Juden in Deutschland*, the Israeli government regarded the speech as a call to the Germans to fight anti-semitism.[37] Large segments of the Israeli public violently rejected any offer from the Germans, and some even rioted to prevent the Knesset from voting to authorize negotiations.[38] However, David Ben-Gurion's cabinet, under severe financial strain, was inclined to discuss reparations with the Germans, and immediately after Adenauer's address, Israeli diplomats around the world adopted a more positive attitude toward their West German colleagues.[39]

West Germans responded in mixed fashion to the chancellor's statement. Politicians such as Franz Blücher, Thomas Dehler, Ludwig Erhard, and Robert Lehr sent warm telegrams to the *Allgemeine Wochenzeitung*. Economics Minister Erhard's response was the most interesting. He greeted the incipient German-Jewish

---

[33] "Unteilbarkeit des Rechts," *Allgemeine Wochenzeitung*, 12 October 1951.

[34] "Text des Briefes des ehem. Oberrabbiners von Berlin, Dr. Leo Baeck, London," in *Deutschland und das Judentum*, 11.

[35] "Das amerikanische jüdische Komitee: 'Von entscheidender Bedeutung,'" in ibid., 9–10; letter from Walter Hallstein to Zachariah Shuster, 14 December 1951, PA-AA, B 10, 308 (Fiche A 2029), 168.

[36] "Statement by the Spokesman of the Government of Israel (Tel Aviv)," 27 September 1951, State of Israel, Israel State Archives, *Documents on the Foreign Policy of Israel*, vol. 6: *1951*, companion volume, ed. Yemima Rosenthal (Jerusalem: Government Printer, 1991), 288–289; "Adenauer Offers to Discuss Restitution," *Jerusalem Post*, 28 September 1951.

[37] "Israels Antwort," *Allgemeine Wochenzeitung*, 28 September 1951.

[38] George Lavy, *Germany and Israel: Moral Debt and National Interest* (London: Frank Cass, 1996), 8.

[39] Trimbur, *De la Shoah*, 42.

reconciliation as a step toward renewed Jewish involvement in the German economy. Before the war, Jews had made great contributions to German economic life, he observed, and now, as the Federal Republic strove to rebuild, it needed their help.[40] On the other hand, the government's declaration unleashed a wave of antisemitic letters to government officials.[41] SPD chairman Kurt Schumacher foresaw great opposition to reparations and predicted that many Germans, as a cover for their latent antisemitism, would claim that their country's poverty precluded reparations.[42] Time would prove him right.

Adenauer's offer to Israel forced the leaders of the Jewish community in Germany to reconsider the manner in which they related to Jewish organizations elsewhere. In October 1951, Karl Marx opined that as an outpost of the international Jewish community, it was the duty of those in the Federal Republic to act as mediators between Germans and Israelis.[43] In fact, the Central Council's leaders hesitated to embrace this role in view of world Jewry's ambivalent or even hostile position on Jewish resettlement in Germany. While Israeli consul Livneh wanted the Jews in Germany to support Israel unconditionally, Julius Dreifuss wanted Israel first to recognize the German Jews.[44] Jewish leaders in West Germany considered Adenauer's new policy to be an opportunity to raise their status in international Jewish circles. Some Jewish leaders in Germany expected that they would conduct the negotiations with Adenauer's government and that these discussions would be their crowning achievement. They aspired to legitimize their presence in Germany through proving their utility to the foreign Jewish community.[45]

Meanwhile, Jewish groups elsewhere took steps that affected the Central Council's position between West Germany and Israel. On 25 October, representatives of the Jewish communities throughout the Diaspora met in New York to establish the Conference

---

[40] "Echo zur Regierungserklärung," *Allgemeine Wochenzeitung*, 5 October 1951.
[41] Various letters, September and October 1951, BAK, B 122, 2086 (29).
[42] "Das 'zentrale Problem,'" *Allgemeine Wochenzeitung*, 5 October 1951.
[43] "Jom Kippur-Tag der Versöhnung-Tag der Besinnung," *Allgemeine Wochenzeitung*, 5 October 1951.
[44] "Protokoll des Direktoriumssitzung des Zentralrates," 7–8 October 1951, ZA, B.1/7, 221.16.
[45] "Die erste Entscheidung zur Aktivierung der Arbeit jüdischer Juristen im Bundesgebiet und Berlin," 28 October 1951, BAK, B 106, 211.

on Jewish Material Claims against Germany, known as the Claims Conference. The sole function of this new organization, in which the German Central Council was not represented, was to negotiate for reparations after Israel had received satisfaction of its claims.[46] Even after joining the group in December 1951, the Central Council remained unsure as to whether it should participate.[47] Van Dam recognized that Israel would have to take the lead in negotiating any agreement on behalf of world Jewry, including Jews who had emigrated from Germany. He informed the leaders of the Central Council that the community in Germany was so weak that it needed to ally with the international Jewish community in order to have any impact. German Jewry did not have the influence or prestige it once had.[48] Despite its difficult position vis-à-vis foreign Jewish groups, the Central Council wanted to strengthen its ties to them and to end its isolation in international Jewish affairs. In January 1952, van Dam informed the Central Council's board members that they would have a seat on the Claim Conference's governing Policy Committee. After some debate, Heinz Galinski of Berlin represented the Jews in Germany at Claims Conference meetings, held in New York.[49] Meanwhile, Karl Marx continued to hope that the government would negotiate with the Central Council or with the Conference of Jewish Jurists. Through Justice Minister Dehler, the government declined Marx's proposal, having established a relationship with Nahum Goldmann.[50] The Jews in Germany, regardless of past disputes, needed to ally themselves with the Claims Conference if they were to have any influence on the negotiations.

Even though Jewish groups in Germany and around the world organized for talks with the Bonn government, the gulf between the two sides remained nearly as great as ever. Neither Israel nor West Germany was prepared to take the first step, and in fact,

---

[46] "Priotität der Ansprüche Israels anerkannt," *Allgemeine Wochenzeitung*, 2 November 1951.
[47] "Telegramm Dr. Nahum Goldmanns an den Zentralrat," *Allgemeine Wochenzeitung*, 9 November 1951; "Besprechung Dr. Goldmann-Zentralrat," *Allgemeine Wochenzeitung*, 14 December 1951; "An die Mitglieder des Rates: Referat auf die Tagung des Zentralrates," 31 August 1952, ZA, B.1/7, 221.23.
[48] Letter from Hendrik George van Dam to Central Council directorate, 15 November 1951, ZA, B.1/7, 121.
[49] Letter from Hendrik George van Dam to Central Council directorate, 7 January 1952, ZA, B.1/7, 120; "Die Biltmore-Entscheidung," *Allgemeine Wochenzeitung*, 1 February 1952.
[50] Letter from Thomas Dehler to Karl Marx, 21 January 1952, ADL, N 1, 774.

the Israelis persisted in turning to the western Allies with their claims.[51] This attitude placed the Germans, in particular, in a precarious position. They needed the approbation that would come with reconciliation. The Israelis' rejection was both embarrassing and potentially disastrous for West Germany's efforts to garner international recognition as a liberal democracy worthy of a place in the community of nations.

Faced with this deadlock, Konrad Adenauer took up the burden, aided by Nahum Goldmann. On 6 December 1951, the two men met secretly in London. Goldmann insisted that the issue was "not one of diplomacy but of morality" and set a billion dollars as the starting point for negotiations. Adenauer accepted Goldmann's terms without consulting his cabinet, thus incurring later criticism for having behaved undemocratically.[52] After the meeting, the chancellor adjourned to a neighboring room where he wrote a personal letter to Goldmann requesting that the Jewish leader inform the Israeli government that the West German government wished to begin talks. To please his Jewish critics, Adenauer added:

in the problem of reparations, the federal government sees above all a moral duty and considers it a duty of honor of the German people to do everything possible to make good the injustice committed against the Jewish people.[53]

Despite a vigorous controversy over taking money from Germans in the wake of the Holocaust, the Israeli Knesset approved direct negotiations by a vote of 61 to 50 on 9 January 1952. Israel needed financial aid, and many Israelis, including David Ben-Gurion, were willing to accept payments from the Germans, even in the absence of formal diplomatic relations. The cordial working relationship that developed between Goldmann and Adenauer became the key to the negotiations' success. They met again in London in February 1952 to set the parameters for the negotiations, and over the next year their willingness to intervene personally in negotiations helped to sustain progress toward a final settlement.

---

[51] Sagi, *German Reparations*, 78.
[52] Goldmann, *The Jewish Paradox*, trans. Steve Cox (London: Weidenfeld and Nicolson, 1978), 127–128; Goldmann, *Autobiography*, 259.
[53] Letter from Konrad Adenauer to Nahum Goldmann, 6 December 1951, *Der deutsch-israelische Dialog*, 1:51.

THE COURSE OF NEGOTIATIONS

Despite Konrad Adenauer's commitment to the idea of reparations, negotiating a final settlement proved arduous. The West German government first faced the challenge of assembling a negotiating delegation and arranging for the talks to begin. Some Jews in Germany, not affiliated with the Central Council, wrote to government officials, and even to Jakob Altmaier, offering their services as negotiators with Israel.[54] However, Chancellor Adenauer charged Walter Hallstein, his deputy foreign minister and former rector of the University of Frankfurt, with assembling the negotiating team. Hallstein selected Franz Böhm, his successor as rector in Frankfurt and Protestant co-chairman of the Society for Christian-Jewish Cooperation, as chief West German negotiator, and Otto Küster, head of the reparations office for the state of Württemberg, as deputy negotiator.[55] While the West German Finance Ministry had reservations about Böhm's nomination, both appointments made a very good impression on the Jewish community, even though the Central Council had no role in selecting delegation members.[56] Joining the West German delegation – and keeping watch over Böhm – were representatives of the Finance Ministry, Economics Ministry, and Foreign Office. The delegation's secretary was diplomat Abraham Frowein, a Protestant whose maternal grandfather was Jewish. Before the war, Frowein had been an attorney in Berlin, with numerous Jewish colleagues and friends.[57]

There was also some discussion as to whether Jakob Altmaier should serve on the West German negotiating team, and Karl Marx lobbied the Foreign Office to prevent Altmaier's appointment.[58] Altmaier wrote to Nahum Goldmann that Adenauer wanted him to join the delegation, but Hallstein told Altmaier that Jewish groups were opposing his appointment. Rumors had been circulating that

---

[54] Letter from Adolf Hamburger to Jakob Altmaier, 15 October 1951, AdsD, Nachlass Jakob Altmaier (Abt. I), 3; letter from Rudolf Pick to Thomas Dehler, 23 October and 8 December 1951, ADL, N 1, 1157.

[55] Letter from Herbert Blankenhorn to Theodor Heuss, 11 March 1952, BAK, B 122, 2080 (26).

[56] Hermann J. Abs, *Entscheidungen 1949–1953. Die Entstehung des Londoner Schuldenabkommens* (Mainz: v. Hase und Koehler, 1991), 129–130; "Vermerk," 7 February 1952, PA-AA, B 10, 1665 (Fiche A. 4514); "Schuldner und Gläubiger in Gewissensnot," *Allgemeine Wochenzeitung*, 28 March 1952.

[57] Jochen Abraham Frowein, letter to author, 23 February 2000.

[58] "Vermerk," 7 February 1952, PA-AA, B 10, 1665 (Fiche A. 4514).

Altmaier had informed British intelligence officers about illegal Jewish immigration to Palestine in 1944 and 1945. Altmaier denied the charge and correctly suspected Karl Marx of intervening behind the scenes to block his appointment.[59] The SPD also had concerns about Altmaier's serving as a German negotiator. As a member of the official West German delegation, Altmaier might have to sign a treaty that his own political party might oppose.[60]

The Israelis ran into difficulties with their delegation, which was composed primarily of Israeli citizens who had lived in Germany before 1933. Felix Shinnar, a former Berlin attorney, an Israeli diplomat, and a Progressive Liberal Party member, assumed that he would become delegation head after deputy finance minister David Horowitz declined the post. In fact, foreign minister Moshe Sharett intended to award the post to Giora Josephtal, director of the Jewish Agency's financial section and a member of the governing socialist Mapai Party. Responding to Shinnar's protests, Sharett appointed the two men co-leaders of the delegation, and soon Shinnar became de facto chief negotiator.[61] Shinnar proved to be an excellent choice and quickly won the respect of the German delegation. Additionally, it soon became known that he and German representative Otto Küster had attended high school together in Stuttgart.[62]

Reparations negotiations began on 21 March 1952, in the Dutch town of Wassenaar near The Hague, and from the beginning the West German negotiators came under restraining pressure from finance minister Fritz Schäffer and banker Hermann Josef Abs.[63] Abs, who served as chief West German negotiator at the London Conference for the Settlement of Germany's External Debts, continually represented the position that the Federal Republic could not agree to significant reparations until the question of outstanding debts it had inherited from the German Reich had been resolved. He wished to link the two sets of talks, foreseeing a possible

---

[59] Letters from Jakob Altmaier to Nahum Goldmann, 12 and 19 February 1952, AdsD, Nachlass Jakob Altmaier (Abt. I), 7.
[60] Werner Schiele, *An der Front der Freiheit. Jakob Altmaiers Leben für die Demokratie* (Flörsheim am Main: Magistrat der Stadt Flörsheim am Main, 1991), 75.
[61] Shinnar, *Bericht eines Beauftragten*, 33–35.
[62] Report by Felix Shinnar for Rolf Vogel, *Der deutsch-israelische Dialog*, 1:55.
[63] "Tagebuchnotizen zu den Verhandlungen über den Sühnevertrag mit Israel," 8 March and 5 April 1952, ACDP, I-084, 001.

advantage for West Germany in lowering its debt burden. Chancellor Adenauer, however, wanted to keep the two talks separate. Nahum Goldmann also objected to Abs's linking of the two negotiations, noting that the reparations obligations were of a very different nature from financial debts.[64] Other German officials also voiced objections shortly after negotiations began. The Finance Ministry's observer at the talks protested that the West German negotiators seemed inclined to settle on a sum without a scrupulous evaluation of Israel's claims.[65] Vice Chancellor Franz Blücher expressed similar concerns and asked Adenauer to consider Abs's opinion.[66] On 5 April, at an extraordinary meeting of all German officials concerned with reparations, Adenauer heard Abs's concerns. Despite the widespread reservations among government leaders, Adenauer decided to continue the talks.[67] Throughout the negotiations process, Adenauer remained adamant that financial considerations not take precedence over moral ones, while Finance Ministry officials gave little thought to West Germany's historical responsibility to the Jews, concentrating almost exclusively on budgetary matters.

On 9 April, under the strain of two concurrent sets of negotiations – for reparations to Israel and for regulation of Germany's foreign debts – the discussions in Wassenaar stalled. The West Germans offered three billion marks, but the Israelis wanted 4.2 billion marks. By Israel's estimates, the total reparations claim amounted to 6.3 billion marks, with a theoretical East German share set at 2.1 billion marks.[68] Abs, however, did not want West Germany to pay more than a billion marks.[69] With formal negotiations in abeyance, Adenauer, Blankenhorn, and Goldmann

---

[64] Letter from Konrad Adenauer to Hermann Abs, 12 March 1952, *Briefe 1951–1953*, 188; "Report on a Conversation with Mr. H. Abs on Sunday, 16th March, 1952," 23 March 1952, BAK, N 1351, 16 (Sonderakte Israel I), 28.

[65] Letter from *Regierungsrat* Ludwig to West German delegation, 30 March 1952, ACDP, I-084, 001.

[66] Letter from Franz Blücher to Konrad Adenauer and "Aufzeichnung," 3 April 1952, BAK, N 1080, 80, 45.

[67] "Protokoll über die Sitzung im Palais Schaumburg am 5 April 1952," 6 April 1952, BAK, N 1351, 17 (Sonderakte Israel II), 205–209. Present were Adenauer, vice chancellor Franz Blücher, economics minister Ludwig Erhard, deputy foreign minister Walter Hallstein, adviser Herbert Blankenhorn, Hermann Abs, and Wassenaar negotiators Franz Böhm, Otto Küster, Abraham Frowein, and Bernhard Wolff.

[68] "Eilmeldung," 7 April 1952, BAK, B 136, 1127.

[69] Letter from Hermann Abs to Konrad Adenauer, 7 April 1952, StBKAH, Nachlass Konrad Adenauer, 10.20.1/13–15, 13.

corresponded about private consultations.[70] Böhm wanted to know how much West Germany could pay. While West Germany's worldwide credit depended on the London Conference, its position in world opinion depended on the reparations negotiations. Although the Jews' demands were large, Böhm claimed that "compared to the size of the damages caused, they are without a doubt completely appropriate." On 23 April, he urged Adenauer to consider political factors, not merely economic ones, in deciding what Germany could or could not afford to pay.[71] Abs continued to exert great influence over the reparations talks, however, and the situation worsened. West Germany offered Israel payments of 100 million marks per year over twelve years, but the Israelis wanted at least 400 million marks per year. Furthermore, the Israeli government was under domestic pressure not to reduce its claims beyond a certain minimum level. According to Böhm, that limit was 200–250 million marks per annum. In fact, Israel had consented to negotiations only because Adenauer had accepted a billion dollars (approximately 4.35 billion marks) as a basis for talks.[72]

The situation reached a critical stage in May 1952, as West Germany's chief negotiators resigned their commissions, and Nahum Goldmann came to believe that Adenauer would not commit to reparations. On 7 May, Otto Küster, claiming to have been insulted by finance minister Fritz Schäffer during an argument over supervision of the negotiations, quit as deputy chief negotiator. Küster had repeatedly clashed with Schäffer, who had wanted to limit the scope of the reparations as much as possible, insisting that reparations would threaten the West German economy.[73] The negotiator, however, was incredulous that the government would offer only 100 million marks out of a huge federal budget.[74] Schäffer

---

[70] Letter from Nahum Goldmann to Herbert Blankenhorn, 24 April 1952; letter from Herbert Blankenhorn to Nahum Goldmann, 2 May 1952, inter alia; BAK, N 1351, 17 (Sonderakte Israel II), 64 and 69.

[71] Letter from Franz Böhm to Konrad Adenauer, 23 April 1952, *Der deutsch-israelische Dialog*, 1:63–64. Meanwhile, Jewish groups had begun a public relations offensive aimed at embarrassing the West Germans for their reparations offer. They issued press releases and met with correspondents from the *New York Times* and *The Times* of London, who published sympathetic articles. Sagi, *German Reparations*, 130.

[72] "Aufzeichnung über das jüdische Wiedergutmachungsproblem," 14 May 1952, BAK, N 1351, 16 (Sonderakte Israel I), 93–96.

[73] Letter from Otto Küster to Konrad Adenauer, 7 May 1952, ACDP, I-084, 001; Henzler, *Fritz Schäffer*, 426–442.

[74] Letter from Otto Küster to Konrad Adenauer, 15 May 1952, ACDP, I-084, 001.

frankly expressed to the cabinet his opinion that appointing Böhm and Küster had been a mistake.[75] At a cabinet meeting on 16 May, Böhm told the ministers that a German offer of only 100 million marks per year would lead to a final breakdown in the talks, and Ludwig Erhard also regarded the offer as too low. Adenauer, seemingly indifferent to the purely economic aspect of reparations, was more concerned about the possible failure of the talks, which he feared would be a political disaster for the young West German state anxious to prove its democratic credentials. Herman Abs announced to the cabinet his plans to meet with Felix Shinnar in London on 19 May to sound him out regarding reparations.[76] In fact, Abs offended the Israeli negotiator by tendering an unofficial offer of 100 million marks annually. After this episode, Nahum Goldmann wrote to Adenauer, demanding an immediate meeting and intimating that the Germans were not serious about reparations. He appealed to Adenauer's sense of morality, adding, "One cannot solve a problem of the moral significance of the Jewish reparations with the usual commercial methods of negotiations – and bargaining."[77] In the meantime, the crisis had grown worse, as Böhm resigned on 18 May.

The Social Democratic opposition exerted pressure on the government as well. On 7 May, the party issued a press release welcoming Israel's decision to break off talks.[78] Adolf Arndt, the SPD's expert on reparations, applauded Küster's resignation and accused the government of sabotaging the project for reparations, placing particular blame on Schäffer.[79] Party leader Schumacher, already near death, appealed to Adenauer not to connect the London debt conference and the reparations negotiations. The chancellor had not linked them in his original address on 27 September 1951, Schumacher pointed out, and he should not do so now.[80]

---

[75] "221. Kabinettssitzung," 20 May 1952, Germany (West), Bundesregierung, *Die Kabinettsprotokolle der Bundesregierung*, ed. Hans Booms, vol. 5: *1952*, ed. Kai von Jena (Boppard: Harald Boldt, 1989), 342 n. 36.

[76] "220. Kabinettssitzung," 16 May 1952, *Die Kabinettsprotokolle*, 5:327–329.

[77] Letter from Nahum Goldmann to Konrad Adenauer, 19 May 1952, *Der deutsch-israelische Dialog*, 1:65–67; Konrad Adenauer, *Erinnerungen 1953–1955* (Stuttgart: Deutsche Verlags-Anstalt, 1966), 146–147.

[78] "Bonn soll konkretes Angebot machen," 7 May 1952, AdsD, Bestand Kurt Schumacher (Abt. II), 58.

[79] Letter from Adolf Arndt to Otto Küster, 20 May 1952, ACDP, I-084, 001.

[80] Kurt Schumacher, "Schumacher an Bundeskanzler Adenauer zum Stand der Wiedergutmachungsverhandlungen mit dem Staate Israel," 10 May 1952, in *Reden – Schriften – Korrespondenzen*, 1005–1006.

Realizing that he had no other choice, Adenauer took decisive measures to ensure that the negotiations would not fail, and a final agreement took shape. Goldmann's letter compelled Adenauer to reinstate Böhm.[81] While Adenauer convinced Böhm to stay on as chief negotiator, he could not take Küster back.[82] During the hiatus, Küster had embarrassed the government by going on radio to attack Fritz Schäffer for his resistance to reparations.[83] Schäffer responded on 23 May with his own inflammatory radio address. The finance minister claimed that he had discussed Küster's behavior with foreign diplomats who also considered it outrageous. More shocking was Schäffer's response to Küster's reproach that he was an antisemite. Drawing on a wave of popular resentment at the constant reminders of the Nazi past and the Holocaust, Schäffer seemed to turn the charge of antisemitism into a red badge of courage in a vicious political war on behalf of the German people. He said,

I remember the times of the so-called political jungle war which began in '45 and '46, when one of the most dangerous poison arrows was to defame one's opponent . . . that he either sympathized with antisemites or was himself an antisemite. I would like to remark that every virtuous man who thinks with his heart and his conviction of the want and of the burden of the German people, and who is a spokesman and representative to the entire world of the German people in its need and burden must – if he negotiates honestly and openly – accept being called an antisemite in this political jungle war. I say it [again]: every virtuous man.[84]

Adenauer convened an emergency session of the cabinet on 20 May. The following day, he met with Böhm and Abs, and they agreed on a sum of three billion marks paid in annual installments of 200–250 million marks. Adenauer then sent Böhm to Paris to meet with Goldmann as his personal representative, not on behalf of the government.[85] Böhm met with Goldmann and Israeli negotiators, who hesitated to accept Adenauer's offer of three billion marks as the basis for renewed talks. However, Goldmann persuaded them, and they consented to recommence negotiations.[86]

---

[81] Adenauer, *Erinnerungen 1953–1955*, 145–147.
[82] "28. Mai 1952: Tee-Empfang (Wortprotokoll)," 28 May 1952, Konrad Adenauer, *Teegespräche 1950–1954*, ed. Hanns Jürgen Küsters (Berlin: Siedler, 1984), 284–285.
[83] "Rundfunksansprache," 20 May 1952, ACDP, I-084, 001.
[84] "Ansprache des Ministers Schäffer," 23 May 1952, ACDP, I-084, 001.
[85] "Sondersitzung am 23. Mai 1952," 23 May 1952, *Die Kabinettsprotokolle*, 5:353–354.
[86] Letter from Franz Böhm to Konrad Adenauer, 24 May 1952, *Der deutsch-israelische Dialog*, 1:67–72.

On 10 June, Adenauer met with Böhm, Abs, Hallstein, Goldmann, and Shinnar in Bonn to settle the most important issues regarding reparations. At this decisive meeting, they agreed on a sum of 3.45 billion marks paid in installments of decreasing amounts.[87]

Reflecting on the circuitous course of the negotiations, the *Allgemeine Wochenzeitung* commented that just as a storm clears the air, allowing people to breathe more easily afterward, the chief West German mediators' resignations had cleared the air of the reparations negotiations.[88] Coupled with Abs's ineptitude and Goldmann's indignation, the resignation of Böhm had forced Adenauer to take the initiative through summit diplomacy. All along, reparations had been Adenauer's project, and his determination finally made the project a reality.

With the basic framework of the agreement set, the chancellor presented the deal to his cabinet on 17 June. Finance Minister Schäffer protested vigorously against the tentative settlement. He not been apprised of developments, he complained, and he denounced the basis of the agreement as dubious. Israel claimed that it would use West German payments to resettle Holocaust survivors, but Schäffer argued that most new settlers in Israel were not truly refugees from National Socialism. After the Holocaust, they had chosen to resettle in Eastern Europe and later fled postwar Communist oppression.[89] To convince wavering members of the cabinet, Adenauer, who normally appealed to their sense of morality, made an uncharacteristic reference to supposed Jewish economic power. At a cabinet meeting on 15 July, he noted that the Jews had great international economic power around the world and that making a moral gesture might help the Germans to obtain foreign loans.[90] Despite his dubious appeal, members of the cabinet and governing coalition still had grave concerns. Up until the last minute, Schäffer complained about aspects of the agreement

---

[87] "Niederschrift über Besprechung zwischen den Herren Goldmann, Shinnar, Staatsekretär Hallstein, Prof. Böhm, Dr. Frowein und Herrn Abs am 10. Juni 1952," undated, BAK, N 1351, 17 (Sonderakte Israel II), 46; Shinnar, *Bericht eines Beauftragten*, 46–48; Adenauer, *Erinnerungen 1953–1955*, 152–153.

[88] "Wir kommentieren: Das Wiedergutmachungs-Gewitter," *Allgemeine Wochenzeitung*, 30 May 1952.

[89] "228. Kabinettssitzung," 17 June 1952, *Die Kabinettsprotokolle*, 5:394–398. After receiving the cabinet's fundamental consent on 17 June, the negotiating delegations meeting in The Hague worked out the remaining details.

[90] "235. Kabinettssitzung," 15 July 1952, *Die Kabinettsprotokolle*, 5:456–458.

in an effort to forestall its implementation.[91] In a letter to Franz Böhm, Transportation Minister Seebohm fretted that Germany might not be able to afford both reparations to Israel and rearmament to stave off "further advancements of Bolshevist-Asiatic" aggression.[92] Vice Chancellor Blücher and his Free Democratic party colleague Hermann Schäfer worried that Arab opposition to the agreement might develop into a boycott of German commerce. Seebohm's colleague in the German Party, Hans-Joachim von Merkatz, noted that he could not deliver his caucus's votes for the treaty. Despite these criticisms, the cabinet ultimately approved the final settlement with only two dissenting votes, from Schäffer and labor minister Anton Storch of the CDU.[93]

Once the advantages of the agreement – chiefly increased foreign trade – become known, some Germans rushed to support the settlement and to profit from it. Because West Germany would pay the reparations primarily in goods selected by an official Israeli trade mission (and acting consulate), German cities began competing for the privilege of hosting the mission with its complement of diplomats and their families. In late July 1952, Frankfurt officials began a lobbying campaign by appealing to Jakob Altmaier to use his influence, and they also petitioned Israeli consul Livneh and Nahum Goldmann for their support.[94] West Berlin mayor Ernst Reuter wanted the trade mission for his city, and in October he wrote to Nahum Goldmann, stressing the latter's ties to the city's Jewish congregation.[95] Ultimately, Cologne received the commission, and Israeli reparations negotiator Felix Shinnar became the first mission director.

THE CENTRAL COUNCIL CLASHES WITH WORLD JEWRY

As Israel concluded its agreement with West Germany, the Jewish community in Germany found itself in deep disagreement with

---

91 "242. Kabinettssitzung," 28 August 1952, *Die Kabinettsprotokolle*, 5:530–531; Wolffsohn, "Globalentschädigung für Israel," in *Wiedergutmachung*, ed. Herbst and Goschler, 161–190.

92 Letter from Hans-Christoph Seebohm to Franz Böhm, 21 May 1952, BAK, B 136, 1127, 132.

93 "245. Kabinettssitzung," 8 September 1952, *Die Kabinettsprotokolle*, 5:557–558.

94 Letter from Walter Leiske to Jakob Altmaier, 30 July 1952, AdsD, Nachlass Jakob Altmaier (Abt. I), 8; "Vermerk," 1 August 1952, letter from Walter Kolb to Nahum Goldmann, date unknown, ZA, B.1/13, A.570, 65–66 and 73.

95 Letter from Ernst Reuter to Nahum Goldmann, 13 October 1952, LAB, B Rep. 2, 4873.

Jewish groups around the world. Hendrik George van Dam felt that the Central Council's loyalty during the negotiations should entitle it to a significant share of the settlement. He wrote to Israeli consul Elihau Livneh that the Jews in Germany could very easily have come to a separate agreement with the West German government rather than casting their lot with world Jewry. Despite this loyalty, foreign Jewish groups persisted in ignoring or disrespecting them. The Central Council's discipline and scruples "were not only unappreciated but were met with a policy of representation monopoly and a tiring know-it-all attitude [*Besserwisserei*]." Van Dam accused the Claims Conference of valuing Jewish leaders and Jewish groups based on their wealth, with the result that the impoverished community in Germany could not compete for attention or prestige.[96] Though all officially recognized religious establishments in Germany collected taxes from their members, the small and impoverished Jewish community was simply unable to sustain itself, and German Jewish institutions were unable to profit from the sale of ownerless Jewish property.

Feeling that its concerns were not addressed, the Central Council remained uneasy about its membership in the Claims Conference and considered quitting. Van Dam protested the suggestion that the entire settlement go to foreign Jewish groups to reimburse them for having cared for Jewish refugees between 1945 and 1952. He was also angered that the Claims Conference considered forgoing ratification of the treaty by each of its constituent organizations once it had been signed. On 20 July 1952, some Central Council members, including the delegates from Munich and Stuttgart, proposed that the Jews in Germany withdraw from the Claims Conference and hold their own negotiations with the West German government. Van Dam, however, wanted to stay in the organization and requested that additional delegates join him in The Hague. Ultimately, his view prevailed.[97] Even the West German government's negotiators felt that the Jews in Germany were not receiving their share of the settlement, despite the lobbying of German Jewish émigrés, including Leo Baeck, and German Jews refused to renounce their claims on state

[96] Letter from Hendrik George van Dam to Eliahu Livneh, 17 June 1952, ZA, B.1/7, 126.
[97] "Protokoll über die Sitzung des Zentralrates der Juden in Deutschland," 20 July 1952, ZA, B.1/7, 221.21.

support for their community, despite participation in the Claims Conference.[98]

These protests further soured the relationship between the Central Council and the Claims Conference. Moses Leavitt of the Joint Distribution Committee and the Claims Conference rejected van Dam's objections and threatened to expel the Central Council from the Claims Conference if the German Jews approached the West German government directly. Again, van Dam appealed to Livneh and Goldmann for intervention.[99] While Leavitt wanted the Central Council's unequivocal support in negotiations with the West German government, he refused any aid for the Central Council's efforts to care for elderly Jews in Germany or to maintain local congregations, claiming that those tasks should fall to German groups alone. The Jewish communities of Germany feared that they were soon to lose the subsidies they had been receiving from the state governments, increasing their anxiety over not having any assurance from the Claims Conference. When still more Central Council members expressed a desire to quit the Claims Conference in August, Livneh scolded them and accused them of valuing monetary issues over Jewish solidarity. Galinski responded by challenging Livneh. He insisted on the necessity of finding guaranteed sources of funding before aid to them was cut off. In Berlin, he claimed, the Jews received state money only because it was expected that they would soon find other sources. One board member feared that the reparations treaty might drain away all West German funding for Jewish causes within Germany and pointed out that the community needed government aid to survive. Quitting the Claims Conference and going it alone seemed attractive to Central Council leaders, but Sam Haber threatened to withdraw the American Joint Distribution Committee from Germany if they did so. The Central Council had until 31 August to make a final decision.[100]

In the end, the Jews in Germany decided to remain affiliated, not wishing to jeopardize the agreement that was so critical to Israel

---

[98] "Protokoll der Repräsentanten-Versammlung vom 23. Juli 1952," 23 July 1952, LAB, B Rep. 2, 6845; letter from Central Council to Claims Conference, 20 July 1952, ZA, B.1/7, 120.

[99] Letter from Hendrik George van Dam to Central Council directorate, 3 August 1952, ZA, B.1/7, 120.

[100] "Protokoll der Sitzung des Direktoriums des Zentralrat der Juden in Deutschland," 10 August 1952, ZA, B.1/7, 221.22.

Figure 7. Signing of the Luxembourg Agreement, 10 September 1952. Pictured *left*, on the Israeli side, are (*left to right*), Felix Shinnar, Giora Josephthal (blocked), Moshe Sharett, Nahum Goldmann, Benjamin Ferencz, Gershon Avner, and Eli Nathan. Pictured *right*, on the West German side, are (*left to right*), Jakob Altmaier, presumably Herbert Blankenhorn (blocked), Walter Hallstein, Konrad Adenauer, Franz Böhm (blocked), and Abraham Frowein. *Source:* dpa.

and to Jews around the world. Years later, van Dam wrote that even though the Jewish communities in Germany had feuded with the Claims Conference, they, as German Jews, needed to join the international group so as not to alienate the West German government and its envoys at the negotiations.[101] They also feared renewed social and financial isolation within the international Jewish community at a time when they needed to strengthen their community. The link to world Jewry, weak as it was, was essential to continued Jewish life in Germany. The Jews in Germany could not thrive in isolation, van Dam reflected, particularly once their government cultivated ties to foreign Jewish groups.[102]

THE LUXEMBOURG AGREEMENT

On 10 September 1952, representatives of West Germany, Israel, and the Claims Conference signed the Luxembourg Agreement for reparations (see Fig. 7). Fearing an attack by right-wing Jewish extremists, the signatories held the ceremony in secret, with only a few journalists present. Unable to agree on suitable texts for formal remarks to accompany the signing, no speeches accompanied the solemn event. Still, the signing had great import for Chancellor Adenauer. As West Germany's first major international agreement, it enabled the young state to begin its foreign policy with moral authority. Joining Adenauer in the West German delegation were treaty negotiators Franz Böhm and Abraham Frowein, foreign policy advisers Walter Hallstein and Herbert Blankenhorn, and Jewish Bundestag deputy Jakob Altmaier. Israeli foreign minister Moshe Sharett and Nahum Goldmann led the Jewish representatives.[103] The Jewish deputation contained men who were German by birth, and the German group contained one practicing Jew and another man of partial Jewish ancestry.

---

[101] Van Dam, "Die Juden in Deutschland nach 1945," in *Judentum*, 2:906.

[102] "An die Mitglieder des Rates: Referat auf die Tagung des Zentralrates," 31 August 1952, ZA, B.1/7, 126 and 221.23; "Protokoll der Zentralratstagung in Düsseldorf," 31 August 1952, ZA, B.1/7, 221.25. One historian believes that the Central Council, supportive of Israel but fearful of losing its sovereignty through incorporation in the Claims Conference, largely withdrew from politics and concentrated on the reconstruction of Jewish life in Germany and on its position as a reminder for the German government of the recent past. Trimbur, *De la Shoah*, 208.

[103] Shinnar, *Bericht eines Beauftragten*, 55.

The final treaty and a series of letters clarifying certain points of the agreement provided for three billion marks to Israel, paid in installments over twelve years. An Israeli trade mission in West Germany was to use the reparations funds to purchase goods and services to aid in the settlement and rehabilitation of Jewish refugees in Israel. Adenauer's government pledged to enact legislation compensating individual victims of Nazi persecution living in the Federal Republic, and the chancellor guaranteed that this compensation would not be less than that provided by American occupation law no. 59. This aspect of the agreement led to the Federal Compensation Law, passed by the Bundestag and ratified by the Bundesrat in the summer of 1953. The Luxembourg Agreement also stipulated that former Jewish communal officials would receive reparation payments for their loss of livelihood, just as Jewish or Socialist employees of the German state had received compensation for their dismissal under the Nazis.[104] Prior to September 1952, these officials had received only provisional compensation against future payments.[105] As a result of the ambiguous legal status of a treaty between a state and an organization, West Germany made arrangements to pay an additional 450 million marks to Israel, which the Jewish state would distribute to the Claims Conference. That organization would then divide its settlement between its constituent members; however, as one official at the West German Finance Ministry noted, the Central Council would receive "only an insignificant, small part" of the total.[106] Nevertheless, the Central Council's participation in the Claims Conference helped to establish its credibility within international Jewish circles. Although many years would pass before foreign Jewish groups completely accepted the Jewish community in Germany as an equal partner within the larger international Jewish community, the negotiations leading to the Luxembourg Agreement started the process, and

[104] "Agreement between the Federal Republic of Germany and the State of Israel," in appendix 2 of Sagi, *German Reparations*, 212–229; "Protocol No. 1, Drawn up by Representatives of the Government of the Federal Republic of Germany and of the Conference on Jewish Material Claims against Germany," in appendix 3 of Sagi, *German Reparations*, 231–236.

[105] Letter from Hessian Interior Ministry to *Oberbürgermeister* Frankfurt, 4 September 1952, ZA, B.1/13, 2949.

[106] "Protocol No. 2, Drawn up by Representatives of the Government of the Federal Republic of Germany and the Conference on Jewish Material Claims against Germany," in appendix 3 of Sagi, *German Reparations*, 238–241; "Aufzeichnung," 28 August 1952, BAK, B 122, 507.

German Jewish organizations slowly gained admittance to international Jewish bodies.[107]

West Germany also received a number of guarantees from the agreement and its supporting letters. Israel agreed to forgo any other claims against the Federal Republic of Germany arising from Nazi persecution. Furthermore, the two states agreed to suspend or to reduce payments to Israel temporarily if West Germany's economy faltered. Under no circumstances, however, would the obligation to pay reparations be eliminated.[108]

FROM TREATY SIGNING TO RATIFICATION

Prerequisite to the implementation of the treaty was its ratification by the Bundestag, an event that was by no means certain. Fearing opposition from his conservative associates, Chancellor Adenauer began his efforts to win parliamentary approval for the agreement even before he and Sharett had signed it. At a meeting of the CDU's leadership on 6 September, he pleaded with his party colleagues to approve reparations and attacked antisemitism in the CDU. Noting that the Bundestag had issued a resolution denouncing the persecution of the Jews under the Nazis, he challenged them to back up their words. "Words are cheap. Actions must follow words."[109] However, in the effort to win support, he either pandered to their worst stereotypes of Jews or evinced his own erroneous and superstitious views. Adenauer invoked the bogeyman of a financially omnipotent world Jewry angry at the rejection of the treaty:

Not only would it be a political catastrophe, it would also impair our entire effort to receive foreign credits again. Let us be clear about it. The power of Jewry in the economic field continues to be extraordinarily strong, so that this – well, the expression is perhaps a bit exaggerated – this reconciliation with Jewry is a necessary requirement for the Federal Republic from a moral standpoint as well as a political standpoint and an economic standpoint.[110]

---

[107] For more information, see Burgbauer, *Zwischen Erinnerung und Verdrängung*, 59.

[108] Letter No. 1, from Moshe Sharett to Konrad Adenauer, in appendix 2 of Sagi, *German Reparations*, 229; article 10 of "Agreement between the Federal Republic of Germany and the State of Israel," in appendix 2 of Sagi, *German Reparations*, 220.

[109] Adenauer, "Ansprache vor dem Bundesparteiausschuß der CDU in Bonn," 6 September 1952, in *Reden 1917–1967*, 266.

[110] Ibid., 267.

It is not clear why Adenauer chose this line of reasoning, but it does demonstrate his association of political profit with morally motivated policies. However, not everyone in his own party regarded the matter similarly, and Christian Democratic resistance to reparations was considerable. Eugen Gerstenmaier, speaker of the Bundestag and a strong proponent of reparations, later wrote that despite his wish to ratify the agreement expeditiously, strong opposition in the CDU and CSU caught him by surprise.[111]

One of the most significant hindrances to ratification was a threatened boycott of West German goods by the Arab League should the agreement become reality. Within the federal cabinet, Vice Chancellor Blücher of the FDP took the threat very seriously, and throughout the autumn of 1952, he repeatedly asked the chancellor to address the issue.[112] Only four days after Adenauer signed the agreement with Israel, the Arab League voted to send a delegation to Bonn to argue against reparations.[113] Hallstein, the government's representative dealing with the boycott issue, requested that cabinet members not meet with Arab envoys without notifying the Foreign Office.[114] In October, West German diplomats did meet with the Arab delegation, but Adenauer clearly underestimated the Arabs' dissatisfaction with his support for Israel. While the chancellor felt that through diplomacy he could overcome their opposition, they wanted nothing less than a rejection of the agreement.[115] Some German politicians proposed that the United Nations oversee reparations to Israel and that fulfillment of the reparations agreement accompany a resolution of the Palestinian refugee problem.[116] Ultimately, concluding that the Arabs' goals were incompatible with West German wishes, the government

---

[111] Eugen Gerstenmaier, *Streit und Friede hat seine Zeit. Ein Lebensbericht* (Frankfurt: Propyläen, 1981), 488.

[112] Letter from Franz Blücher to Konrad Adenauer, 5 September 1952, BAK, N 1080, 80, 152; "247. Kabinettssitzung," 16 September 1952, *Die Kabinettsprotokolle*, 5:571.

[113] Peter Hünseler, *Die außenpolitischen Beziehungen der Bundesrepublik Deutschland zu den arabischen Staaten von 1949–1980* (Frankfurt: Peter Lang, 1990), 33.

[114] "253. Kabinettssitzung," 21 October 1952, *Die Kabinettsprotokolle*, 5:633.

[115] Hünseler, *Die außenpolitischen Beziehungen*, 44–46. There was a pattern of long-standing opposition to Jewish settlement and political autonomy in Palestine. During World War II, many Arabs had actively supported Hitler. On Arab affinity for Nazi Germany, see Stefan Wild, "National Socialism in the Arab Near East between 1933 and 1939," *Die Welt des Islams* 25 (1985): 126–173; and Lukasz Hiroszowicz, *The Third Reich and the Arab Near East* (London: Routledge, 1966).

[116] "Ist die Koalition uneinig?," *Allgemeine Wochenzeitung*, 24 October 1952.

ended the talks in Bonn. Hallstein argued that the Arabs would have to recognize the moral necessity of German reparations, and the cabinet agreed not to give in to their demands.[117] On 14 November, Adenauer announced to his cabinet that he would send a delegation to the Middle East to meet with Arab leaders, but he would not consider their demand to abrogate the agreement with Israel.[118] Although West Germany offered Egypt a long-term loan, which it could repay in kind, the Egyptians' demands were far greater than what the West Germans were willing to offer. Ultimately, the presence of a competing East German delegation in Cairo forced West Germany to withdraw its envoys.[119]

Even though the cabinet was still discussing the issue, and the CDU had yet to address it, the SPD Bundestag caucus voted unanimously on 11 November to ratify the settlement, regardless of the Arabs' protests.[120] Through the Socialist International, the Israeli socialist Mapai Party was pressing the SPD for a quick ratification. Julius Braunthal of the Socialist International asked SPD leader Erich Ollenhauer whether Adenauer hesitated to bring the agreement to the Bundestag for a vote because he feared a backlash from antisemitic voters in forthcoming federal elections. Ollenhauer did not doubt the sincerity of Adenauer's support for reparations, but he assumed that other cabinet members worried about the Arab reaction.[121]

In addition to Bonn and the Israeli government, the Claims Conference's member organizations also were required to ratify the settlement. Unhappy with the Central Council's share of the total financial settlement, leaders of that group considered withholding their approval of the agreement, and van Dam carried

---

[117] "257. Kabinettssitzung," 11 November 1952, *Die Kabinettsprotokolle*, 5:677. After the failure of talks with the government, the Arab delegation turned to individual parliamentarians and former Nazis for assistance. The government responded by asking the delegation to leave the country. Lavy, *Germany and Israel*, 26; Hünseler, *Die außenpolitischen Beziehungen*, 46.

[118] "258. Kabinettssitzung," 14 November 1952, *Die Kabinettsprotokolle*, 5:689.

[119] Hünseler, *Die außenpolitischen Beziehungen*, 58–60. On East German–West German competition for Egyptian support, see William Glenn Gray, *Germany's Cold War: The Global Campaign to Isolate East Germany, 1949–1969* (Chapel Hill: University of North Carolina Press, 2003), 18–21.

[120] "11.11.1952: Fraktionssitzung," 11 November 1952, *Die SPD-Fraktion im Deutschen Bundestag*, half-vol. 1:390.

[121] Letter from Julius Braunthal to Erich Ollenhauer, 22 January 1953; letter from Erich Ollenhauer to Julius Braunthal, 29 January 1953; AdsD, Bestand Erich Ollenhauer (Abt. II), 321.

on special negotiations with Nahum Goldmann to rectify the situation.[122] The Central Council's board had authorized van Dam to abstain if the Jews in Germany gained nothing from the settlement, and the Central Council would not relinquish the possibility of negotiating directly with the West German government for aid to its member communities.[123] At last, in December, the Claims Conference began preparations for ratification. Each member organization would have one vote, but van Dam was dissatisfied with the Central Council's representation within the group's leadership, as Heinz Galinski had lost his election for a seat on the Claims Conference executive. The main organization for German Jewish émigrés, the London-based Council of Jews from Germany, received one of eight vice-presidential seats on the Claims Conference board, as did Jewish groups from Britain, France, Canada, and the United States, which offended the Central Council leadership.[124] The Central Council and Claims Conference began to resolve their differences in the spring of 1953, and in conjunction with the American Joint Distribution Committee and Jewish Restitution Successor Organization, the Claims Conference did distribute funds to the Jews in Germany beginning in 1954.[125] Although many Jewish groups around the world did not support the Central Council, Nahum Goldmann remained steadfast in his endorsement of Jewish life in Germany. He did, however, caution the Central Council not to overestimate its contribution to the Luxembourg Agreement's successful negotiation.[126]

By February 1953, momentum had gathered for West German ratification of the agreement. Walter Hallstein was ready to send it to the state governments for ratification in the Bundesrat, and,

---

[122] Letter from I. W. Wreden (for Hendrik George van Dam) to Leonard Baer, Julius Dreifuss, Heinz Galinksi, and Leopold Goldschmidt, 27 September 1952, ZA, B.1/7, 120.

[123] "Protokoll," 14 September 1952, ZA, B.1/7, 221.27.

[124] "Bericht über die Sitzungen on Jewish Material Claims against Germany," 12 January 1953, ZA, B.1/7, 120; letter from Central Council to board members, state associations, etc., 30 January 1953, ZA, B.1/13, A.746, 21. The Council of Jews from Germany, led from London by Rabbi Leo Baeck, was formally known as the Council for the Protection of the Rights and Interests of Jews from Germany.

[125] Letter from Heinz Galinski to Hendrik George van Dam, 13 May 1953, ZA, B.1/7, 120; Ronald Zweig, *German Reparations and the Jewish World: A History of the Claims Conference* (Boulder: Westview, 1987). For more information on Claims Conference support for the Jews of Germany, see chapter 8.

[126] "Protokoll der Sitzung des Direktoriums des Zentralrates," 9 October 1952, ZA, B.1/7, 221.28.

desiring to expedite the process, he pushed the cabinet to give its consent to the agreement.[127] In his opinion, a number of factors favored immediate action. West German talks with the Egyptian government had failed; the SPD had already approved the treaty; and Adenauer wanted the issue fully resolved before his trip to America in late March. Blücher and Schäffer, however, still expressed reservations about the agreement. Blücher protested that the Israelis would not allow the German flag to fly on vessels delivering reparations goods to Israeli ports, and Schäffer claimed that West Germany could not both pay reparations to Israel and bear the costs of Allied occupation.[128] In fact, the issue of the banned German flag threatened to derail the states' ratification of the agreement, and one of the most vociferous critics of the ban was the leader of Bremen, Wilhelm Kaisen – a Social Democrat.[129] Ultimately, Felix Shinnar asked his government to reconsider its position on the German flag, and David Ben-Gurion agreed to forgo this aspect of the agreement. On 20 February, the Bundesrat unanimously approved the agreement. The focus now shifted to the parties represented in the Bundestag.

The largest political party whose decision on ratification remained uncertain was the FDP, a party divided by the threat of an Arab boycott. Party board member Ernst Mayer represented the viewpoint that regardless of such a boycott, the Luxembourg Agreement would open a burgeoning trade with Israel. Furthermore, it was unacceptable to let West Germany be blackmailed. Manager of the FDP Bundestag caucus Fritz Niebel countered that German trade with the Arab lands involved vital goods, such as oil, whereas Israel had nothing critical to export.[130] The FDP's foreign affairs committee took up the issue, acknowledging German responsibility to the Jews but expressing concerns about the fate of Arab refugees from Israel, whom they wanted to aid in conjunction

---

[127] "273. Kabinettssitzung," 3 February 1953, Germany (West), Bundesregierung, *Die Kabinettsprotokolle der Bundesregierung*, ed. Hans Booms, vol. 6, ed. Ulrich Enders and Konrad Reiser (Boppard: Harald Boldt, 1989), 153. Each state government sent a delegation to the Bundesrat, the upper house of West Germany's federal parliament. Votes were apportioned by population.

[128] "275. Kabinettssitzung," 13 February 1953, *Die Kabinettsprotokolle*, 6:171.

[129] "276. Kabinettssitzung," 20 February 1953, *Die Kabinettsprotokolle*, 6:183–184; "Dem Herrn Bundeskanzler vorzulegen," 20 February 1953, ACDP, I-172, 058/1; Wolffsohn, "Globalentschädigung für Israel," in *Wiedergutmachung*, ed. Herbst and Goschler, 186–187.

[130] "Kurzprotokoll Nr. 86," 8 October 1952, ADL, A 40, 804.

with the Luxembourg Agreement.[131] At an FDP party congress, party chairman Franz Blücher denounced antisemitism and religious intolerance and described the reparations agreement as a chance for Germany to restore its reputation in the world. On the other hand, he noted that the treaty must be composed so as to effect "not unrest, but peace in world," presumably a reference to Arab protests against it.[132] In fact, some FDP party congress participants debated whether or not antisemitism really was resurgent in postwar Germany, and all the speakers who addressed the treaty endorsed voting against ratification.[133] Additionally, numerous party activists lobbied against ratification of the agreement, most citing the potential damage to the presumed traditional German-Arab friendship.[134] As late as the day before the final vote in the Bundestag, the FDP continued to debate the matter, and Hallstein met with the FDP Bundestag caucus to field questions about the treaty.[135]

Within Adenauer's CDU, the debate on the treaty reflected deep divisions. Jakob Diel, a leader of the Rhineland CDU and a former colleague of Adenauer in the prewar Prussian state legislature, wrote to the chancellor and party chairman, "The Israel business is not popular!"[136] Although many on the center-right shared Diel's opinion, others, including Eugen Gerstenmaier and Herbert Blankenhorn, pressed the CDU to approve the agreement.[137] Within the party, Adenauer let it be known that he considered the agreement to be of the utmost importance and expressed his wish that it be ratified before his upcoming trip to the United States.[138]

---

[131] "Entschließung zum Israel Abkommen," 20 November 1952, ADL, A 1, 27, 6.

[132] "Der politische Standort und die Ziele der Freien Demokratischen Partei," 20 November 1952, ADL, A 1, 30, 32.

[133] "Vierter Bundesparteitag der FDP 1952 zu Bad Ems," 21 November 1952, ADL, A 1, 31, 45–46 and 41. A speaker from the Hamburg FDP, a liberal branch, raised the issue of antisemitism, while delegates from Lower Saxony were incredulous.

[134] "Tagebuchnotizen zu den Verhandlungen über den Sühnevertrag mit Israel," 26 October 1952, ACDP, I-084, 001; correspondence between Thomas Dehler and Rabentrost, December 1952, ADL, N 1, 1159 and 1184; "28.2.1953: Sitzung des Bundesvorstandes," 28 February 1953, *FDP-Bundesvorstand: Die Liberalen unter dem Vorsitz von Theodor Heuss und Franz Blücher*, half-vol. 2:867.

[135] "Kurzprotokoll Nr. 227," 17 March 1953, ADL, A 40, 733, 27.

[136] Letter from Jakob Diel to Konrad Adenauer, 13 November 1952, ACDP, I-139, 022/6.

[137] "Entwurf," 25 February 1953, ACDP, I-210, 067/2.

[138] "2.3.1953: Fraktionsvorstandssitzung," 2 March 1953, *Die CDU/CSU-Fraktion im Deutschen Bundestag*, 677.

Meanwhile, the CDU's small Bavarian sister party, the Christian Social Union, harbored significant reservations about the treaty.[139] Emerging CSU leader Franz Josef Strauss rejected it, calling the entire negotiations process nothing less than scandalous. He also attacked the manner in which the Bundestag Foreign Affairs Committee had handled hearings on the treaty under the direction of SPD member and committee chairman Carlo Schmid.[140] In a meeting of the CDU Bundestag caucus, no unity on the treaty materialized, and several deputies announced their intention to vote against it. CDU Bundestag caucus leader Heinrich von Brentano supported ratification, stressing the moral arguments in favor of the treaty and the need to stand behind the cabinet.[141]

During the treaty's first reading in the Bundestag, on 4 March 1953, Adenauer eloquently spoke of its moral importance and pleaded, "The name of our Fatherland must once again have a value which corresponds to the historical achievement of the German people in culture and economics." He added that ratification of the agreement would show the world that West Germany, not East Germany, was the good Germany. To please his critics, he noted that payments were to be in goods, not cash, and could be reduced in the event of an economic catastrophe. Additionally, Israel would not receive any war materiel. Collective reparations to Israel and the Claims Conference, he assured the deputies, were only part of a project that the Allies had begun as early as 1947 with military government law no. 59. Furthermore, some sort of reparations to individual Nazi victims in the future would be the centerpiece of West Germany's financial efforts for reconciliation with the Jewish people.[142] The Central Council also applied

---

[139] Letter from Konrad Adenauer to Fritz Schäffer, 19 August 1952, *Briefe 1951–1953*, 268.

[140] "24.2.1953: Fraktionsvorstandssitzung," 24 February 1953; "3.3.1953: Fraktionssitzung," 3 March 1953; *Die CDU/CSU-Fraktion im Deutschen Bundestag*, 674 and 681. Strauss supported Schäffer's arguments that the settlement was too large, that too few Israelis were refugees from National Socialism, that Arab opposition needed greater attention, and that Germany needed the hard currency or goods that were to be sent to Israel. In future years, Strauss became one of Israel's strongest allies in the West German government. Lavy, *Germany and Israel*, 48–53.

[141] "17.3.1953: Fraktionssitzung," 17 March 1953, *Die CDU/CSU-Fraktion im Deutschen Bundestag*, 688–689 and 693.

[142] "Erste Beratung des Entwurfs eines Gesetzes betr. das Abkommen vom 10. September 1952 zwischen der Bundesrepublik Deutschland und dem Staate Israel," during "252. Sitzung," 18 March 1953, *Verhandlungen des Deutschen Bundestages, I. Wahlperiode 1949*, 15:12092–12096.

last-minute pressure for ratification of the treaty and future passage of individual reparations.[143]

On 18 March 1953, the Bundestag voted on ratification of the Luxembourg Agreement. After Count Karl von Spreti of the CSU spoke for the Foreign Affairs Committee, representatives of each party made statements before the final vote. Eugen Gerstenmaier spoke for the CDU, appealing to the deputies to restore Germany's honor. As Germany had become "free of Jews," Germany itself had become a ghetto, ringed by a wall of hate. Now, he added, "this treaty has the goal to bring Germany out of the ghetto completely and forever." He concluded, "It seems to me it is time, it is high time, that we no longer let ourselves be ashamed. The honor of Germany requires it! Therefore we say yes to the treaty."[144] Carlo Schmid spoke for the SPD, citing his party's repeated support for reparations. He also reminded his listeners that among the victims addressed by this treaty were countless German citizens, including some of the country's most famous former inhabitants.[145] Walther Hasemann, speaking for the FDP, claimed that the government had not adequately addressed the Arabs' concerns. Furthermore, the moral impact of the treaty had been weakened by the haggling over the German flag in Israeli ports. In the end, he announced that the FDP deputies were free to vote their consciences, and party discipline would not be enforced.[146] Hans-Joachim von Merkatz of the German Party claimed that his party preferred individual payments to "Germans of the Jewish faith and to the European Jews" and called for similar reparations for ethnic Germans deported from their former homes in Eastern Europe.[147] Speakers for the Communist Party and the political right wing attacked the treaty. Adolf von Thadden, formerly of the German Reich Party (DRP) and now independent as a result of a ban on his party, acknowledged the deaths of "over one million" Jews but denounced collective reparations and payments to non-German Jews. Oskar Müller of the Communist Party claimed that reparations payments would benefit above all "the American armaments industry and

---

[143] "Aktionen unautorisierter Elemente," *Allgemeine Wochenzeitung*, 6 March 1953.
[144] "Zweite und dritte Beratung des Entwurfs eines Gesetzes betr. das Abkommen vom 10. September 1952 zwischen der Bundesrepublik Deutschland und dem Staate Israel," during "262. Sitzung," 18 March 1953, *Verhandlungen des Deutschen Bundestages, I. Wahlperiode 1949*, 15:12276–12277.
[145] Ibid., 15:12277–12278.   [146] Ibid., 15:12278–12279.   [147] Ibid., 15:12279.

Table 1. *Bundestag vote on Ratification of the Luxembourg*
Agreement (including 19 Berlin delegates)

Political party	For	Against	Abstention
Christian Democratic/Christian Social Union	89	5	39
Social Democratic Party	134	0	0
Free Democratic Party	19	5	22
German Party	5	5	10
Bavarian Party/Federalist Union	3	0	13
Communist Party	0	13	0
Others	5	7	5
TOTAL	255	35	89

Source: "Namentliche Abstimmungen," during "262. Sitzung," 18 March 1953,
Verhandlungen des Deutschen Bundestages, I. Wahlperiode 1949, 15:12290–12293.

high finance," turning Israel into an American base of operations
in the Middle East.[148] Despite these criticisms, the Luxembourg
Agreement passed with an overwhelming majority (see Table 1).

SUPPORTERS AND CRITICS OF REPARATIONS

While many individuals contributed to the Luxembourg Agreement, two statesmen all but willed it into creation: Konrad
Adenauer and Nahum Goldmann. Goldmann, raised in Germany,
considered himself both very German and very Jewish, and he took
great pride in having brought the two sides closer together.[149] However, he reserved the greatest praise for Konrad Adenauer, whose
role in bringing reparations to fruition cannot be overestimated.[150]
The Allies, displaying a marked disinterest in the whole matter, exerted virtually no pressure on the West Germans, particularly after
the Cold War began. Thus, Adenauer acceded to Jewish demands
for reparations of his own accord.

However, ever since the event, historians have inquired after
Adenauer's intentions. Was he motivated by a sense of moral obligation, or was there an ulterior motive for his desire to reconcile

---

[148] Ibid., 15:12280–12281.   [149] Goldmann, *Jewish Paradox*, 121.
[150] Nahum Goldmann, "Adenauer und das Jüdische Volk," in *Konrad Adenauer und seine
Zeit. Politik und Persönlichkeit des ersten Bundeskanzlers, Beiträge von Weg- und Zeitgenossen,*
ed. Dieter Blumenwitz et al. (Stuttgart: Deutsche Verlags-Anstalt, 1976).

with Israel? There is no doubt that Adenauer was determined to ensure the negotiations' success. Adenauer was a deeply moral man, and this morality drove his policy decisions regarding the eastern bloc, Israel, western Europe, and other issues. However, as Yeshayahu Jelinek has shown, Adenauer also intended to reap all possible political benefit from morally driven political acts. He considered reconciliation with Israel, and specifically making reparations for the Nazis' crimes, a vital step in Germany's rehabilitation.[151] He remained personally involved throughout the process, always fearing it would degenerate into horse trading and thus lose its high moral tone.[152]

Other Germans contributed greatly to the negotiations' success, Franz Böhm chief among them. Böhm had the moral strength to defend reparations against the persistent resistance of Fritz Schäffer and Hermann Abs. Blankenhorn later praised Böhm's courage to resign rather than support an agreement he found deficient, and Shinnar called him the best possible choice for the position of West German negotiator.[153] SPD chairman Erich Ollenhauer later cited parliamentary adversary Böhm as the driving force behind reparations.[154] Theodor Heuss and Konrad Adenauer, however, did not recompense Böhm. In 1953, they declined to grant Böhm an honorific decoration for his service as chief negotiator, bowing to popular opinion, which was then running against the Luxembourg Agreement.[155] In 1959, when Heuss nominated Böhm to be his successor as West German president, Adenauer rejected the suggestion. The former negotiator's legendary philosemitism and open criticism of former Nazi fellow travelers in West German political life certainly alienated some

[151] Yeshayahu A. Jelinek, "Political Acumen, Altruism, Foreign Pressure or Moral Debt: Konrad Adenauer and the Shilumim," *Tel Aviver Jahrbuch für Deutsche Geschichte* 19 (1990), ed. Shulamit Volkov and Frank Stern (Gerlingen: Bleicher, 1990): 77–102; Sagi, *German Reparations*, 66; Jena, "Versöhnung mit Israel?," 480; cf. Gardner Feldman, *Special Relationship*, 60 and 65.
[152] Adenauer, *Erinnerungen 1953–1955*, 144.
[153] Herbert Blankenhorn, *Verständnis und Verständigung: Blätter eines politischen Tagebuchs 1949 bis 1979* (Frankfurt: Propyläen, 1980), 141; Shinnar, *Bericht eines Beauftragten*, 36.
[154] Letter from Erich Ollenhauer to Franz Böhm, 16 February 1955, AdsD, Bestand Erich Ollenhauer (Abt. II), 412.
[155] "Verdienstorden der Bundesrepublik Deutschland," 15 June 1953, *Unter vier Augen*, 120. In contrast, they did nominate Hermann Josef Abs for an award for his successful representation of Germany at the London Debt Conference.

on the political right, and the political left probably found his advocacy of West German nuclear armament unacceptable.[156] Böhm's deputy, Otto Küster, suffered even more than Böhm had. In his account of the negotiations, Herbert Blankenhorn assigned credit for the negotiations' success to Böhm and Heinz Trützschler von Falkenstein, Küster's replacement on the West German delegation. He omitted any mention of Küster.[157] In 1954, Küster lost his position as Baden-Württemberg's commissioner for reparations. To liberals in Baden-Württemberg and to Jews throughout the world, it seemed as though Küster had lost his job as retribution for his progressive stance on reparations and relations with the Jews.[158] Küster remained cynical about the Luxembourg Agreement's importance. While many Germans opposed it at the time, he claimed that "in a few years everyone will be very relieved because of it – if his children ask, what did you really do before 1945?"[159] For the Jewish communities of Hesse, the hero was Hessian Jew Jakob Altmaier.[160]

Opposition to reparations, even within the federal cabinet, had been substantial. Cabinet ministers Thomas Dehler and Fritz Schäffer, both of whom emerged politically untainted from the Nazi era, proved to be vigorous opponents of the Luxembourg Agreement. Their active resistance to the agreement, coupled with dubious public remarks, has given rise to some question as to whether they were, in fact, antisemites.[161] Although neither was probably a Judeophobe, both were profoundly insensitive to Jewish needs and desires, placing the pedestrian concerns of daily

---

[156] 4 February, 6 March, and 10 June 1959, *Unter vier Augen*, 292–293, 296–297, 307; Franz Böhm, "Zerfällt die freie Welt oder zerfällt die Kommunismus?," 1957, in *Reden und Schriften über die Ordnung einer freien Gesellschaft, einer freien Wirtschaft und über die Wiedergutmachung*, ed. Ernst-Joachim Mestmäcker (Karlsruhe: C. F. Müller, 1960); Pross, *Paying for the Past*, 6.

[157] Blankenhorn, *Verständnis und Verständigung*, 140–141.

[158] Letter from Franz Böhm to Wolfgang Haußmann, 20 September 1954, BAK, B 122, 2076 (20).

[159] "Tagebuchnotizen zu den Verhandlungen über den Sühnevertrag mit Israel," 19 September 1952, ACDP, I-084, 001.

[160] Letter from Landesverband Hessen to Jakob Altmaier, 23 November 1954, AdsD, Nachlass Jakob Altmaier (Abt. I), 4.

[161] Wolffsohn, "Globalentschädigung für Israel," in *Wiedergutmachung*, ed. Herbst and Goschler, 161–190; Goldmann, *Jewish Paradox*, 128–130; Henzler, *Fritz Schäffer*, 430. They both routinely claimed to oppose collective reparations in favor of individual reparations, but neither man pushed for these in the Bundestag.

politics above important historical gestures. Hermann Abs, West German negotiator at the London debt conference, also opposed Adenauer's efforts for a quick agreement with Israel; however, Abs did favor collective reparations in theory. He merely wanted to wait until West Germany knew the extent of its preexisting foreign debt obligations. Moreover, once Adenauer made his final decision to accept Israel's terms, Abs offered no more opposition.[162] Several cabinet ministers from parties other than the CDU foresaw opposition within their own parties against the agreement and hesitated to support it. Among these fence-sitters were Franz Blücher (FDP) and Hans-Christoph Seebohm (DP).[163]

After the agreement's ratification, those who had worked to make West German reparations to the Jews a reality congratulated and thanked one another. Central Council general secretary van Dam wrote to Adenauer to express his gratitude, and Adenauer thanked Nahum Goldmann.[164] Goldmann wrote to Walter Hallstein, expressing his appreciation of the deputy foreign minister's efforts.[165] For his efforts in furthering German-Jewish reconciliation, Karl Marx received the very same high civilian decoration that Heuss and Adenauer denied to Franz Böhm.[166] For the Jews in West Germany, the ratification of the Luxembourg Agreement represented a landmark, celebrated by the *Allgemeine Wochenzeitung* as a "new beginning after 20 years."[167]

---

[162] Wolffsohn, "Globalentschädigung für Israel," in *Wiedergutmachung*, ed. Herbst and Goschler, 167 and 189.

[163] Ibid., 177–178.

[164] Letter from Hendrik George van Dam to Konrad Adenauer, 19 March 1953, ZA, B.1/7, 101; letter from Konrad Adenauer to Nahum Goldmann, 27 March 1953, *Briefe 1951–1953*, 353.

[165] Letter from Nahum Goldmann to Walter Hallstein, 23 March 1953, BAK, N 1266, 1858.

[166] "Aufzeichnung für Karl Marx," *Allgemeine Wochenzeitung*, 30 January 1953.

[167] "Neubeginn nach 20 Jahren," *Allgemeine Wochenzeitung*, 27 March 1953.

CHAPTER 8

The Central Council's External Relations and Internal Reforms after the Luxembourg Agreement

Since the Central Council's foundation in 1950, political issues had preoccupied its leaders, and in pursuit of the group's goals, they had developed a good relationship with individual government officials – most notably with Theodor Heuss and his staff. While concentrating on political affairs, however, the Central Council had neglected internal matters of great concern, including relations between Jewish communities and the issue of their funding. Moreover, the coordinating body had almost totally overlooked cultural programs and the regulation of religious issues within the communities. In 1953, the Central Council wished to reorganize itself and to place its relationship with the government on a new basis.

With reparations to Israel assured, Central Council board members now looked to the federal government for domestic reparations and financial subsidies. While their cordial relations with leading politicians made such aid feasible, their poor relations with Jewish groups abroad made it imperative. Furthermore, federal officials debated how best to develop the government's relationship with the Jewish community, opting eventually for ministerial supervision to complement the existing informal ties to Theodor Heuss. Meanwhile, newspaper editor Karl Marx acquired more influence in the president's office and served as an unofficial consultant on Jewish affairs.

The Central Council faced internal challenges, as well. With the aim of moving beyond its function as a mere political pressure group, the Central Council began a process of reorganization and reorientation under a cadre of new leaders. Additionally, the influx of East German Jews fleeing to western Germany demonstrated to Central Council leaders the necessity of supervising and coordinating the Jewish community's welfare activities.

TIES TO THE FEDERAL MINISTRIES AND
FUNDING FOR JEWISH AFFAIRS

The Central Council, which had opened formal ties to the Bonn government as early as March 1952, now looked to it – not to foreign Jewish groups – for critical financial support. The group had always operated on a limited budget, and its relations with the Claims Conference gave German Jewish leaders little reason to believe that their organization would profit significantly from the Luxembourg Agreement or would receive financial aid from Jews in America or Israel. Thus, on 9 October 1952, a month after the treaty signing, Central Council board members decided to request funding from the government.[1] At a diplomatic reception a few weeks earlier, Julius Dreifuss had informally approached Chancellor Adenauer about financial aid for the various Jewish communities, and the chancellor had indicated his willingness to help. Adenauer's aide Herbert Blankenhorn then asked Dreifuss to put the appeal in writing.[2] Acting on this request, on 5 January 1953, Hendrik George van Dam sent a report to the interior minister, Robert Lehr, arguing that Jewish groups needed financial aid from the West German government. The Jews in Germany had founded communities and a unitary representative organization in the face of foreign opposition, and for funding they remained at the mercy of the designated successor organizations, such as the Jewish Restitution Successor Organization and the Jewish Trust Corporation. Van Dam wrote,

> Therefore, it is our opinion that the central representation of the Jewish communities should be granted a federal subsidy which would enable it to complete its tasks independent [of foreign aid]. Today, the Central Council's activities can take place only in an atmosphere which is both provisional and uncertain, serving neither the independence nor the strength of the body.[3]

At a meeting with van Dam and Dreifuss, Lehr, who had expressed a desire to show the outside world that Jews could live in Germany again, indicated his willingness to support aid for Jewish communal

[1] "Protokoll der Sitzung des Direktoriums des Zentralrates," 9 October 1952, ZA, B.1/7, 221.28.

[2] Letter from Julius Dreifuss to Hendrik George van Dam, 25 September 1952, ZA, B.1/7, 120; "Beschlussprotokoll der internen Direktoriumssitzung," 12 November 1952, ZA, B.1/7, 221.30.

[3] "Memorandum," 5 January 1953, BAK, B 106, 21407.

officials. He was, however, perplexed when the two Jewish leaders showed an interest in the long dormant proposal to have an official adviser for Jewish affairs appointed by the government. Dreifuss and van Dam then explained that they wanted the Interior Ministry to reallocate funds earmarked for the Jewish adviser's office to provide a subsidy for the Central Council.[4]

In the absence of an officially designated adviser, federal officials remained uncertain which ministerial office was responsible for the government's ties to the Jewish community. German Jewish leaders had been appealing directly to Heuss, Adenauer, and federal cabinet ministers, but a midlevel official would have to maintain the relationship and to administer the disbursement of subsidies once they began. The varying opinions on ministerial funding for Jewish groups reflected differing views of the government's relationship with the Jewish community. Erich Wende, director of the Interior Ministry's cultural affairs division, continued to argue that a special adviser for Jewish affairs could best supervise these matters. Furthermore, since the Jewish community of Bavaria was no longer represented in the Central Council as a result of Philipp Auerbach's death, Wende was uncertain how to aid Jewish groups there.[5] His opinion reflected the belief that the government's relationship with the Jewish community required extraordinary supervision.

Wende corresponded with his subordinate Carl Gussone on the issue of administrative responsibility for the Jews, and in April numerous Interior Ministry officials met to settle the issue. They resolved to transfer supervision of funding for the Central Council to the ministry's bureau for reparations, while care for Jewish cemeteries and oversight of interfaith projects would remain under the cultural affairs division. However, Hans Berger, the official supervising domestic reparations to individuals, protested that support for Jewish institutions was a cultural matter, falling under the purview of cultural affairs administrator Gussone.[6] Gussone later countered that the government needed to support the Jewish community only because of the Nazis' crimes, making

---

4 Report by Robert Lehr, 5 January 1953, BAK, B 106, 21407.
5 Report by Erich Wende (division III, cultural affairs), 21 January 1953, BAK, B 106, 21407.
6 Letter from Erich Wende to Carl Gussone (division III 3), 25 February 1953; "Akten-vermerk," 16 April 1953; memorandum from Hans Berger (division I A 7, reparations), 30 April 1953; BAK, B 106, 21407.

the subsidies a form of reparations.[7] As this meeting revealed, there was still no consensus on whether government support of Jewish life in Germany was compensation for the past or maintenance of a contemporary relationship.

The Luxembourg Agreement stipulated that the West German federal government was to pay reparations to Jewish communal officials who had lost their jobs as a result of Nazi persecution, and in early January 1953, Jewish groups negotiated with West German officials over the modalities of payments. Affected institutions included religious congregations, representative bodies (including the Nazi-era Reich Union of Jews in Germany), seminaries, orphanages, hospitals, schools, and rest homes.[8] The Central Council and Claims Conference, jointly negotiating with the government, proposed that former officials from a wide variety of Jewish institutions be eligible to receive pension payments amounting to 80 percent of their salary in 1933. Widows would receive 48 percent of their husband's salary, orphans 20 percent.[9]

With the issue of funding for the active Jewish communities in Germany still under discussion, several Jewish communities, including that in Berlin, found themselves in increasing financial difficulties. They would not begin receiving funding from the Claims Conference until 1954, and the official successor organizations were parsimonious with their aid.[10] Siegmund Weltlinger, adviser for Jewish affairs within the Berlin state government, had been in contact with his fellow Christian Democrats Heinrich Vockel, Adenauer's envoy in Berlin, and Walter Schreiber, deputy mayor, about aid for the Jewish community there. Schreiber was willing to grant the community 250,000 marks as part of a future reparations payment, while Weltlinger wanted it to be an outright gift. It also seemed possible that the government would file a lawsuit against the Jewish Restitution Successor Organization, which wanted to sell the Jewish hospital in Berlin against the wishes of the community's leaders.[11] The leaders of Berlin Jewry feared that Schreiber might replace the recently deceased Social Democrat Ernst Reuter

7 Memorandum from Carl Gussone, 20 May 1953, BAK, B 106, 21407.
8 "Vermerk (Der Staatssekretär des Bundeskanzleramtes)," 8 January 1953, BAK, B 136, 504, 203.
9 "Entwurf," 9 February 1953, BAK, B 136, 504, 206–208.
10 "Protokoll der Repräsentanten-Versammlung vom 10 Juni 1953," 10 June 1953, LAB, B Rep. 2, 6845.
11 "Aktennotiz," 12 August 1953, LAB, E Rep. 200–22, 38.

as mayor of West Berlin. While Reuter had adopted a reconciliatory approach in dealing with the JRSO, Heinz Galinski, charged with consulting with the successor organization regarding increased support for the Jews in Berlin, feared that Schreiber might simply sue the JRSO to achieve that goal, jeopardizing his efforts for negotiations.[12] By 9 October, the Berlin Jewish community had still not received any of the money promised from the city government, and Galinski turned to CDU Bundestag representative Ernst Lemmer, a well-known friend of the community, to arrange a meeting with Schreiber. Lemmer was also willing to intervene with Adenauer to ensure that the Jewish hospital would not be closed.[13] Even in Berlin, the once-proud Jewish community had little choice but to look to German officials, not foreign Jewry, for increased support, and the Berlin Jews traded on their connections in the CDU to win help.

In western Germany, Jewish leaders also began making explicit demands on the government, causing confusion among administrators. In early June 1953, van Dam and his assistant, Norbert Schäfer, met with Interior Ministry officials and requested over 100,000 marks per year, reiterating that the German Jews needed to be independent of international Jewish organizations and observing that their relationship with the successor organizations was poor. Carl Gussone replied that the ministry had not budgeted any funding for the Jewish communities. They would have to seek special funds from one of the ministry's divisions, making it essential first to determine who had purview over relations with the Jewish community.[14] The Central Committee's request only highlighted the need to resolve the question of administrative prerogative. Even though it seemed that ministerial officials had come to a provisional decision on the matter in April, in late June deputy interior minister Hans Ritter von Lex opined that support for Jewish groups fell under the cultural affairs division, not the reparations office, as it related to future care rather than past injustices.[15] Gussone accepted the decision, but the ministry failed to settle the

---

[12] "Protokoll der Repräsentanten-Versammlung vom 7. Oktober 1953," 7 October 1953, LAB, B Rep. 2, 6845.

[13] "Aktennotiz. Betr.: Bericht des Vorstandes der Jüdischen Gemeinde über die augenblickliche Lage in einer nichtöffentlichen Repräsentanten-Versammlung am 7.10.1953," 9 October 1953, LAB, E Rep. 200–22, 38.

[14] "Vermerk," 3 June 1953, BAK, B 106, 21407.

[15] "Vermerk" from State Secretary Hans Ritter von Lex, 22 June 1953, BAK, B 106, 21407.

issue definitively, and Wende decided that his cultural affairs division would administer the funding until the ministry resolved otherwise.[16] While financial support of the Central Council and the Jewish community resulted from the legacy of Nazi Germany, the government chose to administer its relationship with the Jews as it might maintain its ties with any other ethnic or cultural minority group.

As a part of the Central Council's own project for redefining its relationship with the government, it made a concrete appeal for subsidies. In August, Central Council business manager Norbert Schäfer submitted to the Interior Ministry a budget totaling 145,800 marks. After Jewish state associations contributed 22,800 marks to the Central Council, the group was left with an operating deficit of 123,000 marks, an amount that it asked the Interior Ministry to cover.[17] In October, Schäfer wrote to Gussone to request a one-time grant of 25,000 marks to establish a cultural department, to operate the organization's office, and to fund the legal division, which was flooded with inquiries about reparations. He added that the grant should be in addition to the 123,000 marks he had already requested.[18] The ministry approved the grant, and by the end of 1953, the Central Council had received the first 12,500 marks. Van Dam wrote in his report for the board, "The undersigned is of the opinion that the [Central Council's] central activities should be financed and can be financed without difficulties by the resources of the successor organizations and, above all, by the federal government."[19] Having established this link to the Interior Ministry, van Dam invited Gussone to a Central Council meeting, but the latter could not attend.[20] The Ministry for Refugees (*Vertriebene*) also wanted to establish a tie to the Jewish community and to this end invited the Central Welfare Office to appoint

[16] "Vermerk" from Carl Gussone, 27 July 1953; letter from Erich Wende to Theodor Bleek, 31 July 1953; BAK, B 106, 21407.

[17] "Erläuterungen," 1 August 1953, BAK, B 106, 21407. The largest single expense was staff salaries: 80,400 marks.

[18] Letter from Norbert Schäfer to Carl Gussone, 2 October 1953, BAK, B 106, 21407. The funding was to be distributed as follows: religion and culture department, 7,200 marks; legal division, 7,200 marks; economic and tax department, 4,200 marks; automotive costs, 5,100 marks; and miscellaneous, 1,300 marks.

[19] Letter from Interior Ministry to Central Council, 28 October, BAK, B 106, 21407; "Tätigkeitsbericht des Generalsekretärs," 10 December 1953, ZA, B.1/7, 120.

[20] Letter from Carl Gussone to Hendrik George van Dam, 5 October 1953, BAK, B 103, 36, 42; ZA, B.1/7, 101.

a representative to the ministry's civilian advisory board. Even though many of the Jews in postwar Germany came from Eastern Europe or from formerly German cities such as Breslau (Wrocław), few identified with the ethnic Germans who had flooded in from the east at the end of the war, and the ministry specified that the individual named as liaison need not have been deported himself.[21]

Despite this governmental recognition, the Central Council felt threatened by the continuing activity of the JRSO, the Claims Conference, and Israeli diplomats in Germany. These three had developed a strong working relationship with the West German government after the ratification of the Luxembourg Agreement, and the nascent Israeli-West German relationship became the focal point of German-Jewish reconciliation for many governmental authorities.[22] The prestige that these groups enjoyed in official West German circles compelled the leaders of the Central Council to assert their claim to be the exclusive representatives of the Jews in Germany. Neither the successor organizations nor the Claims Conference, they insisted, had the right to speak for the interests of Jews who chose to remain in the Federal Republic.[23]

THEODOR HEUSS AS PATRON, MARX AS MIDDLEMAN

It is worth noting that, for the most part, when the representatives of foreign Jewish groups – including the Israelis and the Claims Conference – sought contact with the West German government, they looked to Chancellor Konrad Adenauer. Adenauer was clearly interested in foreign relations and relations with foreign Jews. On the other hand, as the Jewish community within West Germany sought to stake its claim vis-à-vis foreign organizations, it looked to the West German president, Theodor Heuss.[24] Moreover,

---

[21] Letter from Central Welfare Office to Jüdische Gemeinde Köln and Landesverband Nordrhein, 17 November 1953, ZA, B.1/11, 218 (Zugang 93/01). While many of the German Jews were from the formerly German city of Breslau (now Wrocław), they identified more with the western German Jewish community than with the expellees.

[22] Letter from Foreign Office to ministries, 26 January 1953; memorandum, 27 June 1953; BAK, B 136, 1154, 13–15.

[23] Letters from Carl Katz and Hendrik George van Dam to *Ministerialrat* Dr. Fiegel (Interior Ministry), Abraham Frowein (Foreign Office), and Walter Roemer (Justice Ministry), 2–3 November 1953, ZA, B.1/7, 101.

[24] For more on the contrast between Adenauer and Heuss regarding this issue, see Geller, "Das Bild Konrad Adenauers vom Judentum und seine Beziehungen zu Vertretern jüdischer Organisationen nach 1945," in *Adenauer, Israel und das Judentum*, ed. Küsters.

with reparations settled by Adenauer and the Bundestag, Heuss once more became the focal point of the government's efforts for German-Jewish reconciliation.

Among the most important contributions made by Heuss to that effort after the signing of the Luxembourg Agreement was his dedication of a memorial at the former concentration camp Bergen-Belsen in November 1952. To most observers of West German politics and to all those engaged in the public discourse over memory of the Holocaust, it was clear that the episode would receive international attention. Even before the event took place, the West German Foreign Office stressed the need to make a favorable impression on world opinion by means of the ceremony.[25] The president did not disappoint the Foreign Office, which long after the event continued to distribute copies of his speech.[26]

In the presence of Jewish dignitaries, including Nahum Goldmann, Heuss spoke at Bergen-Belsen of the obligation to admit the crimes committed by Germans. He claimed that although he had known of Dachau, Buchenwald, and Oranienburg, the first concentration camps, he had not known about Bergen-Belsen and Auschwitz until the spring of 1945. However, he warned his fellow Germans, "This observation should not be a crutch for those who willingly claim, we knew nothing about any of that. We knew about such things." The Belsen monument was to serve as a reminder of the fate of Jews – both German and foreign.[27] The nations whose members had suffered in the camps could never forget what had happened, but Heuss commented that the Germans should never forget the acts their compatriots had committed. Thus, *they* needed a monument. The president also denounced those who wanted to dwell on the Soviets' postwar injustices against the Germans to distract from the Nazi past.[28] He then discussed the roots of the virulent Judeophobia responsible for the Holocaust, recognizing that religious or purely economic antisemitism was insufficient to induce mass murder. The perversion of science, particularly biology, enabled men to become thoughtless murderers. That such a development could occur in the land of Kant, Goethe, and Schiller

---

[25] Letter from Heinz Trützschler von Falkenstein to Luitpold Werz, 15 November 1952, BAK, B122, 2082 (28).

[26] Letter from Abraham Frowein to Luitpold Werz, 16 June 1953, BAK, B122, 2082 (28).

[27] Heuss, "Das Mahnmal," in *Die grossen Reden*, 225.

[28] Ibid., 226–227.

shamed Heuss and the Germans, and in his words, "no one, no one will take this shame away from us."[29]

Heuss's remarks drew a mixed response. While some, such as American senator Jacob Javits and German-American editor Manfred George, applauded the president, many non-Jewish Germans wrote to him to complain that they had known nothing of what had transpired in the camps. Heuss's personal assistant, Hans Bott, handled most of the correspondence, and over time he grew ever more annoyed with such letters. It was clear that most German critics of the president had not read the speech but had relied instead on hearsay. In his responses, Bott reminded letter writers that Heuss had actually said that he, too, had not heard of Belsen or Auschwitz until after the war. However, he added, in one case, "if you knew nothing of the events of that time then you must have led a life of withdrawn idleness."[30]

Despite Heuss's long history of philosemitism and general sagacity, he did not act in Jewish affairs without guidance. On such a thorny issue, he received particular help from the Jewish journalist Karl Marx (see Fig. 8). Between 1949 and 1953, Marx acquired considerable influence in the president's office. On 25 February, he asked presidential aide Luitpold Werz whether Heuss could arrange for Leo Baeck to receive an honorary doctorate on the occasion of his eightieth birthday. Heuss responded by inquiring at several German universities whether it might be possible, and ultimately he came to such an arrangement with the Free University of Berlin.[31] Additionally, the president wrote a contribution for Marx's *Allgemeine Wochenzeitung,* expressing his admiration for Baeck.[32] On occasion, Marx would forward to Heuss letters of particular interest on German-Jewish affairs.[33] Marx also defended the president before his Jewish critics. In November 1953,

---

[29] Ibid., 228.

[30] Correspondence, especially letter from Hans Bott to Adolf Linke, 1952–1953, BAK, B 122, 2083 (29).

[31] Letter from Karl Marx to Luitpold Werz, 25 February 1953; letter from Theodor Heuss to Helmut Gollwitzer, 27 February 1953; letter from Theodor Heuss to Georg Rohde, 18 April 1953; letter from Georg Rohde to Theodor Heuss, 7 May 1953; BAK, B 122, 2083 (29).

[32] "Für Leo Baeck," *Allgemeine Wochenzeitung,* 22 May 1953. For Manfred George's birthday, he did the same. "Bundespräsident Heuss an Manfred George," *Allgemeine Wochenzeitung,* 23 October 1953.

[33] Letter from German-Jewish émigré Alfred Cohn, forwarded on 23 April 1953, BAK, B 122, 2080 (26).

Figure 8. (*Left to right*) West Berlin mayor Ernst Reuter, Karl Marx, Theodor Heuss, and West Berlin Jewish Community chairman Heinz Galinski at a reception in Berlin-Schöneberg city hall, 14 April 1953. *Source*: ullstein bild dpa.

Norman Salit, president of the Synagogue Council of America, visited West Germany on a tour sponsored by the Bonn government. On his return home, the American Jewish leader accused Theodor Heuss of indifference or latent antisemitism. He claimed that Heuss had told him that keeping former SS men in the federal cabinet, namely Waldemar Kraft and Theodor Oberländer, would keep them too busy to organize antisemitic campaigns. Karl Marx rushed to Heuss's defense, and the presidential aide who received Salit's press release read it and labeled it "false!"[34]

On occasions when the president's high profile in Jewish questions brought him unwanted attention, he turned to Marx for advice. On 16 April 1951, Munich editor Heinz Ganther met with Heuss to gain his support for a planned almanac, *Die Juden in*

---

[34] Letter from Karl Marx to Theodor Heuss, 26 November 1953, BAK, B 122, 2084 (29). Although Oberländer had been an active Nazi and probably participated in wartime massacres, he had not actually been a member of the SS. Philipp-Christian Wachs, *Der Fall Theodor Oberländer (1905–1998). Ein Lehrstück deutscher Geschichte* (Frankfurt: Campus, 2000), 184–190.

Deutschland. Armed with a letter of support from the president, Ganther began soliciting contributions. Karl Marx and the Central Council, not having authorized such a project, opposed Ganther and warned potential contributors against him. Furious, Ganther sued Marx and the Central Council, losing his case on 22 December 1952. Nonetheless, he continued with his project, and when his book did appear nearly a year later, it caused an uproar. Not all the advertisements paid for by sponsors appeared in the final edition, leading to criminal proceedings initiated by the public prosecutor in Düsseldorf. Completely unfazed, Ganther sent Heuss a copy of the almanac and asked for his reflections on it. Presidential aide Luitpold Werz turned to the Central Council and Marx for advice. The Central Council regretted that the almanac had appeared, and Marx called Ganther "a swindler." After soliciting these opinions, Werz decided that Heuss should not respond to Ganther, lest his reply be misused as his initial letter of support had been.[35]

Heuss, who often received requests from Jewish organizations for funding, even found himself in the middle of a reparations dispute.[36] In the spring of 1953, the Maccabi World Union, the international Jewish sports organization, wanted restitution for property taken from Jewish sports clubs in Germany under the Nazis. Without first consulting the Israeli mission in Cologne, the Jewish group demanded 100,000 dollars in reparations from the Deutscher Sportbund, which appealed to Heuss to intervene in June 1953. Heuss looked to Marx for advice on the matter, and Marx tried to carry on negotiations but managed to lose the confidence of both sides. The matter dragged on for four years before the German sporting organization paid the Maccabi Union 10,000 dollars.[37]

DOMESTIC REPARATIONS

Just as the agreement for reparations to Israel allowed for a shift in the focal point of German-Jewish dialogue from Adenauer to

---

[35] Judgment by Landesgericht Düsseldorf, 22 December 1952; "Aktenvermerk," 2 September 1953, et al.; BAK, B 122, 2086 (29).

[36] On requests for funding, see correspondence between Foreign Office and Federal President's Office regarding Jewish National Fund, summer 1953, BAK, B 122, 2084 (29), and correspondence between Federal President's Office and Verband für Freiheit und Menschenwürde, spring 1953, BAK, B 122, 2080 (26).

[37] Correspondence, 1953–1957, BAK, B 122, 2085 (29).

Heuss, the agreement's conclusion also permitted the leaders of the Jewish community in Germany to concentrate on the passage of a law providing reparations to individual victims of Nazi persecution still living in Germany. Van Dam and Marx regularly wrote articles in the *Allgemeine Wochenzeitung* on the issue.[38] Although the SPD had proposed a law for the indemnification for victims of the Nazis as early as June 1952, only after the signing of the Luxembourg Agreement did the federal Finance Ministry begin work on its own proposal for domestic payments.[39] By the spring of 1953, Finance Minister Schäffer was nearly ready to have the cabinet's bill undergo review by the Bundestag and the Bundesrat, the house of West Germany's federal parliament representing the states. However, his version was not the only one in circulation. As early as April 1952 the Bundesrat had begun work on its own proposal, largely authored by Otto Küster, and the SPD's separate proposal was still languishing in committee. Jealous of his prerogatives, Schäffer informed Wilhelm Laforet, a CDU member and chairman of the Bundestag committee handling the bill, that as responsible minister he would have to approve any bills dealing with reparations.[40] When the proposal for the so-called Federal Compensation Law (*Bundesentschädigungsgesetz*) reached Laforet's Committee for Legal Affairs and Constitutional Law in March 1953, the SPD was quick to attack the long delay in bringing the issue forward. Social Democratic deputy Otto Heinrich Greve accused the government of expressing more concern for former Nazis dismissed from the civil service than for victims of fascism. Hermann Kopf of the CDU defended the delay, arguing that the recently ratified Luxembourg Agreement had specified a number of conditions for a domestic reparations law. Regardless of the SPD's criticism of the government's bill, most Bundestag deputies favored some form of domestic reparations and thus supported the

---

[38] For example, "Wann kommt das Bundesentschädigungsgesetz?," *Allgemeine Wochenzeitung*, 13 February 1953; "Die innere Wiedergutmachung an den NS-Opfern," *Allgemeine Wochenzeitung*, 20 February 1953.

[39] "Drucksache Nr. 3472, Antrag der Fraktion der SPD," 18 June 1952, Germany (West), Bundestag, *Verhandlungen des Deutschen Bundestages, I. Wahlperiode 1949, Anlagen zu den stenographischen Berichte*, vol. 18: *Drucksachen Nr. 3401 bis 3499* (Bonn: Bonner Universitäts-Buchdruckerei, 1952); "Entwurf des Entschädigungsgesetzes vom Bundesfinanzminister fertiggestellt," *Allgemeine Wochenzeitung*, 20 February 1953.

[40] Letter from Fritz Schäffer to Wilhelm Laforet, 19/24 March 1953, ACDP, I-122, 096/3.

Federal Compensation Law, which was considerably weaker than the bills put forward by either the SPD or the Bundesrat.[41]

Within Jewish circles, disagreement arose over how to greet the government's proposal. Even before the Bundestag had passed the bill, van Dam was working to improve it. In an article published in the *Allgemeine Wochenzeitung*, he argued that the new law would provide for compensation ("Entschädigung") for incarceration, loss of career, and bodily harm but not restitution ("Rückerstattung") for lost property, and he began lobbying for a change to correct that omission. Additionally, he feared that through an overly strict interpretation of the law, many Jews who had suffered under the Nazis would be excluded from receiving reparations payments.[42] Meanwhile, Nahum Goldmann worried that various parties were hindering the bill's speedy passage by burdening it with amendments. He asked SPD Chairman Erich Ollenhauer to forgo any amendments and to accept the government's proposal, even though the SPD had proposed its own bill almost a year earlier and was loath to concede precedence to the government.[43] Goldmann also petitioned the federal chancellery to expedite action on its proposal.[44]

The federal cabinet approved Schäffer's bill on 29 May and sent it to the Bundesrat, but after the long delay, many observers feared that the Bundestag would not approve it before the upcoming federal elections in September 1953.[45] Within the governing coalition, Adenauer was under pressure from some to pass the law quickly and from others to delay its passage.[46] Complicating the matter were the competing proposals, including those from the Bundesrat and the SPD. On 18 June, the SPD, desiring passage

[41] "Protokoll der 249. Sitzung des Ausschusses für Rechtswesen und Verfassungsrecht," 27 March 1953, Parlamentsarchiv, I:537, A:2, 21; Pross, *Paying for the Past*, 36–38. In an ancillary letter accompanying the Luxembourg Agreement, Chancellor Adenauer pledged to enact domestic reparations. Although the letter did specify minimum requirements for the reparations, West Germany could have initiated them earlier, as suggested by Otto Küster in the Bundesrat.

[42] Letter from Central Council to state associations, 20 April 1953, ZA, B.1/15, 522; "Wiedergutmachung und Begriffs-Jurisprudenz," *Allgemeine Wochenzeitung*, 22 May 1953.

[43] Goldmann, *Autobiography*, 275–276.

[44] Telegram from Nahum Goldmann to Konrad Adenauer, 21 May 1953, BAK, B 136, 1154, 122.

[45] "295. Kabinettssitzung," 29 May 1953, *Die Kabinettsprotokolle*, 6:316; "Protest gegen Verschleppung des Bundesentschädigungsgesetz," *Allgemeine Wochenzeitung*, 29 May 1953.

[46] Letter from Eugen Gerstenmaier to Konrad Adenauer, 29 May 1953, BAK, B 136, 1154, 27; "Die Deutschen und die anderen!," *Allgemeine Wochenzeitung*, 5 June 1953; Pross, *Paying for the Past*, 38.

of a law before federal elections in late summer, agreed to accept the federal cabinet's submission, clearing the way for a speedy resolution of the matter despite its deep misgivings about the bill.[47] With overwhelming support, the Bundestag approved the Federal Compensation Law on 2 July 1953.[48]

Taking effect on 1 October 1953, the new law complemented the Luxembourg Agreement and addressed many concerns of the government's critics, who had considered reparations to Israel either inappropriate or insufficient in view of the lack of a domestic reparations program. Before its later modification, the law provided for over four billion marks in payments, in addition to the 500 million marks already paid by the state governments. Largely patterned on the reparations legislation issued in 1949 by the American occupation authority for its zone, the new law standardized disparate state laws for reparations, many of which had been deficient, particularly in the British occupation zone. Unlike the West Germans' reparations to the Claims Conference, which were transferred to Jewish organizations, the Federal Compensation Law addressed the needs of individuals, not groups, and the Central Council did not profit from its passage. Those who had lost their careers or educational opportunities as a result of Nazi legislation could receive either a lump sum payment or a pension. Émigrés would receive partial compensation for the Reich Flight Tax that the Nazis had made them pay in order to leave Germany. The law also allowed for claims based on damage done during the Jewish boycott of 1 April 1933. Moreover, resistance fighters against the National Socialist regime were now eligible for reparations.[49]

While Jewish groups applauded the passage of a reparations statute, they found much to fault in the Federal Compensation Law with its idiosyncrasies and desiderata. Stuttgart Jewish leader Benno Ostertag complained that the requirements to qualify for

[47] Letter from Wilhelm Laforet to Heinrich von Brentano, 19 June 1953, ACDP, I-122, 096/3.

[48] "279. Sitzung," 2 July 1953, Germany (West), Bundestag, *Verhandlungen des Deutschen Bundestages, I. Wahlperiode 1949*, vol. 17: *Stenographische Berichte von der 274. Sitzung am 19. Juni 1953 bis zur 282. Sitzung am 29. Juli 1953* (Bonn: Bonner Universitäts-Buchdruckerei, 1953), 14013. The Communist Party caucus and the Bavarian Party caucus did not support the law, nor did most German Party deputies.

[49] Goschler, *Wiedergutmachung. Westdeutschland*, 298–300; "Ohne Aussprache verabschiedet," *Allgemeine Wochenzeitung*, 10 July 1953; "Ein Minimum an Entschädigung," *Allgemeine Wochenzeitung*, 31 July 1953; "Bonn Votes Payment to Victims of Nazis," *New York Times*, 3 July 1953.

compensation for the loss of a spouse were overly stringent and mean-spirited. Only impoverished widowers would qualify, and widows had to have employment, if physically able. While those who had survived the Nazi era living underground after 31 December 1937 qualified, Germans who had illegally emigrated before then did not. Ostertag also protested the limits on payments for lost pensions as unfair.[50] Later critics noted that the new law strictly limited qualification for claims on compensation for inability to work by requiring a high level of damage to health for eligibility. Furthermore, claimants had to prove they had been personally targeted by "officially approved measures," a provision that disqualified many victims of indirect persecution, including the elderly, who had lost their provisions for old age when Jewish-owned pension funds were closed, or workers, who had failed to register their unemployed status after their dismissal by pro-Nazi employers.[51] Van Dam expected that additional legislation would have to complement the law. In his opinion, it simply had "extraordinary weakness and loopholes."[52] He felt a particular sense of urgency about establishing an acceptable program for reparations under West German governmental administration. In the spring of 1954, American State Department officials told van Dam that they were transferring as much responsibility and power to the Germans as they could, and he feared that under these conditions, the West Germans would neglect reparations and Jewish questions.[53]

Although the SPD had wholeheartedly supported individual reparations, many of that party's leaders attacked the new law as inadequate. In November 1953, the SPD organized a conference to deal with ways to improve it.[54] After the law went into effect, the party proposed that a special office responsible directly to the

---

50 "Kritische Bemerkungen zum Bundesentschädigungsgesetz," *Allgemeine Wochenzeitung*, 30 October 1953.
51 Pross, *Paying for the Past*, 39–40. The new law required a 30 percent loss in earning capacity as a result of damage to one's health for eligibility.
52 "Beschlussprotokoll der Direktoriumssitzung," 28 June 1953, ZA, B.1/7, 221.38; "Ein Minimum an Entschädigung," *Allgemeine Wochenzeitung*, 31 July 1953; "Summarischer Tätigkeitsbericht des Generalsekretärs für die Zeit vom 15. Okt. 53 bis 1. Juli 54," undated, ZA, B.1/7, 246.
53 Goschler, *Wiedergutmachung. Westdeutschland*, 305.
54 "Vorarbeiten zur Besserung des BEG," *Allgemeine Wochenzeitung*, 20 November 1953. For more on Social Democratic commentary on the law, see Pross, *Paying for the Past*, 39.

chancellor administer reparations payments.[55] Many of the gaps in the Federal Compensation Law were addressed by modifications and additional domestic reparations legislation in the years to come, and for the next forty years many former victims of Nazi persecution benefited from pension payments stipulated by the law and its later amendments.[56]

THE EXODUS OF EAST GERMAN JEWRY

Reparations were not the only challenge facing the impoverished Jewish community and its overburdened leadership. Just as domestic reparations and federal subsidies dominated the agenda in the west, antisemitic purges in East Germany induced a significant westward migration. In December 1952, in the wake of the show trial of Jewish communist Rudolf Slánský in Czechoslovakia, the East German Communist Party began a purge of Jews and philosemites in its own ranks. Many Jewish leaders in East Germany, including community chairman Julius Meyer, were Communist Party members, but they were nevertheless detained for interrogation by the secret police in early January 1953. As soon as they were released from custody, most of them fled to West Berlin. At that time, the Jewish communities of East Berlin and West Berlin shared a common administration under Heinz Galinski, and as events began to unfold in December 1952, Galinski counseled the joint congregation to remain politically neutral.[57] However, Rabbi Nathan Peter Levinson defied Galinski. On 14 January 1953, in a

---

55 "9.11.1954: Fraktionssitzung," 9 November 1954, Germany (West), Bundestag, Fraktion der SPD, *Die SPD-Fraktion im Deutschen Bundestag: Sitzungsprotokolle 1949–1957*, half-vol. 2: *182–328. Sitzung 1953–1957*, ed. Petra Weber, Quellen zur Geschichte des Parlamentarismus und der politischen Parteien, fourth series: Deutschland seit 1945, ed. Karl-Dietrich Bracher, Rudolf Morsey, and Hans-Peter Schwarz, no. 8/I (Düsseldorf: Droste, 1993), 128.

56 Bark and Gress, *A History of West Germany*, 1:314. The law's shortcomings led to a major revision in 1956, which rendered more victims eligible for compensation. In accordance with the new law, by 1957 the West German federal and state governments were disbursing over 2 billion marks per year and continued to annual make payments between 1.5 and 2.5 billion marks well into the 1980s. The total paid in compensation will be well in excess of 100 billion marks. Saul Kagan, "A Participant's Response," in *Holocaust and Shilumim: The Policy of Wiedergutmachung in the Early 1950s*, ed. Axel Frohn, German Historical Institute Occasional Paper No. 2 (Washington, D.C.: German Historical Institute, 1991), 59.

57 "Protokoll der Repräsentanten-Versammlung vom 10. Dezember 1952," 10 December 1952, LAB, B Rep. 2, 6845.

press conference broadcast by radio, he advised the Jews of East Germany to flee. Galinski fired Levinson immediately, but it was too late. His public comments had convinced several hundred Jews to flee to West Berlin.[58] Dealing with an influx of immigrants strained the community's resources and revealed the tensions between the central organization and local groups.

In late January 1953, as East German Jews streamed into West Berlin, Galinski realized, "We remained quiet, and perhaps history will one day proclaim us guilty because nothing was undertaken [to prevent the situation]." Community board members fiercely debated whether they should remain neutral or issue a statement denouncing their Communist coreligionists, whom they partially blamed for the crisis. Above all, they agreed, it was their duty to aid the refugees.[59] On 27 January 1953, the Central Council met to discuss the state of affairs in East Germany. Galinski blamed Julius Meyer for the severity of the situation but acknowledged that Central Council leaders had always paid too little attention to their cousins behind the Iron Curtain. Now that the situation was dire, "We can only give one piece of advice: come to us." Even though Galinski now endorsed the migration of Jews from eastern Germany to western Germany, he continued to blame Berlin rabbi Levinson for exacerbating the predicament:

Rabbi Levinson should have kept quiet on all these matters. Through his speech he put us in a terrible situation. It makes a very bad impression when a rabbi speaks and the community stays quiet.[60]

Galinski knew that West Berlin could not accommodate all the refugees, even with emergency aid from the American Joint Distribution Committee, and he wanted West German Jewry to help with housing them. Berthold Simonsohn, chairman of the Central Welfare Office, wanted those communities to devise a plan to deal with the crisis and to approach the federal government for help. He asked representatives of each local group how many people their community could accommodate.[61] Dealing with the Berlin crisis

---

[58] Nathan Peter Levinson, "The Functions of a Rabbi in Postwar Germany," interview by Michael Brenner, *After the Holocaust*, ed. Brenner, 110; Burgbauer, *Zwischen Erinnerung und Verdrängung*, 181.

[59] "Protokoll der Repräsentanten-Versammlung vom (ausserordentliche) 21. Januar 1953," 21 January 1953, LAB, B Rep. 2, 6845.

[60] "Protokoll über die Sitzung des Zentralrates," 27 January 1953, ZA, B.1/7, 221.32.

[61] Ibid.

occupied most of the Central Council's attention, and it resolved to aid each Jewish refugee. Still, the politically savvy board members resented the difficult position in which they found themselves, and they denounced "unauthorized declarations in connection with the events in East Germany," a veiled reference to Levinson's address, which, they believed, had unnecessarily worsened the crisis.[62]

Reacting to the emergency, the West Berlin Jewish community turned its main assembly hall into a refugee center, and the influx of refugees became a burden on the Central Welfare Office. The Central Council began funding the welfare agency, and West German communities were asked to report the amount of money they could contribute and the number of refugees they could accommodate.[63] On 5 February, Galinski reported that 400 refugees were already in West Berlin, and he expected another 400. Elderly refugees would remain in Berlin, while younger ones would be absorbed by the West German states.[64] In the divided former capital, there existed an established program to aid refugees from the east, but it was unclear how the Jewish communities in western Germany would fund support for refugees. Soon, the topic of refugees dominated the agendas of communal boards throughout West Germany, and the issue strained their relations with the Central Council.[65] The Central Welfare Office struggled to convince them to accept refugees, but many resisted. Jewish welfare officials therefore issued an appeal: "We ask all communities to accept seriously this fortunately not very large number of Jewish refugees and to treat them as we wanted to be treated by others during the years 1933–1945."[66] On 18 February, the various Jewish communities did agree to accept a fixed number of refugees, though it was still far fewer than needed accommodation.[67]

---

[62] "Protokoll der Repräsentanten-Versammlung vom 29. Januar 1953," 29 January 1953, LAB, B Rep. 2, 6845.

[63] Ibid.; "Rundschreiben Nr. 12," 30 January 1953, ZA, B.1/11, 15 (Zugang 96/10).

[64] "Vorstandssitzung der Jüdischen Gemeinde Frankfurt am Main vom 5.2.1953," 5 February 1953, ZA, B.1/13, A.10, 73.

[65] "Vorstandssitzung der Jüdischen Gemeinde Frankfurt am Main vom 10.3.1953," 10 March 1953, ZA, B.1/13, A.10, 68.

[66] "Rundschreiben Nr. 15," 27 February 1953, ZA, B.1/11, 15 (Zugang 96/10).

[67] "Rundschreiben Nr. 13," 18 February 1953, ZA, B.1/11, 218 (Zugang 93/01). The distribution was as follows: North Rhine-Westphalia, 80; Bremen, 10; Bavaria, 30; Rhineland-Palatinate, 10; Hamburg, 25; Hesse, 30; and Württemberg-Baden, 15.

At the height of the exodus, Nahum Goldmann went to Berlin to offer his support to the beleaguered and divided community. He recognized that the East German purges were part of a larger wave of antisemitism sweeping across Eastern Europe, and in March he held an emergency meeting of the Jewish Agency to discuss the situation and to coordinate the international Jewish response.[68] Meanwhile, the number of refugees entering West Berlin had increased again. On 8 March, Galinski reported to the Central Council that 520 had fled since 15 January, and approximately twenty-five more were arriving in the west every day. The Central Council, uncertain as to who should support the new refugees and where to house them, could scarcely manage the situation. The Berlin Jewish community gave them pocket money on arrival, but the situation was untenable.[69] Every refugee arriving in the Federal Republic was required to register with the state employment office, and the Central Welfare Office hoped that they would receive unemployment benefits.[70] On 25 March, each state association of Jewish communities agreed to increase its quota of refugees by 50 percent over the number accepted on 18 February.[71] By April, the communities in West Germany began to protest against the burgeoning number of refugees they were forced to accommodate. Even though 350 refugees still needed homes in western Germany, Stuttgart refused to take any; North Rhine-Westphalia asserted it was full; and Cologne claimed it was too preoccupied with the Israeli trade mission to accept refugees from the east. Galinski, however, ascribed their recalcitrance to jealousy of the West Berlin Jewish community's prestige and success in handling the situation.[72]

The communities also faced a complication resulting from a common pattern of German Jewish life. Many of the families fleeing East Germany had only one Jewish spouse. However, the Central Welfare Office advised against housing families with non-Jewish

---

[68] "Protokoll der Repräsentanten-Versammlung vom 29. Januar 1953," 29 January 1953, LAB, B Rep. 2, 6845; letter from Hendrik George van Dam to all Central Council board members, 17 February 1953, ZA, B.1/7, 120.

[69] "Beschlussprotokoll der erweiterten Direktoriumssitzung," 8 March 1953, ZA, B.1/7, 221.35.

[70] "Rundschreiben Nr. 16," 10 March 1953, ZA, B.1/11, 218 (Zugang 93/01).

[71] "Rundschreiben Nr. 19," 25 March 1953, ZA, B.1/13, 2121.

[72] "Protokoll der Repräsentanten-Versammlung vom 29. April 1953," 29 April 1953, LAB, B Rep. 2, 6845.

children in communal buildings, and the Frankfurt group did not want to accept any non-Jews into its housing.[73] The American Joint Distribution Committee regulated stipends for Jewish refugees in West Germany and decreed that in marriages in which the husband was not Jewish, the Central Welfare Office would support only the Jewish spouse. Additionally, refugees with regular employment would cease receiving aid payments before they began receiving a salary.[74] At last, in late 1953, the West German federal government began to help with administering aid for the refugee crisis. All refugees from East Germany were to receive "Identification Card C," and with the proper identification card, refugees could apply for reparations in accordance with the Federal Compensation Law.[75]

After the initial crisis, Jewish life began to return to normal in East Germany. New leaders replaced communal chairmen who had fled to the west, and the Jews in East Berlin established their own separate organization, known as the Jewish Community of Greater Berlin. By October, the East Germans were included in the Central Council once again.[76]

RELATIONS WITH FOREIGN JEWRY AND THE REPARATIONS SETTLEMENT

The crisis in East Germany had strained the unity of the Jewish community in West Germany, but it drew the Germans closer to the wider, international Jewish community. That respite from the prevailing tensions was brief, however. Soon, events would draw the Jews in Germany together against groups abroad. In fact, throughout much of 1953, the Central Council fought with the Claims Conference for a greater share of the reparations settlement regulated

---

73 "Rundschreiben Nr. 19," 25 March 1953, ZA, B.1/13, 2121; "Protokoll der Sitzung des erweiterten Direktoriums des Zentralrates der Juden in Deutschland," 3 May 1953, ZA, B.1/7, 221.37.

74 "Ostflüchtlinge, Joint-Regelung für die Monate April, Mai, Juni 1953," undated, ZA, B.1/13, 1; "Rundschreiben Nr. 24," 22 June 1953, ZA, B.1/13, 2121. The AJDC resolved that a single person should receive 25 marks' pocket money per month, a couple 40 marks, and a family with one child 50 marks. Housing allowances were 60 marks, 120 marks, and 180 marks, respectively.

75 "Rundschreiben Nr. 38," 26 October 1953, ZA, B.1/15, 283; "Rundschreiben Nr. 43," 4 December 1953, ZA, B.1/13, 2121. Ethnic Germans deported from former German territories in East-Central Europe received "Identification Card A."

76 "Protokoll der Zentralratstagung in Bremen," 12 October 1953, ZA, B.1/7, 221.40.

by the Luxembourg Agreement. Initially, Central Council board members had expected their group would receive between 15 and 20 percent of the payment to the Claims Conference. They soon lowered their expectations.[77] Meeting in May 1953 to discuss the matter, they decided to request an annual grant on behalf of the Central Welfare Office, which would distribute aid to the communities and state associations. While many of the board members wanted the Central Council to adopt a more confrontational stance vis-à-vis the Claims Conference, most preferred quiet negotiations conducted by Heinz Galinski. Ultimately, they requested that a representative of the Claims Conference come to Europe to negotiate with them and agreed to submit the issue to arbitration.[78] Galinski's negotiations seemed to bear fruit, for on 12 May, Claims Conference treasurer and negotiator Moses Leavitt accepted most of the Central Council's demands.[79] By late June, the Central Council was drafting a budget to submit to the Claims Conference on behalf of the Central Welfare Office. Van Dam, stressing that the budget would be closely scrutinized, insisted that it be accurate; still, he felt that should include proposals for anticipated cultural activities in addition to contemporary social projects. Berthold Simonsohn, director of the Central Welfare Office, thought that funding future projects from the reparations settlement was wrong, as those funds were intended for victims of the Nazis. Van Dam acknowledged Simonsohn's point but argued that if the Claims Conference was going to fund cultural and religious projects in America and Israel, it should fund similar activities in Germany as well.[80]

Meanwhile, the focus of Central Council efforts for a share of German reparations payments to Jews shifted to the Jewish Restitution Successor Organization. In June, Central Council board members decided that they also needed to approach the JRSO about a share of the yield from the liquidation of property formerly owned by Jewish Holocaust victims. They were angry that many Jewish

77 Report to the Jüdische Gemeinde Frankfurt on the Central Council, 3 April 1952, ZA, B.1/13, A.9, 24.
78 "Beschlussprotokoll der erweiterten Direktoriumssitzung des Zentralrates der Juden in Deutschland" and "Protokoll der Sitzung des erweiterten Direktoriums des Zentralrates der Juden in Deutschland," 3 May 1953, ZA, B.1/7, 221.36 and 221.37.
79 Letter from Heinz Galinski to Hendrik George van Dam, 13 May 1953, ZA, B.1/7, 120.
80 "Beschlussprotokoll der Direktoriumssitzung," 28 June 1953, ZA, B.1/7, 221.38.

communities in the American zone had made separate agreements with the JRSO, rather than negotiating as a group through the Central Council, which would have taken a share of any settlement. The national organization needed JRSO funds, in addition to federal subsidies, to survive.[81] At the same time, the Central Council had an uneasy relationship with the World Jewish Congress, despite its amiable ties to Nahum Goldmann. In July 1953, Abraham Frowein of the Foreign Office noted in a report that the Central Council had "still not formally joined the WJC despite numerous invitations. The Central Council apparently wants to maintain its independent position." He added, "The World Jewish Congress is decidedly Zionist." Although the Central Council had not joined the WJC, the various state and zonal Jewish organizations had already sent delegates to the international body.[82] Despite the misgivings of many WJC leaders regarding Jewish settlement in Germany, WJC president Nahum Goldmann strove to maintain ties to the Central Council.[83] Meanwhile, van Dam worked to cast doubt on the political orientation of the WJC, presumably to deflect attention and prestige away from it and toward the Central Council. He told Frowein that the WJC accepted the Oder-Neisse line as the final German-Polish border and added that even the famous German-born rabbi Leo Baeck had great reservations about the organization.[84]

Despite Frowein's analysis of the split between the Central Council and the WJC, most of the Jews in the Federal Republic supported the Israeli state and wanted closer ties to world Jewry, even if they wished to remain in Germany. The *Allgemeine Wochenzeitung* ran a full-page obituary on page one for Chaim Weizmann, the deceased president of Israel.[85] At a meeting of the Central Council board in October, Harry Goldstein of Hamburg spoke passionately of the German Jews' need to win foreign acceptance, and Maurice Weinberger of Munich proclaimed that it was their duty to help with the construction of Israel, just as it was the duty of foreign Jewish organizations to give the Jews in Germany a chance. He

[81] Ibid.
[82] "Aufzeichnung," 24 July 1953, PA-AA, B 10, 310 (Fiche A 2033), 7.
[83] Shafir, *Ambiguous Relations*, 114–115.
[84] "Aufzeichnung," 24 July 1953, PA-AA, B 10, 310 (Fiche A 2033), 7–8.
[85] "Tiefe Trauer um Chaim Weizmann," *Allgemeine Wochenzeitung*, 14 November 1952.

wanted them to work with the JRSO and the Claims Conference to find solutions to their problems.[86]

Most local community leaders soon came to regret their earlier settlements with the JRSO. By late 1953, many of the communities were going bankrupt, and they had concluded agreements with the successor organization at a time when they were uncertain as to how long Jews would remain in Germany. Central Council leader Carl Katz wanted to ensure that they renegotiated their agreements through the auspices of the Central Council, but Central Welfare Office director Simonsohn felt that they were at a distinct disadvantage in the negotiations because they did not have access to the same property records used by the JRSO.[87] Contrary to the wishes of Central Council leaders, the Frankfurt Jewish community conducted its own negotiations with the successor organization.[88] The Central Council protested any attempt to usurp its influence or to play one Jewish group in Germany against another, and it demanded that any agreement have the approval of the Central Welfare Office. Meanwhile, the Jewish groups in the French occupation zone had begun negotiating with the Jewish Trust Corporation-Branche Française, and the Central Council wanted van Dam to ensure that at least one-quarter of any settlement with the Branche Française went to the Central Welfare Office.[89]

The disagreement between the Central Council and foreign organizations receiving communal reparations and restitution payments continued, and the two sides reached an agreement only toward the end of 1954. By the middle of that year, with the conflict lingering, van Dam was growing despondent. In an internal report, he noted that Leo Baeck's Council of Jews from Germany was having no success in its own negotiations with these groups, asking what hope the little-regarded Jewish community in Germany could have if such an august body could not successfully prosecute its claims. Even though "the legal and political situation of the Jewish

---

[86] "Protokoll der Tagung des Zentralrates der Juden in Deutschland," 12 October 1953, ZA, B.1/7, 221.39.

[87] "Protokoll der erweiterten Sitzung des Direktoriums des Zentralrates der Juden in Deutschland," 2 November 1953, ZA, B.1/7, 221.42.

[88] "Tätigkeitsbericht des Generalsekretärs," 18 November 1953, ZA, B.1/7, 246.

[89] "Entwurf Beschlüsse des Direktoriums auf der Sitzung vom 13. Dezember 1953," 13 December 1953, ZA, B.1/7, 221.44.

community in Germany [had] certainly stabilized and improved," van Dam noted, Jewish groups in Germany found themselves in "a destructive struggle of Jewish organizations against each other."[90]

In 1954, the Jewish Restitution Successor Organization began distributing some restituted communal assets to Jewish groups in West Germany, but it did not cease to represent the viewpoint that the communities had no legal right to the assets, and only a very small proportion was given to the Jews living in Germany. The Council of Jews from Germany did come to an agreement with the JRSO whereby the émigré group would receive approximately 10 percent of all funds collected by the JRSO.[91] The Jews in Germany also received funding from the Claims Conference and AJDC, with the Central Welfare Office being the principal recipient. In 1954, the Claims Conference distributed 1,463,000 dollars of aid in West Germany. As West German reparations payments to former victims of the Nazis began to accrue, the Claims Conference decreased its aid, which was merely 117,000 dollars in 1964. From 1954 to 1964, the Jewish community in Germany received a total of 6,660,386 dollars from the Claims Conference, and support from that organization and the AJDC comprised 90 percent of the Central Welfare Office's budget in the late 1950s.[92] As the Claims Conference resisted agreeing to contractually fixed amounts of funding for member organizations, there was a considerable amount of annual negotiating involved in securing increased amounts of support.[93]

DISUNITY AND REORIENTATION OF THE CENTRAL COUNCIL

Just as the Central Council had begun to achieve its political goals of reparations to Israel and individual Jews in Germany, it suffered

[90] "Summarischer Tätigkeitsbericht des Generalsekretärs für die Zeit vom 15. Okt. 53 bis 1. Juli 54," undated, ZA, B.1/7, 246.

[91] Zweig, *German Reparations and the Jewish World,* 115–116. The Council of Jews from Germany also received funding from British Jewish groups, who themselves were a party to the Jewish Trust Corporation and Claims Conference settlements.

[92] Conference on Material Claims against Germany, *Twenty Years Later: Activities of the Conference on Material Claims against Germany, 1952–1972* (New York: Conference on Material Claims against Germany, n.d.), 81; Zweig, *German Reparations and the Jewish World,* 122–123. The Central Welfare Office received 511,671 dollars in 1957 and 411,488 dollars in 1958.

[93] Zweig, *German Reparations and the Jewish World,* 113.

a series of internal crises that threatened the group's unity. Its leadership, focusing on external political relations, had often neglected relations with other Jewish organizations in Germany, including the state associations. Moreover, the group was not truly representative of the Jewish community in Germany. Although German Jews dominated the Central Council, at least half of the Jews in Germany, and a vast majority in Bavaria, were recent immigrants from Eastern Europe. They were greatly underrepresented on the Central Council board, and in the summer of 1952 the Bavarian state association withdrew from the organization. For years, Philipp Auerbach and Rabbi Aaron Ohrenstein had dominated Jewish communal life in Bavaria, but in the wake of the Auerbach controversy, the Central Council refused to seat the Bavarian state association's newly elected delegate, an associate of Auerbach. While van Dam sent envoys to Munich in June 1952 to negotiate a compromise, the agreement did not last, and van Dam grew sensitive to increasing criticism that the Central Council was undemocratic. The Central Council represented not individual Jews in Germany, but rather the Jewish state associations. They were the Central Council's real constituency.[94] By autumn, the dispute threatened to split the organization. Heinz Galinski of Berlin remained one of the most steadfast opponents of the Bavarians, but the Frankfurt Jewish community wanted to recognize the Bavarians' decision, even if most of the Jews in Bavaria were from Eastern Europe. The communities in north Germany, including Berlin, dominated by German Jews, did not want to accept the Bavarians' choice. Galinski justified his position as protecting the Central Council from further embarrassment after the Auerbach affair, and the north German Jewish communities threatened to quit if the Bavarians prevailed.[95] By February 1953, the Frankfurt group gave up its opposition, and van Dam informed the Bavarians that they could have a seat on the Central Council board provided they chose another delegate, acceptable to the other board

---

94 Letter from Goldschmidt to Hendrik George van Dam, 16 June 1952; letter from Hendrik George van Dam to Goldschmidt, 11 June 1952; ZA, B.1/7, 120.
95 "Beschlussprotokoll der internen Direktoriumssitzung," 12 November 1952, ZA, B.1/7, 221.30; "Vorstandssitzung der Jüdischen Gemeinde Frankfurt am Main vom 18.11.1952," 18 November 1952, ZA, B.1/13, A.9, 5; "Vorstandssitzung der Jüdischen Gemeinde Frankfurt am Main vom 18.12.1952," 18 December 1952, ZA, B.1/13, A.9, 1; "Protokoll der Sitzung des Direktoriums (erweiterte)," 27 January 1953, ZA, B.1/7, 221.33.

members.[96] With no other choice, the Bavarians relented, and at last, on 13 May 1953, van Dam notified the Central Council office that Bavaria, represented by Max Diamand and Baruch Graubard, would occupy seats on the board.[97]

Despite the large eastern Jewish presence in West Germany, native German Jews nevertheless continued to dominate the representative institutions. Having lived in Germany before 1933, these Jews took a keen interest in restitution of lost property and in German domestic politics. Thus, political and economic issues preoccupied the Central Council leadership for its first three years. After having achieved the goals of collective reparations for world Jewry and domestic reparations for individual Jews in Germany, the group began to lose its focus. Founded primarily as a political representative organization, it had overlooked cultural and religious issues.[98] In addition, during the second half of 1953, several of its most prominent members relinquished their board seats, including Julius Dreifuss of Düsseldorf and Leopold Goldschmidt of Frankfurt, who had become disillusioned because of the internal conflicts burdening the group.[99] As part of a reorientation of the Central Council, new board members assumed the reins of leadership in October 1953. While Heinz Galinski of Berlin and Leonhard Baer of Koblenz remained in office, they were joined by Maurice Weinberger of Munich, Ewald Allschoff of Frankfurt, and Carl Katz of Bremen, who served as chairman for a six-month term – a new position for the Central Council.[100]

Katz, the new *primus inter pares*, brought a new leadership style and new agenda to the organization, and he soon clashed with van Dam, who had been administering the Central Council since 1950. While van Dam was technically an administrator, he had assumed a more political role and had actively made decisions

[96] Letter from Hendrik George van Dam to Landesverband Bayern, 25 February 1953, ZA, B.1/7, 120.
[97] Letter from Hendrik George van Dam to Central Council secretariat, 13 May 1953, ZA, B.1/7, 120.
[98] More than half of the communities' budgets went to social welfare functions and another quarter for administration. Less than 20 percent went to religious functions and less than 5 percent for educational projects. Maor, "Über den Wiederaufbau," 134.
[99] Letter from Leopold Goldschmidt to Hendrik George van Dam, 10 July 1953; letter from Hendrik George van Dam to Julius Dreifuss, 16 October 1953; ZA, B.1/7, 120.
[100] "Protokoll der Zentralratstagung in Bremen," 12 October 1953, ZA, B.1/7, 221.40.

regarding Central Council policy. Katz wished to change this aspect of van Dam's employment. On 4 November 1953, immediately after assuming his position, the new chairman made it clear that van Dam would report to him and keep him informed of all his activities. When Katz began learning of community activities only from reports in the *Allgemeine Wochenzeitung*, he became irate and wrote to van Dam, "I do not intend to belong to a mere pro forma committee."[101] Slowly, Katz began to take control of the group's finances and cultural affairs.[102] Galinski, too, had grown displeased with van Dam's activities. The general secretary had been too independent in negotiating with political authorities for Galinski, who wanted to see him limited to administrative duties. He also criticized van Dam's nearly sole oversight of the Central Council's budget.[103] However, it seems that van Dam began to fight back. An anonymous commentator, presumably van Dam, attacked Galinski's letter, noting that the Berlin community contributed far less than its proportional share to the Central Council's maintenance. Additionally, Galinski had not availed himself of many opportunities offered him to review the group's accounts.[104]

The mounting discontent among board members culminated in a change of the group's system of management. On 1 November 1953, board members decided to distribute portfolios rather than have a single permanent official administer all its tasks, and Allschoff was asked to investigate gaining the legal status of a *Körperschaft des öffentlichen Rechts*, allowing it to levy taxes on members. Although Galinski did not attend the meeting out of protest against the false direction in which he saw the Central Council heading, he received the portfolio for education.[105]

[101] Letter from Carl Katz to Hendrik George van Dam, 4 November 1953; letter from Carl Katz to Hendrik George van Dam, 13 November 1953; ZA, B.1/7, 120.
[102] Letter from Hendrik George van Dam to Carl Katz, 17 November 1953, ZA, B.1/7, 120.
[103] Letter from Heinz Galinski to all Central Council board members, 29 October 1953, ZA, B.1/7, 120.
[104] "Sachliche Gesichtspunkte zu Brief Galinski vom 29.10.53," 30 October 1953, ZA, B.1/7, 120.
[105] "Protokoll der Sitzung des Direktoriums des Zentralrates der Juden in Deutschland," 1 November 1953, ZA, B.1/7, 221.41. Portfolios were: finance and administration, Katz; worship, culture, and education, Galinski; welfare, Allschoff; economics, Baer; reparations and foreign relations, van Dam; politics, Weinberger; cemeteries, Baer; and provisional chairman, Katz. The Central Council finally became a *Körperschaft des öffentlichen Rechts* in 1963.

He believed that the organization's leaders spent too much time focusing on reparations and judicial matters to the detriment of other, more important matters. He told the Berlin community's assembly,

We do not need a Central Council for that [purpose]. The scope of the Central Council's duties must be broadened so that the Central Council deals with all areas of Jewish life. Only then will it have the possibility of dealing with the Jewish world and winning a certain prestige.[106]

Another problem, he mentioned, was that that one person had too much control over the organization's budget.[107] Presumably, Galinski meant van Dam, but the reforms initiated at the November meeting lessened van Dam's power. They also signaled a change in orientation away from purely political functions. In the aftermath of the East German purges and migration of Jews to western Germany, social welfare and relief activities had assumed greater importance than ever before, and this was most apparent to the West Berlin community.

Katz grew determined to reform the Central Council by April 1954, stating that the "office must be set up so that it really is the central office of the Jewish communities in Germany." Baruch Graubard proposed a plan to place the Central Council at the head of Jewish life in Germany. The board would reorganize the small office, hire a permanent manager, and establish two principal departments: one for culture and worship, the other for finance, economics, statistics, and labor. Although van Dam and Norbert Schäfer, his assistant, would work out the details of the reorganization, the general secretary felt that he still had much work to do regarding reparations.[108] Despite the plan for reorganization and distribution of portfolios, van Dam would retain control over the group's political activities, which included continued lobbying for improvements to existing reparations law. However, as reflected in the group's budget, cultural affairs became increasingly vital to the Central Council. The Central Council was changing its orientation

---

[106] "Protokoll der Repräsentanten-Versammlung vom 11. November 1953," 11 November 1953, LAB, B Rep. 2, 6845.

[107] Ibid.

[108] "Protokoll der Direktoriumssitzung," 12 December 1953, ZA, B.1/7, 221.43.

from a mere lobbying and legal organization to one more concerned with cultural and social work.[109]

As 1953 ended, the Central Council faced large tasks, and resolving them would not be easy. Differences of opinion still divided board members, but the group now had strong leadership under Carl Katz, who was determined to carry through his restructuring plan. As an elected official, he was wary of van Dam's institutional authority. Still, the Central Council was becoming more than a mere political pressure group. After its success in winning domestic reparations, it could concentrate on social, cultural, and religious aspects of Jewish life in Germany. Furthermore, distributing portfolios to board members representing the different Jewish communities and state associations, rather than relying on the efforts of a single official to run the entire organization, helped to promote cooperation among Jewish groups and leaders throughout western Germany. The organization also worked to define its relationship with the German Conference of Rabbis, and it fought against bans on kosher slaughtering.

The group, which had long relied on personal relationships between van Dam and Marx and leading federal officials, now had a regular governmental interlocutor in the Interior Ministry, and federal subsidies would help to ensure its continued existence. In 1954, the Claims Conference also began supporting the Central Welfare Office and cultural affairs within the communities, including schools for children and adult education classes.[110] Although funding for the organization had been secured, and the Central Welfare Office was to receive a significant settlement from the Claims Conference, the state associations continued to contest distribution of the funds.[111]

Despite internal conflicts, the group had achieved much. As 1953 drew to a close, van Dam reminded the board members,

---

[109] "Protokoll der Sitzung des Direktoriums des Zentralrates der Juden in Deutschland," 1 November 1953, ZA, B.1/7, 221.41; letter from Norbert Schäfer to Carl Gussone, 2 October 1953, BAK, B 106, 21407.

[110] Conference on Material Claims against Germany, *Twenty Years Later*, 82; BAK, B 106, 21407. For the fiscal year 1954–1955, the Central Council received 45,000 marks from the government and 50,200 marks from the AJDC and the state associations. Maor, "Über den Wiederaufbau," 126.

[111] "Protokoll der Sitzung des Direktoriums des Zentralrates der Juden in Deutschland," 7–8 March 1954, ZA, B.1/7, 221.47.

"The Central Council emerged from nothing and succeeded practically without means against the resistance of numerous powers. With a small apparatus we could only achieve something because we did not split up. In 1950, we began with nothing."[112] With a secure source of funding, it now enjoyed prestige within the West German government and could henceforth concentrate on religious work and cultural projects. The Central Council had stabilized the postwar Jewish community in Germany and set it on a course that would last many years.

[112] "Protokoll der Direktoriumssitzung," 12 December 1953, ZA, B.1/7, 221.43.

Conclusion

Despite the devastation experienced by German Jewry from 1933 to 1945, Jewish life returned to Germany. Against considerable odds and under adverse conditions, the Jews living in Germany established roots and even acquired influence in political life out of proportion to their numbers. Additionally, Jewish issues or Jewish-related issues became the subject of political discourse in both Germanys. In East Germany, the community struggled to survive even as the dominant political group seemed opposed to it. In West Germany, the community found supporters, who themselves wished for a German-Jewish reconciliation, and together they created the preconditions for the contemporary Jewish community in Germany.

At its most basic level, this study has attempted to answer a number of questions about the nature of the Jewish community in Germany after the Holocaust, the obstacles it initially faced, the relations between Jewish groups in Germany, and the relations between that community and Jewish groups abroad. It has also attempted to elucidate relations between Jewish organizations and non-Jewish political leaders, as well as the manner in which these leaders viewed Jewish and Jewish-related issues in the decade after the Nazi era. This examination has addressed many of these issues for the first time or in new ways. While this is a German and German-Jewish story, the surprising success of the community in reestablishing itself and finding a place in political society might have implications for the study of other social groups and their efforts for interest representation.

After 1945, the size and composition of the Jewish community in Germany remained unsettled. In fact, the question of whether Jews should remain in Germany developed into an international controversy. The World Jewish Congress overtly called for an end to Jewish life Germany. Meanwhile, the western Allies selected Jews living outside Germany as the heirs to formerly Jewish-owned property, signaling that they, too, did not consider the viability of continued Jewish life in Germany to be a priority.

In fact, the majority of the approximately 200,000 Jews in postwar western Germany shared these sentiments and wished to emigrate as soon as the international political situation allowed. These displaced persons of Eastern European origin considered Germany merely a way station. Most wished to settle in Palestine, where Zionist groups were working for the establishment of a Jewish state. While waiting to emigrate, the displaced persons established a highly developed society, featuring educational institutions, hospitals, theaters, and even a political system that, in many ways, represented a microcosm of the world they had left behind and the land to which they hoped to gain admittance. Meanwhile, they remained largely uninterested in domestic German affairs, and for support they looked to the western Allied occupiers, particularly to the Americans, who appointed a special adviser for Jewish affairs. This official helped to mitigate the worst misunderstandings between the displaced persons and military authorities.

In the British zone of occupation, in northern Germany, the community quickly reached a stable size as migration to that zone abated. The British, wishing to limit unauthorized Jewish settlement in Palestine, would not permit displaced persons to leave the zone once they got there. Thus, after an initial influx, few Jewish refugees chose to migrate to the British zone. In contrast, the American zone, in southern Germany became crowded with Jewish refugees largely because it was porous. As Jews fled antisemitism in Eastern Europe in 1946 and 1947, they came to the American zone. Some waited in United Nations refugee camps until the British opened Palestine to them, while others attempted the hazardous onward journey without permission.

In contrast to the displaced persons, whose presence in Germany was both new and largely temporary, several thousand Jews who had lived in Germany before the Holocaust planned to remain there. Unlike the Eastern European displaced persons, who largely spoke Yiddish, these Jews were acculturated to Germany. Both in eastern and western Germany, they resettled primarily in cities and refounded their disbanded congregations. As they had done before 1933, they looked to German municipal and state authorities for support as they rebuilt their lives in Germany. Their political ties, many of which predated the Nazi era, provided a basis of interlocution with German authorities, and they depended on favorably disposed administrators for aid.

Meanwhile, tensions prevailed between the German Jews and the displaced persons in western Germany. The latter had ties to the Allies, whose sanction of the Jewish Restitution Successor Organization as the heir to ownerless property benefited the Zionists at the cost of German Jewish communities. Additionally, longstanding religious and cultural differences separated the two groups. In northern Germany, these tensions were overcome, but in southern Germany, namely the American occupation zone, with its large displaced-persons population, the friction prevented fruitful cooperation at a time when the Jewish community arguably needed it most.

Only the creation of the state of Israel broke the stalemate. Israel's existence as an independent state permitted an exodus of Jewish displaced persons from Germany, which had the ultimate effect of stabilizing the community's size – virtually a prerequisite for permanent organization. Meanwhile, pressure from the withdrawing American occupiers coupled with a potentially active Jewish policy by the new West German government induced the remaining community to unite. In 1949, the Americans, no longer wishing to maintain an active role in Jewish policy, urged the remaining Jews to organize themselves. A few months later, Chancellor Adenauer proposed appointing an official Jewish interlocutor for German-Jewish dialogue. Jewish groups found his plan unacceptable. As a result, in 1950, Eastern European Jews who did not or could not emigrate came together with German Jews in a single organization: the Central Council of Jews in Germany. The Central Council, whose origins and initial functions have heretofore received insufficient attention, became the primary representative body for the West German community and its highest coordinating body. It was critical to the success of Jewish life in Germany after the Holocaust.

In eastern Germany, the various Jewish communities also united for representative purposes. The small Jewish community in the Russian occupation zone was comprised primarily of Jews who had lived in eastern Germany before the war and Jews who chose to settle there after 1945 for ideological reasons. With the exception of Berlin, there was no significant Jewish DP population. In a society increasingly organized along corporatist lines, the Jews found representation in the State Association of Jewish Communities, doing so even before the ethnically and culturally divided Jewish community in the west united. Julius Meyer, a well-connected Communist and Holocaust survivor, led the organization and came to embody its success. Despite the importance of the organization for eastern German Jewish life, neither this group nor Meyer have previously featured prominently in studies of postwar German Jewish life.

Even with representative bodies bringing unity and organization to the Jewish community, German Jewry remained in poor condition. The community was generally impoverished and in need of social welfare services. With limited resources, Jewish groups found it hard to restore and to maintain synagogues, schools, hospitals, and cemeteries. Moreover, the designation of foreign Jews as heirs to unclaimed property complicated the financial situation. Outside help was desperately needed. For this aid, Jewish groups looked to the German governments.

It would be hard to overstate the impact of relations with non-Jewish, political elites on the community or the efforts made by Jewish communal leaders to cultivate relations. Personal ties between Jewish leaders and key individuals in government, administration, and the political parties clearly furthered Jewish interests. In West Germany, the careful supervision of Central Council administrator Hendrik George van Dam was complemented by the political activities of Berlin Jewish community chairman Heinz Galinski, Jewish politician Siegmund Weltlinger, and, above all, the well-connected journalist Karl Marx. Together, they led the most efficacious efforts to stabilize the community and to lobby on behalf of the Central Council's West German constituents. Their intricate relationships with leaders such as Theodor Heuss, Konrad Adenauer, and Kurt Schumacher were indispensable, yet have largely gone overlooked. In eastern Germany, the State Association worked to cultivate support within the communist Party of Socialist Unity (SED), which dominated society. Julius Meyer and the State Association looked to leading Communists for succor. After the establishment of the German Democratic Republic in 1949, Meyer and his staff worked with non-Communist administrators and officials in East Germany's nominally multiparty governing coalition.

As Jewish groups attempted to develop ties to political leaders, societal and political discourse on Jewish and Jewish-related issues was of critical importance. This discourse reflected the manner in which leading politicians regarded the Nazi past and its legacy for postwar Germany, which, naturally, impacted relations with Jewish groups. At a time when German political discourse was focused on victimhood and entitlement, there was no consensus in favor of aiding the struggling Jewish community. Moreover, competing segments of society sought to shape the public memory of the Nazi years, especially in West Germany. Jewish leaders were fortunate to find powerful political allies. While some politicians had enjoyed ties to the Jewish community before the Nazi years, others sought to atone for the past through postwar support. Others had yet more complicated agendas. The intricate relationships with these unofficial patrons were indispensable.

In West Germany, few politicians took an overt interest in Jewish matters. The Social Democrats, sharing the legacy of persecution under the Nazis and wishing to make a complete break with the past, did, however, support reparations and other issues of vital interest to the Jewish community. Party leader Kurt Schumacher spearheaded this effort. Chancellor Adenauer, who was both a morally upright man and an astute politician, wished to make amends for the past, but he delayed publicly addressing such topics for fear of alienating his political base at a time when his electoral position remained uncertain. Unlike the Social Democrats, Adenauer's fellow Christian Democrats were reluctant to address the Nazi past. Many wished to leave the past behind, while others represented groups that considered themselves victims of events between January 1933 and May 1945. The third political force in West Germany, the liberal FDP, seemed particularly disinterested in examining society's culpability for the Nazi era and redressing past wrongs. However, President Theodor Heuss, an FDP member, did make a number of open statements about German responsibility for the past and obligations to the victims of persecution. Though his position was largely ceremonial and his statements remained symbolic, his staff did aid the Jewish community immeasurably, and Heuss became the unofficial patron of the Jewish community within West Germany. After 1951, Konrad Adenauer renewed his efforts for German-Jewish reconciliation, focusing primarily on ties to Israel and Jewish groups abroad. Among German leaders, he bore the primary responsibility for the West German-Israeli dialogue that began in 1951 and culminated over a year later with an agreement for reparations.

The political situation in the east entailed far greater complexities and perils for the Jewish community. The SED's attitude was the chief factor in determining the Jewish community's survival. When the SED was indifferent to Jewish issues, the community could manage, if not thrive. On the other hand, Communist obstructionism was detrimental to the community. Jewish groups had difficulty navigating bureaucratic issues or even reclaiming their former property, often as a result of a general Communist disinclination toward religious groups, and often as a result of Communist unwillingness to reprivatize nationalized properties, even "Aryanized" Jewish ones. After 1949, as East Germany maintained the façade of multiparty, coalition government, the State Association could seek support from non-Communist officials within the government, most notably deputy prime minister Otto Nuschke, a Christian Democrat, who also headed the Main Division for Ties to the Churches. His staff aided the Jewish community in reconstructing or restoring destroyed Jewish communal properties. This critical relationship must be reincorporated in the story of the reconstruction of East German Jewish life.

Despite the fruitful cooperation with the Christian Democrat Nuschke, by 1952, the SED's attitude toward the Jewish community was too negative for even non-Communist allies to mitigate. The governing Communists predicated their claim to leadership on the legacy of persecution by the Nazis and resistance to National Socialism. However, the issue of victimhood was an automatic point of friction between the regime and East German Jewry, for the Jews also made claims to victimhood. After their experience of persecution by the German state, they demanded reparations from their contemporary government – the very Communist-led government that claimed no responsibility for the past. It is important to note that Jewish Germans did receive assistance from leading Communists Paul Merker and Leo Zuckermann, who supported Jewish claims and who drafted a law that would have provided for compensation to Jewish victims of Nazi persecution. These two men had spent the war years in exile in Mexico, where they had met many German Jews who had fled Hitler's regime. However, the leading faction in the party, led by Walter Ulbricht and those who had spent the war years in Moscow, rejected reparations. The combination of such a rejection and intraparty conflict between Ulbricht's clique and its opponents had serious ramifications for the Jewish community.

This story begins in 1945 and concludes in 1953. By the end of that year, the Jewish communities in both Germanys had achieved a state of stability and greater self-awareness. These conditions were as much a function of external influences as actions taken by the Jews in Germany themselves. After arduous negotiations, in 1952, the West German government and Israel signed the Luxembourg Agreement for reparations to Israel and to the Conference on Jewish Material Claims against Germany. The treaty became reality in 1953. Despite strong opposition within the government and within political society, Chancellor Adenauer had achieved his goal of reconciliatory reparations. Additionally, the treaty both forced the Jewish community of Germany to reevaluate its ties to its foreign coreligionists and offered an opportunity to gain critical financial support from the government. The Central Council had initially not been included in the Claims Conference, West Germany's primary nongovernmental negotiating partner regarding reparations.[1] German Jews did not feel welcome within international Jewish organizations, and they realized that they could not depend on these groups for material support. As a result, the Central Council drew even closer to the West German federal government, whose subsidies effectively ensured the Jewish group's survival.

The year 1953 was also pivotal for East German Jewry. In late 1952, the regime adopted the overtly antisemitic posture that was prevailing in Eastern Europe, and by 1953, the very existence of organized Jewry in East Germany came into question. Merker, Zuckermann, and Jewish Communists found themselves unwelcome in the party that they had loyally served. Soon, the leaders of the State Association and individual Jewish communities were threatened. Arrests and SED purges became widespread. Both

[1] Additionally, many years would pass before the Jews of Germany were generally welcome at international Jewish conferences, including those for women's groups, students, and Zionist organizations. On anti-German sentiment at the International Council of Jewish Women, see Lilli Marx, "Renewal of the German-Jewish Press," in *After the Holocaust*, ed. Brenner, 127. On the position of German Jewry in other Jewish groups, see Shafir, "Der Jüdische Weltkongreß und sein Verhältnis zu Nachkriegsdeutschland (1945–1967);" Burgbauer, *Zwischen Erinnerung und Verdrängung*, 58–61; Cohn, *Jews in Germany*, 93.

Jewish SED members and non-Communist Jewish communal officials fled to the west in fear of their lives. Only the end of the purge and Stalin's death in 1953 saved the Jews of East Germany and Eastern Europe from a more severe fate. Meanwhile, the State Association experienced a change of leadership and an end to its autonomy. However, this transformation ended the fundamental conflict with the regime and led to a relatively stable, if quiet existence for the community.

Incidentally, the events of 1953 drew the Jewish communities in both Germanys closer together in a number of ways. The East Germans did have representation in the Central Council, and that body claimed to speak for all Jews in Germany. When the arrests of Jewish leaders began, the East Germans found themselves cut off from the Central Council. Moreover, the Jewish community of Berlin split into two autonomous groups. A few months later, the reassociation of East German Jewry with the Central Council served as one important indicator of the purge's end. Meanwhile, hundreds of East German Jews fled in the face of persecution. Their reception in the west created possibly the greatest challenge theretofore faced by the still-young Central Council and its associate, the Central Welfare Office.

In the years following 1953, lasting at least until the trauma of the 1960s, a certain pattern of relations between both German governments and the Jewish community was set. As characterized by sociologist Michal Bodemann, it was an era of "bureaucratic reconsolidation."[2] In West Germany, the Central Council's agreement with the federal government, dating from 1953, typified this state of affairs. A stable, bureaucratic leadership cadre emerged, largely confirmed in its authority as a result of its connections to governmental officials, many of whom were bureaucrats themselves. Internal voices of dissent or protest did not receive approbation. The Central Council's relations with the state centered on the community's modest maintenance and interest representation. A secondary function was to bear vigil against neo-Nazi manifestations and to push for continued efforts to prosecute war criminals. In East Germany, the question of Jewish advocacy of reparations and attempts to foment public debate on victimhood ended with

---

[2] Bodemann, "'How can one stand to live there as a Jew...,'" in *Jews, Germans, Memory*, ed. Bodemann, 30–34.

the purges in 1953. Moreover, the community effectively lost its autonomy. From 1953 to 1967, Jewish issues did not concern the East German leadership. In both Germanys, the community experienced stagnation or only moderate growth and generally did not play a prominent role in German public life.

The 1960s saw a gradual change to this pattern. A series of events altered the basis of German-Jewish rapport. From 1963 to 1965, largely at the instigation of Fritz Bauer, several former guards at Auschwitz concentration camp stood trial in Frankfurt, pushing the issue back into the limelight. The Six Day War of 1967 revolutionized German perceptions of Israel. While many politically leftist Germans had embraced Israel as the representative of a formerly oppressed European Jewry, after the war, they considered the Jewish state to be an oppressor regime. Coinciding with the political turmoil of 1968, these Germans – many of whom were members of the postwar generation – sympathized with so-called Third World liberation movements. Considering themselves freed of their parents' culpability and need for reconciliation, they vilified Israel and lauded the Palestinians. Some compared the Israelis' actions to Nazi persecution. At the same time, many politically conservative Germans gained a new appreciation for the militarily assertive Israelis. They also regarded the Jewish state as an outpost of Western liberal democracy in a region dominated by socialist, pro-Soviet Arab states. Meanwhile, the Six Day War had an impact on East German sentiment. In the east bloc, anti-Zionist invective reached an all-time high, once again affecting the small Jewish community of East Germany.

Events also shaped the Jewish community. In post-1968 Germany, a new cohort of Jewish leaders emerged. Regardless of their politics – ranging from Green to liberal to conservative – they were more publicly assertive. They did not abjure protests and demonstrations, and by the 1990s, several Central Council and local community leaders were active participants in German public life and in the discourse on the memory of the past.

Although the years 1945 to 1953 were difficult ones for the Jews in Germany – probably the most difficult the community has experienced since the war – they represent a triumph. After the chaos of the immediate postwar years, when Holocaust survivors struggled to survive with dignity and Jewry's continued existence in Germany remained in doubt, an organized community established roots in

Germany. Respected and active leaders, working with or through the Central Council, built ties to key political leaders. Together they enabled the Jewish community to make plans for a permanent presence. Reparations to many Jewish victims of Nazi atrocities became a reality; Jewish groups in Germany received steady governmental support; and West Germany, at least, established the basis for a larger reconciliation. After the near total extirpation of German Jewry by the Nazis, the land of Mendelssohn, Heine, and Einstein had an established, diverse Jewish community.

Bibliography

PRIMARY SOURCES, UNPUBLISHED

American Jewish Archive, Cincinnati
World Jewish Congress
Central Files, 1919–1975, Series A, sub-series 1
Amherst College Library/Archives and Special Collections, Amherst, Mass.
John J. McCloy Papers
Correspondence, Series 33
Germany File, Series 14
HICOG, Series 13a and 13b
Speeches, Series 4
Archiv des Liberalismus (Friedrich-Naumann-Stiftung), Gummersbach
Bundesparteitage, A 1
Nachlässe (personal papers)
Franz Blücher, A 3
Thomas Dehler, N 1
Hertha Ilk, N 2
Reinhold Maier, A 34
Erich Mende, A 26 and A 31
Hans Reif, N 19
Präsidiumsprotokolle, no file number
1. FDP-Bundestagsfraktion, A 40
Bundestagsfraktionsplenumsprotokolle
Bundestagsfraktionsvorstandsprotokolle
Archiv der sozialen Demokratie (Friedrich-Ebert-Stiftung), Bonn
Abteilung I: Nachlässe und Deposita (Division I: Personal papers and depository)
Jakob Altmaier
Adolf Arndt
Walter Auerbach
Otto Ostrowski
Heinrich Putzrath
Heinrich Ritzel

Carlo Schmid
Jean Stock
Abteilung II: SPD-Parteiführung (Division II: SPD Party Leadership)
　Bestand Erich Ollenhauer
　Bestand Kurt Schumacher
　Parteivorstand, Sekretariat Fritz Heine
Archiv für Christlich-Demokratische Politik (Konrad-Adenauer-Stift-
　ung), St. Augustin
　Abteilung I: Nachlässe und Nachlaßsplitter (Division I: Personal Papers
　　and Fragments)
　　Franz Böhm, I-200
　　Jakob Diel, I-139
　　Eugen Gerstenmaier, I-210
　　Hans Globke, I-070
　　Otto Küster, I-084
　　Wilhelm Laforet, I-122
　　Ernst Lemmer, I-280
　　Otto Lenz, I-172
Bundesarchiv, Berlin
　Bestände (Institutional Collections)
　　Büro des Präsidiums des Ministerrates-Stellvertreter des Min-
　　　isterpräsidents – Otto Nuschke, DC 20
　　Ministerium des Innern, 11.0 Hauptverwaltung Deutsche Volkspoli-
　　　zei (HVDVP), DO 1
　　Staatssekretär für Kirchenfragen, DO 4
　Bestände, SAPMO (Stiftung Archiv Parteien und Massenorganisatio-
　　nen) (institutional collections)
　　Ausschüsse "Opfer des Faschismus," DY 54/V 277/1
　　Politbüro des Zentralkomitees der SED, DY30/IV 2/2
　　Protokolle der Sitzungen des Sekretariats, DY 30/J IV 2/3
　　SED Arbeitsgruppe Kirchenfragen 1946–1962, DY 30/IV 2/14
　　SED Sekretariat Helmut Lehmann, DY 30/IV 2/2.027
　　Vereinigung der Verfolgten des Naziregimes in der DDR, DY 55/V
　　　278/1–3
　　Zentrale Parteikontrolkommission, DY 30/IV 2/4
　Nachlässe, SAPMO (Stiftung Archiv Parteien und Massenorganisatio-
　　nen) (personal papers)
　　Otto Grotewohl, NY 4090
　　Albert Norden, NY 4217
　　Wilhelm Pieck, NY 4036
Bundesarchiv, Koblenz
　Bestände (institutional collections)
　　Bundeskanzleramt, B 136
　　Bundesministerium des Innern, B 106
　　Bundespräsidialamt/Amtzeit des Prof. Dr. Theodor Heuss, B 122

Deutscher Koordinerungsrat der Gesellschaft für christlich-jüdische
Zusammenarbeit, B 259
Office of Military Government of the United States (OMGUS),
Z 45
Nachlässe (personal papers)
Herbert Blankenhorn, N 1351
Franz Blücher, N 1080
Walter Hallstein, N 1266
Theodor Heuss, N 1221
Robert Lehr, N 1244
Hermann Pünder, N 1005
Fritz Schäffer, N 1168
Hans-Christoph Seebohm, N 1178
Center for Jewish History/YIVO, New York
AJC Foreign Affairs Division, Foreign Countries (FAD 1), RG 347.7.1
American Joint Distribution Committee, Reports, RG 335.1
Displaced Persons Camps and Centers in Germany, RG 294.2
Leo W. Schwarz Papers, RG 294.1
Landesarchiv Berlin
Nachlass Siegmund Weltlinger, E-Rep. 200–22
Referat für Jüdische Angelegenheiten, B-Rep. 2
National Archives and Record Administration, College Park
Foreign Service Posts, RG 84
U.S. Political Advisor – Berlin
Office of Strategic Services, RG 226
Research and Analysis, Jewish Desk
U.S. Occupation Headquarters, World War II, RG 260
Office of Military Government for Germany, U. S.
Civil Affairs Division
Office of the Adjutant General
U. S. Army Commands 1942– , RG 338
European Theater of Operations/U. S. Forces European Theater
G-5 Assistant Chief of Staff
NARA website
Parlamentsarchiv des Deutschen Bundestages, Berlin (formerly Bonn)
Materialen zum Bundesergänzungsgesetz zur Entschädigung für Opfer
der nationalsozialistischen Verfolgung (BEG), I:537
Materialen zum Gesetz betreffend das Abkommen vom 10. September
1952 zwischen der Bundesrepublik Deutschland und dem Staate
Israel, I:394
Verhandlungen des Deutschen Bundestages, I. Wahlperiode 1949
Politisches Archiv, Auswärtiges Amt, Berlin (formerly Bonn)
Abteilung II (Politische Angelegenheiten), B 10
Abteilung III (Länderabteilung), Referat 305/II A 6 (USA and
Canada), B 32

Abteilung V (Rechtsabteilung), Referat 501/V 2 (Konsularrecht), B 81

Stiftung Bundeskanzler-Adenauer-Haus, Bad Honnef
Nachlass Konrad Adenauer
Korrespondenz [misc.], 10
Privatbestände H: D. Heineman

Stiftung "Neue Synagoge-Berlin Centrum Judaicum" Archiv
Verband der Jüdischen Gemeinden in der DDR, 5 B 1

U.S. Holocaust Memorial Museum Archive and Library, Washington
Articles and U.S. military Records relating to displaced persons in post-war Germany mss., RG 19.024
Earl G. Harrison Papers, RG 10.088
Oral history interview with Norbert Wollheim (Part II), RG 50.030*0267

Zentralarchiv zur Erforschung der Geschichte der Juden in Deutschland, Heidelberg
Bestände – Institutionen (institutional collections)
Jüdische Gemeinde Düsseldorf, B.1/5
Jüdische Gemeinde Frankfurt am Main, B.1/13
Landesverband Nordrhein, B.1/15
Zentralrat der Juden in Deutschland, B.1/7

Frowein, Jochen Abraham. Letter to author, 23 Feburary 2000.

Heine, Fritz. Letter to author, 7 April 1999.

Kaff, Brigitte (Archiv für Christlich-Demokratische Politik). Letter to author, including dossier on Richard Kantorowicz, 7 Decmber 2000.

Marx, Lilli. Interview by author. Düsseldorf, 14 April 1999.

PRIMARY SOURCES, PUBLISHED

Abs, Hermann Josef. *Entscheidungen 1949–1953. Die Entstehung des Londoner Schuldenabkommens.* Mainz: v. Hase und Koehler, 1991.

Adenauer, Konrad. *Briefe 1945–1947.* Ed. Hans Peter Mensing. Rhöndorfer Ausgabe, ed. Rudolf Morsey and Hans-Peter Schwarz. Berlin: Siedler, 1983.

———. *Briefe 1947–1949.* Ed. Hans Peter Mensing. Rhöndorfer Ausgabe, ed. Rudolf Morsey and Hans-Peter Schwarz. Berlin: Siedler, 1984.

———. *Briefe 1949–1951.* Ed. Hans Peter Mensing. Rhöndorfer Ausgabe, ed. Rudolf Morsey and Hans-Peter Schwarz. Berlin: Siedler, 1987.

———. *Briefe 1951–1953.* Ed. Hans Peter Mensing. Rhöndorfer Ausgabe, ed. Rudolf Morsey and Hans-Peter Schwarz. Berlin: Siedler, 1987.

———. *Erinnerungen 1953–1955.* Stuttgart: Deutsche Verlags-Anstalt, 1966.

———. *Reden 1917–1967: Eine Auswahl.* Ed. Hans-Peter Schwarz. Stuttgart: Deutsche Verlags-Anstalt, 1975.

————. *Teegespräche 1950–1954.* Ed. Hanns Jürgen Küsters. Rhöndorfer Ausgabe, ed. Rudolf Morsey and Hans-Peter Schwarz. Berlin: Siedler, 1984.

Adenauer, Konrad, and Theodor Heuss. *Unter vier Augen: Gespräche aus den Gründerjahren 1949–1959.* Ed. Hans Peter Mensing. Rhöndorfer Ausgabe, ed. Rudolf Morsey and Hans-Peter Schwarz. Berlin: Wolf Jobst Siedler, 1987.

Albrecht, Willy, ed. *Die SPD unter Kurt Schumacher und Erich Ollenhauer 1946–1963: Sitzungsprotokolle der Spitzengremien,* vol. 1: *1946–1948.* Bonn: J. H. W. Dietz Nachfolger, 2000.

Blankenhorn, Herbert. *Verständnis und Verständigung: Blätter eines politischen Tagebuchs 1949–1979.* Frankfurt: Propyläen, 1980.

Böhm, Franz. *Reden und Schriften über die Ordnung einer freien Gesellschaft, einer freien Wirtschaft und über die Wiedergutmachung.* Ed. Ernst-Joachim Mestmäcker. Karlsruhe: C. F. Müller, 1960.

Brandt, Heinz. *Ein Traum, der nicht entführbar ist. Mein Weg zwischen Ost und West.* Munich: Paul List, 1967.

Bubis, Ignatz. "Gedanken an Heinz Putzrath." In *Heinz Putzrath – Gegen Nationalsozialismus, Für soziale Demokratie. Skizzen zu Leben und Wirken,* ed. Johannes Rau and Bernd Faulenbach. Essen: Klartext, 1997.

Christlich-Demokratische Union Deutschlands (Germany, West). Bundesvorstand. *Adenauer: "Es mußte alles neu gemacht werden." Die Protokolle des CDU-Bundesvorstandes 1950–1953.* Ed. Günter Buchstab. Forschungen und Quellen zur Zeitgeschichte, ed. Klaus Gotto, Hans Günter Hockerts, Rudolf Morsey, and Hans-Peter Schwarz, vol. 8. Stuttgart: Klett-Cotta, 1986.

Christlich-Soziale Union. *Die CSU 1945–1948: Protokolle und Materialien zur Frühgeschichte der Christlich-Sozialen Union,* vol. 1: *Protokolle 1945–1946,* ed. Barbara Fait and Alf Mintzel. Texte und Materialen zur Zeitgeschichte, vol. 4. Munich: R. Oldenbourg, 1993

————. *Lehrjahre der CSU: Eine Nachkriegspartei im Spiegel vertraulicher Berichte an die amerikanische Militärregierung.* Ed. Klaus-Dietmar Henke and Hans Woller. Schriftenreihe der Vierteljahreshefte für Zeitgeschichte, ed. Karl Dietrich Bracher, Hans-Peter Schwarz, vol. 48. Stuttgart: Deutsche Verlags-Anstalt, 1984.

Clay, Lucius D. *Decision in Germany.* Garden City: Doubleday, 1950.

Conference on Material Claims against Germany. *Twenty Years Later: Activities of the Conference on Material Claims against Germany, 1952–1972.* New York: Conference on Material Claims against Germany, n.d.

Dahlem, Franz. *Ausgewählte Reden und Aufsätze, 1919–1979: Zur Geschichte der Arbeiterbewegung.* Berlin: Dietz, 1980.

Dahlem, Franz, and Karl Raddatz. *Die Aufgaben der VVN: 2 Referate gehalten auf der Zonendelegiertenkonferenz am 22./23. Februar 1947 in Berlin.* Berlin: Neues Deutschland, 1947.

Dam, Hendrik George van. "Die Juden in Deutschland nach 1945." In *Judentum: Schicksal, Wesen und Gegenwart*, ed. Franz Böhm and Walter Dirks. Vol. 2. Wiesbaden: Franz Steiner, 1965.

Deutsches Komitee Pro Palästina zur Förderung der jüdischen Palästinasiedlung. *Tagung in Köln am 22. November 1927*. Berlin: Siegfried Scholem, [1927].

Ehlers, Hermann. *Hermann Ehlers: Präsident des Deutschen Bundestags, Ausgewählte Reden, Aufsätze und Briefe, 1950–1954*. Ed. Karl Dietrich Erdmann. Boppard am Rhein: Harald Boldt, 1991.

Eschwege, Helmut. *Fremd unter meinesgleichen: Erinnerungen eines Dresdner Juden*. Berlin: Ch. Links, 1991.

Freie Demokratische Partei. Bundesgeschäftsstelle. *Politisches Taschenbuch*. Ed. Fritz Niebel. N.p., n.d. [1953?].

————. Bundesvorstand. *FDP-Bundesvorstand: Die Liberalen unter dem Vorsitz von Theodor Heuss und Franz Blücher: Sitzungsprotokolle 1949–1954*, half-vol. 1: *1.-26. Sitzung 1949–1952*, ed. Udo Wengst. Quellen zur Geschichte des Parlamentarismus und der politischen Parteien, Fourth Series: Deutschland seit 1945, ed. Karl Dietrich Bracher, Rudolf Morsey, and Hans-Peter Schwarz, vol. 7/I. Düsseldorf: Droste, 1990.

————. Bundesvorstand. *FDP-Bundesvorstand: Die Liberalen unter dem Vorsitz von Theodor Heuss und Franz Blücher: Sitzungsprotokolle 1949–1954*. Half-vol. 2: *27.-43. Sitzung 1953/54*, ed. Udo Wengst. Quellen zur Geschichte des Parlamentarismus und der politischen Parteien, Fourth Series: Deutschland seit 1945, ed. Karl Dietrich Bracher, Rudolf Morsey, and Hans-Peter Schwarz, vol. 7/I. Düsseldorf: Droste, 1990.

Galinski, Heinz. "New Beginning of Jewish Life in Berlin." Interview by Michael Brenner. In *After the Holocaust: Rebuilding Jewish Lives in Postwar Germany*, ed. Michael Brenner, trans. Barbara Harshav. Princeton: Princeton University Press, 1997.

Germany (East). *Gesetzblatt der Deutschen Demokratischen Republik: Jahrgang 1949*. Berlin: Deutscher Zentralverlag, 1949.

Germany (Territory under Allied Occupation, 1945–1955). Parlamentarischer Rat (1948–1949). CDU/CSU-Fraktion. *Die CDU/CSU im parlamentarischen Rat: Sitzungsprotokolle der Unionsfraktion 1948–1949*. Ed. Rainer Salzmann. Forschungen und Quellen zur Zeitgeschichte, ed. Klaus Grotto et al., vol. 2. Stuttgart: Klett-Cotta, 1981.

Germany (Territory under Allied Occupation, 1945–1955: Russian Zone). Deutsche Justizverwaltung der sowjetischen Besatzungszone in Deutschland. *Zentralverordnungsblatt. Amtliches Organ der Deutschen Wirtschaftskommission und ihrer Hauptverwaltungen, sowie der Deutschen Verwaltungen für Gesundheitswesen, Inneres, Justiz u. Volksbildung*. Berlin: Deutscher Zentralverlag, 1949.

Germany (West). Bundesregierung. *Die Kabinettsprotokolle der Bundesregierung*. Ed. Hans Booms. Vol. 2: *1950*, ed. Ulrich Enders and Konrad Reiser. Boppard am Rhein: Harald Boldt, 1984.

————. Bundesregierung. *Die Kabinettsprotokolle der Bundesregierung*. Ed. Hans Booms. Vol. 4: *1951*, ed. Ursula Hüllbüsch. Boppard am Rhein: Harald Boldt, 1988.

————. Bundesregierung. *Die Kabinettsprotokolle der Bundesregierung*. Ed. Hans Booms. Vol. 5: *1952*, ed. Kai von Jena. Boppard am Rhein: Harald Boldt, 1989.

————. Bundesregierung. *Die Kabinettsprotokolle der Bundesregierung*. Ed. Hans Booms. Vol. 6: *1953*, ed. Ulrich Enders and Konrad Reiser. Boppard am Rhein: Harald Boldt, 1989.

————. Bundestag. *Verhandlungen des Deutschen Bundestages, I. Wahlperiode 1949*. Vols. 6 and 15. Anlage Vols. 1, 7, 9, and 12. Bonn: Bonner Universitäts-Buchdruckerei, 1950–1953.

————. Bundestag. Fraktion der CDU/CSU. *Die CDU/CSU-Fraktion im Deutschen Bundestag: Sitzungsprotokolle 1949–1953*. Ed. Helge Heidemeyer. Quellen zur Geschichte des Parlamentarismus und der politischen Parteien, Fourth Series: Deutschland seit 1945, ed. Karl Dietrich Bracher, Rudolf Morsey, and Hans-Peter Schwarz, vol. 11/I. Düsseldorf: Droste, 1998.

————. Bundestag. Fraktion der SPD. *Die SPD-Fraktion im Deutschen Bundestag: Sitzungsprotokolle 1949–1957*, half-vol. 1: *1.-181. Sitzung 1949–1953*, ed. Petra Weber. Quellen zur Geschichte des Parlamentarismus und der politischen Parteien, Fourth Series: Deutschland seit 1945, ed. Karl Dietrich Bracher, Rudolf Morsey, and Hans-Peter Schwarz, vol. 8/I. Düsseldorf: Droste, 1993.

————. Bundestag. Fraktion der SPD. *Die SPD-Fraktion im Deutschen Bundestag: Sitzungsprotokolle 1949–1957*, half-vol. 2: *182–328. Sitzung 1953–1957*, ed. Petra Weber. Quellen zur Geschichte des Parlamentarismus und der politischen Parteien, Fourth Series: Deutschland seit 1945, ed. Karl Dietrich Bracher, Rudolf Morsey, and Hans-Peter Schwarz, vol. 8/I. Düsseldorf: Droste, 1993.

————. Presse- und Informationsamt der Bundesregierung. *Deutschland und das Judentum*. Bonn: Deutscher Bundes-Verlag, 1951.

Gerstenmaier, Eugen. *Streit und Friede hat seine Zeit. Ein Lebensbericht*. Frankfurt: Ullstein Verlag, 1981.

Goldmann, Nahum. "Adenauer und das Jüdische Volk." In *Konrad Adenauer und seine Zeit. Politik und Persönlichkeit des ersten Bundeskanzlers, Beiträge von Weg- und Zeitgenossen*, ed. Dieter Blumenwitz et al. Stuttgart: Deutsche Verlags-Anstalt, 1976.

————. *The Autobiography of Nahum Goldmann: Sixty Years of Jewish Life*. Trans. Helen Sebba. New York: Holt, Rinehart and Winston, 1969.

————. *The Jewish Paradox*. Trans. Steve Cox. London: Weidenfeld and Nicolson, 1978.

————. *Mein Leben als deutscher Jude*. Munich: Albert Langen-Georg Müller, 1980.

Heuss, Theodor. *An und über Juden. Aus Schriften und Reden (1906–1963).* Ed. Hans Lamm, Foreword by Karl Marx. Düsseldorf: Econ, 1964.

———. *Die grossen Reden. Der Staatsmann.* Tübingen: Rainer Wunderlich, 1965.

———. *Hitlers Weg. Eine historisch-politische Studie über den Nationalsozialismus.* Stuttgart: Union Deutsche Verlagsgesellschaft, 1932.

———. *Die Machtergreifung und das Ermächtigungsgesetz. Zwei nachgelassene Kapitel der Erinnerungen, 1905–1933.* Ed. Eberhard Pikart. Tübingen: Rainer Wunderlich, 1967.

Jelinek, Yeshayahu, ed. *Zwischen Moral und Realpolitik. Deutsch-israelische Beziehungen 1945–1965, Eine Dokumentensammlung.* Gerlingen: Bleicher, 1997.

Küster, Otto. "Deutsche Wiedergutmachung, betrachtet Ende 1957." In *Judentum: Schicksal, Wesen und Gegenwart,* ed. Franz Böhm and Walter Dirks. Vol. 2. Wiesbaden: Franz Steiner, 1965.

Levinson. Nathan Peter. "The Functions of a Rabbi in Postwar Germany." Interview by Michael Brenner. In *After the Holocaust: Rebuilding Jewish Lives in Postwar Germany,* ed. Michael Brenner, trans. Barbara Harshav. Princeton: Princeton University Press, 1997.

Marx, Karl. "Zur Judenfrage." In *Deutsch-französische Jahrbücher,* ed. Arnold Runde and Karl Marx. Paris: Im Bureau der Jahrbücher, 1844.

Marx, Lilli. "Renewal of the German-Jewish Press." Interview by Michael Brenner. In *After the Holocaust: Rebuilding Jewish Lives in Postwar Germany,* ed. Michael Brenner, trans. Barbara Harshav. Princeton: Princeton University Press, 1997.

Mende, Erich. *Die FDP: Daten, Fakten, Hintergründe.* Stuttgart: Seewald, 1972.

Office of Adviser on Jewish Affairs, ed. *Conference on "The Future of the Jews in Germany."* Heidelberg: Office of Adviser on Jewish Affairs, [1949].

Office of Military Government of the United States (OMGUS). *Public Opinion in Occupied Germany: The OMGUS Surveys, 1945–1949.* Ed. Anna J. Merritt and Richard L. Merritt. Urbana: University of Illinois, 1970.

Office of the U.S. High Commissioner for Germany. *Report on Germany: Sept. 21, 1949–July 31, 1952.* Cologne: Greven and Bechtold, 1952.

Patton, George S. *The Patton Papers, 1940–1945.* Ed. Martin Blumenson. Vol. 2. Boston: Houghton Mifflin, 1974.

Putzrath, Heinz. "Brief an Stefan Blass, Sao Paulo." In *Heinz Putzrath – Gegen Nationalsozialismus, Für soziale Demokratie. Skizzen zu Leben und Wirken,* ed. Johannes Rau and Bernd Faulenbach. Essen: Klartext, 1997.

———. "Heinz Putzrath über Restauration und Neubeginn." In *Heinz Putzrath – Gegen Nationalsozialismus, Für soziale Demokratie. Skizzen zu Leben und Wirken,* ed. Johannes Rau and Bernd Faulenbach. Essen: Klartext, 1997.

Reuter, Ernst. *Aus Reden und Schriften.* Ed. Hans E. Hirschfeld and Hans J. Reichhardt. Berlin: Colloquium, [1963].

———. *Schriften, Reden.* Ed. Hans E. Hirschfeld and Hans J. Reichhardt. Vol. 4: *Reden, Artikel, Briefe, 1949 bis 1953,* ed. Hans J. Reichhardt. Berlin: Propyläen, 1975.

Ruhm von Oppen, Beate, ed. *Documents on Germany under Occupation, 1949–1954.* London: Oxford Univeristy Press and Geoffrey Cumberlege, 1955.

Schmid, Carlo. *Erinnerungen.* Bern: Scherz, 1979.

Schoeps, Julius. "Never Forget Thy People Israel! Autobiographical Remarks." In *Speaking Out: Jewish Voices from United Germany,* ed. Susan Stern. Chicago: edition q, 1995.

Schumacher, Kurt. *Grundsätze sozialistischer Politik.* Hamburg: Phoenix, 1946.

———. *Reden – Schriften – Korrespondenzen 1945–1952.* Ed. Willy Albrecht. Berlin: J. H. W. Dietz Nachfolger, 1985.

Shinnar, Felix. *Bericht eines Beauftragten: Die deutsch-israelischen Beziehungen 1951–1966.* Tübingen: Rainer Wunderlich, 1967.

Slánská, Josefa. *Report on My Husband.* Trans. Edith Pargeter. New York: Atheneum, 1969.

Sozialistische Einheitspartei Deutschlands (Zentralkomitee der SED). *Dokumente der Sozialistischen Einheitspartei Deutschlands.* Vol. 4. Berlin: Dietz, 1954.

State of Israel. Israel State Archives. *Documents on the Foreign Policy of Israel,* vol. 6: *1951,* companion volume, ed. Yemima Rosenthal. Jerusalem: Government Printer, 1991.

Vogel, Rolf, ed. *Der deutsch-israelische Dialog: Dokumentation eines erregenden Kapitels deutscher Außenpolitik.* Part 1: *Politik,* vol 1. Munich: K. G. Saur, 1987.

VVN-Verlag. *Befreiungstag Buchenwald: 9. bis 11. April 1948.* Berlin: VVN-Verlag, 1948.

Weizmann Institute of Science. *Konrad Adenauer Ehrenmitglied des Weizmann-Instituts: Ein denkwürdiger Tag in Rehovoth.* Zurich: European Committee of the Weizmann Institute of Science Rehovoth, [1966].

Wollheim, Norbert. "Jewish Autonomy in the British Zone." Interview by Michael Brenner. In *After the Holocaust: Rebuilding Jewish Lives in Postwar Germany,* ed. Michael Brenner, trans. Barbara Harshav. Princeton: Princeton University Press, 1997.

World Jewish Congress. *Resolutions Adopted by the Second Plenary Assembly of the World Jewish Congress, Montreaux, Switzerland, June 27th–July 6th, 1948.* London: Odhams Press, [1948].

———. *Unity in Dispersion: A History of the World Jewish Congress,* 2nd ed. Foreword by A. Leon Kubowitzki. New York: Institute of Jewish Affairs of the World Jewish Congress, 1948.

PRIMARY SOURCE PERIODICALS

Jerusalem Post, Jerusalem
Jüdisches Gemeindeblatt für die Nord-Rheinprovinz und Westfalen, Düsseldorf (later called *Jüdisches Gemeindeblatt für die britische Zone, Jüdisches Gemeindeblatt: Die Zeitung der Juden in Deutschland,* and *Allgemeine Wochenzeitung der Juden in Deutschland*)
Jüdischer Presse Dienst, Düsseldorf
Neuer Vorwärts, Hanover
New York Times, New York
Der Weg, Berlin

SECONDARY LITERATURE

Ahonen, Pertti Tapio. "The Expellee Organizations and West German Ostpolitik, 1949–1969." Ph.D. diss., Yale University, 1999.

Albrecht, Willy, "Ein Wegbereiter: Jakob Altmaier und das Luxemburger Abkommen." In *Wiedergutmachung in der Bundesrepublik Deutschland,* ed. Ludolf Herbst and Constantin Goschler. Munich: R. Oldenbourg, 1989.

———. "Jeanette Wolff – Jakob Altmaier – Peter Blachstein. Die drei Abgeordneten jüdischer Herkunft des Deutschen Bundestages in den 50er und zu Beginn der 60er Jahre." In *Menora. Jahrbuch für deutsch-jüdische Geschichte* 6 (1995), ed. Julius H. Schoeps et al. Munich: Piper, 1995.

Aschheim, Steven E. *Brothers and Strangers: The East European Jew in German and German Jewish Consciousness, 1800–1923.* Madison: University of Wisconsin Press, 1982.

Assmann Aleida, and Ute Frevert. *Geschichtsvergessenheit/Geschichtsversessenheit. Vom Umgang mit deutschen Vergangenheiten nach 1945.* Stuttgart: Deutsche Verlags-Anstalt, 1999.

Balabkins, Nicholas. *West German Reparations to Israel.* New Brunswick, 1971.

Bark, Dennis L., and David R. Gress. *A History of West Germany,* vol. 1: *From Shadow to Substance, 1945–1963,* 2nd ed. Oxford: Blackwell, 1993.

Bauer, Yehuda. *Flight and Rescue: Brichah.* New York: Random House 1970.

———. *Out of the Ashes: The Impact of American Jewry on Post-Holocaust Europe.* Oxford: Pergamon, 1989.

Bauer-Hack, Susanne. *Die jüdische Wochenzeitung Aufbau und die Wiedergutmachung.* Düsseldorf: Droste, 1994.

Baumel, Judith. *Kibbutz Buchenwald: Survivors and Pioneers.* New Brunswick: Rutgers University Press, 1997.

Becker, Winfried. *CDU und CSU 1945–1950. Vorläufer, Gründung und regionale Entwicklung bis zum Entstehen der CDU-Bundespartei.* Mainz: v. Hase und Koehler, 1987.

Benz, Wolfgang, ed. *Zwischen Antisemitismus und Philosemitismus. Juden in der Bundesrepublik.* Berlin: Metropol, 1991.

Berthold-Hilpert, Monika. "Die frühe Nachkriegsgeschichte der jüdischen Gemeinde Fürth (1945–1954)." In *Menora. Jahrbuch für deutsch-jüdische Geschichte* 9 (1998), ed. Julius H. Schoeps. Munich: Piper, 1998.

―――. "Jüdisches Leben in Franken nach 1945 am Beispiel der Gemeinde Fürth." In *Jüdisches Leben in Franken,* ed. Gunnar Och and Hartmut Bobzin. Würzburg: Ergon, 2002.

Bloch, Sam E. *Holocaust and Rebirth: Bergen-Belsen 1945–1965.* New York and Tel Aviv: Bergen Belsen Memorial Press of the World Federation of Bergen Belsen Associations, 1965.

Broszat, Martin, ed. *Zäsuren nach 1945. Essays zur Periodisierung der deutschen Nachkriegsgeschichte.* Munich: R. Oldenbourg, 1990.

Bodemann, Y. Michal. *Gedächtnistheater. Die jüdische Gemeinschaft und ihre deutsche Erfindung.* Hamburg: Rotbuch, 1996.

―――. "'How can one stand to live there as a Jew...': Paradoxes of Jewish Existence in Germany." In *Jews, Germans, Memory: Reconstructions of Jewish Life in Germany,* ed. Y. Michal Bodemann. Ann Arbor: University of Michigan Press, 1996.

―――. "'Ich verlasse dieses Land mit Verbitterung, doch vor keinem Volke darf man die Fenseterläden zuschlagen...': Zur Abschiedspredigt von Rabbiner Dr. Wilhelm Weinberg (1901–1976) in Frankfurt/ Main, am 11. November 1951." In *Menora. Jahrbuch für deutsch-jüdische Geschichte* 6 (1995), ed. Julius H. Schoeps et al. Munich: Piper, 1995.

―――. "Staat und Ethnizität: Der Aufbau der jüdischen Gemeinden im Kalten Krieg." In *Jüdisches Leben in Deutschland seit 1945,* ed. Micha Brumlik et al. Frankfurt: Jüdischer Verlag bei Athenäum, 1986.

Borneman, John, and Jeffrey Peck. *Sojourners: The Return of German Jews and the Question of Identity.* Lincoln: University of Nebraska, 1995.

Brandes, Mechthild. Introduction to *Bundespräsidialamt/Amtszeit Prof. Dr. Theodor Heuss Bestand B 122. Findbücher zu Beständen des Bundesarchivs.* Vol. 38. Koblenz: Bundesarchiv Koblenz, 1990.

Brenner, Michael. *After the Holocaust: Rebuilding Jewish Lives in Postwar Germany.* Trans. Barabra Harshav. Princeton: Princeton University Press, 1997.

―――. "East European and German Jews in Postwar Germany, 1945–1950." In *Germans, Memory: Reconstructions of Jewish Life in Germany,* ed. Y. Michal Bodemann. Ann Arbor: University of Michigan Press, 1996.

Broder, Henryk. *Der Ewige Antisemit. Über Sinn und Funktion eines beständigen Gefühls.* Frankfurt: Fischer, 1986.

Broder, Henryk, and Michel R. Lang, eds. *Fremd im eigenen Land. Juden in der Bundesrepublik.* Frankfurt: Fischer, 1979.

Brumlik, Micha. "Zur Identität der zweiten Generation deutscher Juden nach der Shoah in der Bundesrepublik." In *Jüdisches Leben in*

Deutschland seit 1945, ed. Micha Brumlik et al. Frankfurt: Jüdischer Verlag bei Athenäum, 1986.

———, ed. *Zuhause, keine Heimat? Junge Juden und ihre Zukunft in Deutschland*. Gerlingen: Bleicher, 1998.

Brumlik, Micha et al., eds. *Jüdisches Leben in Deutschland seit 1945*. Frankfurt: Jüdischer Verlag bei Athenäum, 1986.

Bubis, Ignatz. *Juden in Deutschland*. Berlin: Aufbau, 1996.

Bullock, Allan. *Ernest Bevin: Foreign Minister, 1945–1951*. London: William Heinemann, 1983.

Bundeszentrale für politische Bildung. *Deutsche Juden – Juden in Deutschland*. Bonn: Bundeszentrale für politische Bildung, [1991].

Burgbauer, Erica. *Zwischen Erinnerung und Verdrängung – Juden in Deutschland nach 1945*. Reinbeck bei Hamburg: Rowohlt, 1993.

Büttner, Ursula. "Not der Befreiung: Die Situation der deutschen Juden in der britischen Besatzungszone, 1945–1948." In *Das Unrechtsregime. Internationale Forschung über den Nationalsozialisimus.* Vol. 2, ed. Ursula Büttner. Hamburg: Hans Christians, 1986.

Chernow, Ron. *The Warburgs: The Twentieth Century Odyssey of a Remarkable Jewish Family*. New York: Random House, 1993.

Childs, David. *From Schumacher to Brandt: The Story of German Socialism, 1945–1965*. Oxford: Pergamon, 1966.

Cohn, Michael. *The Jews in Germany, 1945–1993: The Building of a Minority*. Westport: Praeger, 1994.

Confino, Alon, and Peter Fritzsche, eds. *The Work of Memory: New Directions in the Study of German Society and Culture*. Urbana: University of Illinois Press, 2002.

Czichon, Eberhard. *Der Bankier und die Macht: Hermann Josef Abs in der deutschen Politik*. Cologne: Pahl-Rugenstein, 1970.

———. *Hermann Josef Abs. Porträt eines Kreuzritters des Kapitals*. Berlin: Union, 1969.

Dawidowicz, Lucy. *The War against the Jews, 1933–1945*. New York: Holt, Rinehart and Winston, 1975.

Deutschkron, Inge. *Israel und die Deutschen. Das besondere Verhältnis*. Cologne: Wissenschaft und Politik, 1983.

———. "Das Verhalten der bundesrepublikanischen Politiker ist eine Schweinerei gegenüber NS-Opfern." In *Blick zurück ohne Haß: Juden aus Israel erinnern sich an Deutschland*, ed. Dieter Bednarz and Michael Lüders. Cologne: Bund, 1981.

Diehl, James H. *The Thanks for the Fatherland: German Veterans after the Second World War*. Chapel Hill: University of North Carolina Press, 1993.

Dinnerstein, Leonard. *America and the Survivors of the Holocaust*. New York: Columbia University Press, 1982.

Dubiel, Helmut. *Niemand ist frei von der Geschichte. Die nationalsozialistische Herrschaft in den Debatten des Deutschen Bundestages*. Munich: Carl Hanser, 1999.

Dunker, Ulrich. *Der Reichsbund jüdischer Frontsoldaten 1919–1938: Geschichte eines jüdischen Abwehrvereins.* Düsseldorf: Droste, 1977.

Eder, Angelika, "Kultur und Kulturveranstaltungen in den jüdischen DP-Lagern." In *Leben im Land der Täter: Juden in Nachkriegsdeutschland (1945–1952),* ed. Julius H. Schoeps. Berlin: Jüdische Verlagsanstalt, 2001.

Edinger, Lewis. *Kurt Schumacher: A Study in Personality and Political Behavior.* Stanford: Stanford University Press, 1965.

Epstein, Catherine. *The Last Revolutionaries: German Communists and Their Century.* Cambridge: Harvard University Press, 2003.

Faulenbach, Bernd, ed., *"Habt den Mut zu menschlichem Tun." Die Jüdin und Demokratin Jeanette Wolff in ihrer Zeit (1888–1976).* Essen: Klartext, 2002.

Fliszar, Fritz. "Mit der FDP regieren: Ein Gespräch mit Erich Mende." In *Verantwortung für die Freiheit, 40 Jahre F. D. P.,* ed. Wolfgang Mischnik. Stuttgart: Deutsche Verlags-Anstalt, 1989.

Foschepoth, Josef. "German Reaction to Defeat and Occupation." In *West Germany under Construction: Politics, Society, and Culture in the Adenauer Era,* ed. Robert Moeller. Ann Arbor: University of Michigan Press, 1997.

————. *Im Schatten der Vergangenheit. Die Anfänge der Gesellschaften für Christlich-Jüdische Zusammenarbeit.* Göttingen: Vandenhoeck und Ruprecht, 1993.

Fox, Thomas C. *Stated Memory: East Germany and the Holocaust.* Rochester: Camden House, 1999.

Frei, Norbert. *Vergangenheitspolitik. Die Anfänge der Bundesrepublik und die NS-Vergangenheit.* Munich: Beck, 1996.

————, ed. *Karrieren im Zwielicht. Hitlers Eliten nach 1945.* Frankfurt: Campus, 2001.

Friedrich, Jörg. *Der Brand. Deutschland im Bombenkrieg 1940–1945.* Munich: Propyläen, 2002.

Fritz Bauer Institut. *Überlebt und unterwegs. Jüdische Displaced Persons in Nachkriegsdeutschland.* Frankfurt: Campus, 1997.

Frye, Bruce. *Liberal Democrats in the Weimar Republic: The History of the German Democratic Party and the German State Party.* Carbondale: Southern Illinois University Press, 1985.

Fülberth, Georg. *KPD und DKP 1945–1990. Zwei kommunistische Parteien in der vierten Periode kapitalisticher Entwicklung.* Heilbronn: Distel, 1990.

Fulbrook, Mary. *Anatomy of a Dictatorship: Inside the GDR, 1949–1969.* Oxford: Oxford University Press, 1995.

Füllgrabe, Jörg. "'Ich fühle mich so deutsch wie früher' – Die Briefe Dr. Siegfried Guggenheims an Dr. Karl Kanka 1947–1960." In *Zur Geschichte der Juden in Offenbach am Main,* ed. Magistrat der Stadt Offenbach am Main. Vol. 3: *Werden und Vergehen – Aufstieg, Buchdruck, Friedhöfe, Erinnerungen.* Offenbach: Beltz, 1994.

Ganther, Heinz, ed. *Die Juden in Deutschland: Ein Almanach 1951/1952.* Hamburg: Gala, 1951.

————. *Die Juden in Deutschland: Ein Almanach 1951/52–5712, 1958/59–5719.* Hamburg: Gala, [1959].

Gardner Feldman, Lily. *The Special Relationship between West Germany and Israel.* Boston: George Allen and Unwin, 1984.

Gärtner, Marcel W., Hans Lamm, and E. G. Löwenthal. *Vom Schicksal Geprägt. Freundesgabe zum 60. Geburtstag von Karl Marx.* Düsseldorf, 1957.

Gay, Ruth. *Safe among the Germans: Liberated Jews after World War II.* New Haven: Yale University Press, 2002.

Geis, Jael. *Übrig sein. Leben "danach": Juden deutscher Herkunft in der britischen und amerikanischen Zone Deutschlands 1945–1949.* Berlin: Philo, 2000.

Geller, Jay Howard. "Das Bild Konrad Adenauers vom Judentum und seine Beziehungen zu Vertretern jüdischer Organisationen nach 1945." In *Adenauer, Israel und das Judentum,* ed. Hanns Jürgen Küsters. Bonn: Bouvier, 2004.

————. "Representing Jewry in East Germany, 1945–1953: Between Advocacy and Accommodation." In Leo Baeck Institute, *Year Book* 47 (2002), ed. J. A. S. Grenville. Oxford: Berghahn, 2002.

Gershon, Karen, ed. *Postscript: A Collective Account of the Lives of Jews in West Germany since the Second World War.* London: Victor Gollancz, 1969.

Gimbel, John. *The American Occupation of Germany: Politics and the Military, 1945–1949.* Stanford: Stanford University Press, 1968.

Ginsburg, Hans Jakob. "Politik danach – Jüdische Interessenvertretung in der Bundesrepublik." In *Jüdisches Leben in Deutschland seit 1945,* ed. Micha Brumlik et al. Frankfurt: Jüdischer Verlag bei Athenäum, 1986.

Ginzel, Günter, ed. *Der Anfang nach dem Ende. Jüdisches Leben in Deutschland 1945 bis heute.* Düsseldorf: Droste, 1996.

Giordano, Ralph. *Narben, Spuren, Zeugen. 15 Jahre Allgemeine Wochenzeitung der Juden in Deutschland.* Düsseldorf: Verlag Allgemeine Wochenzeitung der Juden in Deutschland, 1961.

————, ed. *Deutschland und Israel. Solidarität in der Bewährung.* Gerlingen: Bleicher, 1992.

Goldhagen, Daniel Jonah. *Hitlers willige Vollstrecker. Ganz gewöhnliche Deutsche und der Holocaust.* Trans. Klaus Kochmann. Munich: Siedler, 1996.

Gorschenek, Günter, and Stephan Reimers, eds. *Offene Wunden – brennende Fragen: Juden in Deutschland 1938 bis heute.* Frankfurt: Knecht, 1989.

Goschler, Constantin. "Der Fall Philipp Auerbach. Wiedergutmachung in Bayern." In *Wiedergutmachung in der Bundesrepublik Deutschland,* ed. Ludolf Herbst and Constantin Goschler. Munich: R. Oldenbourg, 1989.

————. *Wiedergutmachung. Westdeutschland und die Verfolgten des National-sozialismus (1945–1954).* Munich: R. Oldenbourg, 1992.

Goschler, Constantin, and Jürgen Lillteicher, eds., *"Arisierung" und Restitution. Die Rückerstattung jüdischen Eigentums in Deutschland und Österreich nach 1945 und 1989.* Göttingen: Wallstein, 2002.

Granata, Cora Ann. "Celebration and suspicion: Sorbs and Jews in the Soviet Occupied Zone and German Democratic Republic, 1945–1989." Ph.D. diss., University of North Carolina, Chapel Hill, 2001.

Grass, Günter. *Crabwalk.* Trans. Krishna Winston. New York: Harcourt, 2003.

Gray, William Glenn. *Germany's Cold War: The Global Campaign to Isolate East Germany, 1949–1969.* Chapel Hill: University of North Carolina Press, 2003.

Groehler, Olaf. "Antifaschismus und jüdische Problematik in der SBZ und der frühen DDR." In Olaf Groehler and Mario Keßler, *Die SED-Politik, der Antifaschismus und die Juden in der SBZ und frühen DDR.* Berlin: Gesellschaftswissenschaftliches Forum, 1995.

Grossman, Kurt Richard. *Germany's Moral Debt: The German-Israeli Agreement.* Washington: Public Affairs Press, 1954.

――――. *The Jewish DP Problem: Its Origin, Scope, and Liquidation.* New York: Institute of Jewish Affairs of the WJC, 1951.

Grossmann, Atina. *Victims, Victors, and Survivors: Germans, Allies, and Jews in Occupied Postwar Germany, 1945–1950.* Princeton: Princeton University Press, forthcoming.

――――. "Victims, Villains, and Survivors: Gendered Perceptions and Self-Perceptions of Jewish Displaced Persons in Occupied Postwar Germany." *Journal of the History of Sexuality* 11, nos. 1/2 (January/April 2002).

Gruenewald, Max. "The Beginning of the 'Reichsvertretung.'" In Leo Baeck Institute, *Year Book* 1 (1956), ed. Robert Weltsch. London: East and West Library, 1956.

Gurland, A. R. L. *Die CDU/CSU. Ursprünge und Entwicklung bis 1963*, ed. Dieter Emig. Frankfurt: Europäische Verlagsanstalt, 1980.

Hamburger, Ernest, and Peter Pulzer. "Jews as Voters in the Weimar Republic." In Leo Baeck Institute, *Year Book* 30 (1985), ed. Arnold Paucker and Robert Weltsch. London: Secker and Warburg, 1985.

Hamburger Institut für Sozialforschung. *Vernichtungskrieg. Verbrechen der Wehrmacht 1941 bis 1944. Ausstellungskatalog.* Ed. Hannes Heer and Birgit Otte. Hamburg: Hamburger Edition, 1996.

Hansen, Niels. *Aus dem Schatten der Katastrophe. Die deutsch-israelischen Beziehungen in der Ära Konrad Adenauer und David Ben Gurion.* Düsseldorf: Droste, 2002.

Hartewig, Karin. *Zurückgekehrt. Die Geschichte der jüdischen Kommunisten in der DDR.* Cologne: Böhlau, 2000.

Haury, Thomas. *Antisemitismus von links. Kommunistische Ideologie, Nationalismus und Antizionismus in der frühen DDR.* Hamburg: Hamburger Edition, 2002.

Hehl, Ulrich von. "Der Beamte im Reichsministerium: Die Beurteilung Globkes in der Diskussion der Nachkriegszeit, Eine Dokumentation." In *Der Staatssekretär Adenauers. Persönlichkiet und politisches Wirken Hans Globkes*, ed. Klaus Gotto. Stuttgart: Klett-Cotta, 1980.

Heidenhammer, Arnold. *Adenauer and the CDU: The Rise of the Leader and the Integration of the Party.* The Hague: Martinus Nijhoff, 1960.

Heil, Johannes, and Rainer Erb, eds. *Geschichtswissenschaft und Öffentlichkeit. Der Streit um Daniel J. Goldhagen.* Frankfurt: Fischer, 1998.

Hein, Dieter. "Der Weg nach Heppenheim 1945–1948." In *Verantwortung für die Freiheit, 40 Jahre F. D. P.*, ed. Wolfgang Mischnik. Stuttgart: Deutsche Verlags-Anstalt, 1989.

Heineman, Elizabeth D. *What Difference Does a Husband Make?: Women and Marital Status in Nazi and Postwar Germany.* Berkeley: University of California Press, 1999.

Hellmich, Wolfgang. "Peter Blachstein: Zur Rekonstruktion des politischen Lebensweges eines Linkssozialisten von der Weimarer Republik bis zum Wiedereintritt in die SPD 1947/48." Staatsexamen-Hausarbeit, Universtiät Münster, 1986.

Henke, Hans-Gerd. *Der "Jude" als Kollektivsymbol in der deutschen Sozialdemokratie 1890–1914.* Mainz: Decaton, 1994.

Henzler, Christoph. *Fritz Schäffer (1945-1967): Eine biographische Studie zum ersten bayerischen Nachkriegs-Ministerpräsidenten und ersten Finanzminister der Bundesrepublik Deutschland.* Munich: Hans-Seidel-Stiftung, 1994.

Herf, Jeffrey. *Divided Memory: The Nazi Past in the Two Germanys.* Cambridge: Harvard University Press, 1997.

Hildesheimer, Esriel. *Jüdische Selbstverwaltung unter dem NS-Regime. Der Existenzkampf der Reichsvertretung und Reichsvereinigung der Juden in Deutschland.* Tübingen: Mohr, 1994.

Hiroszowicz, Lukasz. *The Third Reich and the Arab Near East.* London: Routledge, 1966.

Hoffmann, Christhard, Werner Bergmann, and Helmut Walser Smith, eds. *Exclusionary Violence: Antisemitic Riots in Modern Germany.* Ann Arbor: University of Michigan Press, 2002.

Hughes, Michael L. *Shouldering the Burdens of Defeat: West Germany and the Reconstruction of Social Justice.* Chapel Hill: University of North Carolina Press, 1999.

Huhn, Rudolf. "Die Wiedergutmachungsverhandlungen in Wassenaar." In *Wiedergutmachung in der Bundesrepublik Deutschland*, ed. Ludolf Herbst and Constantin Goschler. Munich: R. Oldenbourg, 1989.

Hünseler, Peter. *Die außenpolitischen Beziehungen der Bundesrepublik Deutschland zu den arabischen Staaten von 1949–1980.* Frankfurt: Peter Lang, 1990.

Illichmann, Jutta. *Die DDR und die Juden: Die deutschlandpolitische Instrumentalisierung von Juden und Judentum durch die Partei- und Staatsführung der SBZ/DDR von 1945 bis 1990.* Frankfurt: Peter Lang, 1997.

Jacobmeyer, Wolfgang. "Jüdische Überlebende als 'Displaced Persons.' Untersuchungen zur Besatzungspolitik in den deutschen Westzonen und zur Zuwanderung osteuropäischer Juden 1945–1947." *Geschichte und Gesellschaft* 9, no. 3 (1983).

———. *Vom Zwangsarbeiter zum Heimatlosen Ausländer. Die Displaced Persons in Westdeutschland 1945–1951.* Göttingen: Vandenhoeck und Ruprecht, 1985.

Jarausch, Konrad H., and Michael Geyer. *Shattered Past: Reconstructing German Histories.* Princeton: Princeton University Press, 2003.

Jelinek, Yeshayahu. "Israel und die Anfänge der Shilumim." In *Wiedergutmachung in der Bundesrepublik Deutschland,* ed. Ludolf Herbst and Constantin Goschler. Munich: R. Oldenbourg, 1989.

———. "Konrad Adenauer and the State of Israel: Between Friendship and Realpolitik, 1953–1963." *Orient: Deutsche Zeitschrift für Politik und Wirtschaft des Orients* 43, no. 1 (March 2002).

———. "Like an Oasis in the Desert: The Israeli Consulate in Munich, 1948–1953." *Studies in Zionism* 9, no. 1 (spring 1988).

———. "Political Acumen, Altruism, Foreign Pressure or Moral Debt: Konrad Adenauer and the Shilumim." *Tel Aviver Jahrbuch für Deutsche Geschichte* 19 (1990), ed. Shulamit Volkov and Frank Stern. Gerlingen: Bleicher, 1990.

Jena, Kai von. "Versöhnung mit Israel? Die deutsch-israelische Verhandlungen bis zum Wiedergutmachungsabkommen von 1952." *Vierteljahreshefte für Zeitgeschichte* 34, no. 4 (October 1986).

Johr, Barbara. "Die Jüdische Gemeinde Bremen – Neugründung und Wiederaufbau 1945 bis 1961." *Arbeiterbewegung und Sozialgeschichte. Zeitschrift für die Regionalgeschichte Bremens im 19. und 20. Jahrhundert* 7 (July 2001).

Kaack, Heino. "Die FDP im politischen System der Bundesrepublik Deutschland." In *Verantwortung für die Freiheit, 40 Jahre F. D. P.,* ed. Wolfgang Mischnik. Stuttgart: Deutsche Verlags-Anstalt, 1989.

Kagan, Saul. "A Participant's Response." In *Holocaust and Shilumim: The Policy of Wiedergutmachung in the Early 1950s,* ed. Axel Frohn. German Historical Institute Occasional Paper no. 2. Washington: German Historical Institute, 1991.

Kaltefleiter, Werner. *Wirtschaft und Politik in Deutschland. Konjunktur als Bestimmungsfaktor des Parteiensystems.* Cologne: Westdeutscher, 1966.

Katcher, Leo. *Post-Mortem: The Jews in Germany Today.* New York: Delacorte, 1968.

Kaufmann, Uri. *Jewish Life in Germany Today.* Trans. Susan Schwarz. Bonn: Inter Nationes, 1994.

Keßler, Mario. *Die SED und die Juden – zwischen Repression und Toleranz. Politische Entwicklungen bis 1967.* Berlin: Akademie, 1995.

Kleinmann, Hans-Otto. *Geschichte der CDU 1945–1982.* Ed. Günter Buchstab. Stuttgart: Deutsche Verlags-Anstalt, 1993.

Kloke, Martin. *Israel und die deutsche Linke. Zur Geschichte eines schwierigen Verhältnisses,* 2nd ed. Frankfurt: Haag und Herchen, 1994.

Königseder, Angelika. "Jüdische Displaced Persons in Berlin." In *Leben im Land der Täter: Juden in Nachkriegsdeutschland (1945–1952),* ed. Julius H. Schoeps. Berlin: Jüdische Verlagsanstalt, 2001.

Königseder, Angelika, and Juliane Wetzel. *Lebensmut im Wartesaal. Die jüdischen DPs (Displaced Persons) im Nachkriegsdeutschland.* Frankfurt: Fischer, 1994.

Koppelmann, Stefan. "Die Auerbach-Affäre." In *Leben im Land der Täter. Juden in Nachkriegsdeutschland (1945–1952),* ed. Julius H. Schoeps. Berlin: Jüdische Verlagsanstalt, 2001.

––––––. *Bedingungen jüdischen Lebens in der Bundesrepublik Deutschland.* Marburg: Remid, 1993.

Koshar, Rudy. *Germany's Transient Pasts: Preservation and National Memory in the Twentieth Century.* Chapel Hill: University of North Carolina Press, 1998.

Kraushaar, Wolfgang. "Die Affäre Auerbach. Zur Virulenz des Antisemitismus in den Gründerjahren der Bundesrepublik." In *Menora. Jahrbuch für deutsch-jüdische Geschichte* 6 (1995), ed. Julius H. Schoeps et al. Munich: Piper, 1995.

Kreikamp, Hans-Dieter. "Zur Entstehung des Entschädigungsgesetzes der amerikanischen Besatzungszone." In *Wiedergutmachung in der Bundesrepublik Deutschland,* ed. Ludolf Herbst and Constantin Goschler. Munich: R. Oldenbourg, 1989.

Kurlansky, Mark. *A Chosen Few: The Resurrection of European Jewry.* Reading, Mass.: Addison-Wesley, 1995.

Kusch, Katrin. "Diskussion nach den Referaten von Maxwell, Shafir und Hartwig." In *Kurt Schumacher als deutscher und europäischer Sozialist,* ed. Willy Albrecht. Bonn: Abteilung Politische Bildung der Friedrich-Ebert-Stiftung, 1988.

Lappin, Elena, ed. *Jewish Words, German Voices: Growing Up Jewish in Postwar Germany and Austria.* Trans. Krishna Winston. North Haven, Conn.: Catbird, 1994.

Lavsky, Hagit. *New Beginnings: Holocaust Survivors in Bergen-Belsen and the British Zone in Germany, 1945–1950.* Detroit: Wayne State University Press, 2002.

Lavy, George. *Germany and Israel: Moral Debt and National Interest.* London: Frank Cass, 1996.

Levy, Richard S. *The Downfall of the Anti-Semitic Political Parties in Imperial Germany.* New Haven: Yale University Press, 1975.

Lorenz, Ina. "Jüdischer Neubeginn im 'Land der Mörder'? Die Wiederanfänge der Hamburger Jüdischen Gemeinde in den Nachkriegsjahren." In *Leben im Land der Täter. Juden in Nachkriegsdeutschland (1945–1952),* ed. Julius H. Schoeps. Berlin: Jüdische Verlagsanstalt, 2001.

Major, Patrick. *The Death of the KPD: Communism and Anti-Communism in West Germany, 1945–1956.* Oxford: Clarendon, 1997.

Mankowitz, Zeev W. *Life between Memory and Hope: The Survivors of the Holocaust in Occupied Germany*. Cambridge: Cambridge University Press, 2002.

Maor, Harry. "Über den Wiederaufbau der jüdischen Gemeinden in Deutschland seit 1945." Dr.phil. diss., Universität Mainz, 1961.

Marcuse, Harold. *Legacies of Dachau: The Uses and Abuses of a Concentration Camp, 1933–2001*. Cambridge: Cambridge University Press; 2001.

Maurer, Trude. "Die Juden in der Weimarer Republik." In *Zerbrochene Geschichte. Leben und Selbstverständnis der Juden in Deutschland*, ed. Dirk Blasius and Dan Diner. Frankfurt: Fischer, 1991.

_____. *Ostjuden in Deutschland 1918–1933*. Hamburg: Hans Christians, 1986.

Mertens, Lothar. *Davidstern unter Hammer und Zirkel. Die Jüdischen Gemeinden in der SBZ/DDR und ihre Behandlung durch Partei und Staat, 1945–1990*. Hildesheim: Georg Olms, 1997.

_____. "Schwieriger Neubeginn. Die Jüdischen Gemeinden in der SBZ/DDR bis 1952/1953." In *Leben im Land der Täter. Juden in Nachkriegsdeutschland (1945–1952)*, ed. Julius H. Schoeps. Berlin: Jüdische Verlagsanstalt, 2001.

Meyer, Michael A., ed. *German-Jewish History in Modern Times*, vol. 2: *Emancipation and Acculturation 1780–1871*, by Michael Brenner, Stefi Jersch-Wenzel, and Michael A. Meyer. New York: Columbia University Press, 1997.

_____. *German-Jewish History in Modern Times*, vol. 3: *Integration in Dispute, 1871–1918*, by Steven Lowenstein, Paul Mendes-Flohr, Peter Pulzer, and Monika Richarz. New York: Columbia University Press, 1997.

_____. *German-Jewish History in Modern Times*, vol. 4: *Renewal and Destruction 1918–1945*, by Avraham Barkai and Paul Mendes-Flohr. New York: Columbia University Press, 1997.

Meyn, Hermann. *Die Deutsche Partei: Entwicklung und Problematik einer national-konservativen Rechtspartei nach 1945*. Düsseldorf: Droste, 1965.

Miquel, Marc von. "Juristen: Richter in eigener Sache." In *Karrieren im Zwielicht. Hitlers Eliten nach 1945*, ed. Norbert Frei. Frankfurt: Campus, 2001.

Mitchell, Maria. "Materialism and Secularism: CDU Politicians and National Socialism, 1945–1949." *Journal of Modern History* 67, no. 2 (June 1995).

Moeller, Robert G. *War Stories: The Search for Usable Past in the Federal Republic of Germany*. Berkeley: University of California Press, 2001.

_____. "What Has 'Coming to Terms with the Past' Meant in Post–World War II Germany? From History to Memory to the 'History of Memory.'" *Central European History* 35, no. 2 (June 2002).

_____, ed. *West Germany under Construction: Politics, Society, and Culture in the Adenauer Era*. Ann Arbor: University of Michigan Press, 1997.

Morris, Leslie, and Jack Zipes, eds. *Unlikely History: The Changing German-Jewish Symbiosis, 1945–2000*. New York: Palgrave, 2002.

Moß, Christoph. *Jakob Altmaier. Ein jüdischer Sozialdemokrat in Deutschland (1889–1963)*. Cologne: Bohlau, 2003.

———. "Jakob Altmaier, Jeanette Wolff, Peter Blachstein." M.A. thesis, Universität Duisburg, 1999.

Mosse, George. *German Jews beyond Judaism*. Bloomington: Indiana University Press, 1985.

Nachama, Andreas. "Der Mann in der Fasanenstraße." In *Aufbau nach dem Untergang. Deutsch-jüdische Geschichte nach 1945*, ed. Andreas Nachama and Julius H. Schoeps. Berlin: Argon, 1992.

Naimark, Norman. *The Russians in Germany: A History of the Soviet Zone of Occupation, 1945–1949*. Cambridge: Harvard University Press, 1995.

Neumann, Franz. *Block der Heimatvertriebenen und Entrechteten 1950–1960. Ein Beitrag zur Geschichte und Struktur einer politischen Interessenpartei*. Meisenheim: Anton Hain, 1968.

Niewyk, Donald L. *The Jews in Weimar Germany*. Baton Rouge: Louisiana State University Press, 1980.

———. *Socialist, Anti-Semite, and Jew: German Social Democracy Confronts the Problem of Anti-Semitism, 1918–1933*. Baton Rouge: Louisiana State University Press, 1971.

Offenberg, Ulrike, "Die jüdische Gemeinde zu Berlin 1945–1953." In *Leben im Land der Täter. Juden in Nachkriegsdeutschland (1945–1952)*, ed. Julius H. Schoeps. Berlin: Jüdische Verlagsanstalt, 2001.

———. *"Seid vorsichtig gegen die Machthaber." Die jüdischen Gemeinden in der SBZ und der DDR 1945 bis 1990*. Berlin: Aufbau, 1998.

Ostow, Robin. *Jews in Contemporary East Germany: The Children of Moses in the Land of Marx*. New York: St. Martin's, 1989.

———. *Jüdisches Leben in der DDR*. Frankfurt: Jüdischer Verlag, 1988.

Pease, Louis. "After the Holocaust: West Germany and Material Reparations to the Jews." Ph.D. diss., Florida State University, 1976.

Pross, Christian. *Paying for the Past: The Struggle over Reparations for Surviving Victims of the Nazi Terror*. Trans. Belinda Cooper. Baltimore: Johns Hopkins University Press, 1998.

Quast, Anke. *Nach der Befreiung. Jüdische Gemeinden in Niedersachsen seit 1945, das Beispiel Hannover*. Göttingen: Wallenstein Verlag, 2001.

Rabinbach, Anson, and Jack Zipes, eds. *Germans and Jews since the Holocaust: The Changing Situation in West Germany*. New York: Holmes and Meier, 1986.

Rapaport, Lynn. *Jews in Germany after the Holocaust: Memory, Identity and Jewish-German Relations*. Cambridge: Cambridge University Press, 1997.

Rau, Johannes, and Bernd Faulenbach, eds. *Heinz Putzrath – Gegen Nationalsozialismus, Für soziale Demokratie. Skizzen zu Leben und Wirken*. Essen: Klartext, 1997.

Reilly, Joanne. *Belsen: The Liberation of a Concentration Camp.* London: Routledge, 1998.

Reuter, Elke, and Detlef Hansel. *Das kurze Leben der VVN von 1947 bis 1953. Die Geschichte der Vereinigung der Verfolgten des Naziregimes in der sowjetischen Besatzungszone und in der DDR.* Berlin: edition ost, 1997.

Richter, Michael. *Die Ost-CDU 1948–1952. Zwischen Widerstand und Gleichschaltung.* Düsseldorf: Droste, 1990.

Rogers, Daniel E. "Transforming the German Party System: The United States and the Origins of Political Moderation, 1945–1949." *Journal of Modern History* 65, no. 3 (September 1993).

Ross, Ronald. *Beleaguered Tower: The Dilemma of Political Catholicism in Wilhelmine Germany.* Notre Dame: University of Notre Dame Press, 1973.

Rütten, Theo. "Von der Plattform-Partei zur Partei des liberalen Programms 1949–1957." In *Verantwortung für die Freiheit, 40 Jahre F. D. P.,* edited by Wolfgang Mischnik. Stuttgart: Deutsche Verlags-Anstalt, 1989.

Sagi, Nana. *German Reparations: A History of the Negotiations.* Trans. Dafna Alon. New York: St. Martin's, 1986.

––––––. "Die Rolle der jüdischen Organisationen in den USA und die Claims Conference." In *Wiedergutmachung in der Bundesrepublik Deutschland,* ed. Ludolf Herbst and Constantin Goschler. Munich: R. Oldenbourg, 1989.

Schiele, Werner. *An der Front der Freiheit. Jakob Altmaiers Kampf für die Demokratie.* Flörsheim am Main: Magistrat der Stadt Flörsheim am Main, 1993.

Schissler, Hanna, ed. *The Miracle Years: A Cultural History of West Germany, 1949–1968.* Princeton: Princeton University Press, 2001.

Scholem, Gershom. "Wider den Mythos vom deutsch-jüdischen 'Gespräch.'" In *Auf gespaltenem Pfad. Zum neunzigsten Geburtstag von Margarete Susman,* ed. Manfred Schlösser. Darmstadt: Erato, 1964.

Schreiber, Ruth. "New Jewish Communities in Germany after World War II and the Successor Organizations in the Western Zones." *Journal of Israeli History* 18, nos. 2–3 (autumn 1997).

Schumacher, Martin, ed., *M.d.R., Die Reichstagabgeordneten der Weimarer Republik in der Zeit des Nationalsozialismus. Politische Verfolgung, Emigration und Ausbürgerung 1933–1945,* 3rd ed. Publication of the Kommission für Geschichte des Parlamentarismus und der politischen Parteien. Düsseldorf: Droste, 1994.

Schwab-Trapp, Michael. *Konflikt, Kultur und Interpretation. Eine Diskursanalyse des öffentlichen Umgangs mit dem Nationalsozialismus.* Opladen: Westdeutscher, 1996.

Schwartz, Thomas A. *America's Germany: John J. McCloy and the Federal Republic of Germany.* Cambridge: Harvard University Press, 1991.

Schwarz, Hans-Peter. *Adenauer,* vol. 1: *Der Aufstieg, 1876–1952.* Stuttgart: Deutsche Verlags-Anstalt, 1986.

————. *Adenauer*, vol. 2: *Der Staatsmann, 1952–1967*. Stuttgart: Deutsche Verlags-Anstalt, 1991.

————. "Dannie N. Heineman und Konrad Adenauer im Dialog (1907–1962)." In *Staat und Parteien. Festschrift für Rudolf Morsey zum 65. Geburtstag*, ed. Karl Dietrich Bracher et al. Berlin: Dubker und Humblot, 1992.

————. *Geschichte der Bundesrepublik Deutschland*, vol. 2: *Die Ära Adenauer: Gründerjahre der Republik, 1949–1957*. Stuttgart: Deutsche Verlags-Anstalt, 1981.

————. *Vom Reich zur Bundesrepublik. Deutschland im Widerstreit der Außenpolitischen Konzeptionen in den Jahren der Besatzungsherrschaft 1945–1949*. Stuttgart: Klett-Cotta, 1980.

Sebald, W. G. *On the Natural History of Destruction*. Trans. Anthea Bell. New York: Random House, 2003.

Seemann, Birgit. *Jeanette Wolff. Politikerin und engagierte Demokratin (1888–1976)*. Frankfurt: Campus, 2000.

Sellenthin, H. G. *Geschichte der Juden in Berlin und des Gebäudes Fasanenstraße 79/80*. Berlin: Max Lichtwitz, 1959.

Shafir, Shlomo. *Ambiguous Relations: The American Jewish Community and Germany since 1945*. Detroit: Wayne State University Press, 1999.

————. "Der Jüdische Weltkongreß und sein Verhältnis zu Nachkriegsdeutschland." In *Menora. Jahrbuch für deutsch-jüdische Geschichte* 3 (1992), ed. Julius H. Scheops. Munich: Piper, 1992.

————. "Die SPD und die Wiedergutmachung gegenüber Israel." In *Wiedergutmachung in der Bundesrepublik Deutschland*, ed. Ludolf Herbst and Constantin Goschler. Munich: R. Oldenbourg, 1989.

————. "Das Verhältnis Kurt Schumachers zu den Juden und zur Frage der Wiedergutmachung." In *Kurt Schumacher als deutscher und europäischer Sozialist*, ed. Willy Albrecht. Bonn: Abteilung Politische Bildung der Friedrich-Ebert-Stiftung, 1988.

Sichrowsky, Peter. *Strangers in Their Own Land: Young Jews in Germany and Austria Today*. Trans. Jean Steinberg. New York: Basic Books, 1986.

Siegfried, Detlef. "Zwischen Aufarbeitung und Schlußstreich. Der Umgang mit der NS-Vergangenheit in den beiden deutschen Staaten 1958 bis 1969." In *Dynamische Zeiten. Die 60er Jahre in den beiden deutschen Gesellschaften*, ed. Axel Schildt, Detlef Siegfried, and Karl Christian Lammers. Hamburg: Hans Christians, 2000.

Silbermann, Alphons, and Herbert Sallen. *Juden in Westdeutschland. Selbtbild und Fremdbild einer Minorität*. Cologne: Wissenschaft und Politik, 1982.

Simon, Hermann. "Die Jüdische Gemeinde Nordwest: Eine Episode aus der Zeit des Neubeginns jüdisches Lebens in Berlin nach 1945." In *Aufbau nach dem Untergang. Deutsch-jüdische Geschichte nach 1945*, ed. Andreas Nachama and Julius H. Schoeps. Berlin: Argon, 1992.

Spannuth, Jan Philipp. "Rückerstattung Ost. Der Umgang der DDR mit dem 'arisierten' und enteigneten jüdischen Eigentum und die Gestaltung der Rückerstattung im wiedervereinigten Deutschland." Dr.phil. diss., Universität Freiburg, 2001.

———. "Rückerstattung Ost. Der Umgang der DDR mit dem 'arisierten' Vermögen der Juden und die Gestaltung der Rückerstattung im wiedervereinigten Deutschland." In *"Arisierung" und Restitution. Die Rückerstattung jüdischen Eigentums in Deutschland und Österreich nach 1945 und 1989*, ed. Constantin Goschler and Jürgen Lillteicher. Göttingen: Wallstein, 2002.

Stern, Frank. "The Historic Triangle: Occupiers, Germans and Jews in Postwar Germany." In *West Germany under Construction: Politics, Society, and Culture in the Adenauer Era*, ed. Robert G. Moeller. Ann Arbor: University of Michigan Press, 1997.

———. *The Whitewashing of the Yellow Badge: Antisemitism and Philosemitism in Postwar Germany*. Trans. William Templer. Oxford: Pergamon, 1992.

Stern, Fritz. "Adenauer and a Crisis in Weimar Democracy." *Political Science Quarterly* 73 (March 1953).

Stern, Susan, ed. *Speaking Out: Jewish Voices from United Germany*. Chicago: edition q, 1995.

Strathmann, Donate. *Auswandern oder Hierbleiben? Jüdisches Leben in Düsseldorf und Nordrhein 1945–1960*. Essen: Klartext, 2003.

Tauber, Alon. "Die Entstehung der Jüdischen Nachkriegsgemeinde [Frankfurt am Main], 1945–1949." In *Wer ein Haus baut, will bleiben. 50 Jahre Jüdische Gemeinde Frankfurt am Main. Anfänge und Gegenwart*, ed. Georg Heuberger. Frankfurt: Societäts-Verlag, 1998.

Tauber, Kurt. *Beyond Eagle and Swastika: German Nationalism since 1945*. Middletown, Conn.: Wesleyan University Press, 1967.

Tetzlaff, Walter. *2000 Kurzbiographien bedeutender deutscher Juden des 20. Jahrhunderts*. Lindhorst: Askania, 1982.

Theis, Rolf. *Wiedergutmachung zwischen Moral und Interesse. Eine kritische Bestandsaufnahme der deutsch-israelischen Regierungsverhandlungen*. Frankfurt: Verlag für akademischen Schriften, 1989.

Thiele, Hans-Günther. *Die Wehrmachtsausstellung. Dokumentation einer Kontroverse: Dokumentation der Fachtagung in Bremen am 26. Februar 1997 und der Bundestagsdebatten am 13. März und 24. April 1997*. Bonn: Bundeszentrale für Politische Bildung, 1997.

Timm, Angelika. *Hammer, Zirkel, Davidstern. Das gestörte Verhältnis der DDR zu Zionismus und Israel*. Bonn: Bouvier, 1997.

Trimbur, Dominique. *De la Shoah à la reconciliation? La question des relations RFA-Israël [1949–1956]*. Paris: CNRS Éditions, 2000.

Turner, Henry Ashby. *Germany from Partition to Reunification*. New Haven: Yale University Press, 1992.

Unger, Ilse. *Die Bayernpartei. Geschichte und Struktur, 1945–1957*. Studien zur Zeitgeschichte, vol. 16. Stuttgart: Deutsch Verlags-Anstalt, 1979.

Verein EL-DE Haus. *Unter Vorbehalt. Rückkehr aus der Emigration nach 1945*, ed. Wolfgang Blaschke, Karola Fings, and Cordula Lissner. Cologne: Emons, 1997.

Wachs, Philipp-Christian. *Der Fall Theodor Oberländer (1905–1998). Ein Lehrstück deutscher Geschichte*. Frankfurt: Campus, 2000.

Wasserstein. Bernard. *Vanishing Diaspora: The Jews in Europe since 1945*. Cambridge: Harvard University Press, 1996.

Weiler, Peter. *Ernest Bevin*. Manchester: Manchester University Press, 1993.

Wengst, Udo. *Thomas Dehler 1897–1967. Eine politische Biographie*. Munich: R. Oldenbourg, 1997.

Wetzel, Juliane. *Jüdisches Leben in München, 1945–1951. Durchgangsstation oder Wiederaufbau?* Munich: Stadtarchiv München, 1987.

Wiesen, S. Jonathan. *West German Industry and the Challenge of the Nazi Past, 1945–1955*. Chapel Hill: University of North Carolina Press, 2001.

Wild, Stefan. "National Socialism in the Arab Near East between 1933 and 1939." *Die Welt des Islams* 25 (1985).

Winkler, York. *Flüchtlingsorganisationen in Hessen 1945–1954. BHE – Flüchtlingsverbände – Landsmannschaften*. Wiesbaden: Historische Kommission für Nassau, 1998.

Witt, Kurt. "Wie die Union entstanden ist." In *Politisches Jahrbuch der CDU/CSU* 1, ed. Bruno Dörpinghaus and Kurt Witt. Publication of the Generalsekretariat der Arbeitsgemeinschaft der CDU/CSU Deutschtlands. Frankfurt: K. G. Lohse, 1950.

Wojak, Andreas, ed. *Schatten der Vergangenheit. Deutsche und Juden heute*. Gütersloh: G. Mohn, 1985.

Wolffsohn, Michael. *Eternal Guilt?: Forty Years of German-Jewish-Israeli Relations*. Trans. Douglas Bokovoy. New York: Columbia University Press, 1993.

———. "Globalentschädigung für Israel und die Juden? Adenauer und die Opposition in der Bundesregierung." In *Wiedergutmachung in der Bundesrepublik Deutschland*, ed. Ludolf Herbst and Constantin Goschler. Munich: R. Oldenbourg, 1989.

Woodbridge, George. *UNRRA: The History of the United Nations Relief and Rehabilitation Administration*. 3 vols. New York: Columbia University Press, 1950.

Wright, Jonathan. *Gustav Stresemann: Weimar's Greatest Statesman*. Oxford: Oxford University Press, 2002.

Wroblewsky, Vincent von, ed. *Zwischen Thora und Trabant. Juden in der DDR*. Berlin: Aufbau, 1993.

Wyman, Mark. *DP: Europe's Displaced Persons, 1945–1951*. Philadelphia: Associated University Press, 1989.

Yahil, Leni. *The Holocaust: The Fate of European Jewry.* Trans. Ina Friedman and Haya Galai. Oxford: Oxford University, Press, 1990.

Zentralrat der Juden in Deutschland [H. G. van Dam]. *10 Jahre Zentralrat der Juden in Deutschland 1960.* Düsseldorf: Zentralrat der Juden in Deutschland, 1960.

Zieher, Jürgen. "Kommunen und jüdische Gemeinden von 1945 bis 1960. Studien zu Dortmund, Düsseldorf und Köln." Dr.phil. diss., Technische Universität Berlin, 2002.

Zimmerman, Mosche. *Die Deutschen Juden 1914–1945.* Munich: R. Oldenbourg, 1997.

Zweig, Ronald. *German Reparations and the Jewish World: A History of the Claims Conference.* Boulder: Westview, 1987.

Index